Spanish Colonial Tucson

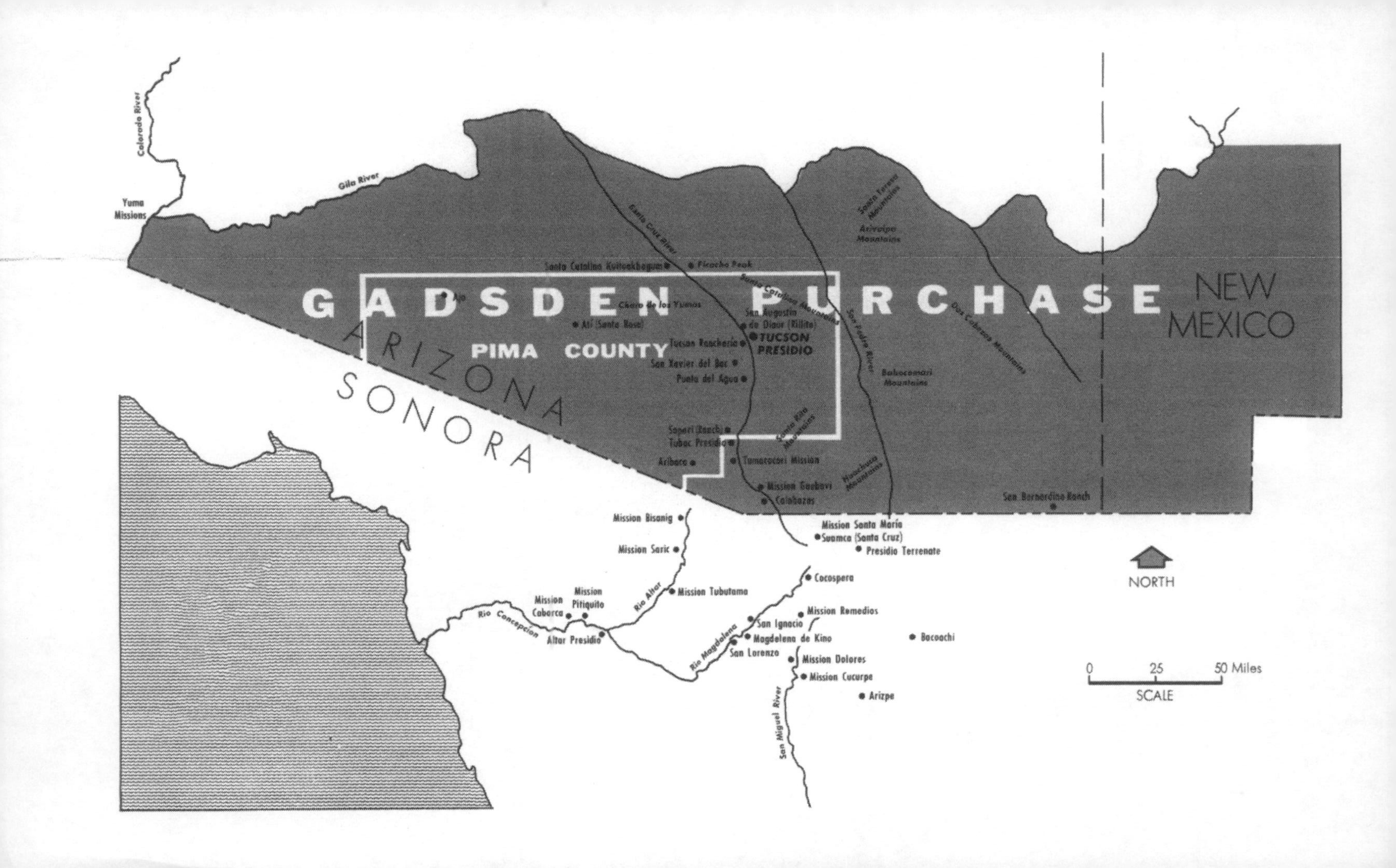
GADSDEN PURCHASE
NEW MEXICO
ARIZONA
SONORA
PIMA COUNTY
TUCSON PRESIDIO
Colorado River
Gila River
Yuma Missions
Santa Cruz River
San Pedro River
Santa Catalina Mountains
Santa Teresa Mountains
Aravaipa Mountains
Dos Cabezas Mountains
Babocomari Mountains
Santa Rita Mountains
Huachuca Mountains
Santa Catalina Kuitoakbagum
Picacho Peak
Ajo
Charo de los Yumas
Ati (Santa Rosa)
San Augustin de Oiaur (Pitito)
Tucson Ranchería
San Xavier del Bac
Punta del Agua
Sopori Ranch
Tubac Presidio
Aribaca
Tumacacori Mission
Mission Guebavi
Calabazas
San Bernardino Ranch
Mission Santa María Suamca (Santa Cruz)
Presidio Terrenate
Mission Bisanig
Mission Saric
Mission Tubutama
Rio Altar
Mission Caborca
Mission Pitiquito
Altar Presidio
Rio Concepcion
Cocospera
Mission Remedios
San Ignacio
Magdalena de Kino
San Lorenzo
Rio Magdalena
Mission Dolores
Mission Cucurpe
Bacoachi
Arizpe
San Miguel River
NORTH
0
25
50 Miles
SCALE

Henry F. Dobyns

Spanish Colonial Tucson

A Demographic History

THE UNIVERSITY OF ARIZONA PRESS
TUCSON, ARIZONA

About the Author . . .

Henry F. Dobyns, a Tucson native son, has contributed distinguished publications to the fields of anthropology and history since 1948. Among the most widely recognized of his numerous works are more than 20 books and articles reporting research and action on rural development in Peru, several analyses of cultural change, and various studies of the Spanish colonial period. Scientific editor of Indian Tribal Series, he has written or collaborated in writing books on the Havasupai, the Navajo, the Hopi, the Papago, and the White Mountain and Mescalero Apaches. His work in demography has won him recognition for bringing to light the extent of Native American depopulation under colonial conditions. Dobyns holds a Ph.D. degree from Cornell University, and has received the Bronislaw Malinowski Award from the Society for Applied Anthropology and shared the Anisfield-Wolf Award from the *Saturday Review* for his writing.

The University of Arizona Press
www.uapress.arizona.edu

Century Collection edition 2016

Printed in the United States of America
21 20 19 18 17 16 7 6 5 4 3 2

ISBN-13: 978-0-8165-0546-3 (cloth)
ISBN-13: 978-0-8165-0438-1 (paper)
ISBN-13: 978-0-8165-3519-4 (Century Collection paper)

L.C. No. 75-10344

♾ This paper meets the requirements of ANSI/NISO Z39.48-1992 (Permanence of Paper).

Contents

Preface

TUCSON, ARIZONA, is one of those Southwestern cities where Native Americans pioneered habitation of the metropolitan site. A European settlement grew up around an original nucleus of native habitation. Within the sprawling 20th century city lies an area of a few blocks that spawned the whole colossus. This native site has been continuously occupied by man for an unknown number of centuries extending far back into prehistoric times.

This book examines the dynamics of ethnic diversification within the city of Tucson, the largest urban settlement within the Gadsden Purchase area which the United States acquired from Mexico in 1853. It analyzes those dynamics during the period of Spanish colonial rule in Tucson because the foundations of its 20th century ethnic diversity were laid then.

Tucson possesses some distinctive advantages as a laboratory for studying inter-ethnic relations, not because it is completely representative of U.S. cities, but because it is not typical. Tucson contained in 1970 the tenth largest urban Native American population in the United States, whereas it was only the fifty-third largest city.[1] Moreover, Tucson held the second highest proportion of Native Americans among the fifteen cities with over 5,000 such residents. Only Tulsa, Oklahoma, had a higher percentage.[2] (See Table 1, Appendix.)

Another advantage Tucson holds as a laboratory of inter-ethnic relations is that its Spanish-ancestry population constitutes a major urban component. At mid-century, Pima County, in which Tucson is located, ranked seventeenth in number of persons with Spanish surnames among 192 Southwestern counties with 1,000 or more such individuals. Seven California counties held more such persons, as did seven counties in Texas, one other in Arizona and only one in New Mexico.[3] (See Table 2, Appendix.)

Nonetheless, little has been published about the Spanish history of Arizona and Pima county's metropolis, Tucson, compared to the numerous studies of other southwestern areas. Perhaps because Spanish colonization of the upper valley of the Río Bravo del Norte occurred at an earlier date than Spanish colonization at Tucson, historians have long devoted especially extensive attention to colonial settlement and rule in New Mexico. Perhaps residual pride of New Mexicans in their Spanish heritage helped to motivate interest in that state's colonial antecedents. Whatever the causes, the intellectual community has already made the history of Spanish New Mexico abundantly available.[4] As a consequence, numerous intellectual treatments of contemporary Spanish-American ethnic minority problems and conditions rely very heavily on New Mexican historic data and interpretations. One summary of the Spanish-speaking groups in the United States,[5] for example, devotes one chapter to New Mexican Hispanos, three to Mexican-Americans in Texas, California and northern cities for the most part, one to Filipinos and one to Puerto Ricans. It barely mentions Arizona.

Farther east, the bitterness of local inter-ethnic relations between Anglo-Americans, Spanish-Americans and Mexican-Americans in Texas early stimulated studies by members of the intellectual community.[6] Social scientists have focused on consequences rather than causes in studying some of the most complex and emotional inter-ethnic relations in the United States.[7]

To the west of Tucson, the very rapid U.S. conquest of California followed by quick settlement by overwhelming numbers of U.S. citizens soon allowed Californians to romanticize that state's colonial heritage. Rather large numbers of books and articles extolling California's colonial Spanish and Mexican heritage have long rolled off the art presses of California as well as those of major national publishers.[8] A few polemicists and social scientists have analyzed such dimensions of contemporary California as health-service delivery to Mexican-Americans.[9]

Between coastal California, with its picturesque Spanish missions and Mexican ranchos, and mountainous Spanish-American villages irrigating subsistence farms in the headwaters of tributaries of the Río Grande, Arizona simply has not yet received adequate attention as a frontier of Spanish colonial settlement.[10]

Arizona's largest ethnic minority is that either speaking Spanish or descended from Spanish-speaking ancestors. Even at mid-century, persons with Spanish surnames numbered 128,580 in Arizona.[11] Native Americans living in Arizona give it the largest Indian population of any state, yet they constitute only the second largest ethnic minority within Arizona. The largest ethnic minority nationwide, blacks, are numerically only the third largest of Arizona's subordinate groups.

Thus, understanding the genesis of Spanish-American and Mexican-American and Native American minority populations, their historic and present conditions, problems and aspirations, clearly deserves scholarly priority. Yet social historians have not yet carried out the studies that would place accurate knowledge of the Spanish-speaking peoples and urban Native Americans of Arizona on a par with that available for other states.

This book, then, attempts to expand the store of knowledge about the ethnic foundations of Arizona's second largest metropolis. It endeavors to analyze at least some aspects of Spanish colonial society and economy as well as to chronicle events at Tucson.[12]

The understanding of what occurred in this one small area contributes to the comprehension of how the United States as a whole achieved its multi-ethnic character. In 1975, persons with some Spanish genetic or cultural heritage constituted numerically the second largest ethnic minority in the country. Persons of pure or partial Native American ancestry, while not nearly so numerous, constituted the fastest growing major ethnic minority in the U.S. Discrimination toward members of these two minorities did not spring from the same causes as that directed toward blacks, nor did it necessarily take entirely identical forms.

To deal fairly and effectively with these ethnic minorities, American policy-makers and the citizens who elect them must base public policy and private actions upon an accurate understanding of the historic genesis of the present Spanish-American and Native American ethnic groups. This book contributes to that objective by describing how Spaniards, Mestizos from New Spain, and Native Americans of various tribal antecedents laid the ethnic foundations of one modern city in the United States.

I originally set out to study Tucson's past in order to assemble historical information about the site of San Cosme-San José-San Agustín del Tucson mission branch after taking part as a volunteer in archeological explorations carried out there in 1949. That analysis later expanded to provide similar data about the partially explored site of the Spanish-Mexican military post of San Agustín del Tucson. Reports to the Arizona State Museum remained unpublished. Searching for information about Tubac for the Arizona State Parks Board in 1958–59, I encountered additional information about Tucson in spare moments. I partially published these in 1962 and 1964. Since that time, other researchers as well as myself have located additional documentation concerning Spanish Tucson utilized in preparing this study. Incorporating much previously unpublished data, this book is essentially a new volume compared to earlier texts by the author.

One way in which this book adds to previously published understanding of ethnic foundations of Tucson is by including numerous colonial documents that have long lain hidden in archives. Usually translated in their entirety, these documents allow Spanish colonial residents of Tucson and officials dealing with this imperial outpost to speak for themselves. This approach resembles the one used by Robert F. Heizer and Alan J. Almquist in their discussion of *The Other Californians: Prejudice and Discrimination Under Spain, Mexico, and the United States to 1920.*[13] It echoes the judgment of France V. Scholes[14] that "the most solid achievements" of historians of the Spanish borderlands in recent decades "may be attributed to wide-ranging archival investigations in Mexico and Spain."

Despite the retrieval of numerous documents from the obscurity of dusty archives, one still cannot prepare a balanced social history of the Spanish colonial period based firmly on primary materials. One can, nonetheless, write a far fuller account of biological, military and ecclesiastical transformations in colonial Tucson than has previously been possible. This book is one such effort.

ACKNOWLEDGMENTS

THE FOUR PHASES that went into developing this volume were stimulated by Terah L. Smiley, the late William L. Wasley, George W. Chambers and especially Mrs. Jane Harrison Ivancovich.

I am indebted to no end of helpful individuals who aided me in discovering parts of the mosaic of Tucson's colonial past. Outstanding are Paul H. Ezell and his wife Greta S. Ezell, and James E. Officer. The Ezells have collaborated with me in reconstructing the history of the Northern Piman-speaking peoples for many years. Officer has frequently discussed Tucson's history with me, and his critical reading of the manuscript of this book greatly improved it.

The late Victor R. Stoner preserved crucial information about Tucson ecclesiastical affairs for many historians. The late Donald W. Page first advanced several interpretations of scanty data, and I benefited from stimulating discussions of Tucson history with him in the scholarly precincts of the Bancroft Library.

The late Thomas A. Segundo, twice a multiple-term chairman of the Papago Tribal Council during crucial periods of self-government, besides offering me his personal friendship, contributed key interpretations of Northern Piman language and culture.

Charles C. DiPeso, director of the Amerind Foundation at Dragoon, aided me by his long-range program of archeological and archival research on the Northern Piman Indians, and his discussions of historic changes in the Gadsden Purchase Area. Bernard L. Fontana, Arizona State Museum, reminded me of several archival sources.

I found the staffs of several research libraries and archives ever courteous and helpful, in addition to the library personnel of the University of Arizona, Cornell University and Prescott College.

As citations in this volume make clear, I owe my principal debt for source material to the staff of the Bancroft Library of the University of California at Berkeley. Most citations to Bancroft Library holdings are made with the permission of its former director, George P. Hammond. Vivian Fisher, head of the microfilm division, has long, enthusiastically, pleasantly and patiently aided me. Julia McCloud painstakingly helped to make the Pinart collections usable. John Barr Tompkins has many times facilitated my consultation of this library's unmatched resources.

The research library of the Arizona Historical Society has been my second base of operations in reconstructing Tucson history. Hilda Overpeck; the late Edith Kitt, historical secretary emeritus; Eleanor Sloan, former executive secretary of the Arizona Pioneers' Historical Society; and Sidney Brinckerhoff, director of the Arizona Historical Society, as well as Winifred Smiley and Margaret Bret Harte all helped to make this book possible. Brinckerhoff read it in manuscript and suggested numerous improvements.

I copied documents in the archive of the Diocese of Sonora through the courtesy of Juan María Navarette, then bishop of Sonora. Luis Baldonado and Bernard L. Fontana provided helpful and good company.

I copied extensively from the archive of the Parish of Santa María Magdalena with the cooperation of its amiable curate, José Santos Sainz, and his parish secretary, Jesús Contreras.

Other individuals with whom I have beneficially discussed materials in this book include Margaret Hees, Edward Ronstadt, Kieran McCarty, O.F.M., and the late Dorothy MacNamee.

For patient psychological and material support during the evolution of this volume, I am deeply indebted to Zipporah P. Dobyns, Cara R. Dobyns, and Mary Faith Dobyns.

Henry F. Dobyns

Part I
The Mission

1.

Founding a Jesuit Mission Near Tucson, 1694-1756

IN 1954, ARCHEOLOGISTS DISCOVERED Native American potsherds dating from A.D. 800-900 on a pithouse floor ruin directly beneath the sun-dried brick wall of the Spanish colonial military post at Tucson.[1] This discovery showed that Native Americans had settled this site at least a millenium ago.

We cannot, of course, ever know exactly who these first pioneers were, but their descendents who were living at Tucson when Spaniards first reached the site were Northern or "Upper" Piman Indians. That is, they spoke a language called "Piman," and belonged to the northern division of speakers of Piman. They were almost separated from the southern or "Lower" Pimans by Opata tribesmen who spoke a related but quite distinct language.

Evolution of a Place Name

The Northern Piman name for Tucson may be written a number of ways. One is *schookson,* pronounced with an *s* as in English *sin, ch* as in *chin, oo* as in *cool, k* as in *key, o* as in *owe,* and *n* as in *now.* This would reproduce the modern *Tautaukwañy* or *Kokololoti* Papago dialect pronunciation of the place name. Other modern dialects would pronounce it *schook shon* with an initial *sh* instead of *s* on the final syllable. Another way of writing this term is *stjukshon.*[2]

As the resemblance between *schookson* or *stjukshon* and *Tucson* indicates, the name now applied to this city was directly derived from the original Northern Piman term. English pronunciation, having modified the sound of the borrowed word, differs in sounding more like *Too sahn,* accented on either syllable. The Piman place name was always accented on the first syllable and the *k* was always sounded. *Tucson* became the Spanish written form of the Northern Piman place name. The Spaniards who first came into the area used *s* for the sound which was *s* in some Northern Piman dialects and *sh* in others, and they used an initial *t* for the double consonant cluster *s-ch* or *s-tj* of Northern Piman. This choice was probably influenced by Lower Piman Indians working as interpreters for the Spaniards.

Schook or *tjuk* is the Piman word which designates the color called *black* in English. The suffix *son* or *shon* designates a place "at the foot of."[3] This specific place name is still understood by Northern Piman speakers hearing it to refer to the hill or mountain rising from the Santa Cruz Valley bottom just off Congress Street in modern Tucson. Usually called "A" Mountain today after the large white-washed stone letter maintained on its slope by University of Arizona students, this peak has been called *Sierra de la Frente Negra* (literally, "Black-Browed Range"), *Picacho del Sentinela* or Sentinel Peak, and Warner's Hill.[4]

A Christian Saint's Name

The first non-Indian who saw the Northern Piman Indian *ranchería* of scattered homes at Tucson, as far as anyone knows now, was the Reverend Eusebio F. Kino. This locally famous Jesuit missionary pushed forward the mission frontier of Spanish Sonora between 1687 and 1711, exploring extensively what the historian Herbert E. Bolton felicitously labeled a "rim of Christendom."

Kino probably passed by Tucson on his way to the Gila River in November of 1694, inasmuch as he traveled along the Santa Cruz River.[5] The missionary explorer surely saw Tucson in November of 1697.[6] Then, on 27 September 1698, Kino and his military escort leader, Captain Diego Carrasco, made the first known written references to Tucson. Kino called it "San Cosme de Tucsón," and Carrasco "San Cosme de Tucsiom."[7] Kino greeted the people of Tucson again on 7 March 1699. Lieutenant Juan Matheo Manje, his military escort commander on this journey, mentioned passing "four settlements one league apart" between Oiaur and Bac — one of them evidently Tucson.[8] Kino again identified "San Cosme del Tucson" on 1 November 1699, while showing his superior, Father Visitor Antonio Leal, the northern frontier country.[9]

When Kino and Manje began writing the history of Spanish penetration into this area, Tucson was certainly a small and unimportant settlement. Kino traveled through the place at least twice before he gave it a saint's name.[10] The good priest, who was something of a real estate and foreign mission promoter, had a penchant for applying a Christian saint's name to every likely-looking Northern Piman Indian settlement. So his delay in naming Tucson implies it was not impressive.

On the other hand, Kino gave a saint's name only to Tucson of the four Native American rancherías recorded between San Xavier del Bac and San Agustín de Oiaur at this time. Thus it was not the least important settlement in this stretch of scattered habitation along the Santa Cruz River.

Ranchería Life

Tucson was at that time clearly much like a modern Papago Indian ranchería in settlement pattern. That is, people lived scattered through the brush in clusters of houses near the Santa Cruz River barely within sight of one another. Kino wrote that it had "splendid" fields which were similar to the ones at San Xavier del Bac.[11]

Manje remarked that the entire five to six leagues between Oiaur and Bac contained numerous cultivated, ditch-irrigated fields.[12] Clearly the Europeans had some difficulty in defining a sufficient concentration of dwellings to qualify in their minds as a "settlement," in such a long stretch of rural farmsteads. Kino's assignment of the name "San Cosme" to Tucson could reflect growth in population there between his visits, or his growing familiarity with local territorial terminology that enabled him to recognize an Indian identification with Tucson regardless of dispersion of residences.

It seems likely that the Tucson natives raised maize, beans, squash, melons, wheat, cotton, amaranth, chenopodium, devil's claw and tobacco[13] on fields irrigated from the river and the springs flowing from the valley's margins. They depended, on the other hand, upon the semi-arid desert for some of their vegetable foods and all of their meat.

About the only record of direct contact between Kino and Tucson's inhabitants is his notation that they gave him six children and one sick woman to baptize at "San Cosme."[14] Manje did note that the Spaniards "greeted" the heathens of the four small rancherías between Bac and Oiaur on 1 November 1699.[15]

Kino also pronounced those characteristic words of Spanish frontier conversion policy, "I baptize thee in the Name..." in the course of another journey from Bac to Oiaur. He left Bac, where he was laying the stone foundations of the first Christian church there, after Mass on the 30th day of April in 1700, stopped at Tucson, continued on to San Agustín de Oiaur and returned to Bac that afternoon. Quite clearly Kino spent a very short time in Tucson.

There are no available records to indicate that Kino ever conducted a funeral at Tucson, or that his rare presence affected the burial practices of its people. Nor did he mention any special structure being built by the Native Americans there for holding Mass. Lack of such information from Kino's pen, inasmuch as he was an inveterate letter writer about changes toward European norms by Native Americans, seems a good indication that his rare visits changed the aboriginal culture of the inhabitants of Tucson very little. They accepted the curative value of the black-robed magician's baptismal shell, holy water, oil and salt applied to ailing adults and infants with the impressive incantation, "I baptize thee in the Name...." Thus, these Native Americans fell under the sway of the peaceful prong of Spanish imperialism symbolized by the little silver baptismal shell.

Initial contact with Jesuit missionaries and Spanish troops left the people of Tucson essentially unchanged. Far more important influences on the Tucson natives probably had been Old World diseases transmitted to them by other Indians even before Kino reached them. Smallpox and other diseases, Jesuit and army explorers, constituted merely a prologue to Spanish imperial colonization, ethnic differentiation and urbanization at Tucson.

Early Jesuit Efforts

Real cultural impact upon the Northern Piman Indian ranchería known as Tucson did not begin until a Christian missionary from Europe began regularly to visit its residents. Like many Native American settlements on the northern frontier of New Spain, Tucson entered into recorded history as a *visita*. That is, the people of Tucson received more or less regular visits from a priest stationed at a nearby mission. The clerical campaign to convert

Native Americans to Christianity generated the first changes in the Tucson native community that can be attributed to contact with Europeans.

Spanish colonial policy relied heavily on the mission as a frontier institution. Colonial officials depended upon missionaries to concentrate scattered native populations at a relatively few mission sites, and there to foster Indian farming and stock-raising, and teach European crafts while firming neophyte military allegiance to Spain. Ideally, at least, the missionary's goal was legally to prepare Native Americans to become tribute-paying Christian subjects of the Crown in one decade.[16]

As an instrument of colonial policy, the Christian mission under the Spanish Crown relied upon clerics belonging to various religious orders. Secular priests ministered to parishioners in the settled diocesan areas, leaving the regular clergy (priests belonging to orders whose lives were specially regulated) to convert the heathens.

When the northwestern frontier of New Spain reached Northern Piman Indian territory, that portion of the missionary effort had been assigned to the Society of Jesus. Founded in 1531 by Ignatius Loyola, the Society entered New Spain in 1572 and the Indian mission field in 1591.[17] Jesuits began seeking converts among the mountain tribes of the Sierra Madre Occidental in Sinaloa. In 1604, the Jesuits advanced to the Fuerte River.[18] In 1617, the powerful Yaqui Indians, who defeated Spanish military expeditions attempting to subjugate them, invited the black-robed Jesuits to enter their country.[19] While radically transforming Yaqui social organization and settlement patterns, the Jesuits advanced northward into Opata country in 1628.[20]

After several decades of expansion of Opata missions, Eusebio Francisco Kino in 1687 carried Jesuit mission activity into the southeastern edge of Northern Piman territory at Dolores, in the San Miguel River Valley.[21] He explored most of Northern Piman territory before he died at Magdalena in 1711, opening the way for later mission expansion.

Changes of the sort sought by Spanish colonial officials possibly began at Tucson in 1701 when Francisco Gonzalvo, a 28-year-old native of Valencia, arrived at Mission San Francisco Xavier del Bac as its first resident priest.[22] On the other hand, his reception was not overly friendly. Manje wrote that Gonzalvo "had to leave" Bac in 1702 because the Native Americans of Juaxona and Tunortaca began to kill his mission livestock.[23] Gonzalvo died on 10 August 1702 and was buried at San Ignacio de Cabórica,[24] so he could have had but little lasting effect on the conservative farmer-hunter-gatherers living at Tucson.

When Eusebio F. Kino wrote to the viceroy of New Spain in 1703 urging appropriation of funds for ten more missionaries for Upper Pimería, he did not even mention Tucson. In the second year of the War of the Spanish Succession, the ranchería was merely one of "two other settlements dependent" on Bac,[25] similar to the scores of other small settlements to which Kino referred without names.

The coming of European-stimulated cultural change was, however, only a matter of time for the Native American inhabitants of the lower Santa Cruz

River Valley. Because these people known to the Spaniards as Sobaipuris[26] were to some extent sedentary irrigation farmers, missionaries stationed farther south could visit them occasionally. Crusty Father Joseph Agustín de Campos did visit Tucson during the 1720s from his San Ignacio Mission.[27] The partially fixed nature of Northern Piman settlement acted as a lure for Spanish colonization and missionization. The Spanish New World empire was built upon a food-producing native agricultural base. Thus, settled natives to be economically exploited and converted to Christianity comprised a magnet leading to new Spanish frontiers, along with the search for new mines, stock ranches, and commerce.[28]

Only in 1732 did the Crown-supported and controlled colonial church finally prove able to supply additional priests for the northern Sonoran missions envisioned by Kino. Spain by that time had recovered from the War of the Spanish Succession and enjoyed half a dozen relatively peaceful years after Philip V's abortive abdication. In that year, Philip Segesser took charge of Bac.[29]

Philip Segesser von Brunegg was a native of Lucerne, Switzerland, born on 1 September 1689. He entered the Society of Jesus in 1708[30] and came to New Spain in 1730.[31] Assigned to Mission San Ignacio in the late fall of 1731 for training in missionary work among Northern Piman Indians under the veteran Joseph Agustín de Campos, Segesser was escorted north to Bac in 1732.[32] He continued to assist the ailing Campos at San Ignacio until at least 7 March 1733, however,[33] so his impact on the people of Tucson must have been slight. He considered their settlement of little importance, listing it only as among the "other small rancherías to the north" of Bac.[34] Perhaps Tucson had lost population since the turn of the century like most other Northern Piman communities, which declined in numbers as their inhabitants succumbed to Old World diseases the Spaniards transmitted to them.

Another Swiss missionary followed Segesser to Bac. He was Kaspar Stiger, a slightly younger Jesuit born 20 October 1695 at Oberried in the Diocese of Constance. Stiger entered the Society in 1725 and reached New Spain in 1729, going first to a Tarahumara[35] mission. This priest had a difficult time with the Bac native religious leaders, especially in 1734. So the veteran Campos came north to control the Native American opponents of conversion.[36] Because Stiger's energies seem to have been largely absorbed in staying alive and struggling with his native competitors at Bac, he affected the Tucson Indians very little, except insofar as results of his survival struggle at Bac provided conversation farther north.

Stiger remained at Bac, also ministering to Guebavi from 1733, until ordered to San Ignacio to replace Campos in 1736.

The Bac missionary's transfer to San Ignacio was an emergency call occasioned by the ouster of Father Campos by Jesuit superiors who could not brook his "insubordination" and independence. Apparently the hierarchy was caught somewhat by surprise in 1736 without a spare missionary immediately available to carry the baptismal shell among the Native Americans of the northernmost mission. Not until the following year was a newly arrived recruit named Joseph Fabier sent from Cucurpe[37] to Bac. Fabier died very shortly after his coming at the age of 31,[38] leaving the Tucson natives still relatively unchanged.

Alexander Rapicani, a Neopolitan educated at Bremen, took over responsibility for ministering to Bac on 1 June 1737. The church furnishings were still in sad estate as a result of native destruction in 1734.[39] Rapicani's mission station was Guebavi,[40] so his influence on the people of Tucson was even less than on those at Bac. While Rapicani professed his final vows in the summer of 1740, there is no known documentation to indicate that he significantly influenced the Native Americans at Bac and Tucson before his transfer to the Seri mission at Pópulo later that year.[41]

On the other hand, the doughty missionary at Suamca, Ygnacio Xavier Keller, did visit *Tuxshon* as he wrote it, in mid-July of 1737 and baptized people there.[42]

A much younger Jesuit, Joseph de Torres Perea, took charge of Guebavi Mission and its outlying settlements early in 1741. Born at Chalchicomula in the Province of Puebla, in 1713, Torres Perea joined the Society in 1729.[43] The governor of Sonora suggested that José Miquio be sent to Bac in 1742,[44] but there is no evidence that he actually went. It was Torres Perea who reported the condition of Bac in 1744. Because his description of the slow pace of cultural change at Bac would have applied equally to Tucson, it is worth translating here:

MISSION OF SAN XAVIER DEL BAC

> This Mission, which is ministered to simultaneously with that of Guebavi in Pimería Alta, is 25 leagues distant from Guebavi toward the North over a road scant in water and dangerous because of the enemy. Toward the North there no longer are Christians, but various gentile nations without the Light of the Gospel nor knowledge of Christ. This Mission was founded the same year as Guebavi, that is 1732, and since then until the present year 1744 shows on its baptismal register 2,142 without counting those whom other Fathers baptized before, in whose books I think they were recorded.
>
> It is a well-populated Mission. There are more than 400 families. It is a Mission of Indians who are still mountain-dwellers, little or not at all amenable to the subjection of the gentle yoke of Christ. They are Christians more in name than reality. Only two Missionary Fathers lived in this Mission. They bewitched one in the year 1734; they rose up and profaned the vestments and chalices. Afterwards they surrendered, and now live quietly. Since then they have been ministered to by those who are Missionaries of Guebavi (because of the scarcity of Missionaries) who cannot do what is necessary fully to teach and minister to them, because of the distance and risky terrain.
>
> These Indians still appear to live like gentiles with the difference that in their paganism they were not baptized as they are now, without any change in their way of life. They know not how to pray, not even the "our Father" nor the "Hail, Mary," nor to cross themselves. Many adults flee from baptism, and I have found old and very old gentiles. The majority, and nearly all, marry according to their pagan rite: they

really work at avoiding being married by the Church. In this matter they hide the truth from the Missionary Fathers, telling them that they had been married by the Church by previous Fathers. This is not true, because I convince them with the marriage registers in which one does not find thirty couples married by the Church, there being more than 400 families. Yet they are not convinced. The poor Fathers work hard in this, but because the jurisdiction is large, it is not remedied according to one's wishes. Dated in Pimería Alta on the sixteenth day of March of 1744.

JOSEPH DE TORRES PEREA[45]

In 1744, Father Ildefonso de la Peña joined Torres Perea at Guebavi. Soon Torres Perea moved to Caborca. In May, Father Visitor Juan Antonio Balthasar visited Guebavi, and it can be concluded that de la Peña departed in his entourage.[46]

The visiting clerical inspector wrote another description of the Native Americans at Bac, which undoubtedly also applied to Tucson. To Father Juan Antonio Balthasar, the natives were a "bad lot." Some "abandoned" the mission — almost surely in the age-old Northern Piman economic pattern of transhumance.

This regular seasonal movement to enable exploitation of economic resources constituted a major block to the missionaries, who strove to make the Northern Pimans a sedentary people. Water supply largely governed Northern Piman transhumance. These Native Americans wintered at either "well villages" located near permanent springs in the mountains, or on the Magdalena-Concepción, Santa Cruz-Gila or Colorado Rivers. They carried water in baked clay vessels to the thick stands of giant cactus for the rich mid-summer fruit harvest. When summer thundershowers filled earth tanks out in the alluvial valleys between the permanent streams, some moved to their "field villages" to till soil softened by rain or flood to plant maize and other crops. Despite a close juxtaposition of fields and permanent domestic and irrigation water at Bac and Tucson, their residents had to travel to stands of giant cactus, oak groves and yucca stands for edible fruits and fibers. They also moved out to good deer and mountain sheep hunting hills, minimizing their residence in fixed abodes well known to hostile Western Apaches, or Yavapais.

In view of such ingrained native cultural patterns, the clerical inspector claimed that the mission at Bac needed colonial troops to "force" the Northern Pimans to live in the pueblo, to labor in the fields, "to punish" the medicine men, and "to drive forth" undesirables. Balthasar advocated obtaining a viceregal order authorizing the deportation of Native American "troublemakers" to Mexico City's workhouses. He viewed the "many and powerful medicine men" who killed one another and bewitched even missionaries as the worst troublemakers.[47]

Another father visitor, Carlos Rojas, reported in 1748 that Bac had had clerical attention only on a fill-in basis for the previous decade, meaning that Tucson had received even less. He pinned an "unlucky" label on the Bac mission.[48]

The missionary who filled in beginning in 1745 was evidently Joseph Garrucho, stationed at Guebavi. He was born 27 March 1712 on Sardinia, and entered the Society in 1731.[49] He came to New Spain in 1744 after being captured at sea by British pirates,[50] and was sent to learn Northern Piman mission work from Father Ygnacio X. Keller at Santa María Suamca.[51] He took over Guebavi the following year,[52] with responsibility for visiting the downriver Native Americans.

Thus, the Bac-Tucson stretch of the Santa Cruz River remained quite peripheral to the Jesuit mission effort in northwestern Sonora until new missionary reinforcements arrived from Europe a decade and a half after Stiger left Bac. It was not until 1751 that the Jesuits once again assigned a resident priest to the mission. This time he was a central European, Franz Bauer, a native of Czechoslovakia. Bauer was born 6 January 1721 and entered the Society on 9 October 1737.[53] He reached New Spain in 1750,[54] and refounded the Bac mission the following year.[55] Apparently Bauer first rode to Bac early in June. Then he divided his time between Bac and San Ignacio.[56] Spaniards spelled Bauer's name in a number of ways, and he himself Hispanicized it to Francisco Pauer.[57]

Northern Piman Nativistic Movement

Franz Bauer re-established part-time missionary work at Bac on the eve of a major nativistic movement among the Northern Piman Indians. This crisis arose in part from competition for control of Spain's colonial government between clerics and civil-military officials.

Royal officials recruited Northern Piman warriors to campaign against hostile Seri Indians on the Gulf of California coast of Sonora in 1749. Led by Luis Oacpicagigua of Saric,[58] the Northern Pimans fought well even by Spanish standards. As a matter of fact, the Northern Pimans seem to have acquitted themselves somewhat better in battle than the Spaniards. Consequently, the Northern Piman veterans returned home feeling less awe for the Spaniards than they had before. Rewarded by the military authorities for their contributions to the Seri campaign, the Northern Piman veterans chafed at authoritarian Jesuit conduct of mission life. A series of untoward incidents between missionaries and Northern Piman neophytes generated a large-scale military revolt led by Captain General Luis Oacpicagigua.

The Pima Revolt of 1751 was typical of nativistic movements[59] seeking to throw the white man out of native territory and bring back the "good old days" before Europeans began ordering natives about. Such armed rebellions occurred again and again on the northern frontier of New Spain as an aftermath of initial Native American contacts with Western Civilization.

The Pima Revolt was unusual, perhaps, in that the rebels enjoyed initial success. They actually did kill or eject all non-Indians from their territory. The evils of missionization from the Northern Piman point of view were incarnate in the Jesuit missionaries Tomás Tello at Caborca, Henry Ruhen at Sonoita, Joseph Garrucho at Guebavi, and above all Ygnacio Xavier Keller at Santa María Suamca.

From a Christian point of view, Tello and Ruhen were martyred by apostate Indians.[60] In the eyes of Northern Pimans, just revenge was wrought on these two Jesuits. Neophytes exacted vengeance for their mistreatment of relatives such as a pregnant woman locked in the stocks at Caborca.[61] Garrucho and Keller escaped death, but transferring Keller out of the area was one of the Northern Piman conditions for restoring peace with Spain.

When the revolt began late in November of 1751, Franz Bauer received a warning from a Native American at Bac loyal to him. The missionary escaped with his Spanish foreman and three or four soldiers stationed at the mission for his protection[62] before the Bac warriors reached a firm decision to join the movement.

So far as Tucson was concerned, the important point is that the natives there had not yet had sufficient experience with missionaries and the harsh inter-cultural clashes of missionization to join in planning the revolt. Even the Bac people were not highly motivated to set off the conflict. They debated for several days before committing themselves to the rebel cause. The Tucson population had had less experience with missionaries, and they surely played a very inconspicuous part in the greatest military action ever carried out by Northern Pimans.

Lieutenant Colonel Diego Ortiz Parrilla, the governor of Sonora, followed an extremely wise course of scouting Northern Piman territory in force, but not provoking hostilities while offering to negotiate peace. His men had to fight one pitched battle against some 2,000 Native Americans, but experienced Apache-fighter Ortiz Parrilla's[63] patience finally paid off in a negotiated peace. Thus the Northern Pimans were brought back into the Spanish colonial orbit with their Apache-fighting power essentially undiminished by battle losses in what could have turned into a very bloody campaign had Ortiz Parrilla chosen to force a military decision. The Northern Pimans who had fled their villages in November and December of 1751 were returning gradually by the spring of 1752.[64]

Locating a Frontier Garrison

As soon as the governor received the first news of the insurrection, he wrote dispatches to the viceroy in far off Mexico City requesting among other things authorization to recruit and equip a new frontier garrison to overawe the Northern Piman Indians. By the spring of 1752, Lieutenant Colonel Ortiz Parrilla had received the requested authority, and he raised the company in March.

Then he had to settle on the best location for the garrison. He held a meeting of military officers and non-commissioned officers with experience in Northern Piman country at his forward headquarters at Mission San Ignacio. Ortiz Parrilla also asked some of the surviving Jesuit missionaries for their opinions as to the most suitable location for a new post to pacify the Northern Pimans and resist Apache incursions. The frontiersmen generally favored two garrisons, one on the Santa Cruz River and the other on the Altar River. The Jesuit recommendations are of especial interest in the ethnic foundation of Tucson, because they constituted a prelude to Spanish settlement there. It is thus significant to note that in 1752 the missionaries already considered Tucson a suitable site for a Spanish military post, as evidenced in their recommendations translated here:

> By order of my Father Visitor Phelipe Segesser I give my opinion on the place or places where there should be placed the new fort or the new forts in the Upper Pimería. Supposing that there is one fort to be located, it is my opinion that this should be put at Aribaca, or if this should not be appropriate from this place being subject to sickness, it should be put toward Aqua Caliente or Arizona or Saric. The reason is that located in any of these places it should be in the middle of the Pimería and more at hand in order to quell the altercations of those Indians and assist the tranquility of the towns. Any of the places mentioned has plenty of water and pasture with which to maintain the garrison horse herds.
>
> If two forts are to be erected, in such case it is my opinion that one should be planted some four or five leagues beyond San Xavier at Santa Cathalina or in *Tucusona*, places abundant in water and pasture, and the other in the Valley of Saric, Caborca and Tubuttama.[65] The first, as adjacent, would intercept the disorders of the Northern Pimas and nearby Papagos, and the second should contain the Pimas of the west and neighboring Papagos. In this lucky event one or the other should come to be where the horde of Pimas has occasioned the past uprisings and where the most caution is necessary. This is how it seems to me, and I sign.
>
> JHS JACOBO SEDELMAYR.[67]
>
> Ures.[66] May 10, 1752.

The veteran missionary Gaspar Stiger wrote a brief note concurring in Sedelmayr's recommendations, and Segesser transmitted both of their opinions to the governor with his own comments:

> Sir Governor and Captain General:
>
> In compliance with Your Honor's order which, with date of May eighth of this year 1752 Your Honor remitted to me in order that opinions might be given by me and the Fathers Jacobo Sedelmayr, Visitor of the Upper Pimería, and Father Rector Gaspar Stiger of the same Pimería, as experienced and informed of its terrain, I make the proper report in accord with the knowledge which I possess and conforming to that which Your Honor asked of me.
>
> I find as appropriate and necessary for the reduction of Upper Pimería the two forts which Your Honor has sited in it. One should be put in the place of Santa Cathalina or in that nearby named *Tucuson* inasmuch as both are abundant in water and pasture for the remount herds and cattle as well as the population. With such a garrison the subjugation and reduction of the most heathen, which embraces the Northern and Eastern part of said Pimería, would be achieved. Not only that part of the Northern Piman Indians which inhabits the banks of the Río Xila, but also the rancherías of the apostate Apaches farther upstream and in the nearby mountains would be curbed. Such a garrison would cover the territory and give a hand to the Post of San Phelipe de Guebavi

at Terrenate, enabling their captains zealously to comply with the civil and politic orders of His Majesty for the education of the Indians.

Thus, the other fort should be situated in the Arizona or Sariqui, places of equal quality as the aforementioned *Tucuson*. Thus, the Papago Indians of the west and the rest would be subjugated as in the center of the Pimería and with the same ease it might give a hand to the two preceding posts, serving not only toward the end of subjugating the Pimería and maintaining its missions in security, but also to parry the hostilities which are executed in it by the Apache tribe.

This is my feeling from the knowledge that I possess with which I have satisfied the request from Your Honor, for whose prudence I pray to God, and that He may preserve the important life of Your Honor for many years. From this Mission of St. Michael of Ures, May 25, 1752.

PHELIPE SEGESSER, JHS[68]

The military experts with whom Governor Diego Ortiz Parrilla conferred at San Ignacio recommended yet another Northern Piman Indian village farther up the Santa Cruz River as the site for the new post. When the governor made his final choice, he settled on Tubac.[69] It received a headquarters unit with a 20-man garrison on detached, rotating duty at Ocuca, between Magdalena and Altar.

Thus Tucson's future was not yet permanently committed to Western Civilization, and its ethnic diversification did not begin in 1752. Nonetheless, the idea that Tucson offered advantages as a garrison site had been planted in the colonial bureaucracy to bear later fruit.

Aftermath of Revolt

The aftermath of the Northern Piman nativistic movement of 1751 appears to have directly affected the future of Tucson as a Native American settlement. The 1751 revolt and Spanish reaction to it produced significant demographic dislocation of Northern Piman local populations. Resettlement of dislocated natives apparently constituted a turning point for Tucson. As Northern Pimans returned from their desert refuges, the Santa Cruz River Valley natives apparently congregated at Tucson instead of spreading along the river as before in four small settlements betwen Bac and Oiaur. Perhaps some of the erstwhile rebels of Bac considered themselves safer farther from the Spanish military frontier and moved to Tucson. Possibly some residents of *Tubaca* moved to Tucson when the Spanish garrison took their lands. At any rate, Tucson began to rival Bac in population, judging from the relative number of baptisms recorded at the two places when a missionary reentered the area with shell in hand.

Even after the Spanish post was established at Tubac, the lower Santa Cruz River Valley did not offer a very inviting prospect to Jesuit survivors of the violent nativistic movement. Not until 1753 did Franz Bauer return northward as far as Guebavi, making that his headquarters for visits farther north to re-convert the recent rebels against Christianity and its cultural implications.[70] He baptized 49 persons at Guebavi and Tumacacori, 50 at

Tucson and 43 at Bac among Native Americans who had returned to peace in 1754.[71]

Bauer visited Tucson infrequently. On 6 August 1754, he baptized 43 persons in Bac and Tucson.[72] He returned again to Bac on 16 February 1755,[73] having just returned to his mission from Arizpe,[74] where he went to make his final profession before Father Rector Carlos de Roxas on 2 February.[75] In October, Bauer came down with chills, probably malaria. The priest might have contracted that illness during his August trip down the Santa Cruz River, inasmuch as that was the rainy season when humid afternoon air favored insect reproduction.[76]

Lack of records of rituals other than baptisms indicates that Bauer continued to be concerned mainly with conversion at this period, as might be expected from the relative lack of previous missionary contact with the Tucson natives. There was, moreover, not too much point in the Jesuit missionaries trying to prepare converts for confirmation. No bishop had visited Sonora for 18 years, and the Jesuits had not then been granted the privilege of confirming, although they hoped to receive it.[77]

The people of Tucson had not yet learned enough Catholic customs to change their marriage ceremonies or funerary or other practices in response to direct prodding by Spaniards. They had, nonetheless, altered some of their customs as a result of indirect European influences, such as wheat seed and various new infectious diseases. Taking into account Bauer's reports to his superiors that rebel Northern Pimans destroyed the church, missionary's house, vestments and livestock at Bac during the revolt, it seems most unlikely that Tucson showed any material signs of Christian conversion in 1754.

After 1755, Tucson and Bac ceased to be mentioned in the Guebavi records, except for the names of random individuals from those settlements who happened to travel south to have a Christian ritual performed. The reason for that change was the 1756 arrival of another resident missionary at the northern settlements in the Santa Cruz River Valley. This new priest, Alonso (Ildefonso) Ignacio Benito Espinosa, was the nearest thing to a native Spaniard yet sent to this frontier post. He had been born in the Canary Islands, which Spain had conquered on the eve of its New World discoveries, on 1 February 1720. Espinosa entered the Society of Jesus and reached New Spain in 1750.[78]

Although the Mexican Jesuit Province had had no immediate replacements for priests slain in the 1751 Bac uprising, it first sent Alonso Espinosa to Caborca.[79] Late in 1754, Jesuit Visitor General Utrera found Espinosa at San Ignacio regaining his health.[80] There he stayed until mid-April of 1755,[81] when he finally went north to Bac.

The new missionary evidently did not stay long at Bac on this first trip. In mid-1756, his immediate superior in the Society reported that Espinosa had charge of Cocospera Mission, while Franz Bauer still cared for Guebavi and San Xavier del Bac.[82]

Already rumor was predicting what was to become a serious setback for Espinosa. Word had it that Gila River Chief Crow's Head intended to rebel with some Papagos. Franz Bauer traveled north to tell this native leader to go reassure the colonial authorities of his peaceful intentions. Pleading that he was too old to make the journey, Crow's Head sent one of his grown sons to declare the rumors false. This son admitted that some "Papagos" at Atí[83] wanted to take advantage of Crow's Head's leadership of the powerful Gileño Pima tribal army to avoid moving. Espinosa may have been pressing the desert dwellers with colonial military backing to migrate to his Santa Cruz River mission to make up population losses there. Crow's Head's son maintained that his father would not accede to the wishes of the uncooperative inhabitants of Atí. This Gila River spokesman further asserted that soldiers who claimed that Crow's Head and his followers had all gone to the Colorado River had not been within 20 leagues of the chief's house.

Tucson clearly continued to be simply one relatively unimportant Northern Piman ranchería among many at this time, a target for Christian proselytization, yet unconverted, and strongly linked to the growing Native American military power on the middle Gila River.

2.

Continued Jesuit Proselytizing, 1756-1767

WHEN FATHER ALONSO I. B. ESPINOSA took up his duties as resident missionary at San Xavier del Bac Mission in 1756, he became the sixth Jesuit actually to reside there. The expansion of Jesuit missionary effort since Gonzalvo entered Bac in 1702 augered well for Espinosa's finally establishing San Xavier as a continuously operating Christian mission with Tucson as its principal branch. Evidently Father Espinosa himself felt that the time had come to alter quickly the traditional behavior of the Native Americans of Bac and presumably Tucson.

More Native Resistance

One might be tempted to assume that Espinosa's Hispanic culture predisposed him toward poor personal relationships with the Northern Piman Indians. Yet that assumption would not be correct. The evidence of the 1751 Northern Piman Revolt makes clear that the Middle-European culture of German Jesuits also set up extreme Native American resistance to clerics wielding great temporal authority. A more reasonable explanation of nativistic movements in both 1751 and 1756 seems to be the inference that the structure of the frontier Christian mission fostered native resistance to forced cultural change.[1] Possibly Espinosa had not been adequately trained to carry out independent proselytization so as to avoid generating a violent reaction.

However lukewarm the Native Americans of Bac may have been about the Northern Piman Revolt in 1751, Father Espinosa goaded them into their own nativistic movement in the fall of 1756. The Native Americans of Bac apparently resorted to violence when Espinosa directly challenged their aboriginal religious beliefs and practices.[2]

The Northern Piman Indians dwelling along the banks of permanent streams in what became the Spanish colonial Province of Sonora had apparently developed in aboriginal times a very important fall harvest festival which they celebrated on a fixed date on or near October fourth.[3] Following long-established Roman Catholic Church policy,[4] Jesuit missionaries set out to capture this native ceremony and integrate it into the Church calendar as a Christian celebration.[5]

Espinosa evidently tried to terminate native ritual elements and "purify" the October fourth observance at Bac in 1756. He restrained the Native Americans from holding their customary dances and festivities.[6] These included ritual intoxication earlier in the year to bring rain through a form of compulsive magic,[7] perhaps also a harvest festival practice of that period.

Judging from the relative sizes of Tucson and Bac at that time, and participation of Tucson Indians in the Bac and Magdalena October fourth festival ever since, there can be little doubt that the Tucson populace assembled at Bac for the 1756 ritual and shared in the bitter native reaction against Espinosa's attempt to change too rapidly centuries-old aboriginal religious rites and beliefs. As another Jesuit put it, the Native Americans went to war thinking "to sate their savage rage by killing Father Alphonso Espinosa and thought to wipe out in deadly destruction the Mission of San Xavier."[8]

When the Northern Pimans of Bac and the area north of it resorted to violence in 1756, Spanish accounts attributed leadership of the Native American fighters to the Gila River Chief Crow's Head (*Havañ mau'au* or as rendered in Spanish orthography, *Jabanimó*).[9] Referring to San Xavier del Bac Mission, one report stated that "Jabanimó assaulted it with his band of rebel Pimas the year 1756, and aided by the Indians of the Pueblo itself, sacked the Missionary Father's house and the loyal Indians' huts. While they were so engaged, the ensign of the Royal Presidio of Tubac[10] arrived with 15 soldiers in relief. Although the rebels received them with the greatest resistance, the latter were defeated with 15 dead and many wounded. They fled precipitously inland, leaving only three soldiers slightly wounded."[11]

Sonoran Governor Juan Antonio de Mendoza[12] quickly collected a punitive expedition. Evidently he passed through Mission San Ignacio, for he enlisted the newly arrived Jesuit Bernhard Middendorff as military chaplain.

Middendorff belonged to a large reinforcement of 42 Jesuits who left Spain on Christmas Day of 1755 and arrived in New Spain on 19 March 1756.[13] Shortly after reaching New Spain, Middendorff rode to Mexico City. He set out from the capital on 11 May[14] and spent four months on the road to Sonora, reaching Mátape in September.[15] Like many later travelers in Mexico, members of Middendorff's party suffered painful diarrhea, so they halted for three weeks at Mátape to recover. Then they proceeded to Ures, and Middendorff continued to Mission San Ignacio, with a large escort for protection against Seri attack.[16] By his own account, Middendorff spent November and December as chaplain with Mendoza's expedition.

Mendoza re-installed Espinosa, a refugee at Tubac, at San Xavier del Bac Mission on his way to the Gila River.[17] Middendorff identified the rebels as "Papagos and Cocomaricopas." That Gila River Yumans formed part of the force seems confirmed by Governor Mendoza's pursuit of hostiles into Coco-Maric-Oopa territory at the Salt and Gila River confluence.[18]

Once Spanish military force had dispersed Northern Piman and Cocomaricopa[19] resistance to forced religious change at Bac, Middendorff felt free to leave. He returned to San Ignacio Mission by a short cut[20] and thus probably missed seeing Governor Mendoza lay the first brick for a new church at Bac on his way south from the Gila River battle.[21]

A Priest for Tucson

Middendorff could have stayed at San Ignacio but a few days, because he soon became the first priest to live north of Bac, starting on 5 January 1757.[22] Rector Carlos de Rojas reported to the provincial in mid-March of 1757 that Middendorff was then "in the Tucson with two pueblos" as mission branches.[23] Inasmuch as Espinosa at Bac also had two branches, Middendorff's would most likely have lain farther north at Oiaur and Santa Catalina *Kuitoakbagum*. Such a situation would account for another Jesuit's memory that Middendorff worked at Santa Catalina. Certainly Middendorff established the northermost mission on this particular rim of Christendom.

The role of the colonial military forces in making the Christian mission function as a frontier institution extending imperial control over Native American populations appeared very clearly in this mission foundation. No less than ten soldiers accompanied Middendorff to provide him security! Small wonder, therefore, that the prospective Christians whom Middendorff lured to his establishment placated him with gifts of wild fruits and birds' eggs!

The German Jesuit encountered the Northern Piman Indians living in the area "scattered in the brush and hills." In other words, they lived in traditional ranchería style with houses barely within sight of each other. Middendorff attracted approximately 70 families to his new mission with gifts of dried meat. The prospective converts included a few "jerky Christians" who had been baptized at Bac by Alonso Espinosa, but sought temporal rather than spiritual rewards.

Middendorff had "to sleep under the open sky" until he could set up a hut made from willow and brush. He celebrated Mass under a typical Sonora-style *ramada* or shade – four posts that supported a reed-and-rush roof.[24]

At the beginning of March, Middendorff was very short on supplies, lacking wine with which to celebrate Mass, and subsisting on grain. He could not taste meat without suffering nausea, he reported to Father Rector Juan Antonio Balthasar. Middendorff remained quite dependent upon Father Gaspar Stiger at Mission San Ignacio for those commodities he did not have.[25]

Even worse, as far as proselytizing success was concerned, Middendorff could not communicate directly with prospective converts. German priests assigned earlier to this mission field were required to learn Northern Piman before receiving independent assignments. For whatever reasons, Middendorff did not spend a year at San Ignacio learning the language before launching his Tucson effort. Consequently, he had to attempt to communicate with his prospective converts through an interpreter. "I had at first to instruct" the natives through an interpreter, Middendorff himself admitted in reporting his relationship to them.

Quite possibly Middendorff alone was surprised one night in May when what he reported as 500 heathen savages attacked his mission. The priest and his military escort fled to San Xavier del Bac Mission with some native Piman families.

Thus ended Middendorff's abortive attempt at proselytizing in the

Tucson area.[26] From Bac, Middendorff soon moved on south to another already-established mission, Saric,[27] leaving Espinosa the entire responsibility for both Bac and Tucson. In other words, Tucson quickly reverted to the status of a branch of the San Xavier del Bac Mission[28] after Middendorff's brief pioneering attempt to found a Christian mission there.

Notwithstanding the brevity of Middendorff's effort, its impact upon the Tucson population should not be underestimated. The five-month mission brought the Tucson people into direct daily contact with Spanish soldiery as well as with a Jesuit missionary. It taught the local Northern Pimans to look to the missionary for food subsidies, as well as to make reciprocal gifts in good Northern Piman fashion. It placed daily Mass on public view and almost certainly brought a fuller perception of baptism, marriage and interment in physical form if not in ritual meaning. It also fostered factionalism by creating a group loyal to the missionary and a group oriented toward aboriginal values.

Whatever broadened perspectives Bernhard Middendorff brought to the inhabitants of Tucson, those Northern Pimans could settle into a more relaxed frame of mind with his departure. The nearest Christian missionary then lived at Bac, and the Indians in and around Tucson still did not see him often enough to remain unduly concerned over the rapidity of cultural change being urged upon them. They could pick and choose what Hispanic behaviors to borrow, and which ones to ignore.

Little of record actually occurred for several years as a consequence of missionary efforts to convert the Northern Pimans. Father Espinosa continued his ministrations despite serious illness, so that in 1761 one of his missionary colleagues labeled him "the Job of the missions."[29]

Forced Northern Piman Migration

The year 1761 proved to be crucial in altering the biological and cultural situation of Native American Tucson. Colonial officials decided on a policy of Northern Piman migration westward from the Apachean frontier.

Apparently the San Pedro River Sobaipuris were disposed to abandon their aboriginal range by progressive loss of manpower and military pressure exerted by hostile Western Apaches. Both of those forces had been set in motion by the colonial activities of Spain. Then, in 1761, Spanish authorities decided on migration as a move to strengthen the frontier of New Spain.

Jesuit Visitor General[30] Ignacio Lizasoaín[31] met Governor of Sonora Joseph Tienda del Cuervo,[32] at San Miguel early in December. They decided to use colonial troops to force Sobaipuris to resettle at existing Jesuit missions.[33]

However pious or however desperate that decision may have been, it actually weakened frontier defense, as Sonorans quickly discovered. The Sobaipuri migration of 1762 did help to assure the eventual biological survival of an aboriginal population in the Tucson area. Sobaipuri migration to Tucson also fostered cultural Westernization by further diversifying the social structure of the settlement.

When retreating Sobaipuris reinforced Tucson, they also brought about the renaming of the place as "San José" by the Spaniards. A report from the colonial officer in charge of the forced Sobaipuri migration related the circumstances:

> Sir Governor Don Joseph Tienda de Cuerbo
> My Dear Sir,
>
> I reply to Your Lordship's dispatch dated March tenth which my Lieutenant Don Ygnacio delivered to me on his return to this post. Seeing in it that Your Lordship would send to this post with the aforesaid Lieutenant six adult Pima women and an infant at the breast, I ought to say that they remain in my charge so that I may practice toward them that which Your Lordship expresses to me in it.
>
> In regard to what Your Lordship wrote me of the Sobaipuris, I notify Your Lordship that I have just arrived from settling them in the town of Tucson. Their number reaches 250, although the missionary and justices informed me that they numbered 400 souls. The place where they are settled offers them appropriate conditions for their labors. They have adequate fields and water assigned to them. They have at no time differed from the natives of that town. The question was raised as to whether they had been prejudiced in the assignment of lands which they had made to the new ones. I asked the Reverend Father Missionary as well as the native inhabitants if they had been prejudiced in any manner.
>
> To this question the Father Minister himself responded as they replied, that they were content. The thought that they had been harmed by the assignment of fields was not to be dignified by belief. The fields allocated to the Sobaipuris were always previously idle. Thus, the migrants as well as the natives, are satisfied with the distribution. This is what I have wished to bring to Your Lordship's notice.
>
> Among them, the first proposition that was mentioned, as Your Lordship knows, did not win their support. It has been most difficult to attain this settlement, because previously they were not inclined to settle in a town, but rather to live always in their native haunts. It was necessary, therefore, to utilize friendly presents and gifts. This does not excuse, nor do I excuse. At present I am proceeding to send them provisions for their maintenance in order to be able to reinforce their choice. Thanks to the presents and affection, I have attained the settlement at Santa María of those about whom I notified Your Lordship, and at Tucson the 250 to whom I have referred. They were enumerated, although as I already told Your Lordship, they reached 400 in number according to the tallies which the justices who govern them brought the Father Minister. Those who were not enumerated roam in the surrounding towns. Only His Divine Majesty knows whether there be the souls they say there are and if Your Lordship shall see them always obedient to the law of God and His Catholic Majesty.
>
> I applied the name of Señor San José to Tucson, because the Sobaipuri settlement occurred on the Feast of the Holy Patriarch.
>
> In regard to that which Your Lordship communicated to me of his departure, I am very happy inasmuch as it will be of much good to the land. At the same time, I shall fulfill the desires I have of serving you

in this, your house. The order which Your Lordship gave, I executed. While awaiting Your Lordship, I shall act as the exigencies and time allow. I desire the health of Your Lordship to be of the best, and pray to God for your prosperity for many years.

I kiss Your Lordship's hand.
Your most attentive and surest servant,
FRANCISCO ELÍAS GONZÁLES[34]

Guebavi. March 22, 1762.

Captain Francisco Elías Gonzáles was at that time commander of the Spanish military post at Terrenate. Governor Tienda del Cuervo had ordered him to carry out the colonial decision to force the Sobaipuris to live at established Jesuit missions.[35] The Sobaipuri migrants had only a limited choice of new homes, settling where Captain Elías would allow them within their preferred band territories. About 30 refugee Sobaipuris settled at Santa María Suamca Mission at that period.[36] Others concentrated their forces as near their aboriginal lands as possible at Sonoita in the highlands west of the San Pedro River. The Jesuit missionary at Guebavi ministered to them as a branch of his mission.[37] In addition, of course, there was the group that relocated at Tucson.

Such dispersion of the San Pedro River Valley natives to various refuge areas seemingly reflected the natives' own social divisions, even though the relocation was carried out under Captain Elías' commands. Possibly these Sobaipuris had not yet developed the kind of integrated war-making organization that later enabled the Gila River Pima Indians to hold their equally exposed riverine frontier against Yavapai and Southern Athapascan aggression.[38] Considering how well the Sobaipuris resisted the Apaches, however, they probably were fairly well coordinated, and Spanish colonial forced migration policy must be awarded the blame for their abandoning the San Pedro River Valley bastion.

The resident missionary at Bac, Father Alonso I. B. Espinosa, became the primary advocate of cultural change for the San Pedro River Valley Sobaipuris settled at Tucson. Espinosa influenced the final outcome of Sobaipuri resettlement, and essayed to incorporate these bellicose frontiersmen into the Jesuit mission model of Christian civilization.

Espinosa was evidently quite ambitious. Yet ambition combined with limited perception of Piman culture has led many an individual attempting to alter the customs of Piman-speaking Native Americans to fail. This priest evidently had become, however, more perceptive of cultural dynamics since his 1756 experience with nativistic rebellion.

In 1763, Father Espinosa tried to change the economic base of the amalgamated native settlement at Tucson by introducing sheep and cattle husbandry. He secured the approval of the leader of the community in the best agricultural-extension-agent style, but the people would have nothing to do with his strange stock.

Espinosa had other matters to attend to in addition to Tucson. On

18 September 1763, Jesuit superiors approved his advancement another step in his status in the Society.[39] Perhaps study for the Order diverted his mind from the hot climate at Bac and Tucson that militated against successful sheep growing there.

The following year Apaches made off with the priest's surplus livestock at Bac. Then he reported "it is necessary to reflect a long time to kill an animal to eat." The rector reported to the provincial that Espinosa built his herds up from a few calves to nearly 1,000 head before Apache raids reduced them to 200.[40] The rector admitted within the Society that what was going on at Tucson occurred in any mission without a resident priest. The Indians wandered everywhere, as "idle" as they wished.[41] In other words, they farmed little, hunted and gathered much.

Some of the wiles of the Northern Pimans employed in fending off missionary control appear in Espinosa's reports:

> There is enough arable land for said town's people and the Sobaipuris. As for water, all these years the neophytes have said that their grain fields dry up for lack of water, and now that they have conceived that they desire to change, they say that there is surplus water. I can only say that before the Sobaipuris came they used to complain about the scantiness of water . . . and the Governor of Tucson asked that I free him from the obligation of cultivating a maize field for the church so that there might be that much more water.[42]

Military Consequences of Sobaipuri Relocation

Espinosa's stock losses illustrate the main strategic defect in the colonial decision to move the San Pedro River Valley Sobaipuris to established missions farther west. As long as the Sobaipuris lived along the San Pedro River, they formed the first line of defense against hostile Apache penetration into Sonora, and an effective defensive line it was. A Jesuit in the frontier missions characterized the Sobaipuris as "the most warlike among all the Pimas."[43]

Sobaipuri resettlement on the Santa Cruz River both converted it into the front line of hostilities and attracted Apache attackers to that previously protected valley. Moreover, the Sobaipuri retreat opened up the San Pedro Valley as a new corridor for Apache raiding south into central Sonora.

Apache thefts during 1763 merely heralded many more and fiercer raids to come. Still, Tubac presidio commander Juan Bautista de Anza[44] detailed only two troopers, on two-week rotation, to protect Father Espinosa at Bac.[45]

Apparently Anza at that time looked south, rather than northward toward his destiny. He sought early in 1764 permission to move the Sobaipuris at Tucson once again. Not long before, Apaches killed three citizens in Buenavista, on the upper Santa Cruz south of Tubac. The remaining citizens petitioned Anza for permission to abandon the valley, which he granted to them.

The new Sonoran Governor Juan de Pineda[46] was not happy with that action. The departure of the citizens left the frontier that much more open to Apache raiding. In an attempt to remedy the weakening frontier defenses, Anza then asked the governor to authorize him to relocate the Sobaipuris at

Tucson in the Buenavista Valley. Anza argued that they lacked adequate irrigation water and fields at Tucson. Anza also charged that Father Espinosa was not able to minister to them, not having been able to collect them together to hear their confessions. Given Espinosa's record of poor health, Anza probably was correct on that score.

When Governor Pineda asked Jesuit officials for their advice, Rector Manuel Aguirre[47] opposed moving these Native Americans again. He pointed out that Tucson had for many years been considered a good spot for settlement. He reported that he had asked his provincial to send a missionary to minister to the people of Tucson.

Aguirre advocated colonizing Santa Catalina and Buenavista with Papagos. He claimed that they had no fields on which to raise food, and not even enough water to drink – something of an exaggeration. Aguirre also predicted that the citizens who abandoned Buenavista Valley would reappear to reclaim their lands as soon as the Sobaipuris might make the area secure. He suggested, therefore, that formal cession of land rights by these citizens to the Native Americans should be a pre-condition for moving Sobaipuris there. Aguirre may well have known or suspected that Anza had ranching interests in the area.

Aguirre criticized the original decision to remove the Sobaipuris from the San Pedro River Valley by emphasizing the degree to which Apache raids increased thereafter. He commented that the colonial authorities should have moved the Tubac garrison to the San Pedro to reinforce its valiant Native American defenders instead of removing the Sobaipuris to the Santa Cruz River Valley.

Missionary Travail

The Jesuit provincial responded to Aguirre's plea for more missionaries. He notified the rector that he would dispatch three more priests for the Sonora-Pimería Province. Aguirre knew from sad experience that most of the missionaries sent to Sonora were intercepted by other manpower-hungry Jesuit officials in the Tarahumara Indian missions or Sinaloa. Nonetheless, Aguirre planned to assign to Tucson a priest (Father Diego Batres) the provincial promised to send.[48]

While Rector Aguirre waited and chafed under Pineda's criticism that the Jesuits collected too many royal stipends for missions without missionaries, his northern staff weakened. Father Alonso Espinosa fell so seriously ill in 1764 that he went to San Ignacio for treatment in the winter. Somewhat improved, Espinosa returned to Bac on 7 January 1765. At that time the native population of Tucson totaled about 220, 70 of the number still learning the catechism, few receiving any sacrament.[49]

Rector Aguirre kept trying to staff a Tucson mission. Once when the ailing German Father Joseph Och recovered sufficiently to leave Baserac to recuperate at Guasave, he reported that he needed no more medicine. Aguirre, always optimistic, then offered Och his choice of Onapa, Atí or Tucson. Och rejected all of these assignments, and Visitor General Roxas then ordered him to Chihuahua to await reassignment by the provincial. Och went on south to a Jesuit institution in Mexico City, where he witnessed the expulsion, still bed-ridden.[50] The rector probably realized he was grasping at straws when he offered Och the Tucson mission.

In 1765, Espinosa relapsed and by mid-May if not earlier was so incapacitated that Rector Aguirre sent another Jesuit missionary to assist him.[51] This replacement-nurse, José Neve, was a native of Calpulalpan in the Province of Tlaxcala, born 10 June 1739. He entered the Society in 1755, and reached Sonora early in 1765. The rector promptly assigned Neve to Atí, which had long been vacant.[52] Hardly had the newcomer to frontier mission work begun to learn his task at Atí when Father Aguirre sent him to Espinosa's assistance.

Neve found Espinosa paralyzed in his bed.[53] The younger priest evidently nursed Espinosa back to enough strength for him to be taken to San Ignacio as ordered by the rector.[54] Espinosa suffered from "one leg already desiccated and continual pains," however, so it was some time before Neve could move him.[55] By October, Espinosa had improved. Neve probably moved him to San Ignacio then, inasmuch as Neve substituted that month for Bauer, who had transferred to San Ignacio in 1760.[56]

Once again, Espinosa improved, and in February of 1766 he transferred west to Caborca Mission,[57] where he remained until the Jesuit expulsion in 1767.[58]

Neve meanwhile returned to Bac. There he was arrested in the summer of 1767 and taken to Mátape to hear read the royal decree of banishment of his Society from New Spain.[59] The *Real Pragmatica Sanción* Charles III issued on 27 February 1767 expelled the Society from his dominions for reasons known but to him. Almost a year before, mobs in Madrid had clashed with royal Waloon guards in protest against the King's Italian ministers, Esquilache and Grimaldi. Then in only his sixth year of rule, Charles left Madrid until its tranquility was assured. Spanish historians tend to credit the new minister, the Count of Aranda, with persuading Charles III to expel the Jesuits, on grounds that they inspired the 1766 riots. Yet, the Order had already been banned from the Portuguese and French empires for what appeared to their sovereigns sufficient reasons. Charles sent Joseph de Gálvez to carry the top-secret decree to New Spain and see that it was executed. In Sonora, Captain Bernardo de Urrea of Altar received the order to round up the Jesuits of Pimería Alta and send them to Mexico City under arrest.[60]

Jesuit Cultural Impact

At the end of the Jesuit ministry, the labors of a resident missionary at Bac were finally beginning to take effect in the native and immigrant population of Tucson. Still, that settlement remained little more than a "field village"[61] where the Native Americans lived during the summer and fall while tending and harvesting their crops. After harvest, these Northern Pimans moved to desert mountains to gather wild foods and hunt. They ranged eastward to collect acorns and roast agave hearts. Some surely ventured to the Gulf of California coast on salt-collecting expeditions.

Such transhumance long confused Europeans who failed to understand Northern Piman Indian cultural adjustment to life in a harsh semi-arid environment. It was most frustrating to Roman Catholic missionaries who viewed such geographic mobility as heathen vagabondage rather than a functional ecological adjustment. As Father Espinosa had put it on 22 July 1764:

> All of them are an unsettled ranchería. At this time they live in their fields, and at the termination of what they have, in other towns in the mountains. Perhaps with the coming of the priest, supported by a good escort, they may be able to confine themselves to living like Christians in their town, which I have never been able to attain with all my diligence.[62]

In other words, Espinosa believed that Northern Pimans had to live in a compact settlement and subsist off their garden produce to be good Christians in Jesuit eyes. Northern Pimans who camped in the giant cactus groves on the south slopes of desert mountains during fruiting season impressed the missionaries as stubborn heathens. The religiosity of the times did not encourage clerical perception of the ecological adjustment to a semi-arid region inherent in movement between areas affording different resources.

The persistence of Northern Piman transhumance in the face of the priests' determination to end it indicates that the Jesuit missionary effort at Tucson was too sporadic and intermittent to have much effect on the Native Americans there beyond nominal compliance with the most outward forms of Catholicism. Even though the settlement had been visited irregularly for nearly 70 years by relays of missionary priests pioneering the Gospel, just one Jesuit priest ever lived at or very near Tucson, and he for only a five-month ministry.

Only seven Jesuit missionaries actually resided at Bac, near enough to Tucson to visit it frequently. Of these seven, only Espinosa, who started off on the wrong foot with the native population, stayed a decade, and during his last couple of years there he was either too ill or in fact absent recovering from severe illness, to minister to the Tucson people.

Before Espinosa, only Stiger stayed more than a few months, and he had Guebavi to minister to, so that his efforts were not channeled north toward Tucson. He barely survived the psychological warfare mounted against him by the Bac native religious leaders, or perhaps their poisons were as effective as their spells. Neve's stay was cut short by Jesuit expulsion, and his early months at Bac must have been devoted largely to Espinosa and the Bac populace.

Thus, Jesuit proselytizing at Tucson provided a prelude to conversion rather than real Christianization. The Society failed to deliver to this rim of Christendom the missionary manpower required to establish a true mission at Tucson.

3.

Garcés' Franciscan Mission Branch, 1768-1779

WHEN THE MEMBERS of the Society of Jesus were expelled from New Spain, civilian commissioners took charge of the physical assets of their missions. The viceroy asked other religious orders to provide missionaries for the former Jesuit frontier Native American missions. The Franciscan College of the Holy Cross at Querétaro accepted the challenge to operate the Upper Pimería missions. Friars started for the Sonoran missions on 5 August 1767.[1] One of them was destined to win considerable contemporary and enduring fame for his exploratory exploits on this frontier.

The "Children's Priest" at Bac

Francisco Tomás Hermenegildo Garcés Maestro was born at Morata del Conde in the Spanish Kingdom of Aragon on 12 April 1738. He was the fourth child of Juan Garcés and Antonia Maestro. Although Juan Garcés farmed, his brother Francisco served the local count as personal chaplain, and his brother Domingo was rector of Chodes, a short walk from Morata. The latter reared Francisco.[2] At 15, young Garcés entered San Cristóbal de Alpartir convent of the Franciscan Order.[3] In 1762, he volunteered for the mission field, and sailed for New Spain shortly after his ordination in 1763.[4] At the College of the Holy Cross in Querétaro, Garcés became known as the "Children's Priest," being considered simple and artless.[5]

Yet the clerical leaders of the College of the Holy Cross recognized the potential of Francisco Garcés as a missionary to Native Americans. Quite possibly they stereotyped Indians as being like Spanish children, and inadvertently chose the best possible friar for the farthest frontier. They assigned him to Mission San Xavier del Bac, the most remote post on this rim of Christendom. Thus, Garcés assumed ecclesiastical responsibility for the Northern Piman Indians of Tucson. Within a month of his arrival at Bac, the friar wrote a courtesy note to the commander of Tubac, the nearest military post. He described the Indians at his new mission to Captain Juan Bautista de Anza from the point of view of a fresh recruit to the mission field:

Don Juan Bautista de Anza
My Dear Sir:
I arrived at this mission the 30th of June having been at your house en route, where your wife and servants elegantly put into practice their

charity as you have instructed and accustomed them to do. There is nothing new here.

The Indians expect to be advised to go out to campaign. They are very wild, without doctrine even in their own language, because, although they pray together, no one by himself understands. Even the most advanced respond with any word, so I endeavor to get them to come to catechism. Yet it is not achieved unless it is in the greater number of youngsters who do it well. On the contrary are those who have already reached adulthood: these only attend on feast days. They say that they have always been reared so that adults go to the fields and the children to catechism. For the present I do not urge earnestly until I see how things are.

The *Tugsones* gave me to understand that they have not wanted any other priest than me, having understood the goal I impose on them that the priest does not come so that they might work for him, etc., with which they are rather happy. They have already built me a little hut among their own. Three times I have been there and I have told them that in the coming month of August I am going to stay some fifteen days, and that they are my children like those of San Javier, and it appears that they are in a good humor.

The soldiers behave divinely, giving a good example in calling these people to the doctrine as any good Christian is obligated to do.

In my harvest time, I expect illnesses and other hardships which everyone has predicted for me. Yet right now only the flies and mosquitoes have moderated. As for the rest, you know how things can go with me.

The Jesuit fathers of San Javier, with all their cows, fields, horses, etc., were occupied with labors, but with my stipend I shall not be, good sire. I commend it to God who alone is able to bring you here, but may it be as soon as possible that we may together enjoy this carefree existence. Here they call one room that of the captain. Thus it has been and shall be, and not for a poor house of St. Francis have they to leave. I await news, and if God aids our arms and some captains or troops are in Pitíc, I should like to know it.

God Our Father, etc.

FR. FRANCISCO GARCÉS[6]

San Javier. July 29, 1768.

In a letter to the governor of Sonora written the same day, Garcés more fully described the situation he perceived at his mission and its branch. Those portions of this missive dealing with Bac and Tucson bear translation here. They add to the evidence as to how rapidly Garcés learned facts pertinent to his ministry, such as the presence of San Pedro River Sobaipuris in Tucson and the extent of Jesuit christening of Papagos not living in the mission or its branch pueblo:

... These missions of San Xavier and of the Tugson are quiet. The Indians are content to see that our King wants them as people and not as slaves. As regards doctrine: in the Tugson, none. They have not prayed nor have they a *fiscal*. In San Xavier, a little less than none, because they do not know it either in Spanish or in their own language.

They have never known it in their own tongue. This is not the worst, because here it has never been possible to assemble the married adults, not even on most occasions our own partisans. Consequently, with great diligence I succeeded in gathering the young people, but few married persons among them. I did not employ violent means to overcome their resistance because things are as they are, and so that I might test other methods. Everyone goes to live in the maizefields and plantings, which they greatly love. This pleases me because thus they eat and halfway clothe themselves. I trust in God that He shall succeed in teaching them the Doctrine with the measures that may be taken.

In the beginning neither children nor adults came until I personally went twice to their *ranchos,* by which means I explained things to them and persuaded most of them to come. The Governor and the justices tell them to come and will make them come, because it is convenient thus. By force or by free choice they must come. Yet I am not inclined to be rigorous. I only threaten the children, and I have begun to spank them so that they should not play hookey. In order to do so, I quieted the scruples of the Governor, who put himself up to telling me that he had read a letter that said that one could not strike Indians. In a word, I am not discontented. The young people do well. If Your Lordship should approve, the adults will be treated a little more forcefully.

The people of the Tugson are content. They told me that they wished no other priest than me — but only when they were well informed that the priest would not make them work as had the Jesuits, that the King greatly cares for them, and that they would not be less than the others. They are a bit flexible. Having closed the old site of the pueblo because of the Apaches, they have made me a little hut at my request. They have given me a youth to instruct. I have told them that in August I am going to spend eight or fifteen days with them and that I shall alternate [between Bac and Tucson]. They do not seem to me to put on a bad face [at that].

The governor and residents of Santa Cruz who are in the Tugson say that they are content, that they live well, plant and remain here happily. This they told me after asking me if [the authorities] wished to remove them from the Tugson. I have assured them that the King wants them to live well and to have a priest, but that he will not treat them violently so that they would go elsewhere.

There are people, but not as many as it seems. The Papaguería makes the population bulk large. Now that the Papagos have gone to their lands, however, one sees that there are not so many. Those whom I have recognized at San Xavier do not number sixty families to date, but there could be more. In the Tugson, there are that many more huts for the inhabitants, which is better to my way of thinking, outside of two rancherías. As they say, there is no doubt that there is a baptized multitude from West of this Mission to the North of it, inasmuch as they are mentioned and evidenced by the registers. The 1,108 baptized yields a great discrepancy from the 213 deaths, 246 marriages, and 500 confirmations, all these since the year 1755.

Some of the country people have given me hopes that they will join the Mission. I have promised that if they are sick and call me to hear their confessions, I will go. I promised that I will go to see their *ranchos* that they say are lacking in water. . . .[7]

After six weeks on the frontier, Garcés wrote to the guardian of his college, "I think they will behave better in Tugson than in San Xavier." The priest found that the Tucson social structure reflected the migration of Northern Piman Indians to that settlement, for he encountered no less than "three Governors who are natives of three former pueblos."

These leaders flattered the new missionary by telling him that they had never before allowed a priest in Tucson — a patent falsehood that Garcés passed on to his superior — but that they wanted no other priest than Garcés now that he had arrived. The fledgling missionary possessed peasant wit enough to perceive that Tucson's governing trio thus complimented him only after they were "well informed that the Father was not going to bother them and that he would feed himself from his stipend." In other words, the Franciscan would not force them to labor as they claimed the departed Jesuits had.

Besides building the priest a hut among their own, the Tucson people assigned him the youth mentioned in Garcés letter to the governor. This boy was to be instructed by the missionary and trained to act as a mission official. Probably the native leaders employed this young man as a spy to provide them with information about the priest.

Garcés clearly suffered from cultural shock after six weeks of dealing with Native Americans behaving in terms of conventional understandings quite different from those the missionary shared. He urged the guardian of his college to assign a full-time missionary to Tucson partly on the grounds a third priest on the Santa Cruz River would greatly "console" the two already there.[8] So great was this initial impact on Garcés that he repeatedly returned to this concept, with rather marked success, as his reputation as an explorer brought him recognition in civil as well as ecclesiastical circles.

One suspects that along with cultural shock, the staunch Catholic conscience of Friar Francisco bothered him because he enjoyed frontier life as much as he did. Later he would venture into the wilderness for long periods during which he seems not to have observed the basic clerical rituals.

After only six weeks among the Northern Pimans, Garcés seems to have perceived his ideological peril. Those very qualities which made him the "Children's Priest" generated in Garcés prompt sympathy for the Northern Pimans. He quickly recognized his personal tendency to identify with these Native Americans. So he pled for clerical reinforcement that would maintain his allegiance to his Order and culture.

If Garcés carried out his intention of spending one or two weeks in Tucson, perhaps that experience reduced his psychological stress from cultural shock. Whatever the explanation, within two months of his arrival, Garcés considered things well enough in hand at Bac and Tucson to embark on the first of the exploring trips which brought him fame.[9] He did so despite a warning from an army officer that the Papagos had rebelled, a report Garcés considered false.

Leaving on 29 August 1768, guided by four pagan Indians, Garcés traversed Papago territory to the Gila River, preaching through the interpreter he took with him. He returned in October, having traveled as long as he had spent at his mission, and fell violently ill.[10] Unconscious for 24 hours, Garcés later suffered severe chills. The Franciscan at Guebavi moved Garcés there to recuperate. While he was gone, Apaches raided Bac, killed its governor and carried off Garcés' two-trooper escort.[11] After Garcés returned to Bac, Apaches again raided it on 20 February 1769.[12]

By March of 1769, however, Garcés was again on the move. Following this second journey, apparently into the San Pedro River Valley, he became ill again. Then Apaches struck Bac in April and on 3 July of 1769. After two weeks of alarm, the ensign of the Tubac garrison led a scout force of 20 soldiers and citizens, 10 Pimas from Bac, 5 from Guebavi "and some who go from the Tugson" to the Gila River. Writing to the governor of the province, Garcés cited a recent bad example of Indian hostilities as a distinct possibility at his mission unless security arrangements improved:

> . . . I say that what happened at Santa María will happen here unless there is a miracle worked by the hand of the Omnipotent. It is not a question of the ordinary goods of the missions, but of the holy vessels and the mission. It seems to me that these would be more valuable than that the presidial remount herds have two, or three or four soldiers, more or less. With regard to this Mission, there have been thought necessary for it at various times twenty, fifteen, ten or five and perhaps fewer troopers when the Sobaipuris were still in their territory. Now, five or six would not be too many, with the responsibility of dividing up, so that even though I might go to the Tugson, [this mission] would still be defended. Now, however, if I should be disposed to travel there, I ought to take with me precisely the present escort, leaving this mission all by itself. In the Tugson there is neither earthen wall nor hut. This is worse than that of the residents so it does not seem prudent to me to go alone and live alone as I did last year.

Having wintered in the Tucson area and learned more about Northern Piman subsistence, Garcés urged on the governor a more authoritarian role for the missionary than he had himself wanted when he arrived in 1768.

> As I wrote to you last year when I had recently arrived, it gave me pleasure to see the maize fields of the residents, and how content they and I were. Having now seen the hunger of the winter, the abandonment of the pueblo and the thievery at the mission, I find myself forced to inform you that although in other areas the Indians can govern themselves, it is not so here unless the priest should govern and other measures be taken than Your Illustriousness ordered. I say this because it is better to struggle with the spiritual and temporal affairs rather than see a poor minister. Those of the Tugson would not object either to having the priests govern the Indians. These poor Indians were so hungry that I told them that if they wished they should plant maize communally. They cleared the ground at once, planted, and it appears that the crop will be lost from too much water. They say that they will sow much wheat.
>
> The measures taken by the Lord Visitor are necessary on the frontier, and benefit the Indians. They do not benefit the merchants and Span-

iards, who are unable to do with a priest what they can with an Indian. For this reason, I know not what events may occur with the temporal affairs. As I say to myself of this land, although I will chant the *Te Deum laudamus* if all the priests there are between here and San Ignacio were to come up here, possibly there would be talent and disposition to develop conversions and found missions with priestly governance. [I have seen] Command and fear where one ought to see love and respect on the part of the recently converted Indians for their minister. I hope to see you. After writing you so many "buts," I shall see whether this disposition [of the Visitor] will have more force and achieve greater observance than that which has achieved such great success in both Americas for these two hundred years!

Finally, the Tugson merits the piety of Your Lordship in order that a priest might come there as I have asked his Illustriouness. Yet the report of the Lord Governor is the most [important]. I also charge you in the name of Jesus Christ, who of course has worked so much personally and with eloquent reports for the good of the Province, that He may render you the greatest service, aiding you to make many new conversions, and [insure] that the missionary fathers, curates, soldiers and merchants remain so that we do not make an end to the sad province. Your Lordship knows very well how many parrots we have in all the estates. Thus it is that this mission has no more than three yokes of tame oxen which are not enough by a wide margin for San Javier much less the Tugson. The plantings appropriate to the two pueblos cannot be made. There are 150 families in these two pueblos, and it is necessary for them to sow like people. It will, therefore, be necessary to have recourse to other missions. If not, the temporal life of this mission may suffer many agonies, and no commission will produce any special effect.[13]

Reading Garcés' correspondence with colonial officials, one sometimes wonders how they reacted to his rather bitter sarcasm. Little wonder that Garcés' ecclesiastical superiors at the college considered him artless!

Factionalism Brings a Church

Friar Francisco Garcés' initial impact on the Tucson Native Americans changed the relationship between them and San Xavier's missionary. Despite Garcés' frequent absences on exploratory trips, his tenure at Bac produced considerable changes in the Tucson community. The Sobaipuri refugees from the San Pedro River Valley who had settled at the ranchería of Tucson in 1762, and feared that Garcés had come to remove them in 1768, were by 1770 thinking of moving to the Gila River. Their leaders claimed that they had always had this thought in mind, although it may have been a purely retrospective interpretation. Part of their disenchantment with Tucson apparently arose from Garcés' failure to subsidize them sufficiently to suit their notions.

Garcés, or someone, got word of the Sobaipuri discontent to Tubac post commander Juan Bautista de Anza early in 1770. Anza was fighting Seris on the Gulf of California coast under Colonel Domingo Elizondo. The expeditionary commander released Anza 60 presidial troops so that he could deal with Spain's Northern Piman allies.[14] Anza hurried this command north to Tubac and left there on 17 April for Bac and Tucson.

Three families had already departed for the Gila River settlements four days before Anza arrived at Tucson. Factionalism clearly had reached some sort of peak. Anza persuaded the Native Americans still at Tucson to remain there. He also ordered the governors of the village to make the three migrant families return. Anza picked out a place for the people to construct a protective wall, which they agreed to do. Building the rampart was the first large-scale community project these Native Americans had undertaken in many decades – perhaps within the lifetimes of all those then resident at Tucson. It was the first major European-style construction at Tucson, the first house the natives built for Garcés' use having been a rather humble structure erected in Northern Piman style.

The Sobaipuri refugees also complained to Captain Anza that they had no church. He told them that was because they themselves had not wanted one enough to build it. The Native Americans offered an alibi. They had long wanted a church and told their missionaries so, but the latter never provisioned them. Anza conveyed this demand for a food subsidy to Friar Garcés. The latter promptly granted the Indians all their own wheat from the church field at Tucson (ten bushels) and half of that from Bac.[15] While the army officer may well have placed Garcés in a position where he could hardly refuse to embark upon church construction at Tucson, the effect was that Friar "Pancho" Garcés significantly favored his Tucson charges over those at Bac.

Whatever measures the Tucson Native American governors may have taken to persuade the migrant families to return from the Gila River, Garcés himself in the end had to try to carry out Anza's orders. Undeterred by previous illnesses, Garcés left Bac on 18 October 1770 to hike to the Gila River. He went to reassure the Pimas, whose numbers were being decimated by a measles epidemic. The friar also wanted to try to bring back a woman who had fled his mission. Possibly she was the carrier who had transmitted the contagion to the Gileños. Garcés returned to Bac on November fifth,[16] after a brief three-week absence.

Apparently the Northern Pimans at Tucson worked on the defensive wall while Garcés was absent, or he kept them at it when in residence. In addition, they completed an adobe structure with towers by 1 February 1771. That afternoon the Tucson people utilized the new complex to repel an Apache attack, although the enemy killed two boys and stole cattle, sheep and horses.[17]

On August 8, when the 1771 rainy season was well advanced, Garcés left Bac to explore westward across Papaguería to the Colorado River. This three-month trip became crucial to his later exploratory exploits, for it served to lay the foundation for expeditions across the Colorado River to upper California. On such journeys, Garcés not only explored Northern Piman territory, but he also began to recruit Papagos to move to Bac and Tucson to replenish their diminishing riverine populations. The wandering missionary returned to the colonial frontier at Caborca Mission on 29 October.[18]

In 1772 a priest at another mission wrote a general description of Sonoran missions apparently based on inventories and enumerations of population that had been made when the Franciscans arrived or soon thereafter. Friar Antonio de los Reyes reported that San José del Tucson had no church nor house for the missionary, concurring with Garcés' own earlier report that he had only a native-style hut.

Reyes noted that some of the Native Americans were still not converted,[19] suggesting that already there had arisen a form of factionalism in addition to that occasioned by the differences between the Santa Cruz River Valley natives and the San Pedro River Sobaipuri refugees. By this time the Native Americans at Tucson had probably been in frequent enough contact with Jesuit missionaries and lay Catholics for somewhat Christianized "progressives" to start being married by the priest, as indicated in Torres Perea's report a generation earlier, wearing cheap crucifixes, telling rosaries of trade beads or at least wearing the beads, adopting some Spanish clothing made from red bayeta cloth supplied by the missionary, possibly burying their dead in an extended position in the church cemetery, and sneering at the unconverted "conservatives."

The Reyes report written in 1772 was, however, almost obsolete for Tucson, evidently based on an earlier Garcés report. That missionary himself reported in 1772 that a church was being constructed and that the fortified village was ahead of Bac.[20]

Tucson apparently can thank Friar Francisco T. H. Garcés Maestro for making Saint Augustine its patron saint. The Franciscan friar seems to have dedicated his church to Saint Augustine. That inference can be drawn from references to Tucson during this part of Garcés' ministry there. Friar Antonio de los Reyes called Tucson "San José del Tucson" in his 1772 report, using the name Captain Francisco Elías Gonzáles had bestowed a decade earlier. In 1774, on the other hand, a Franciscan inspector visited "San Agustín del Tucson" with Garcés' substitute, Friar Juan Gorgoll.[21]

"Pancho" Garcés clearly found Native Americans beyond the colonial frontier congenial and exciting people. Yet, whether in effect forced by Captain Anza or not, Garcés was also a sun-dried brick and mud-mortar friar, at least at Tucson. This Aragonese peasant priest could turn his hand and mind to whatever task demanded doing.

Effects of Franciscan Manpower

Part of the secret of Father Francisco Garcés' success in speeding up the process of cultural change among the Indians of Tucson was the quality of political support and/or competition he received from the young, energetic captain at Tubac. Another part of the secret was Franciscan manpower. Unlike the earlier Jesuit missionaries at Bac, Garcés had assistants and substitutes. This is indicated in numerous documents.

When Garcés first reached Bac and began to learn how to deal with Northern Piman Indians, a civilian commissioner conducted business affairs. Garcés wrote to Governor Pineda on 29 July 1768 that "The Commissary says he will inform Your Lordship of everything."[22] Garcés had a royal commissary for company during his first year as a new missionary. Not until 3 June 1769 did Visitor General José de Gálvez "order each and every one of the Royal Commissaries in whose care the temporal administration of said Missions was provisionally placed that they should immediately turn over to the said Fathers Missionary all the effects, goods, cattle and other things managed by them, with individual inventories."[23]

At the end of Garcés' Tucson ministry, a passage in a military report of 1779 referred to "the two apostles of the Holy Cross of Querétaro who continually are found in the nearby missions of San Xavier del Bac and Tupson. . . ."[24]

When Garcés accompanied the first Anza expedition to California in 1774, Friar Juan Gorgoll, missionary stationed at Atí, temporarily replaced him at Bac and Tucson. Garcés left at the end of the first week of January and returned to Bac on 10 July 1774 after six months of exploration.[25] It is worth noting that Gorgoll, like missionaries previously stationed at Bac, still complained that the Tucson people wandered too much. He noted that they went "in search of food,"[26] but his cultural conditioning prevented his tolerating their aboriginal economic adjustment. Seasonal movement did help to insulate the Northern Pimans against the catechism!

Another Franciscan substitute came to Bac in 1775 when Garcés went off again with Anza's second California expedition. This was Félix de Gamarra,[27] a Cantabrian born in 1747 who came to New Spain in 1770 and was ordained at Querétaro before being sent to the Native American missions. After filling in for Garcés, Gamarra went to Tumacacori in late 1776.[28] He later moved to Tubutama Mission, where he died from a fever in May of 1779, aged only 32 years.[29]

On this major expedition, Garcés departed Bac on 21 October 1775 and did not return until 17 September 1776, almost 11 months later.[30] Then he spent much time at other missions preparing reports. A week after returning to Bac, Garcés wrote to the guardian of his college from Tumacacori Mission.[31] After a short while he probably went on to San Ignacio to write up his nearly year-long fantastic travels over unknown trails among aboriginal peoples far beyond the colonial frontier.

The Father President of the Pimería Alta missions sent Friar Juan Bautista Belderrain to Bac, evidently when Gamarra returned to Tumacacori. When Garcés asked that a second priest be sent to Bac – probably when he went to San Ignacio – the president sent Friar Joaquín Antonio Velarde to reinforce Belderrain.[32] By 3 January 1777, Garcés had completed his report with the aid of other friars at Tubutama. He reported to the guardian again on that date.[33] Garcés probably returned to Bac soon after, and Velarde moved to Tumacacori.

Such frequent changing and reinforcing of mission personnel clearly evidences the fact that the religious Order charged with the spiritual mission to the Northern Pimans after 1767 possessed the manpower to keep sending priests into Upper Pimería with a prodigality that the expelled Jesuits had never achieved. Consequently, the missionary assault on traditional native religion became continuous and much more effective than it had been during the Jesuit period.

In addition, these Franciscans had regular financial support. Missionaries received an annual stipend of 350 pesos paid them from the royal exchequer. They sent this money (paid to them at Arizpe) to the city of Mexico, along with whatever profits they realized from the sale of mission farm produce and cattle once they took over temporal administration from the temporary royal commissaries, to a purchasing agent who procured supplies for the churches and Native American converts.[34]

Thus, Garcés and his alternates really brought the frontier mission institution to bear with full force at Bac for the first time, with significant increase in missionary effort at Tucson. They changed the patron saint of Tucson, and under military pressure supervised construction of a European-style church and defensive works there.

Garcés' Departure for the Quechan Mission

During 1778, Garcés presumably labored at Bac and Tucson. In January and February of 1778, he wrote to the viceroy and guardian of his college from Tucson. Noting Velarde's return to Tumacacori, Garcés commented that his companion, Friar Belderrain, was "applying himself diligently to [learning] the Pima language."[35] Given Garcés' early preference for the people at Tucson over those at Bac, he conceivably divided the evangelical tasks with Belderrain so that he spent more time at Tucson and left Belderrain to learn more Northern Piman and deal with the people at Bac. The presidial garrison had moved to Tucson from Tubac by this time, so the company of other Europeans was available just across the Santa Cruz River from Tucson. There are many indications that Garcés was human enough to enjoy the recognition his explorations won from colonial officials, so that he welcomed contact with Europeans. Moreover, he was urging and planning the establishment of new missions to advance the colonial frontier, so proximity to military communication lines was convenient.

For another year, Garcés likely labored at his assigned mission. In the spring of 1779, however, he was again on the move toward martyrdom. He wrote to the viceroy in mid-March from Los Siete Principes de Atí Mission.[36]

By late March Garcés was churning up affairs at Altar presidio, preparing the mission-founding expedition to the Colorado River Yumas specifying which Tucson soldiers and citizens he wanted as colonists.[37] In August, Garcés left Altar to advance the rim of Christendom to the Yuma crossing of the Colorado River separating Sonora from upper California.

Exigencies of imperial involvement in international warfare producing the independence of the United States from England kept the Colorado River effort small. As a principal architect of the Spanish advance and a missionary with warm relations with the Yuma Indians, Francisco Garcés won assignment to one of the two missions founded across the Colorado River from the mouth of the Gila River, in 1779. There he died two years later in 1781 at the hands of Yuma Indians rebelling against Spanish treatment. Thus, Native Americans on New Spain's northwestern frontier lost a nearly unique friend in colonial councils. Imperial Spain lost one of its great explorers and Christendom one of its gentlest advocates.

4.

Brick-and-Mortar Missionaries, 1779-1790

THE CHURCH AT SAN XAVIER DEL BAC stands as a striking historical monument to the constructive energies of the friars of the Franciscan Order in Pimería Alta during the era of Indian warfare and the decades of relative peace that came at the end of the Spanish colonial period. The priest who began construction of this edifice to his faith at San Francisco Xavier del Bac was Friar Juan Bautista Belderrain, who had joined Garcés at Bac after the latter returned from his long California exploration. Even Belderrain's name was long unknown to historians writing about Tucson, much less the certainty that he deserves the credit for starting the present structure. During the period of preparation of this volume, discoveries in late-18th-century Spanish documents made Belderrain's eminence clear. Yet numerous gaps in knowledge of his career remain to be filled by further archival search.

Probably Friar Belderrain arrived in Sonora with the first Franciscans following the 1767 Jesuit expulsion, or soon thereafter. By 1775, at any rate, he was ministering to the people of Tecoripa and Suaqui in Lower Pimería.[1] There Belderrain gained experience in church construction. He persuaded recently pacified Lower Pimas to work on a church at Suaqui when given rations purchased by the royal exchequer. Belderrain moved to Pimería Alta in 1776, when he at least visited Tumacacori Mission[2] and began ministering to the Native Americans of Bac and Piman Tucson as the companion of Friar Francisco Garcés.

The first direct notices of Friar Belderrain as missionary at San Xavier del Bac occur in the letters of Garcés. On Christmas day in 1776 the explorer-priest reported to the guardian of his college that the president of the Pimería Alta missions had sent Belderrain to Bac.[3] Belderrain had probably been there since September, freeing Friar Gamarra to return to Tumacacori.

Friar Joaquín Antonio Velarde joined Belderrain at Bac for a few months. Then, in early 1777, Garcés returned to his flock after an absence of more than a year. Velarde went back to Tumacacori, where he served as assistant to Friar Pedro de Arriquibar from late 1778 to the summer of 1779.[4]

For two years Garcés and Belderrain labored together at Bac and Piman Tucson, converting the Native Americans to Spanish civilization and Christianity. Then the ever-restless Garcés departed for Altar to prepare for his Colorado River mission, leaving Belderrain alone until he was once again joined by Father Velarde in the summer of 1779.

Neither Belderrain nor Velarde seems to have resembled Garcés in possessing a predilection for exploration among strange aborigines beyond the colonial frontier of settlement. Belderrain, as a matter of fact, seems to have been Garcés' precise opposite. He was a brick-and-mortar priest, a builder of churches. Fortunately for later residents of the Gadsden Purchase area, Belderrain proved to be either as gifted at church design as Garcés was at tribal diplomacy, or able to employ an architect who was.

Mystery of a Church

According to a Spanish oral tradition recorded by one of the first Anglo-Americans to settle in Tucson,[5] Spanish civilian settlers came to Tucson from the San Pedro River Valley. Theirs was reputedly the first church built in the area and was dedicated to San Agustín. Spanish settlers built it with the aid of Native Americans who had fled the San Pedro River Valley with them.[6]

If the oral tradition did not specify Spanish builders aided by Indians, one might think the legend referred to the arrival of the San Pedro River Valley Sobaipuris in 1762, and their subsequent labor on the church at the Pueblo of Tucson financed by Father Francisco Garcés' mission field harvests in the early 1770s. That was certainly the first church building started at Piman Tucson and the first dedicated to San Agustín.

The local historian referred to all the Native Americans east of the Santa Cruz River as *Harneros.* This term could have been derived from *Janos,* a small group of Native Americans absorbed, it has been assumed, by the Chiricahua Apaches who moved into the area during historic times. "A great many of the Indians were Christianized and were baptized. In time they helped herd the cattle and till the soil" at Santa Cruz, according to the oral tradition. Inasmuch as no missionary contact had been established with Apaches prior to the new policy initiated in 1786,[7] it is difficult to understand how any might have been converted earlier.

The Tucson verbal tradition might indicate that some previously converted *Janos* Indians escaped the Apaches and joined the Spaniards in preference to southern Athapascan domination. A Spanish military post was established at Santa Cruz in the San Pedro Valley at the same time the Tubac garrison advanced to Tucson. It lasted for five years at most before retreating. Colonial forces abandoned the post after losing 2 officers and over 80 men. The post could not be defended.[8] It is doubtful whether any attacking Apaches were converted to Christianity there! Santa Cruz civilian settlers with Native American friends might have come to the Tucson area about 1779-1781, then, as refugees.[9]

The verbal tradition might also record a second post-1762 Sobaipuri flight to Piman Tucson. An army adjutant inspector concerned with ways to encourage settlement at Santa Cruz and "cultivation of many lands which the Sobaipuris sow"[10] in 1780 suggested that some Sobaipuris had returned to the San Pedro River Valley with the temporary Spanish military advance. If so, they only had to flee again to the Tucson area.

If there were indeed 1779 refugees who built a Tucson-area church, did they help presidial Captain Pedro de Allande build the military chapel? If not the presidial chapel, did they help erect the Llorens convent at Piman Tucson? If not that, did they erect a chapel on some unknown site in the area? Tucson's oral tradition provides a fascinating mystery not quite solved by known documents.

Builder-Priest Alone

A Cantabrian from Spain, Belderrain's companion Joaquín Velarde was a young man. He had asked to go to the missions in 1770, and was ordained at Cádiz en route to the New World.[11] Evidently not long after his return to Bac in August 1779, Velarde fell ill. Belderrain or the president sent him off to the mining camp at Cienegilla to recover.[12] Still preserved in the parish archives at Altar is a record of the sad outcome:[13]

> In the Year of Our Lord 1781, the Reverend Father Friar Joaquín Velarde, Apostolic Missionary of the College of the Holy Cross of Querétaro, Minister at the Mission of San Xavier del Bac, delivered his soul to God on the Fifth day of March in the house of Don Antonio de Castro, citizen of this *Real* of San Ildefonso de la Cienega, and I gave Ecclesiastical sepulchre to his body in the chancel of the church on the gospel side on the sixth day of said month. He came to this *Real* to cure himself, and as his illness increased, he received all the Holy Sacraments of Penitence, Eucharist and Extreme Unction. All the community attended his funeral rites, and with the assistance of the Superintending Curate and Ecclesiastical Judge Don Josef Nicolás de Mesa, all the rite was solemnized. In order to certify, I sign this day, month, and year as above.
>
> FRIAR THOMAS EYXARCH

Thus, Velarde had but little time between Garcés' departure and his own death early in 1781 to accomplish very much among the Northern Piman Indians of Bac and Tucson. While the royal Spanish post of San Agustín del Tucson was being turned into a true fortification by the construction of an adobe wall and moat, the aboriginal Northern Piman ranchería of Tucson a short half league[14] across the Santa Cruz River followed the less dynamic tenor of semi-mission life. Velarde and Belderrain evidently lost none of the ground gained under Garcés, however, inasmuch as the latter was able to embark upon the most ambitious church construction program yet undertaken within the boundaries of what later became the state of Arizona. In fact, the mission church Belderrain started in 1783 was not to be equaled in size and material for many decades, and in architectural grace not for many years if at all.

By the time Velarde died, the College of the Holy Cross in Querétaro was running short of priests for its frontier missions. The two-priest policy Garcés had managed to win for Bac-Tucson lapsed, and Belderrain manned this mission by himself. His solitary situation helps to explain the nature of the documentary reference to Belderrain in the affidavits collected on orders from Captain Pedro de Allande y Saabedra to reconstruct the events during the Apache attack which carried up to the entrance to the post stockade on

1 May 1782, translated in Chapter 7 of this book. Sections of the affidavit Belderrain wrote describing his view of the battle reveal several interesting details of his relationship to the Tucson people and their position among the frontier Native Americans. He penned his statement at San Xavier Mission on 4 May 1782.

The affidavit of the post chaplain describing the same notable battle provides additional information about mission life at Tucson in the early 1780s. When the ensign charged by the post commander with collecting statements interrogated the chaplain, the latter said that "because he found himself in the Pueblo of Tucson to visit Father Minister Friar Juan Bautista Belderrain after the conventual Mass (with the kind permission of his captain) he was unable to see the number of enemies...."[15] Thus, it appears that the chaplain and the missionary liked to meet one another at Piman Tucson after the Franciscan had celebrated Mass or other ritual for the Native American congregation. Presumably the chaplain had already celebrated Mass for the troops in the military chapel on the post. The two priests evidently felt themselves to be quite intellectually isolated on the far northern frontier of Christendom, and welcomed this weekly opportunity to converse with another man of the cloth.

In 1783, Friar Juan Bautista Belderrain began construction on the monumental church at Bac. During the next six years, he watched the massive walls rise, supervised the barrel vaulting that roofed the nave, the drum and dome that soared across the transept. By the end of 1789, he had brought the fundamental structure of the new church to completion.[16]

Tucson oral tradition credits Ygnacio Gauna with being one of the builders of this magnificent mission. Father Llorens placed him at the head of the list of citizens living at the mission in 1801, as shown in Table 14 in the Appendix. He was reportedly 27 at that time, making him an early teenager in Belderrain's day, a bit young to have been much of a construction worker, much less the designer of the building, as some oral accounts would have it. When Father Llorens took over in 1790, Ygnacio Gauna would have been 16 and perhaps ready to help with the finishing touches over the course of the next seven years. Thus, Gauna's role could have been no more than minor, although his existence is clearly documented. Possibly Francisco Gauna, a soldier in the presidial garrison in 1817 (see Table 10, Appendix) was Ignacio's brother, whose baptismal name oral tradition has lost.

Such fragments of verbal history help to fill in the story of the construction of the beautiful San Xavier church. The practical builder-priest who labored seven years on the grandiose project surely reported progress to his superiors, but his letters have yet to be located.

Then, late in 1789 or early in 1790, Father Belderrain died alone and unconfessed, despite the effort of his colleague at Tumacacori to reach him, reportedly by running the 45 miles between the two missions. Belderrain died without the last rites of his Church, which he administered to many others.[17] Presumably his body was buried at his mission, in a spot unknown today, but most likely under the floor of the new church.

Probably Belderrain did little building at Piman Tucson, even though he celebrated Mass there on Sundays. The manpower of both Bac and Tucson was almost certainly all committed to the construction at Bac, or to growing crops and animals to sell to finance the purchase of construction materials and hiring of journeymen builders. Besides an oral tradition indicating that the Peaceful Apaches participated to some extent in the construction project, (see Chapter 5), traditions are still preserved by the desert-dwelling Papagos that tell of their forebears contributing labor to this cause. Belderrain's monumental plan for Bac mobilized widely scattered resources, but militated against church-building at the Pueblo of Tucson.

Piman Cultural Change

Antonio de los Reyes, who had written the 1772 report on Sonoran missions, composed yet another comprehensive report in 1784. Meanwhile, he had been appointed the first bishop of Sonora, Sinaloa and the Californias. The information about Piman Tucson on which the bishop-designate based his description of the people of that village probably was supplied to him about the time Belderrain began building his Bac church. Thus, it may be taken as a good measure of the impact Garcés, Velarde and Belderrain and interim ministers achieved on the Tucson natives during a decade and a half of conversion and directed cultural change.

The bishop-designate dismissed the Native Americans of Tucson as unambitious beings who would run about practically naked if the missionary did not "succor" them with some clothes. Reyes regarded them as lazy and labeled their customs as uncouth.[18] They did work as a community, however, to raise crops, cattle and horses for the missionary to sell to supplement his stipend from the royal treasury. Apparently the Franciscans had succeeded in introducing animal husbandry where the Jesuits had failed. Moreover, the communal production organization initiated by Garcés clearly was mobilized behind the Bac church construction effort.

All the Tucson natives were still considered to be Northern Pimas, and all of them spoke their own language. None spoke Spanish.[19] This meant that everyone in the village could communicate naturally and easily, but that outsiders could not do so unless they spoke Northern Piman. The Native Americans at the Pueblo of Tucson were still homogenous in the essential cultural bond of common language, even though factions had surely come into existence based on other differences – amalgamation of San Pedro River Sobaipuris and differential conversion most obviously.

By that time, although the Native Americans still lived in beehive-shaped, grass-thatched huts, Tucson presumably had become a walled village as a result of Anza's 1770 efforts[20] to persuade the natives to build a protective wall. In 1785, the Tucson military commander claimed credit for improving the defensive structure, having "formed for the greater security of the Pimería, these nearby towns of adobe walled houses.[21] Thus, the decade and a half following 1770 evidently saw the introduction of Spanish-style, vertical-walled, square-cornered adobe structures in the domestic and public architecture of the Native Americans of Tucson. This period must have been one of rapid change in technology and material possessions of these people.

5.

Franciscans at Work, 1790-1821

AFTER FRIAR JUAN BAUTISTA BELDERRAIN DIED, the father president of the Upper Pimería missions rushed a replacement missionary to Bac early in 1790.[1] Friar Juan Baptista Llorens had been missionary at Oquitoa since 1787.[2] He came to Bac and Piman Tucson to stay for a quarter century of key ministry in the lives of the Northern Pimans there. Llorens completed the construction work initiated at Bac by Belderrain. It took Llorens seven more years, but in 1797 he finished the present church and mortuary chapel.[3]

Taking over the project in 1790, Llorens had to cope with rising prices generated by conditions in Europe. As early as the fall of 1792, the purchasing agent for the College of the Holy Cross was warning the frontier missionaries of inflation. Sugar sold at 6 pesos per *arroba* even though it never before cost over 18 *reales*, for example.

Thus, the national historic monument resulted from the combined local efforts of Fathers Belderrain and Llorens, with the latter responsible for the finishing touches, plus the Franciscan supply system reaching from Vera Cruz to the frontier. Llorens and other Pimería Alta missionaries all signed one power of attorney empowering their agent to collect their royal stipends. The president had to certify to the royal exchequer that each missionary in fact served his mission and was eligible for payment. By 1792, colonial policy had changed so that Llorens could no longer count upon income from mission lands.[4] As the mission Indians' living standards presumably rose, mission building-income fell just when inflation caused construction costs to rise.

During the busy construction period, Llorens had also to try to protect the irrigation water rights of the native population of Tucson against usurpation by the soldiers of the presidio and civilian settlers.[5] He showed himself to be a capable and versatile missionary who accomplished much besides completing the Bac building program.

Western Apache Help

According to Spanish-language oral tradition in Tucson, the peaceful Apaches who had settled at the Piman village (see Chapter 9), picturesquely but probably inaccurately termed "mesquetaires and Coyllatiars" (that is, Mescaleros and Coyoteros), joined in the work of finishing the present magnificent church structure of St. Francis Xavier at Bac, and helped with another dedicated to St. Joseph.[6] Although a Franciscan official wrote in 1793, the year that the Arivaipa Apache band settled in peace at Tucson, that "we hope to see completed this year the church which has been built in the mission of San Xavier del Bac,"[7] it was not actually finished until four years later, even with the possible addition of Apache labor. "The date, 1797, which is seen on one of the doors of this church, is, according to the tradition, the date of the monument's completion."[8] Oral tradition is confirmed in this instance by a report of the father president of the Upper Pimería missions who made an inspection tour that year.[9] According to tradition,

> This mission was built for all Christian Indians, but the Papagos would not let the Apaches have anything to say about the feast[10] or anything about the church but to pay the ties [tithes].[11] So they asked for a mission or convent where they could kind of work for themselves, which was granted them and the place was designated as the line northwest of the Rancho del Tucson and was called San José del Tucson. It was more of an industrial school than a mission. This was built by the Apaches and had but little help from the Papagos. During the building of this mission [a] great many Indians came from the northeast to assist.... It was not very hard work to build the mission as there were so many to do it.[12]

Even so, some of the newly pacified Apaches evidently were not much interested in even light work done by many hands. Before the construction was finished, according to the same oral tradition, "some of the Indians got dissatisfied and a great many of them left, taking horses and cattle with them. That made the others dissatisfied, so they had a fight."

The oral traditions this account follows in dating the construction of the church at Piman Tucson after that of San Xavier del Bac are independently supported by a Forty-Niner's journal. Ygnacio Saenz, one-time civil judge of the Presidio of San Agustín under Mexican sovereignty, told H. M. T. Powell that the two-story building at the Pima Pueblo of Tucson across the valley from the fort was erected after the church of St. Francis Xavier del Bac.[13] The construction of this edifice is treated later in this chapter.

Ministry to the Apaches

It is clear that Llorens took quite seriously his ministry to his Apache helpers, a duty which was eschewed by military chaplains of the presidio of San Agustín del Tucson. That Llorens established his program rather promptly and with some effectiveness appears in the first lines of a report he made to the president of the Franciscan frontier missions in 1795.

Other officials had urged the founding of new missions to the Peaceful Apaches. Father President Barbastro[14] had written to Llorens at Bac and to Arriquibar at Bacoachi for information, considering them the two missionaries under his jurisdiction most knowledgeable of prospects for proselytizing the Apaches:

> Very Reverend Father President
> Friar Francisco Antonio Barbastro,
> I acknowledge receiving yours of 25 April. In view of its contents, I went to the Pueblo of Tucson on the second day of Holy Week, even

though I was not ignorant of the condition of these Apaches. Inasmuch as the Captain was executing his New Mexican commission,[15] the Lieutenant came as is habitual for the commanding officer. We discussed the matter. He told me that the Apaches are very obedient and prompt to carry out what they are ordered to do, and that they are desirous of being Christians. On such evidence, he concludes that there will be no difficulty whatsoever with their settlement. We could not speak to the Apaches because they were out hunting.

Many still have not returned. Others were here today. They did not fail to understand me. They showed themselves to be quite content with what I said, and desirous that it should be carried out promptly. Nevertheless, one cannot make a great point of this, because they are quite enchanted by novelties without penetrating them through and through. They do not understand that they have to give up vicious customs and superstitions. Neither do they comprehend that the enemy Apaches would make war on them as a result.

I know that the yoke of the law will weigh heavily upon them – heavier than it would have when they first came down. This is because today, besides living completely licentiously, they have followed many bad examples that they have seen citizens set. Nonetheless, we could hope probably to reach all the youths, and to settle some of the elders little by little with the patience and industry of the Minister. Yet they must concede the following, in my opinion.

The first thing is that the Father Minister must govern their temporal and spiritual affairs without the Commandant's interfering except when the Father is present, or when he requests help in making them respect and obey him.

The second is that they should immediately try the law, so that they come to know the penalty or punishment which must be handed out to those who break it, so that they are denied all contemplation of doing so.

Third, they must be established in the Pueblo of Tucson with a detachment of ten soldiers and the captive interpreter under the command of the Father, insofar as Indians are concerned. To remove them from the presidio but to leave them far from the view of the Father and the Church is to risk all and to further nothing.

Fourth, they must at once be given a school for all the youths, who are a great many. They have manifested a desire to learn to read.

Fifth, they must be allocated the fields of one citizen and Ensign Sosa[16] which are next to the Pueblo, with those on the Island[17] that are contiguous to these and belong to the Pueblo, in order for them to manage themselves with a quarter part of the water from the irrigation ditch in the middle belonging to the Pueblo. Said citizen, with another who is on the Island, and the Ensign, can obtain the lands that the Apaches hold today far below the Presidio, in order to avoid in this way quarrels and difficulties.

Sixth, that for the first time each family head be given a hatchet, a hoe, a sickle, and a plowshare. Moreover, they should be given provisions for one year from the hand of the Father, so that they may apply themselves to their fields, and lose the drive to go out seasonally to the mountains to hunt. Said agricultural implements must be given to them by the Father, who would take care to collect them so the Apaches do not lose them.

Finally, if these Apaches are put in good order from the beginning, all will be achieved in a short time, because they are not like those at Bacoachi. On the contrary, they are all very polite, greeting one with the *Ave María Santísima,* which makes them exemplary. They have harmed no one. Whenever the occasion has offered to manacle or to put one of them in the stocks, they have all taken it well. Thus, they have known much subordination and docility.

The difficulty that arose among the Pimas over admitting the Apaches to the Pueblo and allowing them entry to the Pima lands I have already conquered, although it cost me some labor. In spite of what I have said, I would not presume to guarantee their loyalty, in view of the contrary examples we have. Your Reverence should report, therefore, what he may judge fitting. Doubtless, all will be achieved if this is God's work.

FRIAR JUAN BAUSTISTA LLORENS[18]

Bac. 2 June 1795.

Problems at Bacoachi

Thus, Father Llorens forwarded a sober, well-reasoned assessment of the prospects for converting the Peaceful Apaches at Tucson to Roman Catholicism. His counterpart at Bacoachi was considerably less restrained. In the following report Friar Pedro de Arriquibar eloquently denounced the terrible example the local Christians were setting for the Peaceful Apaches there:

We must suppose, before everything else, that from the beginning until this very day, there has been continued an error in the political government of these Indians. For this reason, they are full of new vices learned among the very people who are called Christians, besides those they already used to commit in their heathendom. It appears that at least the principal heathen vices such as robbery and murder are already amended by the passage of time and lack of exercise. On the other hand, I consider it very difficult, indeed, to amend the new vices they have learned among our people, principally because the cause does not cease. That cause is the bad example set by Christians!

The heathen Apaches are themselves the most expert and objective witnesses to prove the truth of this conclusion. During the conference I held with them on the afternoon of my visit, I witnessed them playing the game of "*albures*"[19] to which they are addicted, principally the youths but even the women. They told me that this, like the other games of cards that they play, is the first milk that they sucked from the Christians, because in their lands they used to know nothing about these things. They responded in the same vein with regard to dances, swearing, obscene words and the rest of the vices that they display. They said that they had learned them all from the Bacoachi Christians. Thus it is that this cause of their vices does not stop in Bacoachi. There are too many dances where they sing a thousand blasphemies and they make a thousand iniquitous movements, there is no lack of depraved conversations, insolent swearing and curses, injuries, envy and so on. We ought promptly to confess, although with great sorrow, that the settlement of the Apaches at Bacoachi cannot be lasting or true as long as they are kept in the company of the Christians.[20]

Father Arriquibar did not really consider the Bacoachi Mescaleros convertible. Some of his reasons provide insights into Apache cultural stability after military defeat, and the operation of the colonial Apache-control system:

> Besides what I have said, if we learn from experience, we see that the faith enters into this class of heathens more by the mouth than by the ear. Their true settlement will be achieved by no method that does not take special care that they make good use of the rations which the Piety of the King affords them for their maintenance. This point I conceive to be one of the most important ones in the experiment that has been tried, although it is dealt with by much carelessness and omission. What I have observed in this particular is that these unhappy heathens end up with nothing on the very day that they receive their ration. I have seen with my own eyes that they go about throwing away bread, meat, etc., on the same day on which they had just drawn their ration. From this disorder it follows that inasmuch as the unhappy heathens have nothing to eat, they must seek it by hunting in the mountains, roasting mescal, etc., with no stability in their ranchería. All this could be remedied if they were forced to conserve one ration until the next issue.
>
> Yet, even in case these heathens knew how to spread their ration over a week, . . . they would still have to dress themselves. This they do with buckskins. These they seek in the wilds. Thus, their wanderings cannot be denied them, inasmuch as it is not proper for them to present themselves to learn the Doctrine naked – especially the women and their daughters. Thus, we have this great difficulty to overcome on this road.[21]

A Mixed Group of Converts

Unlike the disparaging Arriquibar, Llorens clearly saw the Peaceful Apaches at Tucson as potential converts. He intervened with his Northern Piman neophytes to smooth the path of imperial resettlement of hereditary enemies on Piman Tucson lands. The letter from the father president quoted earlier indicates that Llorens had persuaded the Peaceful Apaches to adopt a religious salutation in the Spanish language. Bringing Apaches within the formal folds of the Church may well have been this missionary's strategy for gaining Northern Piman acceptance of Apache integration into their settlement. Certainly later generations of Papagos have referred to the Peaceful Apaches as the *Waukoñi Aup,* or "baptized enemies."

A decade after initial Apache settlement at Tucson, these migrants formed an integral part of the Tucson Pueblo population. Still hostile Apaches attacked the "Apaches Mansos" who "live in the pueblo of Tucson" in May of 1804, killing four and capturing three.[22] Llorens' prediction of inter-band Apache fighting was confirmed.

Father J. B. Llorens traveled out into the Papaguería like Garcés before him, but to proselytize rather than to explore the country.[23] Llorens obtained Christian results. He persuaded many of the Desert People to come to settle at Bac and at Tucson Pueblo to repopulate those settlements. He baptized fifty-seven Papagos at Piman Tucson in 1795 in two groups, having already christened 53 since 1790 at either San Xavier del Bac or San Agustín del Tucson.[24] A group of 134 Papagos moved from Aquituni to Piman Tucson where 63 of them settled on 19 January 1796. Capt. José de Zúñiga played some role in resettling them. Llorens baptized 51 infants in the migrant group.[25]

Having in mind the rations the viceroyalty gave the Peaceful Apaches, no doubt, an official of the Apostolic College of the Holy Cross of Querétaro asked the commandant general to order these Papago settlers given steers and other foodstuffs so that "they might see effective the advantages this union brought them."[26] Meanwhile, Friar Juan drew on the resources of San Xavier del Bac Mission to ration the new Papago settlers and to clothe them according to European concepts of propriety.[27] The older converts may have talked the new Papago neophytes into flight. In any event, flee they did, so that Llorens had to persuade them all over again to move to the Pueblo of Tucson.[28]

On 25 September 1797, the population of Piman Tucson consisted of only 68 survivors of the area and previous immigrants, and 211 recent Papago settlers.[29] About 107 of the latter group had been brought there and baptized since 1795. Captain Zúñiga reported the flight of the Papago migrants to the commandant general. Consequently, the government "intimated" to Llorens that he should allow no more pagans in his mission. The president of the Pimería Alta missions appealed to the guardian of the college in Querétaro to obtain official approval for relocating Papagos at Bac and Tucson pueblo and founding two missions among the Gila River Pimas.[30]

At that time the adobe church with beam-supported roof at Piman Tucson that Garcés had begun in 1770 was so dilapidated that Llorens hoped to build a new one. Six statues of saints graced the main altar, and sufficient vessels to celebrate Mass were kept in three locked boxes. The old church did possess a baptismal font and a supply of holy oils.[31]

Llorens or his assistant celebrated Mass in the ruinous structure at Tucson on most Sundays and feast days, but required an interpreter to translate the sermon.[32] The continued necessity of preaching through interpreters appears in early Pima County records relating to a field once belonging to the Mission of Tucson. A claimant declared that it "was donated by the priest — Juan Bautista Llorens — to Pedro Ríos for services as interpreter during the conquest of the Indians by the Missionaries."[33]

Clerical Assistance

Friar Diego Bringas de Manzaneda led a fund-raising and revivalistic preaching mission in northwestern New Spain in 1795. His action apparently so rejuvenated his College of the Holy Cross at Querétaro that it was once again able to recruit enough Franciscans to post two missionaries to each Pimería Alta Indian mission. Thus, Father J. B. Llorens had assistance from other priests in his missionary work among the Tucson and other Northern

Piman Indians, after he virtually completed the new Bac church building. This assistance enabled him not only to put finishing touches on the Bac edifice, but also to recruit Papago neophytes and to erect the large adobe convent at Piman Tucson to replace the old chapel Garcés had built.[34] The quarters and chapel constituted an impressive mission plant for this frontier. A description of the chapel and its furnishings has been published and need not be repeated here.[35] Mission economic resources only allowed Llorens and his helpers to build the structure of sun-dried bricks, however, so that it deteriorated rapidly once unroofed.

In 1797, Llorens had Friar Bartholomé Socies[36] for an assistant. This priest had formerly served at Tubutama in 1791,[37] and had been pro-secretary to the president-governor of the *Custodio* of San Carlos in 1793. He transferred to Saric Mission in 1798.[38] By that time Llorens began baptizing the Papagos he persuaded to move to Tucson Pueblo in 1795. On 21 April 1798 he christened 25 of the adults and a dozen more on Holy Saturday.[39] On the Saturday of the Vigil of Pentecost, Llorens baptized 20 adults and 2 infants, leaving 27 migrants still outside the Christian fold. Llorens renewed at this time his affiliation with the College of the Holy Cross.[40]

A young priest born in Puebla, New Spain, Ignacio José Ramirez y Arrellano, arrived at Bac on 15 June 1802, only four years after entering the Order. In letters to his family, Ramirez mentioned that mission Indians from both San Xavier and Piman Tucson joined the Gila River Pimas and Papagos to fight Apaches. He assisted Llorens until his death on 26 September 1805, after a long fever.[41] Later, Friar Diego Gil assisted Llorens in 1814, when the latter still had charge of Bac and Piman Tucson.[42] These assistants allowed Llorens to travel to other missions as well as into friendly Indian country.[43] He baptized a child at Tumacacori Mission on 6 April 1808, for example, signing the register there as "Ministro de S.n Xavier del Bac."[44]

In 1808, Friar Juan B. Llorens also twice acted as an investigator for the Bishop of Sonora into difficulties between the military chaplain and the Tucson post commandant.[45]

Tremblings of a Shaken World

Llorens' tenure at Bac and Tucson Pueblos coincided almost exactly with the period of the French Revolution, the Terror, and Napoleon's regime, exile, and return and final defeat between 1789 and 1815. These were world-shaking events whose effects reached even to the far northern frontier of New Spain and the Northern Piman Indian village at Tucson, undoubtedly shaking to its foundations the settled world of Llorens' youth. Late in 1808, he celebrated the accession of Ferdinand VII to the Spanish throne on orders from the bishop of Sonora transmitted by the father president of the Upper Pimería missions.[46] What must Llorens have thought of the ancient symbolism when the occasion stemmed from social ferment that threw a lowly Corsican to the commanding position in France that enabled him to humble the reigning Spanish king?

One of the products of the French Revolution and French conquest of the Spanish Crown was attempted social revolution in Mexico. Even though loyalist Spanish troops put down the Hidalgo rebellion of 1810, reforms in the colonial Roman Catholic Church advocated by the revolutionists had some effect upon the hierarchy. Certainly the recommendations for action made to Fathers Llorens and Gil by an inspecting Franciscan superior in 1814 represented a departure from traditional Franciscan mission operations. They had, however, been foreshadowed in reforms the bishop of Sonora ordered in frontier military post education as early as 1803.

An Inspector's Report

The visitor, Commissary Prefect Juan Baptista de Cevallos, instructed Llorens and Gil in many areas of endeavor. Because little has been known about ecclesiastical administration of Mission San Xavier del Bac and its branch at Tucson during this unsettled terminal period of colonial rule, the Cevallos affidavit is translated here in full:[47]

> I visited this Mission of San Francisco Xavier del Bac and its branch Pueblo San Agustín del Tucson.
>
> Its Minister is Father President Friar Juan Bautista Llorens. His companion is Father Friar Diego Gil.
>
> After informing myself well, it seemed to me that I ought to order, and I ordered arranged the old registers that there used to be in the Mission and other papers and that all should be placed in order in the archive.
>
> I also ordered folios arranged, and authorized the registers of baptisms, marriages and burials, not only those belonging to this Mission but also those of Tucson and the Ranchería of Santa Ana, plus another register of Royal Orders, of military papers of the Commandancy General, or whatever other non-religious petitions. [I also authorized] this book in which are copied only the Letters Patent of the Order, Decrees and affidavits of Inspection, which bears the seal of my office and [has been] approved by my Secretary.
>
> Thus I also ordered formed four books in which separately according to their titles are to be kept the accounts of the branch to which each one pertains; that is, one for Cattle, another for small stock, a third for horses, and a fourth for the seeds. [I ordered] two more books, one for the population enumerations and the other for the inventories, and moreover a cash book in which is recorded the receipt and expenditure of *reales* using the method which is explained in it.
>
> I charged the Ministers to supervise with great care instruction in Christian Doctrine. For this end there shall be hired as soon as possible a School Teacher to teach the alphabet in the Mission, and another in the branch Pueblo so that the children may learn the Doctrine, to read, to write, and to speak our language. I saw it thus: that the citizens should pay the Teacher for their children according to custom, and the Mission should pay for its children according to arrangements made by the Ministers.
>
> I charged the Father to live in the Mission, and the other in the branch Pueblo alternately at least some days of each week. [I instructed them] that on festive days they should explain personally or through an

interpreter one point of Doctrine. [I instructed them] that they should sometimes visit the School, seeing that the Teacher complies with his obligation and [seeing to] the advancement of the pupils. [I instructed them] that the Ministers should also dedicate themselves to the instruction of the catechists and to the conquest of the Pagans who are ignorant of the Doctrine to attend School, exhort the parents to send their children . . .

I equally ordered that in the future lands should be given to the Indians who do not have them. [I instructed them] that one should take into consideration that the laws give preference in the use of water to Mission Indians. [I indicated] that after they have attended to the heathens who are converted and settled in the Mission, to these and to others should be allotted the indicated land, giving them possessory title. The Minister should do this in accord with the tribal Alcalde and the statement of goals in the matter. Not only should the Indians not be impeded in cultivating their lands by being occupied in other works which distract them, but they should be assisted and motivated to work them. [I indicated] that in no way should the Indians be permitted to alienate by themselves the lands that might have been allotted to them nor to sell other things of value, inasmuch as this should be done only with the approval of the Minister and the tribal Alcalde.

I arranged equally that citizens who wish to settle in the Mission Pueblos should be loaned that extent of land which in the judgment of the Minister and tribal Alcalde can be given to them, keeping in mind that neither the Minister nor the Alcalde has the authority to allot them any Mission lands, and that which may be assigned to them has to be on condition that it not prejudice the plantings and irrigation by the old residents of the Pueblo nor its converted pagans.

Inasmuch as the temporal resources are under the care of the Ministers, I ordered that until the Government may arrange something else, they shall continue to administer them, but in conformity to that which has repeatedly been ordered. This is that the portion of the lands that are said to belong to the Mission must be cultivated at the request of the Minister, by means of manual workers, be they Indians or citizens, to whom an individual salary should be paid according to the rate in this Province. In no manner should they be obliged to work at this task, nor in any other occupation whatsoever, such as steward, cowboy, cook, gardener, sacristan, etc., without paying them a just wage. Because there may be among the Indians those who wish to apply themselves as is convenient, and are sent to learn the skills of a carpenter, blacksmith, mason, soapmaker, and such like, when they are ready to apply in actual labor the skills that they learned, they should also be paid their just price. With regard to the product of the labor of the Mission, the cattle and small stock, horse herd, which are the temporal resources that are in charge of the Ministers, are to be used to pay the manual workers and to help with the costs of construction, the Church, sacristy, wax, vestments, sacred vessels, as well as the payment to the schoolmaster, for the succor of poor widows, orphans, the sick and other necessities and requirements, but, all in proportion to the income derived from said branches [of enterprise] and in conformity with the prudence, Apostolic Zeal and Christian and Religious Charity of the Minister.

I equally charged the Minister to be carefully vigilant that the boys and girls cover their flesh, and [that he exercise] much more care in this regard among adults, especially the women, and that the Indians should make distinct rooms in their houses as demanded by Christian decorum.

Finally, I exhorted the Ministers to comply with their respective obligations. Convoking the Pueblo in the Church, I preached the Divine Word. I explained the Constitution of the Spanish Monarchy, and persuaded them of the necessity for observing it. I exhorted everyone to unite, and pay among themselves the respect for and obedience to the Ministers and tribal Alcalde, and to submit to all that which may be ordered and decreed by the legitimate authorities so that it may be carried out. Nothing else in particular occuring to me, I thanked the Ministers for that part of their obligations which they have fulfilled, and for the trouble they have taken for the spiritual and temporal welfare of the Mission, its branch Pueblo and pagan ranchería. With that I concluded and closed the Inspection Affidavit which I signed in said Mission of San Xavier del Bac on the 7th day of July in 1814.

Friar Juan Baptista de Cevallos
Commissary Prefect

It is interesting to note that despite inter-ethnic conflicts over local resources, the ecclesiastical inspector directed that citizens who wished to settle at the mission pueblos were to be loaned such lands as might be available in the judgment of the priest and the alcalde. The continued depopulation of the native Northern Piman Indians, which is documented in detail in Chapter 13 of this book, was thus important in freeing mission fields for Spanish cultivation.

One of the final instructions to Llorens and Gil from the commissary prefect reflected the rate at which Spanish attitudes and values had been accepted by the mission Indians at Bac and Tucson. Thirty years after Bishop Reyes reported that these Indians ran about practically naked unless supplied clothing by the priest, the inspector found them still not dressed to his pious liking.

Again, the part depopulation played in the Westernization of the mission Indians appears to have been critical. As fast as converts learned to wear European-style clothing in an approved manner, they died. Then the missionaries had to go out and repopulate their missions with new converts, who had to be taught all over again about such things as the proper manner of wearing the trappings of Western civilization. Almost without a doubt the very adoption of clothing helped to foster disease among the mission Indians, who had not yet learned the principles of personal sanitation that went along with European-style clothes.

As the highlight of his inspection, Commissary Prefect Juan Bautista Cevallos assembled the Native Americans and preached to them on the new concept of constitutional monarchy for Spain and the values of unity and obedience to as well as respect for civil and ecclesiastical authority. He formally thanked the priests for their labors on behalf of the people of the Pueblos of Bac and Tucson. All in all, Friar Juan B. Llorens, who had spent a quarter of a century at these two missions, must have been very happy to see Friar Juan B. Cevallos, *tocayo* (namesake) and brother Franciscan though he was, sign his affidavit of inspection and recommendations on 7 July 1814, and then depart.

The End of an Era

How long Fathers Llorens and Gil remained at Bac and Piman Tucson remains unknown. Llorens reportedly died in 1815 near Santa Cruz.[48] By 1818, Friar Juan Bañó had taken charge of the Bac and Tucson mission. This missionary was born in 1781 and became an Indian missionary in 1815,[49] quite possibly at Bac.

Bac and Tucson led the eight Upper Pimería missions in 1818 in production of wheat, garbanzos (chick peas) and lentils, and came second in maize and bean harvests and number of cattle.[50] Crop production fell heavily in 1819,[51] and continued to fall in 1820, except for wheat. The 1820 wheat harvest at Pueblos Bac and Tucson increased by one-third over the 1819 harvest, while maize dropped one-third, beans two-thirds, chick peas over a third and lentils by almost half. Cattle increased to 5,700 head, while sheep and goats dropped to 700. Horses decreased by one-third, and mules and donkeys did not change in numbers.[52]

At the end of the colonial period, then, the Spanish Catholic missions to the Northern Piman Indians had not yet solved the fundamental problems of stabilizing the converted population, and converting the heathen population that managed to reproduce itself. To be sure, a most impressive church had been erected at Bac (and others at a few more places), yet the mission frontier remained as much a frontier in 1820 as it had been in 1720. While earlier imperial policy gained Upper Pimería 30 years of peace and prosperity, the preoccupation of Spain with European wars during the final 30 years of the empire prevented any significant colonial initiatives toward advancing the political frontier in the Gila-Sonoran region.

Part II
The Presidio

6.

Founding the Royal Spanish Post of San Agustín del Tucson, 1766-1779

PART I DEALT WITH a kind of Spanish Borderlands history familiar to many people because a number of eminent historians have chronicled and analyzed the role of the Christian mission as a frontier institution. Part II now turns to a less familiar sort of Borderlands history, that of the military post or *presidio* as a frontier institution. This part analyzes on the one hand "the influence of military officials and presidial garrisons in the internal history"[1] of the Tucson area. In presenting these data, the chapters in this second part also exemplify the function and achievements of all the military garrisons on the northern frontier of New Spain in the last quarter of the 18th century and the first two decades of the 19th.

Spanish colonial military authorities laid the foundations of modern Tucson's ethnic diversity when they established a post a short distance across the Santa Cruz River from the Native American Pueblo of Tucson. Royal defense policy moved the military arm of Spanish imperialism into the Tucson area in the latter third of the 18th century. The garrisons stationed at the new post included not only Mestizo and detribalized Native American troops, but also veterans and non-commissioned and commissioned officers born in Spain and other parts of Europe. Many of these Europeans, moreover, brought their wives and families with them to the post of San Agustín del Tucson.

The Christian missionaries who had insured the survival of Tucson as a Native American settlement did not initiate permanent European settlement at or near that mission outpost. The Roman Catholic requirement that its clergy remain celibate militated against missionary priests founding families of Europeans, or even contributing European genes to the Native American population.[2] Thus, it remained for the Spanish frontier defense forces to institute permanent European settlement, and permanent Mestizo settlement (including mulattos[3]) in the Tucson area.

Even before the military post was established opposite Piman Tucson, the Native Americans there had gained some experience with royal Spanish troops. Not only did passing missionaries usually travel with military escorts, but a small detachment from Tubac was stationed at Bac for the protection of its missionary. Captain Nicolás de Lafora visited Tubac in 1766, and reported that a detachment was maintained at Bac and Piman Tucson for the safety of the Jesuit laboring there.[4] That protection policy continued after Franciscans took over the Pimería Alta missions. It will be recalled that Friar Francisco Garcés wrote to Captain Anza that the soldiers were behaving "divinely" and setting the Native Americans a good Christian example.[5]

Some small force was undoubtedly kept at Bac until the Tubac garrison moved north to protect the exposed mission and its branch as well as the overland route to California in 1776. Then the Tucson natives met Spanish soldiery at mission headquarters at Bac or in their own ranchería.

The Move from Tubac to Tucson

One positive reason for the selection of Tucson as a garrison site was provided by the Native Americans themselves. The social structure of colonial Spanish America had been erected upon a base of food-producing Native Americans. Defense officials could count, they assumed, upon the Native American gardens at Tucson providing the garrison with at least some of its food requirements, in addition to the pasturage and firewood resources noted by Jesuit missionaries in 1752.

The immediate stimulus leading to establishment of a Spanish military post in this particular forward area was, on the other hand, a negative kind of military defense. Characteristically, Spanish colonization of its northern borderlands in New Spain late during colonial times occurred chiefly for defensive motives.[6] New Mexico, first settled in 1598, resulted from initial imperial momentum. New Spain expanded its northern frontiers into Texas, Arizona and Upper California during the 18th century, however, primarily to block the path of England, Russia and other European powers to its riches. Thus, military posts founded in the Santa Cruz River Valley met first a Northern Piman Indian military threat, and later an immediate Apachean threat and remoter Russian threat to Spain's New World empire.

First, the northern military frontier advanced to defend missionaries against the very Native Americans they tried to convert to Christianity. The Sonoran provincial governor founded the posts at Tubac and Altar in the aftermath of the Northern Piman Revolt in 1752.[7] Later, the distant threat of Russian colonization on the Pacific Coast of California and the actuality of hostilities with the non-sedentary Apaches loomed more important in official policy-making. Frontier officials enthusiastically supported the colonization of Upper California by Portolá, Serra and Anza to counter a Russian southward advance.[8]

Once Spanish outposts dotted Upper California, protection of an overland route from Sonora to that frontier province dictated orders to the Tubac garrison to move. Officials sent it north down the Santa Cruz River to the site across that stream from Piman Tucson that Sedelmayr, Stiger and Segesser had recommended a quarter of a century earlier. As a post protecting a communication line against hostile Indian attack, Tucson initially performed precisely the same task the first presidios established on New Spain's silver-mining frontier had been designed for beginning in 1555.[9]

The final advance of the Tubac garrison down the Santa Cruz River to Tucson stemmed directly from an inspection of New Spain's northern frontier posts. The Marqués de Rubí[10] carried out that tour of examination in 1766–1767 as a special assignment from King Charles III. After completing his personal inspection tour, the marqués recommended realigning the conglomerate of posts originally located for local tactical reasons. He envisioned the foremost military problem on the northern frontier of New Spain by that time as keeping hostile Apaches out of settled areas. The marqués thought that could be accomplished by establishing the frontier garrisons at the most defensible points along a line designed to repel hostile Indian incursions and also to guard against invasion by forces of another European power. The king's inspector wanted the frontier posts relocated to form a fairly straight line from the Sea of Cortez to the Gulf of Mexico.[11] King Charles III ordered the Rubí plan put into effect in September of 1772.[12]

The viceroy of New Spain appointed Hugh O'Connor as commandant inspector to carry out the new regulations.[13] Among the changes recommended by the marqués had been the relocation of the garrison stationed at Tubac since 1752, but O'Connor had his hands full in Texas where he was ordered to begin working. O'Connor campaigned almost constantly against various Apachean groups and examined post sites on the eastern sector of New Spain's northern frontier.[14] Not until 1775 had O'Connor made sufficient progress on the Texas-Coahuila border sector to deal personally with Sonora on the west. Meanwhile, O'Connor in 1774 sent Antonio Bonilla to inspect the Sonora military posts and to plan improved defense there.[15] In the course of his inspection, Bonilla examined the proposed site at Aribaca where the presidial garrison located at Tubac was to move according to the Rubí plan. Bonilla reported that spot to be unhealthy, as Sedelmayr had noted 22 years earlier. Bonilla therefore recommended against sending the Tubac garrison there.[16]

At the same time, Captain Juan Bautista de Anza rendered the Marqués de Rubí's conception of the western section of the frontier line obsolete when he succeeded in opening a land route from Sonora to Upper California with the assistance of Friar Francisco Garcés. To protect the new supply route, Spanish posts farther north than Rubí's envisioned straight line from gulf to gulf became necessary.

"El Capitán Colorado"

Credit for founding Spanish colonial Tucson and fixing the multi-ethnic character of its population goes to a red-headed Irishman serving the Spanish king. Hugh O'Connor became famous to the Native Americans of Texas as *El Capitán Colorado,* "The Red Captain," from his flaming red hair.

Hugh O'Connor burst brilliantly upon the scene in military and Indian affairs in northern New Spain during the decade 1768 to 1778. As a captain, he had commanded the Presidio of Adais and acted as interim governor of Texas from 1768 to 1771. Promoted to lieutenant colonel and named inspector of military presidios in Coahila, Nueva Vizcaya and Sonora by Viceroy Bucareli, O'Connor took command on 12 December 1771.

He threw himself energetically into campaigns to defeat the hostile Apache tribes and to relocate the frontier presidios to enable them better to deal with enemy Native Americans. It fell to O'Connor to carry out the policies recommended by the Marqués de Rubí and embodied in the king's

1772 New Regulations for the presidial forces. His dedicated performance of this six-year task eventually won him military and civil honors.[17]

When he finally was able to select new sites for military posts on the western sector of Rubí's defense line, O'Connor determined the location of the post from which grew the modern city of Tucson. Carrying out his duties as commandant inspector of the Frontier Provinces of New Spain, O'Connor finally entered the Province of Sonora on 22 May 1775. By early September, O'Connor was back in Chihuahua. In less than four months, he relocated the four presidios forming the Sonoran sector of the defensive alignment of posts.[18] O'Connor inspected the Tubac garrison, its arms, clothing, accounts, etc., from the 9th to the 18th of August in 1775.[19]

One portion of the lengthy reports then prepared for O'Connor tells something about the type of soldiery that would soon move to Tucson. Table 3 in the Appendix of this book presents data about the ages, birthplaces, ethnic classification and economic situation of troopers known to have served later at Tucson.

Riding north from Tubac, O'Connor personally inspected the Tucson area and marked off the future location of the Royal Post of San Agustín del Tucson. His reasons for choosing this particular site he clearly set forth in his brief report of inspection translated here:

CERTIFICATION

Don Hugo O'Conor, Knight of the Order of Calatrava, Colonel of Infantry in His Majesty's Armies, and Commandant Inspector of all the frontier posts of this New Spain for the King, Our Lord (whom God protect):

I certify: that having carried out the examination which Article 3 of the Royal Instruction inserted in the New Royal Regulation of Presidios issued by His Majesty on the tenth of September of 1772 prescribes for the removal of the company of San Ygnacio de Tubac in the Province of Sonora, I chose and marked out, in the presence of the Reverend Father Friar Francisco Garcés and Lieutenant Don Juan de Carmona, for the new situation of said presidio, with the denomination of San Agustín de Toixon, the place of this name situated at a distance of eighteen leagues from that of Tubac, because the requisite conditions of water, pasture, and wood occur, as well as a perfect closing of the Apache frontier.

In order to certify I sign this with the Reverend Father mentioned and Lieutenant Don Juan de Carmona, in the Mission of San Xavier del Bac on the twentieth of August of 1775.

DON HUGO O'CONOR
FR. FRANCISCO GARCÉS
JUAN FERNANDEZ CARMONA[20]

As is apparent in this report, O'Connor seems to have adopted "San Agustín de Toixon" as the proper local place name and ordered the new post to adopt the same designation as native Tucson (*stjukshon*). In other words, the "old place name took precedence."[21]

The red-haired Irishman did not linger at Tucson nor even Bac on this initial inspection tour. Nonetheless during his brief visit the captain did obtain from Friar Francisco Garcés a pledge that the Native Americans of Bac and Piman Tucson would help to build the new post buildings.[22]

Two days after O'Connor selected Tucson as the future site of the post then at Tubac, he inspected Santa Cruz with the Tubac commander, and decided that the Terrenate garrison should move there.[23] Three days later, he selected the San Bernardino site for the fourth Sonoran unit, again with Lieutenant Oliva as witness.[24]

Then, moving eastward, O'Connor wrote to Viceroy Antonio María Bucareli on August 29 and again on September 7 from Janos, recommending that the Tubac garrison be moved to Tucson. The viceroy approved on October 18, and O'Connor received his message at Carrizal by December 2.[25] O'Connor then ordered the move for December 10, 1775.[26] Consequently, according to Friar Pedro Font, the "following year of 1776 the presidio of Tubac was transferred hither, where it remains still, and is called the Presidio of San Agustín del Tuquison."[27]

Old Commander, Young Ensign

Lieutenant Juan María de Oliva commanded the Tubac garrison at the time of its relocation at Tucson.[28] The titular commander of the post, Juan Bautista de Anza, was at the time absent on his second California expedition.[29] This left Oliva as senior officer present. Oliva had come up through the ranks of the Tubac garrison over the long years that had passed since he joined the then newly organized frontier defense company in 1752. Oliva excelled as a frontiersman and field commander, but he suffered from certain handicaps in background when called upon to exercise independent garrison command. This officer was not literate, for one thing, so depended upon others to handle the abundant correspondence which a Spanish post commandant had to carry on with his superiors. One possible consequence of Oliva's inability to write, and the recommendation O'Connor made that the only subaltern on the post be cashiered, might be that no written report on the precise date the Tubac garrison actually moved to Tucson ever was made to Oliva's superiors.[30]

Commandant Inspector O'Connor recommended on 18 August 1775 that Oliva, who was then 60 years old with over 29 years of service beginning on September 4, 1749,[31] be retired with his salary.[32] On October 27, the viceroy endorsed O'Connor's recommendation,[33] and on 28 February 1776 the king signed the order retiring Oliva with the rank of captain.[34] On 27 May 1776, the viceroy forwarded to O'Connor the king's retirement commission.[35]

Given the usual rate of transmission of royal mail, Oliva probably learned of his retirement about the beginning of August in 1776. Quite possibly he still had to retain command of the post until relieved, a situation complicated by Anza's continued absence. The post commandant journeyed to Mexico City from California to report personally to viceregal officials. Writing to the viceroy on 20 November 1776, Anza referred to "the garrison in my command" stationed at "San Agustín del Tuczón."[36] This reference clearly establishes that the garrison moved no later than a month or so before that 1776 date, and that it had only its acting commander in residence.

After Anza had drained Tubac of its best personnel for his California expeditions, the only subaltern Oliva had left while awaiting retirement was an ensign whose principal claim to office at that period lay in being Anza's godson. This ensign, Juan Felipe Beldarrain, was a son of the original captain of the Pimería Alta company and founder of Tubac, Tomás Beldarrain. Yet the younger Beldarrain's performance during the pioneer Spanish years at Tucson left a good deal to be desired, as will become plain later.

The Spanish pattern of primary dependence upon genetic and ritual relatives to gain advancement clearly operated on the Sonoran frontier in such a way as to place men of questionable competence in responsible commands from time to time when members of the provincial elite succeeded in obtaining royal commissions for their real or fictive relations. On one occasion, a Spanish priest who was provoked by Beldarrain's callous report of Apache depredations accused him of doing nothing but dance, gamble, and sport fancy clothes.[37]

First Physical Structures

For several years following removal of the presidial garrison from Tubac to Tucson, the garrison lived on an open post. A fort was not built immediately at the new location, even though various Apache bands had been stealing horses and killing settlers near Spanish posts farther east since 1773.[38] The first actual fortifications thrown up apparently consisted of a wooden palisade erected by order of the energetic young captain, Don Pedro Allande y Saabedra, after he took command on 12 June 1777.[39] Allande claimed later to have erected a palisade of rough logs with four bulwarks, magazines and a guardhouse without cost to the royal exchequer.[40] The Allande palisade did not, however, enclose all of the dwellings. When Adjutant Inspector Don Roque de Medina inspected this post in the spring of 1779, he reported:

> The area of the presidio houses and *jacales* is fortified with a wide ditch roundabout and a palisade of logs which Captain Don Pedro Allande ordered built, and two ramparts on which the cannon are emplaced. Some of the houses of citizens and soldiers are outside the palisade and under only the defense of the artillery and the low works raised at one side at a greater distance from the water than they could have been put.

Allande built this fortification to follow the specifications laid down in the 1772 New Regulations, even though his stockade was temporary. It has been concluded that such bastions distinguish posts resulting from the 1772 reforms from both earlier and later structures.[41]

At this time, the construction of a permanent fortification languished half-finished, largely because of very poor financial management by the subaltern who had been acting as quartermaster of the presidial company with inadequate supervision from the illiterate former commanding officer.

According to Medina, "Only on two walls is the material structure of this presidio to the height of a scant yard and a half, and it is of adobes. In it there has been consumed, according to the account rendered by Don Juan Felipe Beldarrain, the ensign who was quartermaster, 1,801 pesos 6 reales."

The unfortunate Beldarrain owed the construction fund some 2,150 pesos 2 reales. After selling his property to pay off his total debts, this officer still owed 6,176 pesos 1 real 2 maravedis in the spring of 1779! His default was attributed to lack of experience in handling finances, to poor conduct, lack of an accountant, and lack of a literate superior officer to help him.

The armament of the new post in 1779 included four bronze cannon, for which 66 balls were available. A dozen others sent to the post had been made into musket balls. The powder magazine was built a gunshot's distance from the post where it would not endanger it if this structure caught fire, but the adjutant inspector considered the practice of closing its doorway with adobes quite unsuitable. A new magazine to have a door with two locks was being built in accordance with the 1772 Royal Regulations.[42] A large enough supply of powder was on hand for Captain Allande to sell the settlers at the former Tubac post 25 pounds at one peso per pound. The powder reserve was 694 pounds. Over a three-year period, 140 pounds had been used up in exercises, target practice and actual engagements.[43]

In 1780, reports of Apaches referred still to the stockade.[44] In the report of 27 December 1783 post inspection, Lt. José María Abate was commended for "having at his own cost walled the Presidio on the very terms he offered."[45] Thus, the earthen wall evidently was completed in 1783. When ultimately finished, the presidio walls of sun-dried bricks stood some ten or twelve feet high and three feet wide at the base,[46] although it melted away to a lesser dimension as rains eroded it.[47] A Welshman who settled in Tucson in 1858 remembered the wall when describing it 27 years later[48] as eight to sixteen feet high enclosing 300 square yards.

Settlement and Social Patterns

When colonial authorities stationed a military garrison across the river from Tucson, they determined the specific location of the modern city and set its pattern of early urban development. The post was built as a compact village. A stockade and then an earthen defensive wall surrounded the military post buildings, although both members of the garrison and civilians built houses outside the wall. All clustered together in a compact settlement, however, and the farmers, the ranchers, and even the military guards assigned to protect grazing remount herds all walked or rode from their homes to their fields and pastures to labor.[49] The Spanish presidio followed royal plans drawn up in emulation of Roman military colonies centuries earlier.[50] In practice, Apachean attacks upon the royal Spanish presidio at Tucson gave reality to a constant military threat to that post's population, fostering social solidarity.[51]

Furthermore, the garrison and civilians alike shared a single religion, with an ordained Roman Catholic priest living on post most of the time as military chaplain. The chaplain and the presidial commander shared the social leadership of Tucson. They represented king and Pope, sharing an identification with an older prestige.[52] While not all post commandants possessed a formal education, most had some, so that they stood out as superior to their subordinates and the civilian satellites of the post. Even the illiterate Lieutenant Juan M. Oliva stood out as an Indian fighter. The chaplains possessed considerable formal learning, of necessity. Thus, both military and ecclesiastical leadership at Tucson lay in the hands of men superior in techniques highly approved by Hispanic society – oral facility in Spanish, formal learning, and rather extraordinary physical fighting powers exemplified by such men as Oliva, Pedro de Allande, José María Abate and Ygnacio F. Usarraga.

By keeping the productive population in "ready touch" with the officers and ecclesiastical leaders of Tucson, the compact presidial settlement facilitated cooperation. The size of the garrison and its direct royal financing allowed the religious institution to function on this far frontier of Christendom much as it did in more peaceful urban places.[53]

The Native Americans who farmed along the river felt major social impact from the presence of the presidio. Once established at Tucson, the military post became the primary institution of cultural contact and exchange[54] involving Spaniards and the Santa Cruz River Valley Indians, as well as many Northern Pimans dwelling on the arid lands north to the Gila River and west to the mountains bordering on the Colorado River.

Defense officials in New Spain had garrisoned the new post with a troop of frontier cavalrymen who relied primarily upon the lance to fight Native Americans who possessed few firearms and less ammunition. Arrival of this garrison therefore augmented the cultural alternatives colonial Spain offered to Native Americans on its northern New World frontier. One side of the Santa Cruz River showed imperial might exemplified in the lance wielded by cavalry troopers stationed at San Agustín del Tucson. On the opposite bank of the stream, imperial Christianization policy found its symbol in the baptismal shell of the missionaries who served Piman Tucson from Bac.

Hostile Western Apaches posed a real physical threat to inhabitants of both Tucsons. This seemed to generate inter-ethnic exchange and solidarity. Civilians cooperated with the garrison to defend the post and conduct offensive actions, yet their Hispanic individualism probably survived intact. The Native Americans at Piman Tucson across the river cooperated in defense and raiding, thus forging the kind of social alliance that was fundamentally important in culturally assimilating Northern Pimans into colonial society.[55]

The Santa Cruz River Valley environment imposed one constraint on individualism among Tucson farmers that fostered inter-familial and even inter-ethnic cooperation. That constraint was semi-aridity that required irrigating crops. Many modern studies document how fundamental cooperation between irrigators is for their mutual success.[56] Inasmuch as Native Americans at Piman Tucson quarreled over irrigation water even before the Jesuit 1767 expulsion, one may be sure that settlement of Spanish farmers near the presidio forced inter-familial and even inter-ethnic cooperation in irrigation water management[57] as water demand increased. At the same time, Spanish settlement generated inter-ethnic conflicts over water allocation, as least at a later date than the founding of the post.

Captain Don Pedro de Allande y Saabedra

Fortunately for historians, and evidently for the Tucson garrison, a literate and energetic regular army officer assumed command about a year after the founding of the new post. Captain Don Pedro de Allande y Saabedra was assigned the command of the Tucson post on 11 February 1777, at the age of 35 or 36.[58] His regular commission was dated 12 June 1777,[59] and by coincidence he actually assumed command of the post on that date. Five days later he reported to the commandant of the Frontier Provinces the sad condition in which he found the presidio.

Allande y Saabedra was evidently a martinet, a spit-and-polish officer who was very different from Oliva. Allande had been a lieutenant in the Dragoon Regiment of Mexico and wanted to be reassigned to that outfit. An inspector in 1779 reprimanded him for using cruel and improper punishments to maintain discipline, and for employing soldiers and Indian scouts in his private business affairs, yet he was not then transferred.

Allande y Saabedra was a nobleman born in Spain. He had entered the royal army as a cadet in the Navarre Infantry at the age of 14, and had spent 22 years in the service by the time he assumed command of the presidial company at Tucson. Allande was a veteran of Spain's war with Portugal in 1762, battles against the Moors, and the drawn-out Sonoran campaign against the Seri Indians on the Gulf of California Coast between 1767 and 1777. Probably Allande y Saabedra's behavior was not mitigated by his being a widower when he reached Tucson. Allande belonged, in a word, to that group of frontiersmen developing during the 18th century which has been seriously neglected by historians.[60]

The Soldiers of Tucson

The human component of the Royal Fort of San Agustín del Tucson seems to have been little better or worse in the late 1700s than in the other frontier posts of New Spain. The officer who inspected the presidio in 1779 found a great deal to criticize. Few actual changes of a serious nature were made, however, so it appears that the situation was little worse than that in other posts.

Captain Allande had under his command in the spring of 1779 77 men, but only 59 effectives. His lieutenant served at San Miguel de Horcasitas because of his special knowledge of the still-hostile Seris. Ex-ensign Felipe Beldarrain was in the guard house under arrest and not numbered among the effectives. This left two ensigns and the chaplain, with whom Allande did not get along, for officers.

Lieutenant Miguel de Urrea

Captain Allande's second-in-command was 12 years older than he, and undoubtedly much wiser in frontier Indian warfare. Lieutenant Miguel de Urrea was a native Sonoran, son of Captain Bernardo de Urrea, founder of the Royal Post of Altar. The Urrea family followed a tradition of service to the Crown and produced many competent officers.

Miguel de Urrea had in 1779 spent his entire 37 years of army service in Sonoran frontier posts. This gave him a detailed knowledge of warfare with specific Native Americans, but his provincial birth and service worked against him in the promotion lists. Apparently Allande had recognized the desirability of replacing Lieutenant Oliva with another experienced Indian fighter when the latter retired. Urrea transferred to Tucson five months after Allande took command, after spending 23 years as a lieutenant in the Urrea family operation at Altar.[61] Those years close to the Seri frontier motivated Urrea's transfer to San Miguel, where he could lend Allande no assistance in 1779. Whatever role Urrea's relatives played in obtaining a commission for Miguel, his ability as an Indian fighter seems unquestionable.

Ensign Diego de Oya

The first ensign of the Tucson company in 1779 was Diego de Oya, then 57 years old. A native of Europe, Oya was another veteran of the Portuguese War. He had served 14 years as a soldier and corporal and 5 as a sergeant before becoming an acting ensign on 30 March 1776. The king signed his regular commission on 31 August 1776. Oya took the place vacated by the dismissal of Juan Felipe Beldarrain.[62] When Oya first arrived in Sonora, Lieutenant Colonel Anza prevailed upon the governor not to approve him, reportedly thus winning time for his godson Beldarrain. Oya's superiors then ordered him back to his assigned post and had Beldarrain cashiered.[63]

Ensign José Francisco de Castro

The second ensign of Tucson in 1779 was José Francisco de Castro, only a year older than Allande and a native of Mexico. Like Oya and Urrea, Castro came up through the ranks, where he spent nearly 14 years before becoming an acting ensign in the Tucson company on 30 March 1778. Castro earlier fought in the Caribbean and served as a sergeant with the Dragoon Regiment of Mexico under Hugh O'Connor. King Charles III signed Castro's commission on 26 August 1778.[64]

The Troop

Allande's leather-armored or heavy cavalry consisted of 37 troopers with 2 second corporals paid the same as privates, 2 first corporals and a sergeant plus a master armorer. The light cavalry included 17 soldiers under 2 corporals and a sergeant. The company had 10 Indian scouts under a corporal. Five of the corporals and 29 of the soldiers were Spaniards, the heavy cavalry sergeant a Roman, and the rest were mixed-bloods or detribalized Native Americans.

The list of Tubac troopers who later served at Tucson (Appendix Table 3) gives some interesting insights regarding Spanish colonial ethnic and social perceptions. One column is headed "Social Class," but in fact indicates ethnic make-up. This usage reflects the fact that colonial authorities in 1775 employed the term *class* in a sense very different from the socio-economic group meaning it acquired during the French Revolution and later. In 1775, it meant ethnic status to residents of New Spain. The peninsular Spanish dominant minority in the colonies held the ethnically mixed population in low esteem. Manuel Abad y Queipo, Bishop of Michoacan, in 1799 characterized the people created by miscegenation as "drunks, incontinent, lazy, without honor, grace nor loyalty, without a notion of religion, nor of morality, without class, polish nor decency...."[65]

Racial categories included in Appendix Table 3 are Spaniard, Coyote, Morisco, and Mulatto. The latter term carried the same meaning that it did in the English-speaking colonies in North America: the mating of a Spaniard and a Negro produced a Mulatto. The person termed a *Morisco* in colonial New Spain would be socially defined as a black in the United States 200 years after this document was written. A Spaniard who mated with a *Mulata* produced a Morisco.[66] Both Mulattos and Moriscos would be socially defined as Negros in modern Tucson.

The term *Coyote* probably denoted a person three-fourths Native American and one-fourth European. By a complicated series of matings, a Coyote could also be 7/64 Indian, 257/512 Negro and 271/512 European.[67] It is questioned, however, whether the refined conceptualization required to so define a "Coyote" was employed on the Sonoran frontier.

Clearly race mixture was well advanced in this garrison. Two Opata Indians served in the heavy cavalry. Their presence indicated that in addition to service in three special ethnic Opata companies,[68] these Native Americans now had another social route by which they could lose their tribal identity in their eager adoption of Spanish culture.

Opata Indian scouts were listed in the inspection report with Spanish baptismal names and both Opata and Spanish surnames, reflecting the European standardized system of identifying individuals "as impersonal units" in the military service.[69] Officers clearly assigned Indian scouts serving with Spanish units Spanish names if they did not already possess them. Thus, army service functioned as one of those institutions of cultural contact between Spaniards and friendly Native American tribesmen[70] which facilitated the acquisition of Hispanic traits by the latter, including personal names as well as more complex patterns.

Military Commandant of Sonora Don Juan Bautista de Anza had attached 20 Opatas to the Tucson company in 1777 for service against the Seris. When Adjutant Inspector Don Roque de Medina reviewed the post in May of 1779, he dismissed those Opatas from the service. The summary of Medina's inspection of the Tucson garrison showed the force listed in Appendix Table 4.[71]

Twenty-six of the 58 enlisted men in the Tucson company in 1779 (excluding Indian scouts) can be identified as having belonged to the unit in August of 1775 perhaps six months before it moved. This was only 45% of its 1779 complement. There had been a very large turnover in personnel, apparently, just before or just after the garrison moved.

The Tucson cavalry troop had 289 horses and 52 mules. Its personal spit-and-polish seems not to have extended to horse gear, inasmuch as this was virtually ruined by poor care in the open, according to the inspector.

Medina viewed the Tucson troops as well-clothed. They had received new uniforms in November of 1778. As a result, they had not been receiving the two *reales* in cash per day to which they were entitled under the New Royal Regulations of 1772,[72] because the company's funds had gone to pay for the uniforms. They seemed to be better-than-average musket shots at target practice, but lacked experience in firing pistols. The commandant general of the Frontier Provinces considered the Tucson unit the only one in Sonora well-trained in the use of firearms at this period.[73] They also knew their close order and mounted drill to the satisfaction of the inspector.

Captain Allande considered eight of his men unfit for service in the spring of 1779.

The Roman sergeant, José de Tona, was 47 years of age at the time of the inspection, having served in the Spanish army since 1774. He had come from Tubac with the company, had been demoted to corporal in January of 1778 and made sergeant again in July, probably when Sergeant Pedro Márquez was promoted to ensign and transferred to the Pima Indian company then stationed at Buenavista.[74]

Tona's variations in rank sound typical of non-commissioned officers in other armies at other times and places. Clearly non-commissioned officers formed the backbone of this command as of many others in military history.

Allande seldom had more than a few men under his direct control on the post. Most of his troops served in detachments stationed at the former post of Tubac and the missions of Tumacacori, Calabasas and San Xavier del Bac for their protection. Other troops escorted the pack trains which brought provisions from those places to Tucson, and 25 men spent their time guarding the horse herd.

The large detachment stationed in the settlements farther up the Santa Cruz River Valley to the south represented Captain Allande's attempt to protect Tucson's supply lines. The depredations of hostile Apaches had made the threat to those places very serious. In October of 1777, the Apaches ran off the last of the cattle and horses of the settlers left at Tubac. In November, Apaches grazed their own animals on Tubac's fields with impunity, stealing maize from the *milpas* for three days. Captain Allande had set up stiff penalties for the settlers if they left or sold out, so he felt obligated to provide them with some protection.[75]

A Spanish presidio commander's powers included that of making grants of land within the military reservation. The frontier presidio constituted, therefore, an institution specifically designed to foster civilian settlement on imperial frontiers, as well as a short-term military installation. Allande exercised this power at least once during 1779.[76] In New Spain, military posts and missions became centers of ranching and farming development on generous land grants, and retired solders usually settled in the vicinity of their old posts. "Roman history was repeated" in Spanish royal land policy.[77]

Thus it happened that a civilian settlement remained at Tubac after the military garrison moved to Tucson. Moreover, the civil population at the post of San Agustín del Tucson grew, probably beginning with the transfer from Tubac, and certainly by 1779, as Allande's grant of land then shows. Inevitably, military land policy irked the Tucson Native Americans, who suddenly had to share fields and irrigation waters with strangers.

An idea of the financial status of the soldiers in the Tucson garrison under Allande may be gained from a report on their accounts with the company treasury as of the end of December in 1778. There are stated in terms of the nearest peso in Appendix Table 5. This company accounts statement provides an idea of the antiquity of certain surnames in the Spanish-speaking population of modern Tucson.

Later enumerations and other documents allow some determination of the fate of pioneer Tucson soldiers. Mission records reveal, for example, that Trooper Loreto Amezquita had less than a year to live at the time Medina inspected the garrison. Amezquita died on 7 February 1780, apparently while on detached guard duty at Tubac. About 45 years old at his death, Amezquita left a widow, María Phelipa de León. Friar Pedro Antonio de Arriquibar presided over his burial in the cemetery of Tumacacori Mission the following day.[78] The fate of other members of the Tucson garrison remains shrouded in the fog of forgotten archives.

7.

Fighting Apaches: Offense and Defense, 1778-1782

SUPERVISING CONSTRUCTION OF FORTIFICATIONS at a new post did not absorb all of Captain Pedro de Allande's energies. Fighting Apaches constituted the primary mission of frontier presidial forces in the latter 1770s, and he was quite aware of that fact.

Militarizing the Northern Pimas

Allande began his anti-Apache campaigns, apparently, by hiring Native American reinforcements because he had too few troops. He dipped into his own pocket for a month's pay for Indian warriors.[1] This was likely a May 1779 sortie ordered by Pedro de Tueros,[2] commandant of arms of Sonora. Allande took out 79 troopers, militia and auxiliaries.[3] He found a number of Apache trails, but achieved no success in combat terms. On 1 October, Apaches ran off five horses and a mule, but the troops failed to catch them.[4] Allande then began to move. Six years later it was chronicled:

> The year 1779 he made another campaign in the Santa Catherina mountains in which he attacked two rancherías. They killed some warriors, women and children, and captured six prisoners. He has similarly arranged for Pimas, Papagos and Gileños to make some campaigns. They have always achieved in these some victory against the Apaches. He has regaled and made them gifts from his salary to motivate them.[5]

Within three years of the founding of the Tucson post, its commander had assumed an active role leading to a progressive militarization of Northern Piman society, including that of the Gila River Indians well to the north of Tucson. Thus, its influence spread widely among frontier Indian allies.

On 6 November 1779, an Apache force that Allande estimated at 350 approached the post itself. He formed a command of 15 men to sally forth and engage the enemy. The Spaniards defeated the Apaches in a long running battle. Allande cut off and brought back the head of a slain chieftain carried on a lance as a trophy, after waving it at the surviving Apaches. They reportedly broke and fled at this sight, abandoning their plunder. The Spaniards killed several Apaches, including a brother of Chief Quilcho.[6]

Captain Allande and his men made three scouts in all during the final four months of 1779, and "with the assistance of the Pimas of San Xavier del Bac and the heathens of Aquituni, they killed six Apaches, three women, and captured seven prisoners." This expedition moved the Apaches to retaliate against Piman Tucson, where they killed one trooper and captured another, losing two of their own men in the process.[7]

Northern Piman Indian participation in the expedition is significant evidence of the extent of military cooperation of these Native Americans with Spanish troops only 28 years after they rebelled against Spanish colonial rule. This marked the beginning of integration of significant numbers of Northern Pimans into Spanish frontier forces.

One modern author has commented upon Sonoran acceptance of Papagos as soldiers after Mexican independence,[8] and another has detected a progressive militarization of Gila Pima society in the 1800s with an accompanying professionalization of the soldiery.[9] The 1779 records of the Tucson presidio, the Spanish military post nearest to the Gila Pimas and most Papagos, disclose a much earlier European militarization of Northern Piman culture. The Pimas and Papagos gained 40 years of direct experience in the Spanish army, learning European patterns of warfare and military organization as well as the Spanish language[10] before Mexico gained its independence. Mexico did rely heavily on the military prowess of loyal and friendly frontier Native Americans, following a colonial pattern. Colonial accounts make clear that the Spaniards paid Native American warriors, so that their progressive professionalization is not at all surprising.

Supporting Colonial Expansion

The Tucson post played its expected role in supporting Spanish colonial expansion to the Colorado River. Frontier Provinces Commandant General Teodoro de Croix ordered Tucson to supply 11 of the troopers to be assigned to the two new settlements. Sergeant Juan de la Vega led this contingent, aided by two corporals. Three more troopers came from the Altar presidio along with Ensign Santiago de Yslas, the military commander of the project. Buenavista supplied six troopers. The Tucson garrison drew three replacements from Altar, five from Buenavista and seven from San Miguel de Horcasitas.[11] By replacing the contingent drawn from the Tucson garrison for the Colorado River settlements, Croix could keep the Tucson unit at full strength. Thus he was able to report to the king's minister, José de Gálvez, that he had drawn a subaltern, a sergeant, 2 corporals and 18 men from the presidios of Altar, Horcasitas and Buenavista. This reduced the complement at each of those posts to 64 officers and men.[12]

Ensign Yslas led the troops and settlers to the Colorado River by December 1780.[13] The Yumas received them well. The colonists paid little attention to Yuma land rights in selecting their settlement sites and fields. Worse still, they let their livestock destroy Yuma crops. Consequently, the Yumas refused to sell the colonists supplies when they exhausted their provisions. A California-bound expedition grazed its animals on Yuma fields and mesquite groves, triggering a very effective Indian uprising in July of 1781.[14]

Portents of Warfare

Meanwhile, the year 1780 brought portents of Indian warfare later in the decade for San Agustín del Tucson. Late June proved to be most eventful. On 26 June, Apaches approached the post stockade. They took two girls captive, but presidial gunfire drove them off, and they abandoned the girls.[15]

On that same day but far away, the garrison lost its military chaplain by enemy action. Friar Francisco Perdigon went south to Bacanuchi for the festival of St. John (23-24 June). He returned toward Arizpe with an escort of 11 armed men. When they were attacked by some 30 Apaches four leagues from the provincial capital, the escort broke and ran. The Apaches slew two members of the ineffective escort, captured one, and killed the priest, wounding him from head to foot. When survivors reached Arizpe and notified the authorities, the latter sent 50 dragoons after the Apaches. The cavalrymen were unable to overtake the attackers.[16]

At other times during the early summer of 1780, Apaches killed a friendly Native American at Tumacacori, a Papago and a Gileño. On 10 July a Tucson Pima managed to escape from his Apache captors.[17]

The year of disaster on the Colorado River, 1781, opened with excitement on the Apachean frontier. Early in January, four Apaches tried to steal sheep from Tumacacori Mission with the aid of three captives. The foreman heard them and they fled – save for one of the captives, who hid until daylight, when he was apprehended and conducted to the *presidio* for questioning. Next came an Apache sortie against Tucson's supply lines:

> The 22nd of the same January the Apaches attacked a pack train of the aforementioned Presidio which was carrying supplies from the Mission of Saric escorted by a corporal and a dozen soldiers. They valorously resisted the attack. They killed two of the barbarians, and the rest retired to a nearby hill. The corporal of the party, fearing a second attack on terrain more advantageous to the enemy, dispatched three soldiers to the Presidio seeking aid and munitions. They were cut off by seven Apaches, but dismounting they tied their horses and defended themselves bravely, killing two more barbarians and obliging the other five to flee. They carried out their mission, and the reinforced escort conducted the pack train happily to the presidio.[18]

That civilian Hispanic settlement began at Tucson very soon after the military post moved there seems clear from the fact that Allande could take militiamen into the field in 1779 along with his troops and Native American auxiliaries.

An unexpected and sad female reinforcement came to San Agustín del Tucson in 1781. The Yuma Indians on the lower Colorado River had rebelled against Spanish colonization in their territory in July. The Yumas successfully surprised two settlements and missions which had been founded, killed the men (including Friar Francisco Garcés) and carried women and children off into slavery. A Spanish expedition under Lieutenant Colonel Pedro Fages in December of that year rescued these survivors.[19] At least some of the rescued women went to Tucson. Lieutenant Josef M. Abate wrote on 2 May 1782 that "the women who were on the Colorado say that those nations paint their faces with colors,"[20] indicating the presence of these women at Tucson. Probably they came originally from Tubac, and returned to live with relatives who had moved to Tucson from the former post.

The colonial contretemps at the Colorado River crossing the year Spain invaded Minorca and Florida ended Spanish efforts to maintain overland communication between Sonora and California. That frontier lay too far from the theaters of decision for the empire to divert resources there. Consequently, Tucson remained the most advanced military post on this sector of the frontier of New Spain.

May Day! 1782

That Apache Indians on occasion attacked the Spanish garrison at Tucson has been known for some time. In his study of Juan Bautista de Anza as governor of New Mexico, A. B. Thomas noted that Gila Apaches allied with Navajos stormed both Tucson and Janos in 1784 in retaliation for a Spanish strike deep into Apache territory.[21] That was not, however, the first Western Apache attack on the Tucson post. At least two years earlier, Apaches assaulted the Tucson post with the clear hope of capturing it. The following account of this 1782 assault, reinforced with translations of eye-witness reports, contributes directly to our knowledge of the long-range problems of defending New Spain's northern frontier provinces against marauding tribesmen.[22]

May Day in 1782 dawned peaceably over the Royal Post of San Agustín del Tucson and its neighboring Northern Piman village. There was little to distinguish May Day from any other day in post routine save that it was Sunday. Such of the garrison as was on the post went about its accustomed duties.

The chaplain probably celebrated early Mass in the post chapel. Then he went across the Santa Cruz River to Piman Tucson to visit the missionary from Bac who had come north to the Native American settlement to celebrate Mass for its inhabitants. The company's ensign also crossed over to the Northern Piman village, along with a soldier. The company's lieutenant slept late in his house outside the post stockade. A soldier wandered on who-knows-what errand through the brush a short distance away from the post. Some women and children went walking in the cultivated fields in the valley toward the Indian village.

About 10:00 A.M. a strong force of Apache Indians intruded upon this peaceful frontier scene, achieving nearly complete surprise. They raced for the open entrance to the post stockade and nearly won through. A valiant personal stand by post commandant Captain Pedro Allande y Saabedra held the opening for the Spaniards. The sleepy lieutenant provided an important tactical diversion from his rooftop. The ensign and soldier visiting in Indian town across the river tied down another portion of the Apache force.

Thus, the tactical surprise the Apaches achieved in their initial attack was frittered away by their dispersion of forces against the two settlements, and the unforeseeable pinning down of many of their effectives in the housing outside the stockade. Apparently the Apaches attacked in accord with a pre-concerted plan, but without unified field command.

Certainly the Spaniards fought without a unified battle command. Their senior officer held the stockade gate more by personal efficiency in killing Apaches than by intelligent orders. Each of the other officers also fought virtually on his own, breaking the Apache attack by personal accuracy with firearms, which gave each one some edge in firepower over the bow-and-arrow-armed Apaches. The luck of the position of the various commissioned officers at the beginning of the battle also insured that they would be able to immobilize two large forces of Apaches away from the gravely threatened stockade entryway and thus prevent an all-out Apache mass assault on that weak point. Yet the officers fought independently and without real knowledge of what the others were doing during the conflict.

The next day, Captain Allande ordered his company ensign to collect eye-witness accounts of the battle from its several participants in order to reconstruct events for a report to higher authority.[23] The Spaniards' segmented, personal views of the battle showed clearly in the resulting affidavits. Some of these reports have been translated here to provide a sense of the battle isolation and an understanding of the individual emergency behavior displayed by these men under enemy surprise assault.

Delgado: a Trooper Who Hid In a Tree

> In obedience to the order of my captain, I had appear the soldier José Antonio Delgado, whom I interrogated upon his knowledge of the following points:
>
> Asked, where he found himself when the Apaches fell on this post?
>
> He replied that he found himself in the low brush which is near the post.
>
> Asked, how he escaped from the Apaches?
>
> He replied that as soon as he saw them, he fled through the wheat and hid himself behind the back of a ditch and climbed up a cúmaro tree.[24]
>
> Asked, what he saw from there?
>
> He replied that first some thirteen Apaches passed, and that these were carrying three dead bodies, and that they were resting underneath where he was hidden.
>
> Asked, if he saw anything else?
>
> He replied that when the cannon fired he saw that other Apaches passed with three of them being carried already dying.
>
> Asked if he knew whether the dead and those who carried them were Apaches?
>
> He replied, yes, he knew the living to be because they were talking under the tree, and the dead wore the same clothing as those who carried them.
>
> Asked if he saw anything else?
>
> He replied that he saw nothing more than what he has declared, and that this is true, and he ratified and signed it with me.
>
> YGNACIO FÉLIX USARRAGA
> JOSÉ ANTONIO DELGADO[25]

The Apache surprise, in other words, was complete so far as this trooper was concerned, and he contributed nothing to the Spanish defense, being quite immobilized up in his cúmaro tree. One imagines that Delgado suffered considerable mental torment in his leafy hiding place while the Apaches removing bodies of slain comrades from the battlefield paused to rest and converse under his tree. What if they had glanced up, or he had moved or sneezed?

Because of the number of literate, educated Spaniards visiting in the Native American settlement of Tucson that morning of 1 May 1782, several eyewitness accounts of the battle for the bridge between Indian town and the post were obtained in the next few days. In addition to offering various views of the battle, these documents make clear that much more water flowed in the Santa Cruz River then than did a few decades later, and that the spring which flowed from Sentinel Peak also contributed far more water than in later decades.

There were two stream channels or very large irrigation ditches which created an island on which Piman Tucson was located. The eastern stream flowed so heavily that it was bridged with a permanent structure to carry traffic between the military post and Native American town. Apache horsemen did not attempt to ford or swim this waterway in order to outflank the Spanish defenders of the bridge.

The fact that this heavy streamflow existed on the first day of May emphasizes the difference between the aquatic ecology of the Santa Cruz River Valley in 1782 and that of a century and a half later. The month of May is part of the driest season of the year in southern Arizona, after the winter rains have ended and long before summer thunder showers begin. While the hydrology of the area must be inferred from brief references to the streamflow in accounts of the battle, these references are quite clear.

Non-Combatants: The Missionary and the Chaplain

Father Belderrain of Bac, whose peaceful Sunday visitation was violently interrupted, was able to observe the various encounters from a position at Piman Tucson:

> As for what I saw from the Pueblo of Tucson on the first, between it and the presidio there were many Apaches on foot and some mounted. Those on foot, judging from the body which the Pimas, Papagos and Gileños who are collected for campaigns make, that we have counted, I judge to have been about 180. I did not pay much attention as to how many there may have been on horseback. I judge that these had taken up a position at that site in order to hamper the relief of the Pueblo, because I observed that they were not receiving Your Honor's attention, because I saw that the fire came from the northwest to the northeast, so I inferred that those in those directions were more numerous than those who made an all-out effort to enter inside the stockade....
>
> ... The battle lasted until the remount herd approached near the Pueblo. This was so far as I know quite distant and nearly an hour passed in collecting and herding it.[26]

Very likely Father Belderrain's estimate of the number of Apaches on foot was the most accurate one made that May morning. Apparently the number of mounted enemies was not large, so this estimate is significant in comparison to the higher guesses of combatants who were pinned down where they could see only small portions of the total Apache force, but who probably were more emotionally involved in the battle. Significantly, Belderrain implied that he consciously estimated Apache numbers by comparison with his memory of the bulk of Native American allies when forming to go on campaign, giving his estimate a real base.

The other priest in Piman Tucson that morning was the chaplain of the Tucson presidial garrison. Inside when the first shot was fired, Father Gabriel Franco immediately climbed up onto the mission roof where he could see what was going on. Yet,

> . . . "he was unable to see what the number of enemies who attacked this presidio might have been. Despite the distance, he was able to hear the first shot, and climbing to the roof he immediately commenced to see the Apaches who surrounded the presidio in such numbers that not only was the presidio surrounded, but also one wing occupied the field.
>
> They came straight for the mission cited, for which reason it was unable to give aid, because Ensign Usarraga and the distinguished[27] Don Juan Phelipe Beldarrain who wished to come to the Presidio were attacked by the enemy on the bridge. Without doubt they restrained there the advance of the Apaches onto the island and pueblo. It is certain that although he was unable to distinguish perfectly the number that there might have been, never has there come such a numerous body of enemies, nor have they attacked with such pertinacity and by such places.
>
> Without doubt the number of troops who resisted the assault was very small because really very few were present, and even fewer of them were in the Presidio. The cited Ensign Usarraga, the distinguished Don Juan Phelipe Beldarrain, and a soldier who had gone for grass were in the Pueblo. The latter was unable to enter the Presidio, so entered the Pueblo, from which I watched with Father Velderrain the multitude of enemies who assaulted the north side of the Presidio, where they were met with the major force of fire, while equal case was not made against those to the south and west who were numerous enough.
>
> The time that the battle which I was watching from the Pueblo lasted would have been around two hours. . . . [28]

Even the two priests became too excited during the battle to pay attention to the passage of time. One estimated one hour while the other guessed nearly two hours as the duration of the engagement. Both agreed that the Usarraga-Belderrain defense of the bridge saved Piman Tucson and its mission as well as themselves from attack. Usarraga, with his bravery, clearly made a key contribution to the Hispanic institutions struggling to survive on the banks of the Santa Cruz River.

This subaltern had transferred to Tucson from the Flying Company of the Province of Sonora, in which he also held an ensign's rank. He replaced the deceased José Francisco de Castro. Usarraga's formal commission as first ensign was not signed by the king until nearly a year after this battle.[29] The following report gives Usarraga's own first-hand impression of the bridge defense that saved the Pueblo:

Usarraga: The Ensign Who Held the Vital Bridge

My Dear Sir:

In compliance with Your Honor's order of the second of this month, and in accordance with the questionnaire that accompanied it, I expound the following under my word of honor:

The first day of the present month when the enemies fell on this presidio, I found myself in the Pueblo of Tucson on my own affairs and with Your Honor's permission, accompanied by the distinguished Don Juan Phelipe Beldarrain. At that time, despite the distance of the shots and disturbance, I attempted to return to the presidio. I did not reach it, however, because when I arrived at the Bridge with the distinguished person mentioned, the enemy was already in possession of that site in great numbers. They tried forcefully enough to advance over the Island to the Pueblo, but seeing that those who had come there were many, and that, moreover, if I won through them I should find it necessary to enter another multitude who were covering the lake and ditch, I decided it would be well to make a stand with the distinguished person mentioned, firing on said Bridge as much to impede their advance on the Island and Pueblo as to succor some women and children who found themselves in the ditch. From there we saw the presidio surrounded and notwithstanding that there were very many on all sides, the major resistance from the presidio was directed to the north of it, which made me decide that the greater part of the enemies were there.

When they had abandoned their intention of entering the Pueblo, I returned to it and asked Father Friar Juan Baptista Beldarrain for some Indians whom he gave me immediately. With them and the distinguished person I was able to enter the presidio after the battle ended, although the enemies were still gathered not far distant.

As for their number, I am unable to say definitely (inasmuch as I was not present) what it might have been. Yet I can assure you under the faith of my word that I have not seen such a body in the battles in which I have engaged, nor have I heard said that they have made such an attempt to enter any other presidio.

The troops who were in the presidio that day (including the captain, cadet, and sergeant, who was sick) were eighteen men and two citizens.

The enemy losses [were as follows]: ... From the Bridge I saw one fall in the *Ojito* (spring) and the Apaches picked him up and carried him. Another among those whom the distinguished one and I were firing on at the Bridge fell and the Pimas continued shooting arrows at him and and yelled to us,

'We are going to get him.'

Inasmuch as we did not foresake the Bridge, we left him, and I am sure that this Apache is the one whose head the Pimas cut off which Your Honor placed on the gate of the stockade, because he had a ball in the chest and two arrow wounds in the side according to what those who went to see the body say.[30]

Allande made a practice of cutting the heads off Apaches his troops killed and setting them on the defensive wall of the post "causing terror to the barbarians and an agreeable perspective to this most affectionate and humble vassal of Your Grace," as he wrote to a superior officer.[31]

Ensign Usarraga's account makes clear that although his defense of the bridge with Beldarrain saved Piman Tucson from invasion and pinned down one wing of the Apache force, the battle really was won elsewhere. The one Apache killed for certain near the bridge, and the second either killed or mortally wounded near the spring, discouraged the attackers, but not enough to cause them to disengage.

Lieutenant and Servant: A Key Flank Diversion

Another pair of defenders caught outside the stockade by the surprise Apache attack caused more casualties and pinned down a significant portion of the Apache assault force close to the threatened stockade entrance. In Lieutenant Josef María Abate's own words:

> The Apache attacked this presidio on the first day of May about ten o'clock in the morning while I was dressing. My servant arrived, saying to me, 'The Apaches are here.'
>
> I grabbed my weapons and climbed to the parapeted roof of my house. I saw that the enemies had it completely surrounded. Inasmuch as the latter were not expecting harm from the roof, I was able to kill one with my first shot without being seen. My servant took the opportunity to fell another with an arrow. The Apaches, seeing that those who were firing were only two, and those who had surrounded the house were about a hundred and fifteen, rather more than less, commenced to shoot at us. Returning their fire, I felled another.
>
> Frightened by seeing that I had killed two and my servant one, they retreated and with the bodies of the dead they entered a house which was back-to-back with mine. Although they had retired, it was in such a manner that they remained at a distance which enabled them to shoot arrows at us, but because we were protected by the roof parapet, the wall resisted their arrows although the multitude was large. Firing where they were, my servant with his arrows and I wounded many because every shot was unerring. Continuing to fire, I reached my tenth round when the barrel of my gun plugged up. I ordered my servant to descend to bring me another rifle which he brought me despite having been wounded since the middle of the battle. When I opened fire again they retreated, but, forewarned, I took advantage of this last shot, but only wounded my target, although he fell.
>
> From the roof of my house I saw that in a little space the Apaches took possession of a very large number of houses near the guard, and tried with the greatest perserverance to enter the entryway to the stockade which I thought they had gained because I saw them within less than ten paces' distance and I saw very few of ours in it, although these between the cloud of smoke from powder and dust kept up an unceasing fire.

I did not see how many enemies were killed in the presidio, but I heard that they yelled when they were forming the line that three Apaches had been killed.

I am ignorant of the troops that were in the presidio but I conceive that they would have been very few because at the bulwark which was the most favored there would not have been over six who were in the gate of the stockade. There seemed to me to have been fewer because of their small mass.

I never have seen such a large number of enemies, but it seems to me that those who attacked the presidio were not fewer than 600 and I have heard said that no other presidio has been assaulted with such persistence nor by such large numbers.[32]

The importance of the diversion created by Lieutenant Abate and his Indian servant was very great because they forced a considerable number of Apaches to take cover in houses outside the stockade where they were no assistance to the assault force trying to storm the entrance. Abate could hardly have fought better had he known that his promotion was before the king and that his lieutenant's commission would be signed in far-off Spain on May 14. He had recently been transferred from Altar to Tucson, and promoted from first ensign to acting lieutenant.[33]

Captain Allande: The Entryway Engagement

The bridge defense and roof-top diversion seriously weakened the Apache thrust at the stockade entrance, but the defense of that point clearly proved to be the key to the battle. The man who held the stockade entryway for Spain was none other than the post commander, Captain Pedro Allande y Saabedra:

> The first day of May of 1782 six hundred Apaches approached this presidio (which was without a wall) reaching to the stockade itself, and entering many houses. The deponent found himself with only twenty men including the cadet, his son, who is today ensign of this company, during the first attack which he resisted at the entrance of the presidio. They dangerously wounded three men, one of whom died, running the deponent through the right leg, until he remained with only one soldier....[34]

Apparently the commanding officer felt constrained to exhibit modesty about his brave role in defending the post, leaving it to others to emphasize his fighting efficiency and bravery. Another of his summaries of the action adds but little to that above:

> The first day of May of 1782 I defended the presidio with twenty men including the Cadet, my son Don Pedro María de Allande, against 600 Apaches who tried to dispose of all the inhabitants, taking possession of many houses to attack us and to defend themselves. These served them

at the same time as a hospital in which to put their dead and wounded. They reached the stockade which was without doors nor guardhouse, in their first assault, wounding a soldier, an invalided one and a citizen. They shot the deponent's right leg through and through, despite which he killed two by his own hand after being wounded, continuing to direct from the bulwarks and stockade (a soldier serving him as a support) such a heavy fire that they were obliged to retire with heavy losses. Although the wound weakened the deponent's forces inasmuch as it hit the nerves, nonetheless because of his anxiety that the arms of Your Grace should shine with the greatest brilliance, he did not retire for treatment until the battle ended. . . .[35]

At the very end of the battle, Captain Allande actually remained alone at the stockade entrance despite his serious wound. He sent the soldier supporting him, José Domingo Granillo, who was himself still sick from wounds he had suffered on January 30, to fire the cannon which apparently completed the demoralization of the Apaches and signaled the virtual end of their assault. According to Granillo: "finally he remained alone with his captain in the entrance to the stockade and his captain ordered him to climb to the bulwark to fire a cannon. The numerous arrows gave him pause for a while, but his captain turning to see, said, 'Climb! I will protect your rear!' He climbed up and fired the cannon."[36]

The troops that participated in the defense of the stockade and its entrance concurred in the captain's account. Of the Apache main attack, they said, "They made the utmost effort to gain the entrance to the stockade in order to enter the guardroom, but the heavy fire the captain with four men directed at them dissuaded them." These defenders also estimated that the battle lasted for two hours, and judged from the blood found afterwards in the houses where the Apaches took cover that many of them had been killed, "but those who fell in the view of all were three. The Captain killed two of these and the Paymaster Don Francisco Núñez one." During the key struggle for the entryway, the Apaches "wounded the captain, shooting his right leg through and through, the invalided Juan Espinosa and the trooper Baletín de la Peña. The latter two retired when they were wounded, and only the captain kept up his fire and animated those who accompanied him, without ceasing to attend to all the bulwarks until the battle ended, at which time he issued forth supported by Sergeant Juan Fernandez and a soldier to examine the slaughter which our arms had wrought among the enemy."[37]

The Spanish officers on the post were unanimous in expressing their admiration for their commander's stand. According to Ensign Usarraga:

> The trail which the Apaches left demonstrated that they had reached within eight or ten paces of the guardhouse and exercised every diligence to enter it. Everyone with a single voice says that Your Honor without paying attention to the wound which you received in the leg continued to direct with great animation those who accompanied you without leaving the bulwarks, and that with only four men you defended the entrance to the stockade notwithstanding that it was necessary for you to avail yourself of a soldier to keep yourself on your feet. I myself testify

that after I reached the presidio Your Honor left the stockade, supported by the sergeant, to reconnoitre the havoc which had been wrought by the enemy. Despite our having urged on you going for treatment, only much later did you wish to do so, after seeing that the enemy had retired.[38]

The troops who defended the stockade besides the captain, Paymaster Francisco Núñez, and troopers Juan Espinosa, Baletín de la Peña, José Domingo Granillo and Sergeant Juan Fernandez already mentioned, were Corporal Ygnacio Arias and troopers Joaquín Ortega, Miguel Antonio Talaman, Francisco Xavier Castro, José Antonio Fuentes, Martín Mascareno, Juan María Olvera, José Jesus Baldenegro, Antonio Miranda, Manuel María Mallen, Vicente Pacheco, Procopio Cancio and Thomás Ramón Amesquita. The citizens who joined in defending the presidio were Juan de Dios Marrujo and Pascual Escalante.[39] The commandant general of the Frontier Provinces of New Spain authorized Captain Allande to enter on the service record of every participant in the battle his official commendation.[40]

New Tactics by a Nameless Strategist

While the Spanish estimate of 600 Apaches in the attacking force[41] may have been inflated by fears generated in the stress of battle which affected perception, there can be little doubt that the royal Spanish Fort of San Agustín del Tucson had been savagely attacked by one of the largest Apachean armies ever to attempt to take a frontier post. This 1782 battle was noteworthy for its divergence from customary Apache tactics. Usually the Apaches ambushed isolated, small parties of troopers guarding remount herds or conducting pack trains with animals or goods of immediate economic value to the aggressors. In other words, the southern Athapascan Indians became "raiding robbers" of Spanish herds and flocks in New Mexico, Sonora and Chihuahua.[42] The southern Apaches did not then raise cattle, although they kept horses to ride on their raids. They slaughtered cattle, donkeys and horses soon after capture to cure the meat for later consumption. They thus remained "parasitic" on Spanish livestock,[43] and continual hostilities with Spanish forces thus ensued.

This means that the most noteworthy aspect of the Apache attack on Tucson on May Day in 1782 was that it amounted to a frontal assault upon a Spanish presidio and its associated friendly Native American town. In a complete departure from usual Apachean battle tactics, the attackers struck directly at the poorly defended post and ignored its remount herd. The eyewitness accounts clearly credit the troops guarding the cavalry post's animals with helping to halt the Apache attack on the presidio, in a reversal of the usual roles.

The attack described in the eye-witness accounts translated in this chapter prove that for a brief period, at least, some anonymous Apache leader succeeded in mounting what must be termed a strategic Apache offensive against the Spaniards. Economic raiding was suspended while the Apaches tried an all-out attack on Spanish military posts. Apparently some Apache military genius had perceived that the customary hit-and-run raids harassed the Spaniards but did not stop their northward advance. He perhaps realized that the only way really to halt the Spanish advance and effectively to defeat the Spaniards was to assault and capture their frontier military installations. Then, too, the posts held far more plunder than a single pack train conveyed.

That nameless Apache strategist was undoubtedly correct. Had the Tucson post fallen to the attackers, they could have mopped up the Northern Piman Indians of Tucson at their leisure, and swept west to wreck havoc in the exposed rancherías of the Papaguería. They could have advanced south to annihilate the civilians left at Tubac and the unprotected missions and towns farther south of the frontier. Consternation would have reigned on the Sonoran colonial borders.

In the trials of deadly conflict, superior fire power evidently won the battle of 1 May 1782, combined with a disposition of Spanish officers when the battle opened that prevented effective concentration of Apache forces against the presidio entrance.

Just possibly an Apache strategist had been able to persuade band chiefs not only to concentrate forces for an all-out attack on the presidio, but also to experiment with a unified battle plan. The accounts of the battle by the priests and officer caught in the Pueblo of Tucson by surprise suggest that that Apaches had split their forces foolishly in a twin-pronged assault on both Indian village and military post. It is possible, however, that this was precisely what the Apaches wanted the people at Piman Tucson to think. The fact that the Apaches concentrated on the bridge, suggests that they, like Ensign Usarraga and Don Juan Phelipe Beldarrain, were fighting a holding action there to dissuade the Tucson Native Americans from attacking the rear of their main force striking the presidio. Such an interpretation suggests that the Apache assault on the presidio failed principally because of superior Spanish fire power of firearms over bows and arrows, and the unforeseeable bit of Spanish luck in having a sharp-shooting lieutenant and his accurate bowman-servant outside the stockade in a parapet-roofed house on the Apache flank.

Eventually Apache casualties simply mounted too high for them to maintain the attack, having lost the advantage of initial surprise. The Spanish accounts indicated a minimum of eight Apaches killed — two by Allande, one by the paymaster, two by Lieutenant Abate, one by his servant, one by Ensign Usarraga or Beldarrain, and one by an unknown hand near the spring. Thus, the Apaches sustained far higher proportional casualties in killed and wounded than Apaches customarily suffered before they disengaged in economic raids on flocks and herds.

The total attacking force was probably in the neighborhood of 300 warriors. The priest's estimate of about 180 Apaches on foot based on comparisons of mass with a known number of friendly Indians carries more weight than the guesses of 600. All the Spanish accounts suggest that mounted Apaches numbered fewer than those on foot, who carried the brunt of the battle. Probably the horsemen were deployed to ride rapidly around the post to give the Spaniards the impression of being effectively surrounded while the Apache infantry struck for the entryway. The 8 claimed Spanish kills amounted to some 2.6% mortality for a force of 300, and many other Apaches were badly wounded, as evidenced by Spanish descriptions of bloody houses where the Native Americans were pinned down. Ensign Usarraga took particular note of this bloody evidence of Apache casualties: "The enemy dead, judging from the abundant blood which they lost, were many. In the house of the soldier Juan Santos Lopez (where they deposited the cadavers while the battle lasted) I saw many fresh pools of blood, and the same in that of the soldier Baptista Romero and that of the corporal Francisco Espinosa."[44]

The Spanish casualties consisted of three wounded defending the gate, so amounted 12.5% of their 24 effectives. Yet the Spaniards had no choice but to continue fighting or die. The attackers could choose, and they admitted that their supreme effort failed. The Spaniards did not stress their own losses, and the death of one of their three wounded was mentioned only in passing. Even more casually, the chaplain's comments on possible Apache allies revealed that a woman had also died at the hands of the attackers: "I have heard said by women that the Chacon boy has said he did not flee because he recognized that the one who killed Dona Thadea was a one-eyed Papago Indian.[45]

When interrogated, the Chacon boy replied "that he who wounded him was a one-eyed Indian who wore *Guaraches* [sandals] and for this reason he did not flee. Although he was not acquainted with him, the Indian resembled a Papago whom he had seen a few days before in the Pueblo, but he does not affirm that it was he.[46] Thus, a brief hint in the post-battle accounts raises the possibility that Apaches captives operated as part of the attacking force. At any rate, the presence of hostile warriors wearing Mexican-style sandals rather than Apache boots shows that there was some cultural diversity among members of the assaulting forces.

Battle Epilogue

One of the results of this sanguinary battle seems to have been the completion of the adobe fortification wall by one of the Spanish officers engaged. In rating the post's officers in December of 1783, the adjutant inspector had this to say about the man who fought from his house roof during the battle:[47]

> Lieutenant Don José María Abate has managed the finances of this company with integrity and disinterest enough. He had obeyed the captain's orders according to what the latter tells me. He is capable of disciplining troops, and I believe he would try very hard to carry out any commission with which he were charged, inasmuch as he has walled the presidio at his cost on the same terms which he offered.

Thus, the wooden stockade Captain Allande had thrown up in 1777 and defended in 1779 and 1782 has been replaced by a permanent adobe wall by the end of 1783, making the Tucson post rather more secure against attack. Eight years after the garrison arrived on the Tucson site, its post was physically secure, and it was ready to go over onto the offensive.

8.

Harassing the Western Apaches, 1782-1792

THE YUMA UPRISING OF 1781 and subsequent changes in Spanish colonial expansion policy ended Tucson's function as protector of the land route to Upper California. The post shifted thereafter to become a full-time Apache-fighting garrison. Its success can be evaluated in terms of its diminution of Western Apache military power as one unit in the frontier defense cordon set up by the king's New Regulations of 1772.

Some historians have argued that Spanish involvement in European wars after 1779, and administrative dependence of the commandant general of the Frontier Provinces on the viceroy of New Spain for supplies "almost nullified" the effectiveness of the changes in presidial defense ordered in 1772.[1] One historian reported that King Charles III decreed a halt on aggressive action against Apaches from 1779 to 1783 during Spain's war against England in alliance with rebellious British North American colonies.[2] The example of frontier presidial effectiveness provided by the following case study of Tucson shows on the contrary that the reforms ordered in 1772 did in fact achieve long-range success in carrying out the geopolitical mission assigned to Spanish frontier garrisons.

Recovering from May Day, 1782

During the first decade after establishment of the Royal Post at San Agustín del Tucson, Spanish officials in charge of the Frontier Provinces of New Spain actively pursued a policy of Apache extermination. They strove to break the military might of the hostile Apache bands. They sent frequent armed parties into Apache territory so as to waste Apache manpower in troop engagements, and to destroy Apache crops and settlements in a scorched-earth attrition strategy.[3]

The Royal Post of San Agustín del Tucson seems to have been too weak to participate very effectively in this probing of southern Apacheland during 1782. Captain Pedro Allande y Saabedra appears to have had to fight a purely defensive war, and the relative weakness of the Tucson post in addition to its very forward position in relation to other frontier garrisons may have helped to bring down upon it the all-out Apache assault that occurred on May Day of that year.

Toward the end of November in 1782, the commanding inspector general of the Frontier Provinces inspected the Tucson post and garrison. He found the post recovering from the May Day attack. His inspection summary, Table 6 in the Appendix of this book, indicates the Tucson garrison was at full authorized strength of 72. It consisted of 67 men and 5 officers.[4] This represented a decline in force, however, because the Opata scouts Allande had commanded in 1779 had been discharged.[5] The Tucson company remained one man shy of its authorized complement in fact because Felix Armenta had deserted and was being sent to Buenavista presidio under arrest.

The inspector described First Sergeant Juan Fernandez as good officer material because of his intelligence and knowledge of writing and accounting. The two ensigns, Usarraga and Carrillo, and the other sergeant, the inspector characterized as good field men not fitted for handling accounts.[6] Certainly Usarraga had proved his bravery earlier that year.

On Christmas Day, Apaches again struck to drive off Tucson's cattle herds. When the commanding general of the Frontier Provinces recommended Allande for promotion, he described the Christmas encounter: "More than 200 seized the cattle which were recovered by the parties of troops which he dispatched in their pursuit inasmuch as the wound in his leg was still open. They were able to kill six of the Apache aggressors, whose heads were cut off."[7]

Juan Antonio Oliva, son of the tough old lieutenant, emerged as the hero of this encounter. Two parties totaling only 30 men pursued the Apaches, who had slain three herdsmen. Oliva rode pell-mell into the midst of the aggressors. Armed with only his lance, this young man mortally wounded one of the Native Americans, whom he took to the post. Oliva suffered three minor wounds.[8]

Campaigns and Manpower in 1783

The captain and others wounded on May Day in 1782 gradually recovered. By 1783 Allande was ready to whip his command into shape to take the field. He was able to do so at least three times during the course of the year. The captain himself led a campaign in March which captured two Apaches.

On 6 June, five Indians killed a horse-guard and stole two saddled horses. On 24 to 30 June, Allande took the field again. On this expedition, he led a combined force of presidial troops from Tucson and Santa Cruz, the Catalonian Volunteers and Northern Pimans numbering 96 men. This force killed two enemies in the Santa Catalina Mountains. Allande had the heads cut from the bodies to display at the presidio. He claimed that two Native Americans who escaped "probably" died from their wounds. Most residents of the attacked ranchería had fled beforehand. Even so, the few fighters wounded one trooper.[9]

In December, Allande achieved even greater success, killing "eleven valiant warriors" and capturing nine prisoners between the Santa Teresa and Florida Mountains in a battle which "began at three in the afternoon and ended in the night." Allande's own horse was wounded during that engagement.[10]

Between the end of that campaign and the next, the Tucson garrison received another inspection by the adjutant inspector on orders from the brigadier general commanding the Frontier Provinces. The summary of this inspection (Table 7, Appendix)[11] shows that Allande was keeping his complement at full authorized strength despite a year's hard campaigning.

The human erosion of the previous year's campaigning appeared in the turnover in personnel. Only Captain Allande and Sergeant José María Sosa of the 1784 list of garrison strength had been in Tucson in 1779. Sosa was then a lowly second corporal,[12] whose promotions reflected attrition in frontier garrison leadership in the field. Besides the 5 officers, 2 sergeants and a drummer listed in Table 7, the remainder of the post complement included the 62 men listed in Table 6, with their financial status shown rounded off to the nearest peso.[13] Of these 62 men reported in 1783, 7 had appeared on the 1775 roll, 20 had appeared on the 1779 roll, and 11 had been commended for their bravery during the May Day 1782 encounter (see Appendix Table 7).

At this moment between campaigns in 1783, the troopers of the Tucson cavalry company had 185 horses and 40 mules, not counting officers' mounts. That was considerably short of the 7 mounts per man prescribed by royal regulations,[14] reflecting the success of Apache raiders in keeping down the size of the post remount herd.

The troop accounts showed that the financial situation of the individual troopers in the Tucson garrison had changed sharply for the worse during the four years of active campaigning with horse and mule losses to Apache raiders. In 1779, the company had had 2,414 pesos to its credit compared to debts of only 445 pesos. By the end of 1783, the contingent as a whole was 3,630 pesos in debt because of charges for replacing mounts (Appendix Table 7). Only Juan Felipe Beldarrain seems to have worked himself out of debt, which was a very notable achievement considering how much he had still owed in 1779!

Before the year 1783 ended, Captain Allande took out another column which achieved signal success in the opening days of 1784. His intensive campaigning brought him favorable notice from his superiors and another promotion recommendation to the king's minister Joseph de Gálvez from the commandant general of the Frontier Provinces:

His Excellency Don Joseph de Gálvez — No. 76

My Dear Sir:

In letter No. 64 of December 29th last, I referred to Your Excellency the good results of the campaign which the Captain of the Presidio of San Agustín del Tucson, Don Pedro de Allande, had just finished executing against the enemy. I indicated the measures which he had taken in order to repeat his sally. He did so on the 30th day of that same month, having to endure the harsh rain and snow storms which have occurred generally since the first of this month. On the 5th he attacked two rancherías near the Gila River, killing five Apaches and four women, capturing twenty-four prisoners of both sexes, recovering one female captive, recapturing five riding animals and destroying everything in their miserable habitations. He returned to his presidio on the 8th in order not to mistreat his troop and mounts further, inasmuch as the legs of the latter were swollen from the intense cold and snows which they suffered, giving proof of the greatest devotion.

For this action and that referred to in my aforementioned letter No. 64, as well as for his proved bravery and spirit and twenty-nine years' seniority, I judge Allande worthy that His Majesty might deign to reward him with promotion to Lieutenant Colonel of Cavalry. Moreover, Captain Don Pedro de Allande defended his presidio with valor on the 6th day of November of '79 against a considerable number of barbarians. He defended it especially well with only twenty men on the 1st of May of '82 when it was surrounded by more than 500 enemies who were able to seize some houses which were outside the stockade, which they attempted to break into and enter by the gateway. (My predecessor gave account in the summary of news which accompanied his letter No. 751 of the 30th of the same month.) Allande encouraged everyone with much calmness and boldness, from the beginning of the battle until the enemy retired after two hours. Allande maintained himself among the most active although they wounded him through one leg. He killed two with his own hands. Finally, he has bloodied the enemy on all occasions when they have approached his neighborhood. . . . [See page 83].

I therefore ask Your Excellency that he might serve to contribute his most powerful influence so that Allande might be conceded promotion so that he may continue his useful labors with this satisfaction.

The ensigns Don Ygnacio Felix Usarraga of the Presidio of Tucson, who came out gravely wounded, and Don Joseph Tona of that of Santa Cruz, have distinguished themselves in the two campaigns mentioned, giving proofs of unusual valor. I present them to Your Excellency to the end that they might be brought to the notice of the King so that he might dispense to them the gratitude of his Royal Will.

May God preserve Your Excellency for many years. Arizpe. 26 January 1784.

Your most attentive and loyal servant kisses Your Excellency's hand.

PHELIPE DE NEVE[15]

Ensign Usarraga was, of course, the officer who bravely defended the bridge between Piman Tucson and the presidio on May Day of 1782. This brave subaltern apparently died of his battle wounds, for Juan Carrillo had become ensign of the Tucson company by 31 March 1784,[16] and Usarraga's wife Doña María Antonia Gonzalez de Usarraga was identified as a widow on 31 December 1785.[17]

The other frontier posts shared this problem of maintaining their officer cadres during this period of high mortality. This led to relatively rapid promotions from the lower ranks. The Santa Cruz Ensign Joseph Tona, whom the commandant general also recommended for promotion, was formerly a sergeant in the Tucson company[18] who had been commissioned in the Santa Cruz garrison to maintain its officer strength. The Tucson unit drew on other companies for its officer replacements in like manner.

Fighting With the Lance, 1784

While the commandant general's recommendations progressed up the colonial administrative chain of command to the king of Spain, the frontier troops carried on their bloody battle with the southern bands of the Western Apaches. On 21 March 1784, these enemy Indians retaliated again in the conventional manner against the forward Tucson post. They attacked the post's remount herd. Once again, the commandant general's summary to the king's minister tells the story:

His Excellency Don Joseph de Gálvez, No. 100
My Dear Sir:

At break of day on the 21st day of March last, a multitude of Apaches attacked the remount herd guard of the presidio of San Agustín del Tucson, which was under the command of Ensign Don Juan Carrillo. Although the herd was halted in the corral, which was defended bravely, the Apaches succeeded after a long time in stampeding and carrying off the herd, leaving five soldiers dead and one wounded at the cost of the lives of three of the aggressors in the attack.

Thirteen horses ran away to the presidio and immediately afterwards two soldiers arrived to give notice of what had happened. Without loss of time an equal number of troops mounted them and followed the trail under the orders of Lieutenant Tomás Equrrola, reinforced with thirty Pimas of the neighboring towns of Tupson and San Xavier. Thus, this united force consisted of forty-nine men, including five citizens. With the rest of the remount herd guard which consisted of twelve men, our people succeeded in catching up with the enemy in less than three-quarters of an hour. Confident in their numbers, which according to the dispatches which do not seem exaggerated exceeded 500 on foot and mounted, the latter advanced to receive them and were intrepidly attacked. Equrrola gave the example by killing with his own hands one of the Apaches, and the others mixing it up killed thirteen more, among them Chief Chiquito, who was the one who commanded and stimulated them to sustain the action. They broke off the engagement and took precipitous flight as soon as they saw the massacre and noticed the harm which this handful of men whom they had planned to surround with their mass had caused.

Our small forces retired, carrying to the presidio the seventeen heads of Apaches who died in the two combats, twelve horses which it was able to recapture, and some of the arms and effects of the dead soldiers. The barbarians would have received more harm had the troop been able to pursue them in their flight, but it could not be done because all the horses on which the troop was mounted had been wounded. The troops and the citizens and the Indian auxiliaries gave uncommon proofs of valor in the action. This has been in all circumstances among the most distinguished and advantageous skirmishes that has occurred in the Provinces. It is the most notable for there having been, besides the number with whom it was fought, more than hundred more Apaches placed in ambush on the Santa Catalina River and mountain near Tucson, according to what was found in the reconnoitering which they carried out, noting that the wounded were losing much blood on the trail. It is easy to infer the harm and destruction which the enemy would have wrought had our people been defeated.

The experience there is that said enemies execute their strongest irruptions at the beginning of spring. The knowledge acquired that they direct them toward the presidio of Tucson makes me most fearful that they may strike a blow there to revenge the rebuffs with which they have been repelled the other times when they have tried, and make up for the damage which that garrison has caused them in its campaigns. With this in view, I have thought it wise to order that their remount should not be taken until the middle of last month, although they lack more than 350 mounts to complete their complement. I delayed it partly so the Apaches should have less incentive, and partly so that it should not be so surprised by winter as it would if taken during the cold weather, which maltreats the horses and renders them useless. As a result of this prudent measure, the company of the aforesaid presidio has been freed from the loss of a number of mounts equal to the 150 which, including 40 mules, are those which have now been stolen, a little more or less. Also, this occurrence should not, I believe, delay the projected expedition to the Gila River which should be carried out the middle of this month, nor the later operations. I have taken measures to have the remount mentioned arrive at the presidio of Tucson from the 8th to the 10th.

The members of the company which garrisons Tucson find themselves for the reasons related in the hard necessity of paying with their credit for the entire complement of their horses and mules. This is six of the first for each man, and one of the second. Their replacement will increase the considerable pledges which they already have originating from the equal losses which they have suffered. At present, Tucson is the presidio on this frontier which the enemy strikes most often, desiring vengeance for the damage that unit has inflicted. Since the end of November of last year until today, it has killed thirty-three Apache Indians and four women, and made prisoners of thirty-three of both sexes.

It has seemed to me part of my obligation to inform Your Excellency of all this in order that he may serve to present it to His Majesty with the merit which Lieutenant Don Tomas Equrrola, Ensign Don Juan Carrillo, and the troop have contracted in the battle described in order that the Royal Mercy may deign to dispense to them the gratitude which might be his sovereign will.

May God preserve Your Excellency many years. Arispe. 5th of April of 1784.

Your most attentive, certain servant kisses Your Excellency's hand.

Postscript: I have just received a new dispatch in which I am assured with positive certainty that besides the seventeen Apaches killed in the battle referred to in this letter, a very great many more were slain until the party of troops grew tired of lancing the great number of enemies who traveled on foot.

PHELIPE DE NEVE[19]

This final comment by the commandant general emphasized the key importance of the cavalry lance as the preferred and most effective weapon of Sonoran frontier garrison soldiery. A German Jesuit expelled from Sonora in 1767 wrote that the spear was the only weapon the frontier soldiers were skilled in using, wielding it to advantage when they caught enemy Native Americans in the open. They learned to handle the spear while hunting cattle.[20] The reliance that Tucson troops placed on this weapon may be inferred from the number and condition of the lances reported by military inspectors, compared to other weapons. Neve's own 1782 inspection report[21] contained this notation about Tucson's weaponry:

> The armament has been used since the year 1776, in part, and the rest since '79. Twenty muskets need repairs, and four pairs of pistols, which I ordered done. The guns are of equal caliber, consisting of sixty-six of the first and an equal number of the second. Except a dozen pairs, the latter fire very untruly and are stored for safety. Thirty-eight swords are lacking and the twenty-eight that the troops use are of bad quality because of their inequality and temper. *The company is completely equipped with lances.*

Much the same condition obtained during the adjutant inspector's review of the post at the beginning of 1784.[22]

> The armament which this Company uses consists of sixty-four muskets, thirty-five of which were supplied the year of '75 and twenty-nine have served since September of '79; an equal number of pairs of pistols, twenty-five almost useless from having French-style triggers and very little fire, and the rest of good quality. . . . There are only sixteen medium-quality swords. *All have lances* except four, who are the newest soldiers in the company, whom I ordered supplied from the reserve. I ordered some other short ones replaced with these. Only twenty-two individuals of this company are provided with leather armor, requiring eleven to complete the complement. Twenty-three shields are lacking and there is no prospect of replacing either the one or the other for lack of hides for them.

Lieutenant Tomás Equrrola's distinguished role in the March 21 running battle with Apache raiders emphasized once again the rapid turnover in commissioned junior officers during this period. Tucson Lieutenant José Abate, another of the heroes of the 1782 May Day defense of the post, had been promoted to the captaincy of San Carlos de Buenavista. Commandant General Neve had replaced him with Equrrola. The latter had previously served as a lieutenant under Commandant Inspector Hugh O'Connor in one of the Flying Companies of Nueva Vizcaya in 1775.[23] Neve's letter recommending that Equrrola be recommissioned on the basis that he had reformed his faults helps to clarify an odd situation:[24]

> Excellency Don Joseph de Gálvez
> My Dear Sir:
> A lieutenancy has become vacant in the Company of the Presidio of San Agustín del Tupson because Don Joseph Abate has been promoted. He has obtained the command of the Presidio of San Carlos de Buenavista, as I informed Your Excellency in my letter No. 81 on 26 January. I have settled the lieutenancy upon Don Tomás de Equrrola. He served

in an equal capacity in the companies of the Nueva Vizcaya expedition. In various encounters with the enemy, he exhibited outstanding bravery. He has a special knowledge of the lands the enemy inhabits and of this type of warfare, in which he has distinguished himself and for which he is very useful. He has corrected the defects which obliged my predecessor to terminate his career. Knowing that he has reformed, I recently offered to appoint him again.

I hope that Your Excellency will serve to present him to His Majesty and incline his royal will to order Equrrola commissioned a lieutenant of the aforementioned Presidio of Tupson.

May Our Lord guard Your Excellency many years. Arispe 8 March 1784.

Excellency

I kiss Your Excellency's hands, your most attentive and surest servant

PHELIPE DE NEVE

Joseph de Gálvez indeed followed Neve's recommendation, so the king signed Equrrola's commission late in August.[25] The inevitable time-lag in imperial governance forced Charles III like other Spanish monarchs actually to delegate much decision-making to officials on the spot in his colonies.

Strategic Offensive and Promotion

The commandant general of the Frontier Provinces was in a position by this time to put into effect the intensive Apache extermination policy contemplated by Teodoro de Croix, the first commandant general. This capability stemmed from the power that Croix and his successors had built up in the frontier posts. Don Phelipe de Neve felt that the presidial detachments operating individually close to the frontier had enjoyed considerable success in defeating Apaches. He regarded the next step as going over to a strategic offensive by launching a large-scale, multi-expedition probe into the upper Gila River region where the border Apaches retreated.[26] Neve originally planned a five-pronged invasion of Apachería, but had to divert some troops to the ever-worrisome Seri frontier.

Adjutant Inspector Don Roque de Medina took over command of two of the planned divisions of a combined force, and led 190 men out of the presidio of Fronteras.[27] Adjutant Inspector Don Diego de Borica commanded the third division which entered Apache country from Janos, Chihuahua.[28]

Captain Don Pedro de Allande y Saabedra commanded the fourth division, apparently composed entirely of troops from his presidio of San Agustín del Tucson. He drove into the Apache strongholds from the southwest[29] through the Florida, Santa Teresa, Piedad, Cabezas and Babocomari Mountains.[30] The fifth division came from Velarde on the southeast to bottle up the Mimbres area in modern New Mexico.[31]

Captain Allande proved himself to be the most efficient Apache fighter among the task force commanders. On 26 April 1784, Allande with part of his command slew three warriors, three women and four boys, capturing two youths and freeing a captive Yaqui Indian woman.[32] On his return, the Tucson commander managed to kill six more Apaches at Babocomari.[33] He also recovered 19 animals on this campaign.[34] His superiors felt quite satisfied with the results of the effort, concluding that the Apaches had seen Spanish soldiers in all of their mountain strongholds which had never been scouted before by Spanish troops.[35]

At a somewhat later date, another expedition took Captain Allande into the same middle Gila River area. Some troops came north up the Santa Cruz River Valley to Tucson, probably from Terrenate.[36] From there on Allande apparently commanded the force of 150 men which included two other captains, Echegaray and Azuela, Spaniards, Opatas, Pimas from San Ignacio, Santa Cruz, Tumacacori and San Xavier,[37] not counting Papago and Gileño auxiliaries. The latter ran out of food on the fifth day, and upon receiving rations promptly melted into the brush and returned home.[38] The expedition under Allande captured and beheaded four Apaches on the eighth day out of Tucson,[39] evidently in the Arivaipa Mountains. Three of those executed were women.[40]

At the site of the former post of Santa Cruz on the 13th day of campaigning, Captain Allande found 53 of his men sick. He thereupon abandoned the campaign and marched back to Tucson in three days (two of actual travel).[41]

This campaign in Apache territory achieved very happy results from the Spanish colonial point of view, at least. Consequently, Captain Allande's superiors repeatedly requested promotion for the commander of the Tucson post. The commandant general of the Frontier Provinces recommended him again in July of 1784 along with the other task force commanders:[42]

> Most Excellent Sir Don Joseph de Gálvez No. 124
> My Dear Sir:
>
> In a separate letter of this date numbered 124 I have the satisfaction of informing Your Excellency of the happy results of the campaign carried out to the margins and mountains of the Gila River according to the plan which I remitted in another of March 8th last, numbered 89. The Adjutant Inspectors Don Roque de Medina and Don Diego de Borica, and the Captains Don Pedro de Allande and Don Francisco Martinez have carried out exactly the orders and smallest details of the arrangements that I made for the perfect fulfillment of that enterprise. I consider the four of them worthy of the piety of His Majesty, which might deign to concede them the thanks of the rank of Lieutenant Colonels of Cavalry. Inasmuch as I have asked this for the latter two captains in letters of 25 August 1783, No. 7, and 26 January 1784, No. 76, I shall limit myself in this to soliciting equal ranks for the Adjutant Inspectors Don Roque de Medina and Don Diego de Borica, in reward for the merit which they have accumulated on the campaign mentioned, the punctual fulfillment of their respective present assignments which they serve with distinction. The first has served twenty-nine years, ten as Adjutant Inspector and retired captain, and the second twenty-one years, four years eight months as captain of the presidio of San Elceario and two years nine months as Adjutant Inspector.
>
> Should the superior comprehension of Your Excellency consider them worthy of these thanks, I beseech your generosity in serving to incline the royal will of His Majesty to concede it to them in order that

the prize of their merits and services may excite the emulation of other officers to discharge with exactitude the serious responsibilities committed to them, especially in the continuous war which is waged in these provinces against the enemies who attack them.

Our Lord preserve Your Excellency many years. Presidio of Fronteras. July 6, 1784.

Your most attentive, humble servant kisses your Excellency's hands.

PHELIPE DE NEVE

Apparently the earlier request for promotion for Captain Allande had prompted royal action, for within a short time the commander of the Tucson post requested reassignment to a higher position in part because he outranked Adjutant Inspector Roque de Medina, and in part because his leg wound sustained in the 1 May 1782 action (and probably aggravated by his prolonged refusal to seek treatment) handicapped his efficient discharge of the active leadership required of a frontier post commander:

> I place myself under Your Excellency's most powerful protection and am most anxious to employ all my efforts for the illustrious honor of the arms. I find myself in very poor health and in continual suffering in my stomach from inexperience with this climate and many fatigues, with the sadness of seeing my wife and children ill. The deponent finds it impossible to continue this labor because of the wounds which he received in the right leg which have hurt the nerves, as well as because of the present aggravation of seeing the arms of this Province commanded by Adjutant Inspector don Roque de Medina, who has only the rank of captain, while the deponent who is under his orders holds that of lieutenant colonel. Deponent feels capable of continuing his illustrious career or improving it in some government or regiment of cavalry or dragoons with the salary which the mercy of the King might deign to concede.[43]

Worth noting in this dispatch, along with Allande's jealousy of Medina, is his reference to a wife and children, inasmuch as he had been listed as a widower when he assumed command of the Tucson garrison several years earlier. Perhaps the Santa Cruz River Valley climate agreed less with the new Mrs. Allande and her young children than with the tough officer.

Despite Allande's complaints about his health, he actually continued campaigning against the Western Apaches. During March and April of 1785, this officer again scouted through the Babocomari, Peñascosa, Huachuca, Santa Rita and Santa Catalina Mountains. His command killed eight warriors and recovered stock the enemy had stolen from Cieneguilla. Acting as an example to his troops, the Spanish commander personally dispatched one of the Apaches slain.

Subalterns on the Rise

When fall inspection time came around again in 1785, the summary (Table 9, Appendix) reported a troop composition of 3 officers and 65 men.[44]

The troopers had 356 horses and 51 mules at the time of the inspection, so were in relatively good shape for further mounted campaigning.

The rapid promotion of junior officers during the 1780s was reflected by the fact that the subalterns of the Tucson cavalry company had completely changed since the 1783 inspection. Lieutenant Tomás Equrrola, hero of the running battle with Apache horse thieves, had died and been replaced by Francisco Barrios, who had won rapid promotions during the early part of the decade of the 1780s. His rise from second to first ensign of the Fronteras garrison apparently came in 1783[45] and his transfer and lieutenancy followed within about two years.

The rapid rise of Don Pedro María de Allande, son of the post commander, to the rank of second ensign also points up the rapid promotion of junior officers during these times. His valorous participation in the presidio defense on May Day 1782 stood in his favor, as did his father's position. Yet in a more settled period, young Allande probably could not have risen so fast.

High subaltern mortality brought relatively rapid promotion by commissioning senior sergeants, as well as cadets. This produced in turn relatively rapid promotion of non-commissioned officers from the ranks of veteran soldiers. This process opened opportunities to able individuals whose upward social mobility would have been blocked by their ascribed status in less demanding and rewarding decades.

Such an individual was Francisco Xavier Márquez. Only 27 years of age in 1775, he probably had not then long belonged to the Tubac company when its commander identified him as a *mulato* born in Sinaloa. Márquez would be socially defined, in other words, as a Negro in contemporary Tucson.

In 1779, Márquez was still merely a trooper in the ranks. Allande listed him seventh among the enlisted men, though, implying either seniority or relatively high promotion eligibility. As the Tucson cavalry company shifted to offensive warfare, promotion accelerated. Sometime before the end of 1783, Francisco Xavier Márquez won the rank of corporal. Before the end of 1785, Márquez rose to sergeant. This represented no mean achievement by the man who may well have been Tucson's first "black" resident, in view of colonial Spanish racial discrimination.

New Apache Pacification Policy

While the large-scale, bitterly contested Spanish cavalry sweeps around Apache territory filled the promotion lists, high royal officials in New Spain searched for a better solution to the Apache problem than genocide. Spanish officialdom sought success for colonial goals rather than inflexible adherence to the details of the royal reforms of 1772.

King Charles III utilized to his advantage the knowledge of officials experienced on the colonial frontier. In 1786, his new viceroy of New Spain, Bernardo de Gálvez,[46] concluded that Spain could not militarily defeat the Apaches, so would have to outsmart them. Gálvez enunciated a new concept of Spanish-Apache relations well summarized by H. H. Bancroft.[47]

> The Apaches were to be forced by unceasing campaigns with the aid of friendly Pimas and Opatas, to make treaties of peace, never before permitted with that nation; and so long as they observed such treaties, though closely watched, they were to be kindly treated, furnished with supplies, encouraged to form settlements near the presidios, taught to drink intoxicating liquors, and to depend as much as possible on Spanish friendship for the gratification of their needs. Hitherto war had been the business, as easier than hunting, by which they had lived; now they were to be made to dread war, as sure to cut off their supplies.

This new ethnic policy enabled the augmented military effectiveness stemming from the 1772 royal military reforms to achieve success directly measurable in terms of number of Apaches pacified. The presidial forces continued vigorously to campaign against hostile Apaches year after year, regardless of changes in army command and personnel on the Sonoran frontier.

In pursuit of the goal of Apache pacification, the presidial forces of the Frontier Provinces constituted an Apache-fighting army. These Spanish troops made the year 1788 an especially uncomfortable one for the still-hostile Apaches. As it opened, Captain Manuel de Echegaray of Santa Cruz presidio was assembling forces from the posts at Tucson, Altar, Tubac (which had been re-established as a military post with a Native American garrison), Buenavista, Pitic and Bacoachic for a thrust northward. He led his 186-man force out of the royal post at Santa Cruz on 5 January. The Tucson garrison contributed 30 men to his expedition – 1 ensign, 1 sergeant, 1 corporal, 5 carbineers and 22 troopers.[48] Apparently the Tucson garrison at that time boasted the best marksmen on the Sonoran frontier. In any event, no other garrison sent more than one carbineer on this campaign.

During this hard-riding mission, Captain Echegaray took his command as far east as the Río Grande. On its banks he fought an engagement with a large Apache force. The latter killed Ensign Rafael Tovar. The Spaniards slew 6 warriors, 8 women and 5 children, capturing 1 woman and 2 dozen horses.[49]

On the return journey, the ensign of the Pimas at Tubac died from a fever.[50] An Opata was killed by a shot in the first engagement of the expedition.[51] Compared to this total loss of three killed, two of them officers, Echegaray's command captured 16 Apaches (1 warrior, 4 women and 11 children) and 43 mounts, killing 27 Apaches (7 warriors, 15 women, 5 children). By early February, the expedition's horses were exhausted, and the contingents dispersed to their various posts.

Captain Pablo Romero's turn to hunt Apaches came in early summer 1788. He had been lieutenant at the presidio of Santa Cruz in 1778, staving off abandonment of that post.[52] Also lieutenant in the Flying Company of Sonora in 1780,[53] Romero commanded the Opata Indian Company at Bacoachi,[54] at that rank. He became captain in command of the Buenavista presidio, apparently.[55] When Lieutenant Colonel Pedro de Allande left Tucson, Romero moved there as acting captain.[56] The earliest available record of his coming is an enlistment record dated 10 September 1786.[57]

From 31 May to 24 June 1788, Romero led a 208-man force of Sonoran troops that killed 11 Apache warriors and 4 women and children, capturing 34 men and women. The Apaches slain included a chieftain named *Quilcho*. Romero's expedition recovered 2 captives and 11 animals and lost 2 men. Although Romero did not keep his column in the field as long as Echegaray had, and killed fewer Apaches, he and his subalterns and troops received the thanks of their superiors in the king's name. They singled out Ensign Joseph Moraga for his bravery during the campaign.[58]

The highlight of this mission was a battle in the Pinal Mountains. Ensign Moraga with a few men from the pack-train escort attacked a ranchería, slaying one Apache himself in hand-to-hand combat. Captain Romero, hearing firing, raced to the scene, arriving before the battle ended. The Spaniards lost 1 man, but killed 6 Apache warriors, captured 23 women and children, and recovered 2 captive Pima girls from the native settlement at Tucson.[59]

Captain Romero evidently left straightaway after the expedition ended to report to the commandant of arms in Arizpe how well he succeeded in his sweep. On 30 June, a band of Apaches hunting him caught and killed him on the hill of San Borja between Chinapa and Bacoachi.[60] Thus, Romero did not live to see the king's commission granting him 2,400 pesos salary, because this was not even signed until October 12.[61] Romero left a widow, Doña Luisa Bohorquez, and at least two sons.[62]

The high mortality of junior officers also continued. The Lieutenant Francisco Barrios who replaced Equrrola was himself killed in 1788 and replaced by Lieutenant Francisco Salas Bohorquez, who was promoted from ensign at San Bernardino presidio.[63] Salas himself had won his commission only four and one-half years earlier. The king appointed then Sergeant Salas as second ensign of the Fronteras garrison early in 1784.[64]

Captain Echegaray took the field again during October and November of 1788 with from 400 to over 500 men,[65] as part of a large-scale Apache surrounding operation by Spanish frontier forces. Similar commands moved into the field in Nueva Vizcaya and in New Mexico, driving Apaches toward each other. Early in this campaign, Echegaray picked up some new Peaceful Apaches, one of whom had a brother living with the ranchería whose inhabitants had slain Captain Romero. This chieftain, called *Compa,* claimed to have won some of Romero's effects, including his saber, while gambling with the Apaches who killed him. The Indian politicly gave the saber to Echegaray, who forwarded it to Colonel Juan Bautista de Anza, military commander of arms of Sonora, to send to Romero's heirs.[66]

On this fall search-and-destroy-or-capture mission, at least the third mounted from Sonora within the year 1788, Captain Echegaray achieved notable results, in part because the simultaneous sweep strategy worked. Fifty-four Apaches were killed, almost half of them warriors, and 125 were captured. Most important, Echegaray admitted 55 Apaches to peace as allies, and they rendered excellent service as guides, enabling the Spaniards to locate the rancherías and to kill and capture large numbers of hostiles.[67]

Prosperity and Success

By 1788, the viceroy's new Apache policy had begun really to hurt the hostile aborigines, and imperial Spain began to win its long northern border war. Some *Apaches de Paz* or "Peaceful Apaches" were already congregated at the Opata post at Bacoachic, but the hard-hitting frontier simultaneous search-and-destroy missions of 1788 seem to have been the clinching argument that convinced numerous Apaches on the Sonoran frontier of the advisability of coming into the posts to settle peaceably. The new Apache policy inaugurated in 1786 paid off handsomely for the Spanish colonial empire. Bancroft evaluated it in glowing terms:

> The plan seems to have been remarkably successful; at least for twenty years or more there are but slight indications of Apache depredations . . . in comparison with its condition in earlier and later times, the country in the last decade of the century and the first of the next was at peace. Then it was that the Arizona establishments had their nearest approximation to prosperity, that new churches were built. . . .[68]

Not two but three decades of growth and prosperity for the Spanish communities in Arizona have been similarly described by a more modern historian.[69] Ranchers founded "princely domains," prospectors sought minerals, missionaries put Native Americans to work erecting permanent structures, and Spanish settlers "opened up new farmlands." In conclusion, the final years of Spanish Arizona were "full of hope and peace."[70]

The development of the Presidio of Tucson, and its role in the Spanish offensive from 1783 through 1788, offer further evidence of these several decades of Spanish colonial success. The various reports and letters cited in this chapter indicate that this post built its physical structures, then passed from a defensive posture to far-ranging aggressive sweeps that forced Apaches to surrender.

Tucson and the other presidios in the Frontier Provinces effectively solved the "multitudinous" problems of the colonial frontier. Far from being the "real villian" of what some historians have viewed as failure,[71] "the Spanish colonial system" achieved striking success. Having labored long and diligently to achieve a resurgence of Spanish power overseas, King Charles III lived long enough to learn of at least the first evidence of his success in terms of settling Apaches at frontier presidios.

The commander of the presidio of San Agustín del Tucson who led the people of this frontier community into the new peaceful era was Captain Josef de Zúñiga. After Captain Romero's death, the viceroy reportedly appointed Colonel Juan Bautista de Anza as commandant of the Tucson post. If so, Anza was commander in name only, for he continued as commandant of arms of Sonora until his death on 19 December 1788 in Arizpe.[72]

Then Nicolás Soler was appointed commander of the post. He was adjutant inspector of the Peninsula of Lower California when promoted, so Lieutenant Salas Bohorquez evidently ran the post for some time awaiting

Soler's arrival.[73] The latter soon died in office, and Zúñiga was promoted to the Tucson command. He was at the time lieutenant and commandant of the presidio of San Diego in Upper California. His commission was signed by the new king on 19 May 1792,[74] but Zúñiga did not reach Tucson until 1794 at earliest. He was a veteran frontier officer with wide geographic experience, having been first commissioned ensign at the *Presidio del Norte* on the Río Grande in 1778, after serving in the Mexican Dragoon Regiment.[75]

The high attrition rate among junior officers had, meanwhile, brought about further changes among Tucson's subalterns. Having been breveted a lieutenant, Tucson's First Ensign Josef Ignacio Moraga won promotion to his brevet rank on 1 March 1790, in the Fronteras garrison at San Bernardino.[76] Soon after came the recommissioning of Juan Phelipe Beldarrain, son of the founding captain of the Tubac presidio and godson of Colonel Juan B. de Anza. Commissioned an ensign at a tender age in Anza's garrison, Beldarrain had been cashiered for misconduct by Commanding Inspector Hugh O'Connor, and served in the ranks of the Tucson garrison for over a decade. He participated bravely in the defense of the Pueblo of Tucson at the bridge during the May Day 1782 attack. Finally, when the son of another post commandant, Pedro María de Allande, was promoted, Beldarrain was recommissioned as second ensign with official date from 11 August 1790.[77]

Thus, the quarter of a century following the transfer of the Tubac garrison to Tucson witnessed the Sonoran frontier as it changed from a defensive expansion to a genuine strategic offensive against the Western Apache Indians, carried it to notable victory, and began to enjoy peace. The first decade served to establish the Tucson post firmly and securely at the most advanced permanently held point on this sector of the northern perimeter of New Spain between the provinces of New Mexico and Upper California. The five years following 1786 saw the strategic offensive against the Apachean bands reduce those enemy Native Americans to suing for peace, and settling around the Spanish frontier posts under military supervision, sustained by Spanish rations.

The provincial elite families lost large numbers of junior officer members during the drive to defeat the Apaches in their homeland just beyond the colonial frontier. Thus, the frontier military population became a mixed society of Peninsular natives, creoles and friendly Mestizos and Native Americans with even a few mulattos, as the prosperous decades opened on the Sonoran frontier. Conditions fostered upward social mobility, and then economic prosperity.

9.

Peace With the Western Apaches, 1793-1821

THE ROYAL SPANISH GARRISON AT TUCSON in itself created a bi-ethnic population there. It also led to adding yet another distinctive Native-American component, Apaches, to the local populace. This ethnic increment can be considered to be the best possible index of the resounding success of the military reforms that King Charles III had ordered in 1772, the establishment of the Frontier Provinces by José de Gálvez, and the policy shift that Viceroy Bernardo de Gálvez had instituted on the northern frontier of New Spain in 1786. The Spanish colonial system succeeded so well with these policies that southern Apache bands settled peacefully beside royal posts, including San Agustín del Tucson, ending centuries of inter-ethnic conflict.

The Apachería Achievement

The magnitude of this Spanish colonial achievement was so great, yet remains so little known to residents of old Apachería today, as to bear summation here. One historian has pointed out how rapidly Apache resistance crumpled after Gálvez's pacification policy allowed objective measurement of the effectiveness of the presidial forces of the Frontier Provinces following King Charles III's 1772 model based upon recommendations by the Marqués de Rubí and José de Gálvez.[1]

Some Chiricahua Apache bands sued for peace as early as September of 1786, and moved to Bacoachi in the eastern Sonoran mountains. Other Chiricahua bands followed suit, so by March of 1787 over 250 Chiricahuas under Chief *Tisonsé* lived at Bacoachi. They even began presenting their infants for baptism.[2] After a brief test of Bacoachi Spanish hospitality, another chief the Spaniards called *El Chiquito* led his band back into the Apachería, and fended off Spanish overtures and military pressures alike.[3] By mid-year of 1786, several Chiricahua bands still ranging freely sent emissaries to either Bacoachi or Tucson to excuse their failure to accept an amnesty offered by Don Jacobo Ugarte y Loyola, commandant general of the Frontier Provinces.[4]

Mimbreño Apache leaders appeared at Janos presidio in Chihuahua seeking peace in March of 1787. Commandant General Ugarte required the Mimbreño bands to settle near San Buenaventura. By late May, 800 to 900 Mimbreños had congregated there.[5] Then they fled back into the Apachería where they eluded a number of Spanish search-and-destroy missions later that year.[6] Mescalero Apache bands settled meanwhile at *El Norte* presidio, only to flee after Colonel Juan de Ugalde attacked them.

Over half of the Chiricahua Apaches at Bacoachi fled on 20 June 1787.[7] The independent Chiricahuas attacked those remaining at the post on 7 February 1788, lancing to death Chief *Tisonsé*.[8] Viceroy Flores seriously modified the Gálvez Apache policy in 1788,[9] and more Chiricahuas deserted Bacoachi in September. Captain Echegaray replaced them by others who surrendered during his campaigns in the Apachería.[10]

Continued Spanish military thrusts into Apache territory brought Mimbreño Apache leaders to Janos seeking peace again in March of 1790. Consequently, one Mimbreño band led by Chief *Ojos Colorados* (Red Eyes) settled there at the end of May.[11]

The earliest known settlement of Western Apaches at San Agustín del Tucson presidio occurred in January of 1793.[12] Certainly the presidio seethed with excitement on 5 January, when these enemies of centuries appeared to ask for peace. *Nautilnilce*, recognized by the Spaniards as principal chief of the *Vinictinines,* or Arivaipa Band, brought in 51 men, women and children. Forty-three more individuals followed the next day.[13] This chief later persuaded 13 more Apaches to settle in peace at Tucson on 19 January,[14] bringing the total Western Apache population to 107 persons. That was a significant increment to the local population, especially in view of the continued decline in numbers of native Northern Piman-speaking Indians.

By the first month of 1793, settlement of Apache bands seeking peace at various frontier posts had become more or less routine to superior officers, as the tone of the following dispatch from Manuel de Echegaray, by then promoted to commandant of arms of Sonora, indicates:

> Sir Brigadier Don Pedro de Nava[15]
> Sir Commanding General,
>
> The commander of the Presidio of Tucson, Don José Ygnacio Moraga, on the 6th of this month informed me that the day before the Arivaipa chieftan *Nautilnilce* had presented himself in peace with thirteen warriors and some women and children to the number of fifty-one persons. He informed said captain that the following day the rest of his relatives would come in, as was effectively verified on the day set by forty-one persons, according to the dispatch of the same commander on that date.
>
> In consequence of all this, I am sending that commander the advice which has appeared to me best in order to keep these newly reduced Indians happy, inasmuch as the tranquility of the towns of Upper Pimería depends on it. I have ordered them rationed in conformance with that which Your Honor provided in your Instruction of the 12th of October of '91, that the ordinary people be taken care of with some sweetmeats and that the captain who is the leader of this tribe known as the *Vinictinines* should be taken care of with distinction and should be given a gift of clothes.
>
> Said captain sent me one of the Apaches of this band in order to gain my permission for their admission to peace, and with it Your Honor's superior approval. I have outfitted him completely with clothes. I find that all the reduced Apaches are of good faith, having shown the commander of Tucson the ears of eight warriors whom Chief *Nautilnilce* killed, evidencing their faithfulness.

The ensign Don Agustín Márquez, who belongs to the command of that presidio, is now here as quartermaster for that company. I have given him such advice as has seemed to me in order so as to consolidate the peace which those Indians have contracted, and to assure myself of a successful outcome, inasmuch as it is so important to the good of the state and the province. Within a few days I shall go to that presidio so I can inform Your Honor of the results with more certainty.

In order that the necessities for the subsistence of those Indians shall not be lacking at the place in the interim before the superior measures of Your Honor take effect, I have taken my own steps, one of them being that of purchasing fifty head of cattle to ration them, because without this prerequisite these avaricious ones would live discontented, seeing that they had not bettered their luck. I am hoping that the prudence and long experience of Your Honor shall have the grace to approve these measures, with the assurance that I am moved to them only by the zeal which I feel for the good of His Majesty's service.

God preserve Your Honor for many years. Arispe. 21 January 1793.

MANUEL DE ECHEGARAY[16]

Beef and Sugar Peace

By 1793, the colonial policy toward "Peaceful Apaches" had been well worked out. The Chiricahua Apaches who settled at Bacoachi late in 1786 had stimulated Spanish colonial officials to take a series of actions that set precedents for treatment accorded later bands settling at other presidios.

Quite clearly the "Peaceful Apaches" utilized the threat of their abandoning settled life beside the frontier posts to obtain increasing economic support from colonial officers. The first enumeration of 68 Chiricahua Apaches at Bacoachi showed them receiving a relatively inflexible *almud* of rations per person, or two *almudes* per family, regardless of household numbers. The nature of the rations was not even specified. Probably it consisted of cereal grains. The governor of Sonora and Sinaloa, Pedro Corbalán, established at the beginning of the program the practice of issuing Indian rations weekly. His initial order to the man who became in effect Indian agent to the peaceful Chiricahua Apaches at Bacoachi set sufficient bureaucratic precedents to merit translation here:

> Beginning next Sunday, that is three days from now, Your Honor shall provide those rations indicated on the attached enumeration to the Apaches who are reduced to Peace and settled in that Pueblo up to that date. For that purpose, you shall lay hands on such grains as you may have at your disposal, upon a reimbursable basis, or, with the idea that their value shall be paid at the current price at the expense of the Royal Exchequer.
>
> In case Your Honor does not have enough grain, he shall solicit it on loan from the stores of that garrison, under the same arrangement for reimbursing it as may be convenient, or he shall purchase it at the lowest price that may be possible from whomever has it. You are advised that a list must be drawn up weekly showing the family heads who

receive rations, expressing their names, in order to know what increases or decreases may occur in their number in the future. These are to be remitted to me monthly for my use.

God protect Your Honor for many years. Arizpe, first of December of 1786.

PEDRO CORBALÁN[17]

Whatever rations the Spaniards initially provided the Chiricahua Apaches at Bacoachi, by January of 1787 they had already settled on the pattern that continued. Wheat constituted the mainstay of the ration, supplemented by maize — about five measures of wheat to three of maize. Unrefined brown sugar or *panocha* such as still is sold in Latin American markets in cone-shaped blocks tempted the Apache sweet tooth. Apparently each person received half a cone of *panocha* each ration-day. Finally, the royal tobacco monopoly sold the Indian agent packs of cigarettes to be issued to the Apaches. Chief *Tisonsé,* who received the given name "Leonardo" after the Indian agent, garnered two measures of wheat, two of maize, four *reales* worth of *panocha* and three of cigarettes for eight persons in his family.[18]

The Chiricahua Apaches at Bacoachi parleyed Spanish uncertainty over their motivation to remain settled into augmented rations of freshly killed beef during 1787. The penny-pinching new governor of Sonora attempted to save money on the grain, sugar and cigarette ration when fresh beef was added to the issues. He ordered the agent to allow the Apaches to choose an all-grain-sugar-cigarette or an all-meat ration, or a combination, reducing the amount of the former in proportion to the meat issued.[19] The Chiricahua Apaches quickly blackmailed the commanding general into ordering their full grain, sugar and cigarette ration restored along with the beef. The order is important enough to merit translation here:[20]

No. 7

The Commanding General on the fourth of this month wrote me the following:

The Chief of the Ranchería of Chiricahua Apaches established at Bacoachi and other leading Indians of the Ranchería of the Chiricahua Apaches established at Bacoachi have complained to me that the reduced wheat and maize ration they have been given since they began receiving meat does not suffice even with the latter to feed their families. They attribute the desertions recently experienced to this motive.

In this regard, wishing for my part to remove any reason or pretext that might induce them to abandon their establishment at Bacoachi, I have resolved that they be given the same grain ration as before without prejudice to the current meat ration. I advise Your Honor so that he may issue the corresponding order to this effect.

I transmit this to Your Honor for his information and compliance.

May Our Lord protect Your Honor many years. Arispe. 8 February 1788.

PEDRO GARRIDO Y DURAN[21]

To Don Leonardo Escalante.

The action that Manuel de Echegaray took in purchasing 50 head of cattle to begin rationing the Apaches newly settled at Tucson followed this precedent established by colonial officials trying to keep the first surrendered Chiricahuas at Bacoachi. The commanding general purchased a herd of 250 head of cattle to feed the Chiricahuas. Theoretically, the cows in this herd were to produce enough calves to sustain it, while feeding the Indians steers and culls. In practice, the Indian agent reported having slaughtered two bulls per week for the Bacoachi Apache contingent. The latter augmented their meat ration by consuming additional animals that died or were killed by hostile Apaches from time to time.[22]

Thus, the Apaches settling at Tucson in 1793 received the by-then standard Indian ration of wheat, maize, *panocha,* beef and cigarettes. Royal subsidies to the peaceful Apaches constituted a powerful economic stimulus to production of these commodities in the Frontier Provinces precisely when pacification allowed Spaniards and sedentary Indians to concentrate upon increasing production.

Life in a Peaceful Apache Camp

It is doubtful whether many of the Peaceful Apaches at Tucson ever became serious agriculturalists. It is also doubtful whether they ever lived in the immediate neighborhood of Piman Tucson. They were oriented toward the Spanish post rather than the Northern Piman Indian ranchería, and toward subsidized warfare and idleness rather than earning a living by toil.

They built their wickiups downstream from the presidio.[23] Thus, they drew their domestic water and such irrigation water as they may have used from the presidial and pueblo tailings as well as main Santa Cruz River streamflow. Possibly the Apaches lived on the terrace above the damp river floodplain. All traces of their dwellings have almost certainly been destroyed by later construction of the city of Tucson. The lack of physical traces notwithstanding, they left their mark in the biological make-up of Tucson's population.

As the locally peaceful but imperially turbulent end of the 18th century changed to the 19th, the Spaniards at Tucson continued to make the Apache pacification policy work. That Spanish authorities at the post put forth a genuine effort to maintain good relations with their Indian allies is indicated in the sentencing to prison in 1817 of three soldiers of the San Agustín presidial company for killing one of the Peaceful Apaches.[24] In other words, the Spanish officers faced the same dilemma U.S. officers faced in later wars with Native Americans and in Vietnam. Spanish colonial law and military officers treated murder of uneasy allies belonging to a different ethnic group as murder, thus achieving a significant level of legal egalitarianism within an authoritarian colonial structure.

At the same time, Tucson garrison officers continued to ration the Peaceful Apaches with sugar, beef and cigarettes. Handing out food to friendly Apaches with one hand, they brandished the lance at hostile groups. Tucson's commanders continued the policy of harassing still-hostile bands and inducing them to settle in peace at Tucson and other frontier posts. Even during the period of relative peace and prosperity in frontier Sonora that began during the 1790s, the Tucson garrison continued to fight Indians. In 1812, for example, a large detachment from the Pima Indian Company at Tubac marched to Tucson to join the garrison there for a sortie into Apache territory.[25]

Peaceful Apache Reinforcements

The enduring success of the Gálvez policy toward the Apaches and continued campaigning into hostile territory was evidenced by at least one other large-scale settlement of hitherto hostile bands at Tucson near the end of the colonial period. The Pinal Apache Band under Chief *Chilitipagé* asked for peace and settled at Tucson in 1819.[26] The course of events that added 236 newly pacified Apaches to Tucson's population may be followed in the official reports.

Sir Commandant of Arms Don Antonio Narbona:

The 17th day of this month the General of the Pinals *Chilitipagé* presented himself to me with seventy-eight warriors of his band. Afterwards I conferred with him and told him that all seemed to me just in order to insure that the peace which they promised should be of good faith and enduring. According to the expressions with which this Indian spoke, it appears that the peace should be good. I have given cattle, tobacco and wheat to fourteen women who came in and to the chieftains who have expressed themselves as very content. At the same time the Chieftain Pascual *Navaicagé* and two warriors have asked me for permission to go to that city in order to affirm the faith of their peace and to ask you for the Indian woman whom I dispatched with Coyera, who is a sister of one of them. When I said that I did not know whether she would be returned, he again asked permission and the escort of Sergeant Ramirez with seven men inasmuch as he feared the Apaches de Paz, and [he asked] that they should guard them well. It seemed to me politic not to deny them this permission because it might cause them some annoyance, so I have permitted it, and they leave this very day. All this I communicate to you for your guidance and so that the arrival at that city of the said Indians and escort shall not surprise you.

God preserve you many years. Tucson. February 25, 1819.

JUAN ALEXO CARRILLO.[27]

More of the scene and ensuing events are recorded in the report of the former commander of the Tucson post, Antonio Narbona, who had become head of the Spanish army in Sonora:

No. 140

Brigadier and Commandant General Don Antonio Cordero,

Sir,

The Commander of the Company of the Tucson informs me with a dispatch dated the 25th of last month, original of which I transmit to Your Honor, that the 17th day of the same there came in the General of the Pinal Apache Tribe *Chilitipagé* with seventy-eight warriors of his band seeking peace. In a communication of the fifth of this month I told him to grant them peace, issuing the usual rations only when they subsist on foot in that establishment so that their movements may be observed and their attacking us avoided insofar as possible, as has taken place in the previous peaces on retiring from Tucson for their territory. I included in the same all those notices which seemed to me appropriate with the goal of conserving other peaces because of our present great interest.

The aforesaid general with other chieftains was in this capital to ask me for the six female prisoners whom Ensign Don Juan Alexo Carrillo took as I informed Your Honor in Report No. 123 of January 2d last. I fulfilled [their request] with only the Indian woman and boy who have been held in the warehouse of Fronteras, inasmuch as the other four have already been given employment, but they remained very agreeable, showing particular gratitude. They are going to establish themselves with their people happily at Tucson, the separation of the original *Apaches de Paz* (with whom they did not get along well) having been successfully [achieved by] transferring them from that post to Santa Cruz. They offer to conserve our alliance without fault [in complying with] all the instructions I made. I have rewarded said General as well as the rest of the Indians who accompanied him to this city with fifty-two pesos, six reales worth of various gifts.

I notify Your Excellency of all this for your superior guidance and approval if it should be worthy of meriting it.

God preserve Your Honor for many years. Arispe. March 8, 1819.

ANTONIO NARBONA[28]

The commandant general of the Western Frontier Provinces in turn notified the viceroy of New Spain in Mexico City of the negotiations with *Chilitipagé* and his Pinal Apaches,[29] and the viceroy approved the actions of the frontier officers.[30] Meanwhile, events moved forward on the frontier while the news traveled south to the distant viceregal capital. The next step was actual settlement of Pinal Apaches at Tucson, an event reported by the local commander toward the end of May:

Commandant of Arms Don Antonio Narbona No. 2
Sir:

The 13th day of the current month the General of the Pinals *Chilitipagé* presented himself to me with four chieftains and their bands with their families and everything. There are 236 souls to be established on a fixed footing here the same as the old *Apaches de Paz*. They are already located here building their wickiups to live in, after having been advised of the mode and government with which they should conduct themselves according to the instruction of the Commandant General, to which they remain very agreeable. They show much fidelity in appearance, from which I infer that the peace which they have offered will be durable and stable from the signs which they give, from having come with their families and everything, and the very great pleasure with which they are living among us.

I am rationing them with cattle and the customary ration of wheat. On the day when they finished coming in, which was the 18th, I found it necessary to issue to every one half an *almud* of wheat. In order to give them every Saturday all that to which they are entitled, according to the computation which I have made for rationing them and the old *Apaches de Paz* who come here every fifteen days, there will be necessary for twelve months 1,170 Spanish bushels as Your Honor may see from another dispatch.

I communicate all this to Your Honor for your satisfaction via extraordinary post.

God preserve Your Honor many years. Tucson. 21 May 1819.

José Romero[31]

The final step in the introduction of hitherto hostile Pinal Apaches into the frontier defense system of the Spanish empire was to arrange a reconciliation between these newly allied Native Americans and the older Apaches allies. This occurred within about a month of the ultimate arrival of *Chilitipagé* and his 235 followers at Tucson, judging from the report by the commandant general of the Western Frontier Provinces:

Excellency the Viceroy of this New Spain, No. 298
the Count of Venadito,
Excellent Sir,

According to the correspondence of the line which arrived at this city Tuesday of last week proceeding from the provinces of Sonora and New Mexico, and the military posts of the frontier of this one, there has occurred no news more worthy of the attention of Your Excellency in all the preceeding month than that of there having assembled at the Presidio of Tucson twelve Apache chieftains of those originally established at Santa Cruz with the object of making a complete reconciliation with the Pinal Indians who have recently been admitted to peace at the former of the presidios cited.

I communicate this to Your Excellency for your proper guidance, as well as [the idea] that said reconciliation should help indispensably the security of the peace with the Pinal Indians, which should have been concluded much earlier except for the rancor with which until now some Indians have seen others without certainty of their identity.

God preserve Your Excellency many years. Durango. July 19, 1819.

Alexo Garciá Conde[32]

The Story of a Boy

An elderly Mexican woman interviewed in Tucson in the early 1870s told of an Apache peace treaty which may have been a separate event in her girlhood between about 1800 and 1820, or an old woman's fused memories of more than one occasion:

It seems the Apaches got the worst of a fight on the Aribaca ranch. Several were killed, and the son of a chief was taken prisoner and brought to Tucson, and the Indians opened negotiations to obtain this boy.

Colonel Carbon [i.e., Narbona] in command of the Spanish forces, agreed with them that on a certain day the Indians should all collect here, and to prevent treachery and being overpowered, he brought in at night and concealed within the walls of the fort all the men he could get from all the towns within 150 miles. On the day appointed the Indians came in vast numbers; all the plains around were black with them. The colonel then told them if they had come on a mission of peace, they must lay down their arms and meet him as friends. They complied with his request and then all the people inside the walls went among them unarmed. The Colonel gave them one hundred head of cattle, and the boy prisoner was brought out and given to his father and they embraced each other and cried and an era of reconciliation and peace seemed to have arrived.

The boy told his father that he liked his captors so well that he desired to live with them, and in spite of all the persuasions of the old man he still insisted on remaining, and the Indians were compelled to return to their mountain home without him. The boy was a great favorite with the people. Sometimes afterward he went to visit his people, but before leaving he saw every one in the village and bade them good-by, and promised and did return in fifteen days. [This is acceptable Spanish, but not Apache behavior.] A few days subsequent to his return he took smallpox and died, and very soon afterward the Apaches commenced to murder and rob the same as before.[33]

As one historian has stated, folklore is not history.[34] Nonetheless, the old woman's reminiscence indicated that the dreadful scourge of smallpox loosed upon the Native Americans by a soldier under Panfilo de Narvaez in 1520 continued capriciously to influence human events in Tucson. Fitting this oral tradition to documented events suggests that it could well refer to an earlier attempt to force Western Apaches to settle at Tucson. The reference to Colonel Narbona as the officer in charge could date the occurrence in the period between 1805 and 1815. The death of the Apache youth from smallpox could very well have occurred during the severe epidemic that swept northern Sonora in 1816.

At any rate, all or part of the Arivaipa and Pinal Apache bands settled at Tucson between 1790 and 1820, as recorded in contemporary documents in colonial archives. They reinforced the local population in numbers and in military power relative to still-hostile southern Apache bands. That accretion of military power ensured the continued existence and economic prosperity of the northernmost post on the Sonoran colonial frontier. Moreover, the Apache population increment further diversified the multi-ethnic character of Tucson area population on a large scale, and the *Apaches de Paz* retained a degree of self-governance lost to Apache war captives reared in Tucson households.

Despite all the difficulties of financing the colonial government after the Napoleonic wars diverted Peninsular attention from the Americas, resulting in real poverty and crisis in the missions, the thrust King Charles III and his Viceroy Bernardo de Gálvez had given frontier Apache policy carried the colonial administrators right to the date of Mexican independence.

10.

Peacetime Presidio, 1793-1821

THE APACHE PACIFICATION POLICY initiated in 1786 succeeded so well during the next half-decade that life in the military post at Tucson followed a very different tenor after Apaches settled there in 1793 than it had during the years of the great Apache offensive by New Spain's northern frontier forces. The policies instituted by King Charles III made the reign of his son Charles IV startlingly peaceful on the northern frontier of New Spain, in contrast to his loss of his crown in the aftermath of social revolution that began in France within months of his succession to the Spanish throne after his father's death on 14 December 1788.[1]

Garrison Life in a Decade of Peace

By the early 1790s, the Royal Presidio of San Agustín del Tucson had increased in strength to nearly 100 men. The Tubac post on its supply line south toward the interior of New Spain had been reactivated with an Indian company. Tucson demand stimulated Gila River Pima commercial wheat production, and nearby mission production climbed. As the Apache pacification policy shifted the balance of frontier military power in favor of the Spaniards, the pioneering pace of military action at Tucson seems to have slowed.

In 1793, the captain of the Tucson post served on detached duty in Monterey, Upper California. Higher officials took advantage of José de Zúñiga's experience in California during the relative lull in Sonora.[2] The lieutenant running the Tucson company with two ensigns was Don José Ygnacio Moraga, who had been commended for bravery in Romero's Apache campaign during the summer of 1788 when Moraga was still an ensign. The command again included both a military chaplain and an armorer.

As the presidial forces settled into the life of an old established post, the financial problems and supply difficulties of the pioneering years were solved. The powder magazines contained plenty of powder, and the quartermaster had sufficient grain and other supplies on hand for the entire year.

Still, all was not entirely peaceful and quiet at Tucson. During one month, the second ensign and 24 men went out campaigning and another 30 men guarded the remount herd, leaving 40 men at the presidio. Nine of those men were sick. The ensign taking the field was none other than Don

Juan Felipe Beldarrain. The company was 6 men short of its authorized strength of 105 at this time.

During this same month, Apaches raided the Tucson area on three consecutive nights. The first night they stole some wheat, the second night some other produce, and the third they took a mare from the Northern Piman Pueblo of Tucson. The next day Lieutenant Moraga took nine men out to track these brigands, but was not able to do so.[3]

Apparently Moraga's service at Tucson was temporary. When Lieutenant Francisco Salas Bohorquez retired, Mariano Urrea replaced him in the fore part of 1793. A member of the pioneer premier family of Altar, Urrea was promoted from first ensign at San Miguel de Horcasitas.[4] Don Juan Franco served as first ensign of the Tucson garrison during the first part of 1794. The king signed his promotion to lieutenant at Santa Cruz on 9 May 1794.[5] The officers and sergeants of the Tucson company later in 1794 were Captain José de Zúñiga, Lieutenant Mariano Urrea, First Ensign Juan Felipe Beldarrain, Second Ensign José María Sosa, Sergeant Francisco Usarraga, Sergeant Juan Antonio Oliva (son of the acting commander who moved the post to Tucson), Sergeant José Domingo Granillo, and Cadets José Romero and Bernardo de Urrea.[6]

In 1795, the Royal Presidio of San Agustín del Tucson became the jumping-off place for exploring a trade route through recently pacified Apachería to the New Mexico Indian pueblo of Zuñi. Captain José de Zúñiga personally led the expedition, which symbolized the complete success of the Gálvez Apache pacification policy instituted only nine years earlier. Zúñiga's command included troops from the presidios of Fronteras, Santa Cruz, Altar, Bacoachi and Tubac as well as Tucson, and incorporated some Apaches as scouts.[7] Captain Zúñiga left his own post on 9 April and met the other units in the San Pedro River Valley the following day.[8] On 1 May the advance under Ensign Antonio Narbona entered the Pueblo of Zuñi, where the entire command waited six days for messengers to establish communication with provincial officials on the Río Grande.[9] The expedition returned to Tucson on 29 May after a very successful trip.[10]

By early 1796, 20 years after the Tucson post was founded, if no earlier, its settlers encroached on Native American fields and water rights in the Santa Cruz Valley. A high Franciscan official charged that "because of the nearness of the Presidio to said Pueblo and the plantings the citizens and soldiers make, the water necessary to the Indians becomes scarce. The Indians suffer, moreover, much damage to their plantings from the cattle and horses of the citizens and individuals of said Presidio." The friar therefore petitioned the commandant general of the Frontier Provinces to order the damage made good and the Indians allowed to use as much water as they needed.[11]

The ensign who acted as Zúñiga's adjutant for his 1795 expedition, Don Antonio Narbona,[12] later wrote one of the reports of Apache settlement at Tucson in 1819 translated in Chapter 9 of this book. By that time Narbona was serving as commandant of arms of Sonora. He played a significant role in Tucson affairs during the intervening years. Narbona transferred to Fronteras in 1793 from Santa Cruz, where he had been a cadet since 7 October

1786. His royal commission appointed him to a Tucson ensign's post vacated by Juan Felipe Beldarrain when the latter was promoted.[13] Yet Narbona served at Fronteras from 27 January 1793,[14] not at Tucson.

In September of 1796, Zúñiga had an ensign named Eduardo García and Sergeant Juaquín Berdugo under his command,[15] while Sergeant José Domingo Granillo and Ensign Juan Felipe Beldarrain served at Tucson until at least 3 February 1801.[16] The latter had also accompanied Zúñiga on his Zuñi expedition. Yet another young ensign, Manuel de Arvizu, who also made that journey,[17] was also to direct Tucson's destinies later on.

In 1796, Lieutenant Mariano de Urrea took leave to go to Arizpe to marry Gertrudis Elías Gonzáles. On 30 September 1797, Chaplain Pedro Arriquibar baptized the oldest son of this union of pioneer Sonoran military families José Cosme. Captain José de Zúñiga became little José's godfather, and Doña Loreta Ortiz his godmother.[18] Mariano thereafter spent much time in Arizpe as his company's quartermaster.[19]

During this period, the 106-man Tucson garrison cost the royal exchequer just over 30,000 pesos annually when at full strength. The captain earned 3,000 pesos, a tenth of the complement's payroll. The lieutenant drew only 700 pesos and ensigns 500 apiece. Post Chaplain Arriquibar received 480 pesos. Enlisted men earned as follows: sergeants 324, corporals 276, armorer 272, carbineers 270, soldiers 240 and the drummer 144 pesos.[20]

Captain José de Zúñiga commanded the Tucson presidial unit until some time after 1 January 1803, when his name last appears in available post records, noting a promotion for one of his soldiers.[21] Later that year, the king commissioned a trooper who had served at Tucson since its garrison moved there. Tucson Sergeant Juan Antonio Oliva, son of the doughty lieutenant who moved the post, became second ensign of the Santa Cruz presidio with an 11 May 1803 commission.[22]

An officer named Palacio commanded Tucson from some time before 1 April 1805 to after 12 August 1805. In September 1806, José Romero served at first ensign when he received permission from the Frontier Province commandant general to marry Doña María del Carmen Rodriguez of Arizpe.[23]

Before 10 September 1807, Antonio Narbona took command. He had risen swiftly in rank since the 1795 Zuñi expedition. He held the command until after 18 July 1812. On that date, he promoted to sergeant's rank one José María Gonzales, a Tubac native who had enlisted in the Tucson outfit in 1796 at the age of 19.[24] Later, Narbona became captain of Fronteras Presidio. He frequently visited Tucson as acting commandant in alternation with Manuel de León. This officer transferred to Tucson from the Tubac unit and then furnished command continuity for 20 years.[25]

Murder at the Mission

The alternation between Narbona and León can be followed through documents concerning a murder at San Xavier Mission. The crime was committed 6 July 1813, when Narbona was interim commander. He had the suspected murderer arrested and jailed. Taken out for exercise on 12 July, the prisoner slipped out of his irons, struck his guard, and went over the wall. The post was in a bustle of preparation for a campaign against the Apaches at the time. Perhaps this explains Narbona's presence, inasmuch as troops from other posts assembled at Tucson for the foray. Lieutenant Ygnacio Sotelo, commander of the Tubac company, accidentally apprehended the escaped prisoner when the officer encountered him trying to steal a horse on the road between the two posts. The Tubac troop did not reach Tucson before nightfall, and while it was camped, the prisoner regained his freedom.

Reversing his tactics, the accused man sneaked back into the Tucson post and took sanctuary in the military chapel. When this became known, the authorities formed a ring around the church with armed sentries to prevent the suspect's fleeing farther. The time pressure of the impending campaign prevented their maintaining this blockade very long, so they arranged to have Chaplain Pedro de Arriquibar deliver the fugitive into arrest outside the sanctified limits.

By that time it was 20 August, the second day of the annual festivities for Tucson's patron Saint Augustine. The clash between fugitive and the army interferred with the celebration. Manuel de León acted as military post commandant.[26] He issued a writ to the chaplain demanding the fugitive. At four in the afternoon, Chaplain Arriquibar with all solemnity delivered the suspect to a detachment of soldiers commanded by a sergeant.[27]

Variable Command

In the fall of 1813, the Presidio of Tucson again came under the command of a lieutenant colonel. Manuel de León turned over responsibility to Manuel Ygnacio de Arvizu as interim commander on 19 October.[28] Lieutenant Colonel Arvizu did not stay long on that tour of duty at Tucson, probably only until the end of the year. The last available record of him dates from 27 November.[29] It was Narbona's turn again from sometime before 22 April 1814 to some time later than 6 May of that year.[30]

Manuel de León acted as commander again on 29 January 1815, and he had assisting him as a witness to legal documents a young man who was to become an important figure in Mexican and early American Tucson, Teodoro Ramírez, a godson of the post chaplain.[31] Lieutenant Colonel Manuel Y. de Arvizu returned to Tucson in 1816 and commanded the post into at least 1818.[32] In contrast, a mere ensign was acting commander of the post late in February of 1819. This was Juan Alexo Carrillo, whose report on the Apache settlement under Chief *Chilitipagé* was translated in Chapter 9 of this book. Carrillo joined the Tucson garrison only on 1 February 1817, on orders of the provincial commander issued a month earlier. He had been promoted from sergeant to ensign of the Bacoachi Opata Indian unit.[33] By late May of 1819, Lieutenant José Romero commanded Tucson, as his report on the same affair shows. He still acted as commandant in mid-September of 1820, although his own post was commander of the Opata Indian Company at Bacoachi.[34]

Thus, it is clear that the command situation at Tucson remained highly variable for 15 years. The senior officer on the post ranged from a lieutenant colonel to an ensign. This situation differed markedly from the previous one since the founding of the post to the end of the great Apache offensive. Evidently it reflected changed frontier military conditions following the general pacification of the Western Apaches. The frequency with which higher ranking officers took over command of Tucson on an interim basis suggests some centralization of frontier command that made the post commandant's job less important than it had been when Tucson was the isolated northernmost outpost of Spanish colonial power in Sonora. On the other hand, the frequent devolvement of command on Lieutenant León and even upon ensigns indicates that Tucson played a diminished role in frontier military affairs once the Apache threat terminated.

Early 19th Century Garrison

During the period immediately following King Charles III's promulgation of the New Regulations for frontier posts, field grade officers inspected the garrisons annually. After military success reduced the Apache menace, presidial garrison commanders apparently had to begin making monthly company reports. A set of such reports from the beginning of 1817 indicates the range of duties of officers and men in the Tucson unit. The list and summary of the 1817 review appears as Table 10 in the Appendix.

As in earlier years, only a small fraction of the presidial force actually lived on-post at any given time. Over one-quarter of the garrison guarded the remount herd of this cavalry unit. A sergeant, a corporal and a carbineer led twenty-two soldiers assigned to that duty. One corporal and eight men conducted the pack trains that brought food and other supplies to the post. One carbineer and seven soldiers served as guards. They probably were stationed at San Xavier del Bac Mission and its Piman Tucson branch. Three men cared for the king's cattle, and two for ordinance.

Several individuals were on detached duty elsewhere. One officer served in the Kingdom of Nueva Vizcaya. A cadet, a carbineer and one soldier enjoyed life in Arizpe, the provincial headquarters. One soldier was in Bacoachi with the Opata company, and a sergeant in Tubac with its Pima Indian company. A sergeant, a corporal, a carbineer and eleven soldiers served on the Coast, perhaps on the Seri Indian frontier, although this assignment is not self-evident from the terse company report language. This left only fourteen soldiers, one carbineer and one corporal present for duty on the post, with one sergeant, one carbineer and seven soldiers sick, and two men in the hospital.

With approximately 100 men under arms in the Tucson presidial garrison, that unit's strength fluctuated from month to month regardless of lack of military action. A soldier named Joaquín Berdugo died, for example, during December of 1816.[35] The previous month, Hilario Andrada deserted, but because he served with the group "on the Coast," his commander did not learn of the event until after he made out his January monthly report. Consequently, Lieutenant Colonel Arvizu noted the loss of manpower in his February report. At that time, he also recorded the enlistment of two new recruits. Nineteen-year-old Ysidro Gallegos was born in Tucson, son of Juan

Gallegos and María Burruel. Manuel Chavez, the other recruit, came from Albuquerque.[36] Gallegos' enlistment indicated the biological success of Spanish and Mestizo settlement at Tucson, showing that this population was already able to supply part of the manpower required to maintain the military garrison.

One soldier, José León, was discharged during February. At the beginning of that month, the Tucson company received a new second ensign to fill its vacancy. New Year's promotions of Francisco Romero from carbineer to corporal, and Gerónimo Herran from soldier to carbineer went into effect in time for the March company report.[37] Because these men held the special status of "distinguished" individuals, their surnames suggest that they were relatives of officers in the Tubac and Tucson garrisons at an earlier time serving their apprenticeships for winning commissions. The officer listed as first ensign in 1817,[38] José María Elías Gonzáles, for example, was a member of the frontier military lineage founded by Francisco Elías Gonzáles de Zayas. Born in Arizpe on 2 February 1793, the son of Simón,[39] he enlisted as a cadet in Nueva Vizcaya late in 1809. By 1812 he became an ensign. In September of 1817, José María was promoted to lieutenant at San Buenaventura. During the revolution, he won his captaincy in 1821, becoming a lieutenant colonel the next year in Durango. Returning to Sonora in 1827, he held both military posts and elected office, ascending to colonel in 1835.

In 1840, José María became military commandant of the El Paso District, only to return to Sonora the following year. Elected to the national congress in 1842, Elías resumed military command in Sonora in 1843 and invaded Chihuahua in 1844, assuming command of that province. Deposed by a coup d'état in 1846, Elías nonetheless received command of the relief column sent to Tucson after the U.S. Mormon Battalion under Philip St. George Cooke passed in December. He commanded the garrison for some time, perhaps occasionally remembering the short period of his youth spent there as a lowly ensign. He became inspector of the new "military colonies" on the frontier on 2 September 1848.

Elías retired from the army on 14 March 1851, yet he commanded Sonoran forces in 1854 and in 1857. Moreover, this active elder citizen offered his services to fight the French in 1862 when he was 69 years old![40] A kinship diagram of his illustrious family appears as Chart 1, Appendix.

Although never to achieve distinction like their First Ensign Elías, several of the Tucson troopers in 1817 were also career soldiers. The viceregal court on 1 July 1817 recognized the rewards earned by five Tucson enlisted men for lengthy enlistments. Corporal Vicente Rodriguez had served five terms. Marcos Castro and Gregorio Egurrola each served four, while Juan Bautista Romero and Andrés Ramírez, Manuel Orosco, Francisco Figueroa, Juan José Martín and Francisco Pacheco each had served three terms.[41]

Ethnic Stratification

Despite the social mobility some soldiers achieved through serving in the Tucson military garrison, the population of this frontier post remained socially stratified along ethnic lines. The military mission of Tucson as a

Spanish settlement perpetuated there, even more than in central New Spain, the social and economic supremacy of military officers of noble antecedents and the clergy. Frontier Tucson reflected that Peninsular alliance between church and military nobility which had paralyzed any development of a Spanish middle class during imperial times.[42]

As the northwesternmost outpost of Spanish empire, Tucson attracted none of the doctors, lawyers, barbers, factory workers, notaries public, merchants and artisans who constituted a small urban middle class in the capital and other large cities of New Spain at the end of the imperial era. Being a military post, Tucson did not even require civilian bureaucratic employees, who also formed the emerging middle class in administrative cities.[43] What is not clear is whether Tucson's retail merchandising that decades later distinguished its Spanish-speaking leadership from that in other southwestern U.S. cities had already emerged before the end of the colonial period.

On the other hand, Tucson's frontier location prohibited it from ignoring the aboriginal population as urban New Spain tended to do during the 18th century.[44] Its mission continued to be frontier defense against tribal assaults, carried out in symbiotic relationship to the indigenous community of Tucson and Northern Piman missions in the Santa Cruz River Valley. Thus, Native Americans were never absent from the conscience and consciousness of the Tucson dominant ethnic minority, as their cousins to the south were from the conscience of New Spain's urban elites.

11.

Religion at the Royal Fort of San Agustín del Tucson, 1779-1821

THE FRANCISCAN MISSIONARIES AT BAC responsible for propagating the Christian gospel among the heathen northern Piman Indians living at Tucson enjoyed fairly regularly the company of clerical colleagues from the Royal Spanish Post of San Agustín del Tucson. This situation has been suggested in the description in Chapter 7 of the 1782 attack on the post by hostile Apaches while the Indian missionary and post chaplain watched from the roof of the mission at Tucson Pueblo.

During the 24 years the garrison was stationed at Tubac, it had been ministered to more often than not by first Jesuits and later Franciscans of Guebavi and Tumacacori Missions. It had seldom rated a chaplain of its own. Once the company transferred to Tucson, however, it seems to have been assigned a military chaplain on a permanent basis.

Unfortunate Friar

The first post chaplain of record was Father Francisco Perdigon, who was on duty at Tucson by May of 1779. He set a good example to his parishioners and taught the children their catechism and the fundamentals of reading as well as fulfilling his duties to the soldiers. The chaplain quarreled publicly with post commandant Captain Pedro Allande y Saabedra. So bitter was their antagonism that Perdigon requested Adjutant Inspector Don Roque de Medina to transfer him to any other post whatsoever. Medina in fact recommended that Perdigon be sent to Santa Cruz and that one of the pair of Franciscan missionaries then serving San Xavier del Bac and the Native American Pueblo of Tucson be appointed chaplain of the post.[1] As related in Chapter 7, Apaches killed Friar Perdigon on 26 June 1780 some 12 miles from Arizpe. The armed escort returning the priest to Arizpe from the St. John's Day festivities at Bacanuchi had fled from the attack, abandoning the priest to the Indians. Two of those who fled were also slain,[2] as attested to by 1950s excavations in the Arizpe church. The three were found in a common burial place, wrapped together in a coarsely woven blanket. A burial entry in the Arizpe church records gives further details.[3]

> On 26 June 1780, the Apaches killed on the slope toward Bacanuchi the Reverend Father Chaplain of the Royal Presidio of Tuczon Friar Francisco Perdigón, Franciscan religious belonging to the Province of the Holy Gospel of México. The appropriate funeral honors were paid

to him who was our brother, with Mass and vigil with the body present. It is buried in this Church of the capital of Arizpe. The enemy left him no ecclesiastical property at all because they carried everything off. I have given 60 reales in commissions... [illegible]....

On said day, month and year, they killed in company with the aforesaid Reverend Father, one whom he brought as a servant. It has been impossible to verify his name or marital status. They killed in the same way José de Torres, apparently a mulatto, originally from Chihuahua, who was married, although it has not been possible to discover his wife's name. They are buried in this Church, and in order to attest I signed.

A Church for the Chaplain

Despite his differences with the unfortunate Perdigon, Pedro Allande y Saabedra paid for erecting the first church for the new Tucson post. "Finally, since there was no church, he has made a very large and pretty one, entirely at the expense of his own stipend."[4] Either Spanish colonial standards of military chapel size differed from those of Anglo-Americans or Allande's "large" chapel did not endure. A Texas cattle driver in 1854 estimated the chapel was 20 feet by 10, with plaster only on its facade.[5]

The next chaplain of the Tucson garrison of whom records have been discovered was Friar Gabriel Franco. Father Franco was the chaplain when Apaches attacked the post on 1 May 1782, and part of his account of the battle has already been quoted in translation[6] in Chapter 7. Chaplain Franco was present when the post was inspected in November of 1782,[7] and the end of December in 1783.[8] By October of 1785, the chaplain's post was vacant, however, because "of his having been ordered to suspend the exercise of his functions by the Illustrious Bishop and to go to the presence of the latter at the Real of the Alamos."[9] Unfortunately, nothing more is known of Franco at this writing. A blank in the record of chaplains gaps between 1785 and 1796.

One notable occurrence in presidial religion toward the end of this period was a Franciscan mission, which would be termed a revival by Protestants. The Guardian of the College of the Holy Cross in Querétaro sent ten friars to preach to the clergy-shy populace on the Gulf of California coast to renew its faith and to seek alms for Indian missions. This contingent of hardy priests preached all the way to the northwestern frontier of New Spain, ending their mission at the Presidio of San Agustín del Tucson,[10] evidently around mid-October of 1795. Meanwhile, there was a chaplain on the post in 1793,[11] but his name is unknown.

Wealthiest Man on the Post

A good deal is known about the last royal chaplain of the company of San Agustín del Tucson. He was Pedro Antonio de Arriquibar, a native of the Spanish peninsula born in Viscaya in the Kingdom of Castile. Arriquibar became a Franciscan priest "of the Regular Observance of our Father Saint Francis, Apostolic Preacher"[12] prior to 1770. He arrived in Mexico on 29

May 1770, from Spain.[13] Arriquibar left the City of Mexico in October headed for Tepic, and in February of 1771 sailed for Lower California. His ship ran aground, and Arriquibar was unable to reach the peninsula until 24 November 1771. There ecclesiastical authorities assigned him to the mission of Santa Rosalia de Mulage, where he remained for two years. He sailed from Loreto on 19 October 1773.[14]

Arriquibar's trail then disappears for a couple of years. By 26 February 1775, he had arrived at Tumacacori Mission and was officiating there,[15] meeting the soldiers who would found the post at Tucson the following year. After the garrison moved, Arriquibar stayed on at Tumacacori until late March 1780, when he transferred south to San Ignacio Mission.

When a Pima Indian company was raised and stationed at San Ignacio, Arriquibar became its acting chaplain. Perhaps ministering to soldiers at both Tumacacori and San Ignacio persuaded Arriquibar that his real destiny lay in becoming a chaplain. In any event, Arriquibar obtained from the Pope on 10 February 1784 special dispensation from his vows of poverty so that he could be paid like chaplains who did not belong to an Order, acquire property and bequeath it. Military officials soon transferred the Pima Indian Company to Buenavista in southern Sonora, and then to the former post at Tubac, which it re-activated. Arriquibar remained at San Ignacio, however, until 1794,[16] when he finally entered the Spanish army as chaplain of the Opata Indian company at Bacoachi in eastern Sonora.

The president of the Pimería Alta missions counseled against this move, but Arriquibar had made up his mind. Whatever knowledge the priest may have acquired of the Northern Piman language and customs during the previous 19 years would have stood him in little stead among the Opatas and Peaceful Apaches at Bacoachi. He probably began at once to seek reassignment. Arriquibar was in Bacoachi at least as late as September of 1795.[17] By that time, however, everyone from Adjutant Inspector Pedro Mata to the mission president anticipated that Arriquibar would move to Tucson as its chaplain at any moment. The Father President inferred that Arriquibar obtained this chaplaincy by the intervention of the commandant of arms. Some time in 1796, apparently, Arriquibar achieved his goal and transferred to the Royal Post of San Agustín del Tucson.[18]

The Franciscan charged with leading the Pimería Alta missions characterized Arriquibar as being very *cerrado* on leaving mission work for a military chaplaincy. This term is frequently used by Latin Americans to label Anglo-Americans. In that context it denotes frigidity of social interaction by Latin-American standards. Applied to Arriquibar, it evidently meant that he behaved very individualistically and outside the norm for his Order in his time.

Viewed in the context of later historic departure of Franciscans assigned to Northern Piman Indian missions from their Order, Arriquibar's transfer might be interpreted as disenchantment with the colonial mission institution. In the 1790s, Arriquibar could not very well simply resign from the Order and church and go into another sort of work. The university or hospital administration jobs open to many a modern Franciscan leaving his Order were not available on the Sonoran frontier. A military chaplaincy may well have been the only career alternative open to Arriquibar that would enable him to abandon work that had become quite uncongenial to him.

In March of 1796, Friar Diego Bringas asked the commandant of the Frontier Provinces to assign four of eight new missionaries to act as chaplains to the garrisons at Tucson, Tubac, Altar and Santa María. He sought this change to ease the cost of doubling the number of missionaries in Pimería Alta.[19] While two missionaries thereafter labored in Bac and Piman Tucson, Arriquibar remained as presidial chaplain until his long life ended on 17 September 1820.[20] When the chaplain died, he left about 600 pesos, 40 head of cattle, 27 horses and mules, a house and spartan furnishings, including 50 books and a few clothes.[21] He was considered to be one of the wealthiest men on the post,[22] and his library probably was the largest in the settlement. The royal decree of 26 December 1804 ordering clergymen to divest themselves of their property[23] appears not to have kept Arriquibar from accumulating material goods.

Scarce Supplies and Equipment

From documents written by Arriquibar's own pen we can gain some idea of the state of grace of his parishioners, and the physical plant of his church in the frontier military post. His inventory of the sparse church furnishings made early in 1797 (Inventory 1, Appendix) provides an idea of the state of the military chapel shortly after Arriquibar's arrival in Tucson a little over a decade and a half since its erection.

The presidial chaplain prepared this inventory during an inspection visit by Licenciado Manuel M. Moreno, a representative of the bishop of Sonora. Arriving on the post on 20 January, the bishop's deputy remained there for six days. Undoubtedly he confirmed numerous young people instructed by their parents and perhaps Arriquibar. Unfortunately for the new chaplain, the inspector found nothing to his liking. He noted, "The church [is] very bad. Its utensils [are] not at all good. There is no holy oil nor holy water font. Books very disordered. There are no matrimonial diligences." The visitor added that "appropriate measures were provided and dictated."[24] Unhappily for historical reconstruction of clerical administration of the presidio, the orders evidently were entered on the presidial records which have disappeared, so we know not their import.

Possibly Arriquibar had only recently arrived at Tucson, but he may also have put off preparing an enumeration of population and chapel inventory until Licenciado Moreno arrived and reminded him of the episcopal circular calling for them. Arriquibar himself noted, in a letter translated later in this chapter, that he let his correspondence pile up. Quite probably the bishop's deputy charged Arriquibar with improving the physical equipment of the military chapel. Certainly Arriquibar did so, and informed the bishop of his accomplishment. Within seven years of the date of his first inventory, Arriquibar wrote to the bishop that the military chapel had been provided with at least some more pious images:

> In this Holy Church that is in my charge, a most pious image of Our Lady of Piety located on the main altar in its gilt frame is venerated with tender devotion. I would say its size is more than two yards high and more than a yard wide. I humbly beg that as a result of love for this Mother of Piety, and in order to excite in some devotion to this Mother of Piety and augment it in all, Your Illustrious Reverence may deign to concede the customary indulgences with the endowment which might be the will of Your Illustrious Reverence."[25]

There can be little question that obtaining statuary, vestments and ecclesiastical supplies remained a problem for the military chaplain of the royal post "which is located in the most distant part of Christendom" as the president of the Pimería Alta missions phrased it. Friar Francisco Yturralde thus referred to the Presidio of Tucson in 1799 when he asked the newly consecrated bishop of Sonora for three crystal bottles of Holy Oil.

"By the will of God, Your Most Illustrious Reverence will consecrate the Holy Oils during next Holy Week, but I know not where," wrote the father president. Then he begged, "Here we are very distant, Illustrious Sir. Therefore, I pray with humble affection and due respect that you should order your Secretary to send us in three crystal bottles the quantity you think sufficient for fifteen towns that are comprehended in the eight Missions in my charge, as well as three Presidios to which we presently minister." Then the missionary leader added a request for Arriquibar: "The oils for the Presidio of Tucson, which is located in the most distant part of Christendom and linked to the Mission of San Xavier del Bac, can also come [with this shipment]." Friar Francisco also named agents to receive the Holy Oil in either Alamos or Cieneguilla.[26] A marginal notation on the petition indicates that the bishop sent the Holy Oil to Alamos for transshipment to the frontier priests. Despite apparent difficulties in supplying the presidial chapel with the symbols of religious devotion, new ideas of society diffused to this remote Sonoran frontier.

Manners and Morals of the Tucson Flock

Chaplain Arriquibar on 6 January 1804, acknowledged a decree from the bishop of Sonora promulgated 3 August 1803 ordering extensive reforms in the education of children in the frontier presidios. This followed changes in civil education ordered by the intendent. It made chaplains responsible for supervising basic education of youngsters in such areas as the catechism, moral principles and obedience to duly constituted authority.[27] Probably Arriquibar began to take an active role in educating Tucson's youngsters in accord with this measure designed to counter the spread of ideals of the United States and French social revolutions.[28]

The chaplain had received the bishop's directive on 16 December 1803. When he acknowledged it, he wrote a letter to the bishop and another to his secretary that same day in January, suggesting that he habitually let his correspondence pile up. and answered it all at once. The second letter Arriquibar wrote that day replied to a letter from the bishop's secretary dated 16 September 1803, and dealt with matrimonial affairs and the chaplain's relation to them:

> I have received the very nice and instructive letter of Your Honor of September 16 last year with the petition of José María Syqueiros, Armorer of this Company, against his wife María Jesus Arguelles, caught in adultery, and in answer I say to Your Honor that the said Syqueiros being quite Christian and human and instructed in that maxim of the Sacred Gospel *Dimittite et dimitretur Vobis* [Forgive as you would be forgiven] has seen fit to pardon his wife all offense, and has united with the woman in their matrimony, which has given me the greatest joy. I have given many and very humble thanks to the Most High by whose means I have been freed from taking more measures very strange, repugnant and laborious for me in a country so remote as this is, where scarcely a person is found who knows how to write.
>
> Despite what I have expressed, this couple is now separated because the husband is sick from an accidental contagion which he has communicated to his wife, but when this cause ceases, they will continue their matrimony.[29]

Reading between the lines of the priest's missive, a modern liberated woman could readily infer that María Jesús Arguelles de Siqueiros lived very much under the domination of males dedicated to their own interests. Additional insight into the morals and ethics of the frontier Spaniards and Mestizos at Tucson and their relationship to the chaplain and church comes from a petition for episcopal indulgence formulated by Chaplain Arriquibar:

> Illustrious Sir:
>
> Don Juan Romero, former corporal of the Company of the Tucson, Bachelor and legitimate son of the deceased Don Pablo Romero, former Captain of said Company, and of Doña Luisa Bohorquez, citizeness of said post, wishes to contract matrimony with María Gabriela Ramirez, widow of Ygnacio Contreras, soldier of the same company for five years. The realization of this marriage has the dire impediment of relationship in the first degree, because his own brother has had carnal knowledge of said widow and had by her a daughter. Desiring efficiently and with Christian sincerity to quiet his conscience agitated by much remorse, to end scandals, repair the damage which he has occasioned said widow, to legitimize the embryo which she has in her womb, and take her out of the considerable unhappiness and disrepute in which she finds herself, and in manifest risk of committing equal excesses at the age of twenty-eight years with three daughters without counting the embryo which is newly planted in her womb, he begs Your Illustrious Grace with the greatest submission and most profound humility that as a result

of your well known goodness you might deign to concede him the grace which he implores for the salvation of his soul. Thus he expects this from the pastoral zeal of Your Illustrious Grace, remaining ready to practice whatever may be the superior will of Your Illustrious Grace.

Royal Post of San Agustín del Tucson. March 6, 1806.

FRIAR PEDRO DE ARRIQUIBAR[30]

The chaplain dispatched with this petition a letter to the bishop containing his own sentiments. Despite his continual exhortations and sermons in the military chapel, and his declamation against all vices, but particularly against the abomination of luxury, Arriquibar was unable to end scandals practiced by some individuals of the garrison. "Of this class and Number 1 is without doubt Don Juan Romero mentioned in the petition." Knowing that his own brother had had a daughter by the widow Ramirez, Romero formally betrothed himself to her and then by virtue of this act "made use of her until he impregnated her." She could not marry the first brother because he was an officer and she was poor, "but he suffered his punishment," observed the chaplain. According to the chaplain, this widow had nothing notable about her person, believed the promises the Romero brothers made to her, and was very pious. Although Romero was a captain's son, he had no resources beyond his small carbineer's pay because he had been broken from corporal.

The chaplain's own feelings in this matter were summed up in his discouraged plaint to the bishop: "These excesses, sir, are so regretable to me that they make me ready to abandon the enterprise and retire to my convent, but the consideration of the great scarcity of priests which exists in these remote countries animates me to continue." Apologizing for his lack of proper formality in writing to the bishop, Arriquibar pleaded: "I am only fifty-nine years of age, without a notary, nor any other person whom I can utilize for such purposes." Because of the lack of literates at Tucson Presidio, a salary for a secretary would not help, so "I have to do everything except ring the bells."[31]

Although he did not have to ring them, Arriquibar evidently did have to buy bells for his church. One of three bells recorded at the chapel in 1854 bore the inscription "Vuestra Señora de Guadalupe Año 1807."[32] Quite possibly Arriquibar had it cast that year. Almost certainly he added it to the chapel, hanging it and a companion bell beside the door, with a third suspended from a gable.

They were probably rung loudly at the wedding of a young ensign, whose problems in 1811 were similar to those experienced by Juan Romero five years earlier. Arriquibar once again petitioned the bishop on behalf of his wayward parishioner, who, like Romero, was the son of a former officer of the Tucson post. This young man wanted to marry a girl with whose sister he had already been intimate. The petitioner was José Sosa, a citizen of Tucson and son of Ensign José María Sosa, then deceased, and Rita Espinosa.[33] In a separate letter to the prelate, Arriquibar pleaded in favor of Sosa that the girl with whom he had been intimate was really only a half-sister of his intended, having a different mother although the same father, and they had never lived together, one residing at Altar and the other at Aribaca. Sosa was a poor farmer subject to the vagaries of Apache raiding, claimed the chaplain,[34] although popular opinion rated his mother one of the wealthiest persons in Tucson.[35] Ensign Sosa's widow died at Tumacacori on 16 April 1820[36] only a few months before Arriquibar.

Conflicts: Small-Scale and Worldwide

Echoing the conflict between Captain Allande y Saabedra and Friar Perdigon almost 30 years earlier, Chaplain Arriquibar and post commandant Captain Antonio Narbona were at outs with each other in 1808. Narbona complained to the bishop about Arriquibar's conduct, and hardly had Friar Juan B. Llorens from Mission San Xavier del Bac investigated and placed his report in the hands of the bishop when the latter received a new complaint from the senior officer at Tucson. The bishop wrote to the father president of the missions of Pimería Alta more in sorrow than in anger:

> In the same mail which brought to my hands the report by Father Llorens there came to me a new complaint made by the Commandant Narbona to the Commandant General against his own chaplain Father Arriquibar. I should, therefore, be grateful to Your Reverence for repeating the license to the aforesaid Llorens in order that he may, following the authorized testimony from which with appropriate credentials I send him by Your Reverence's hand, conducting himself in the manner in which he did before, again make a summation of that which he is informed by the specified Commandant Narbona concerning the administration of sacraments and healing of souls, as to having married various strangers without any particular diligence and without publication of banns for whatsoever interest.[37]

The geo-political changes underway in Europe resounded on Spain's far colonial frontier at Tucson. The central governing council of the kingdom tried to raise funds in 1810 all over the colonial empire in order to carry on the war against "the common enemy Napoleon," and the commandant general of the Frontier Provinces and the bishop of Sonora joined in urging the frontier chaplains to contribute. This circular merits full translation here:[38]

> Reverend Fathers, Chaplains of the Frontier Presidios:
>
> The Most Illustrious and Most Reverend Lord Bishop, Don Friar Francisco Rouset de Jesus, on the 22d of February sent me two copies of documents concerning the contributions which all the vassals of Spain justly ought to make to support the war that it conducts against the common enemy Napoleon. One comes from the Central Governing Junta of the Kingdom. The other comes from the Commandant General of these Provinces. The Bishop wishes us, the Clergy, to cooperate on our part with something, and to inspire our parishioners to do the same. To that end, I beg Your Reverences to take up this matter energetically, calling on each one after the exhortation that you make to them in

Church in order to draw up a list showing what each one gave. Send me the list. Remit the money to Arizpe at the disposition of the Illustrious Lord Bishop.

May God protect Your Reverences for many years. Arivechi, March 18 of 1810.

FRIAR YGNACIO DÁVALOS

Chaplain Arriquibar pledged to give a large sum himself, plus what he collected from his parishioners:

> Every year that Our Mother and beloved fatherland Spain continues the just war against the impious Napoleon, I subscribe ninety pesos annually with inclusion of that disposed by the royal order, obligating myself to put the excess at the end of every year at the disposition of the Illustrious Bishop together with that which I shall collect from my parishioners by my persuasions.

The patriotic Arriquibar undoubtedly cheered the final defeat of Napoleon in 1815. The death of his long-time Franciscan neighbor Llorens surely saddened Tucson's post chaplain and reminded him of his own advancing age. Death freed Arriquibar from the sadness of witnessing the end of Spanish rule in New Spain.

Somewhat more than a month prior to his demise in 1820, at the age of 73 or 74, Friar Pedro Antonio de Arriquibar may have felt a premonition of that event and decided to inventory the church furnishings in preparation for the new priest who would follow him. This afforded him an opportunity to note that many additions to the post chapel had been built during his long administration, although he seems not to have replaced Allande's basic structure. The choir loft, baptistry, sacristy and a chapel of Our Lady were constructed while Arriquibar was chaplain, according to this final inventory, which shows a considerable increase in furnishings since 1797. The listing appears in full as Inventory 2 in the Appendix.

The "Integral Code"

While the period of material prosperity toward the end of the colonial era at Tucson permitted Arriquibar to improve the structure and furnishings of the post chapel, other aspects of religion remained fairly constant. Members of the garrison enjoyed, for example, exemption from the general Roman Catholic requirement of abstaining from eating meat on Fridays and certain holy days of obligation. This privilege related to the special legal status of the armed forces of Spain. In 1551, the king granted military jurisdiction over civil and criminal legal cases to certain military units. In 1587, he extended that privilege to the entire regular military and naval establishment. Through the course of time, the full privilege of military court jurisdiction came to be labeled the "integral code."[39]

Published studies show that presidial troops on the northern frontier of New Spain were classified as part of the regular army during the period when what became the Tucson garrison manned the post at Tubac.[40] As regulars, in contrast to the provincial militia units formed during and after the Seven Year's War, they enjoyed the privilege of the "integral code." This distinction meant a considerable difference in the fasting expected by ecclesiastical authorities. The bishop of Sonora spelled out this difference in circulars issued in 1805, 1808 and 1809.

The 1805 circular disseminated the policy set by the vicar general of the Spanish army. The 1808 circular disseminated the determination of Pope Pius Seventh that only members of the regular army who enjoyed the "integral code" had the grace of ignoring fasts. Militiamen or others who did not hold the privilege of the "integral code" were "excluded from the grace with regard to fasting and eating meat specified in our first-cited circular," wrote Bishop Francisco Rouset de Jesús. Then in mid-December of 1809, the bishop of Sonora, Sinaloa and the Californias issued yet another circular aimed toward dispelling all confusion on the subject.[41]

> We declare that military men who according to the rule laid down in our previous circulars enjoy the "integral code" could and can because of their privileges at all times and all days of the year eat without scruple milk products and meats except on Ash Wednesday, the Fridays of every week of Quaresma, and the four final days of Holy Week.

On those days of obligation, the military establishment was to observe the same food regulations as the other American subjects of His Catholic Majesty, admonished the bishop. If, however, military men were actually campaigning or on an expedition on those dates, they could still ignore the fasting rules.

In other words, military men with the integral code were excused from fasting on Saturdays during Quaresma and on three days of Holy Week. They could also eat milk products and meat on the other days of obligation, even mixing meat and fish at the same meal. Moreover, enlisted men who traveled on any of the days of obligation were excused from fasting on those days.

The bishop further granted military men of whatever rank the privilege of combining fish and meat in the same meal, "because of their low pay and because of the circumstances and distance of their posts and scarcity of food supplies which force them to choose for their necessary nutrition that which they encounter or are able to purchase at the lowest price."

Even the families of the specially privileged military man shared to a limited extent in his exemption from church dietary rules. Members of the family and household of military men enjoying the integral code could share the meat purchased by the soldier for his own consumption on days when others abstained. On the other hand, members of the family "ought and are absolutely obliged to observe at that time the obligation of fasting, without being able on those days on which it is generally prohibited to eat meat to mix meat with fish." Apparently this injunction aimed at preventing family members from flavoring their fish with meat gravy so it would taste less like fish and more like meat, thus lessening the penance.

The bishop differentiated even more between members of the family of a military man and other members of his household. "The servants of military men who receive their ration allowance in cash, and guests who do not live for some time in the house and at the expense of said military men are not granted the privilege of eating meat on the above mentioned days."

In order to make sure that these ecclesiastical rules of military conduct would be observed in the numerous military posts in his diocese, Bishop Rouset de Jesús dispatched copies of his circular to the military chaplains. Further, he required them to copy it into their records, countersign it and return it to his office. Even though the copy countersigned by Friar Pedro Arriquibar is not at hand, we can be fairly sure from other countersigned copies that one conveyed the episcopal message to the chaplain of Tucson, and that he admonished his parishioners accordingly.

Even though the Sonoran diocese was vast, the royal mail did carry written messages to the most remote outposts, so that provincial Christians were part of the even vaster communication network of the Roman Catholic Church. Scarce as Arriquibar and other clerics felt priests to be, they achieved an enduring impact upon the Native American and Spanish-speaking population of the Tucson area and the Papaguería beyond.

12.

The End of Spanish Colonial Rule at Tucson, 1821

The Royal Fort of San Agustín del Tucson ceased to exist in the fall of 1821 when Mexico achieved political independence from Spain. The garrison and the fortification remained, but the presidio was no longer a royal institution or a unit in a vast colonial empire. Political revolution converted it into a military unit of a passing monarchy which disappeared in a year to make way for a republic. The process of conversion was orderly at Tucson and other frontier posts because the key events occurred at higher headquarters and overseas.

Citizenship: A Revolutionary Concept

One very necessary although not sufficient condition for the Mexican revolution of 1821 stands out. This is the concept of *citizen.* Official and semi-official letters and reports from the immediate post-revolutionary period in Mexico abound with evidence of the tremendous import of this concept, expressed in Spanish by the term *ciudadano.*

Throughout this book, the Spanish term *vecino* has been translated also as "citizen." That translation corresponds with United States frontier usage of "citizen" as an ethnic, racial term for the politically dominant group in a multi-racial country. A *ciudadano* marches to a different drum than a *vecino,* however, although one English term combines the meanings of two Spanish words. The *ciudadano* was not necessarily a *vecino. Ciudadano* became a socio-political term denoting a political status of every man regardless of his ethnic background.

For that reason the concept of citizen (*ciudadano*) held utmost importance for the Mexican revolution, precisely because it cut across the social barriers inherent in the concept *vecino.* It symbolized a new-found belief in an inherent value and worth in every man as a political being. This socio-political concept reinforced the Roman Catholic Church's doctrine of the worth and value of every individual soul. Thus, it created a climate of opinion and resulting social action in New Spain in the late colonial period which made the 1810 and 1821 revolutions inevitable, and set the pattern of political intercourse and formal interaction for many decades.

The specific concept of *ciudadano* that spread through New Spain at the end of the colonial period came directly from revolutionary France. It stood diametrically opposed to pre-existing principles of differential and hierarchical ranking of individual men in terms of political roles with a king at the apex of a pyramid of lesser valued persons. It opposed previous principles of differential social stratification of individuals in a manner parallel to the political pyramid. It clashed with traditional principles of religious ranking of clerics and laymen on scholastic and ethnic grounds. This revolutionary new concept was all the more congenial and plausible to the Mexicans because French troops provided objective verification of it when they chased the king of Spain from his throne. Napoleon's conquests in Spain toppled a centuries-old faith in the Spanish king and the immutability of the imperial system.

The concept *citizen* became a revolutionary one, given the previous ordering of political and social action. It can be viewed as equally important as gunpowder, cannon, dynamite and other tools of violence. These technological items were only means to ends. One of the most important concepts defining ends toward which they are applied was that of *citizen.*

European Background

A necessary condition for successful Mexican revolution, although remote at first thought, may have been the international relationships in Western Europe late in the 18th and early in the 19th centuries. Franco-British hostility can be traced back into medieval times. A Norman duke sailed across the English Channel and landed an expeditionary force on English soil. It made him king of England by winning a decisive battle at a place called Hastings in 1066 A.D. The French dynasty thus created in England retained a lively interest in the governance of France.

Eventually personal ambitions overrode emerging national ties. When a problem arose in the French succession, English kings thought they should assume the French throne. French claimants disputed that thought, and the dispute degenerated into one of the longer hostilities in recorded history. Armed conflict between England and France became predictable in almost any circumstance in which the ruler of either country thought he saw an opportunity to weaken the other.

Without complicating this analysis more, one may trace the course of events that converted the Royal Post of San Agustín del Tucson into a Mexican republican presidio. The concept *citizen* had been operating on men's minds in the British Isles for several centuries, reducing the autocratic powers of English monarchs. The reality of citizenship steadily expanded to begin to approximate the ideal of equality advocated by political philosophers. In the North American colonies of the English king, the reality of citizenship expanded as social equality increased through selective migration. Autocrats, well-satisfied with their existing situations or seeking betterment through the hierarchical system, left the lower classes to emigrate to the colonies and Continent.[1] Consequently, colonial society became somewhat less stratified than that in the metropolis. The colonial system of governance maintained metropolitan social distinctions in the face of growing colonial equality. A consequent lack of "fit" generated sufficient stress among key colonials in seaboard cities that they rebelled to bring their government into closer congruence with their social structure.

Inspiration from the French Revolution

The North American colonial rebels achieved political independence only with much external help, primarily from France and Spain. France succumbed to the temptation handed down from the past to twist the lion's tail. Losing its North American colonies would weaken the English, ergo, the king of France would aid rebel English colonists.

In the hindsight of history, that decision appears to have been possibly the worst thing the French king could have done in terms of his own self-interest. Once freed from English control, the colonists proved that citizens equal under the law could govern themselves, so a traditional hierarchy was not necessary. Once that proof of the viability of citizenship became manifest to the world, many people hastened to abandon the medieval concept of hierarchical society with a monarch at the apex.

The French war effort brought economic suffering to the people of France, already oppressed by their nobility. Tempted by the few tastes of citizenship they had enjoyed, and reacting against worsening economic conditions, the commoners of France launched another revolution. Their successful effort translated the local and limited success of the North American colonials into a worldwide message of citizenship and egalitarian political forms. The French Revolution put the success of the North Americans into terms understandable to Spanish colonials. The Anglo-Saxons were not very sympathetic models for Mexicans. The French revolutionists, on the other hand, spoke a Romance language closely resembling Spanish, and brought to earth the strongest royal system in Europe save that of Spain.

The French Revolution further directly precipitated the political independence of Mexico when Napoleon intervened in Spain. Accustomed for generations to viewing the Spanish monarchy as the next thing to divinity, the colonials suddenly learned that a diminutive ex-corporal of French artillery sent two kings of Spain scurrying for their lives with a few rag-tag French republican troops nipping at their royal heels.[2]

The nerve-center of Spanish imperialism, the colonial administration and home government disintegrated into chaos. Peninsular Spaniards suddenly became far too busy trying to free their country from French invaders to work very hard at imposing their will on New World colonials. They had to establish local governments to replace the vanished monarchy. These necessarily functioned more democratically than the dispersed court. Thus, colonial Spaniards and subject peoples witnessed the emergence of a model of local self-government at the very time they necessarily made decisions for the first time that the colonial administrators had always made for them.

The Napoleonic changes in European society, then, moved New Spain toward increased de facto independence from Spain and the traditional monarchy. By the time the latter institution was restored on the Peninsula, colonials had experienced more than a decade of greater freedom than ever before. Attempts to re-impose royal authority in New Spain along ancient lines fostered the same kind of lack of fit between tradition and reality that proceeded the rebellion of Great Britain's North American colonies. In Argentina, Venezuela and then Mexico, colonials moved to achieve a more comfortable fit. They discarded the king of Spain and his viceroys and colonial administrations. Often they did so with urban militia forces created beginning with King Charles III to protect the New World colonies against European invasions.[3]

Techniques of Successful Rebellion

New Spain became independent Mexico by a course of revolutionary action different from that in other colonies. The northern frontier forces, long dedicated to fighting Native Americans, played key roles in the independence movement. The nature of that movement is best grasped, perhaps, by comparing how the men who achieved political independence in 1821 defeated the social revolution launched by Hidalgo in 1810.

In British North America, loyal subjects of the king were called "Tories" by the rebels, who labeled themselves "patriots." In New Spain, most loyal subjects of the King were *Gauchupines* (Peninsular-born Spaniards), while the rebels began terming themselves *Mexicanos*, adopting what they took to be an old Native American terminology. The 1821 political rebellion remained relatively bloodless because many men who would have been Tories in North America were patriots in Mexico.

In 1821, the upper class carried out a palace revolt by means of which colonial leaders seized control of the machinery of government and continued to operate much as they had prior to independence. These members of the elite leadership wanted independence from political interference from Spain, but they were not the sort of radicals who could rally to the banner that Hidalgo had raised. In fact, they were often the very royal officers who had stopped Hidalgo's radical social revolution in its tracks.

They learned after 1810 and wider dissemination of the ideals of the French Revolution that colonial society could never be restored to its pre-1810 ridigity.[4] It could never again be as oblivious to the aspirations of the lower class as it had been. Yet the rebel leaders intended to maintain their own power to rule.

Rebel Leaders in the Frontier Provinces

The true character of the 1821 Mexican political revolution may be grasped from the careers of a sample of the men who carried it out in the Western Frontier Provinces.

Alexo García Conde

The senior imperial administrator in the Frontier Provinces had for many years been Intendent-General Alexo García Conde. This African-born Spaniard[5] had become chief of the provinces toward the end of 1796 as colonel of fuseliers. In 1802, he received a promotion to brigadier general.

In 1810, when Hidalgo's popular revolt threatened to overturn colonial government, revolutionists dispatched an expeditionary force under Colonel

Gonzalez Hermosillo from central New Spain toward the northwest. Intendent-General García Conde learned of the rebel advance through Sinaloa from Lieutenant Colonel Pedro Villaescusa. Sweeping the remaining royal garrisons before him, Hermosillo defeated Villaescusa at Rosario.[6] The intendent-general collected troops from the frontier posts under his command, and adding a large contingent of Opata Indians, marched south to intercept the rebel column.

General García Conde had not won his military rank solely as an administrator. He had learned his primary trade in the hard school of active fighting in the Old World. Wounded during the Algerian campaign, García Conde spent four years in the siege of Gibraltar. He understood very well how to fight decisive battles with massed troops. The rebel colonel led his numerically superior force, well armed with captured hand arms and artillery and well provisioned from captured royal stores, against General García Conde's chosen position at San Ignacio Piaxtla in Sinaloa on 8 January 1811. When the smoke cleared from the field, Hermosillo's enthusiastic thousands were either dead or fleeing for their lives. García Conde's few hundreds celebrated their victory which shattered the rebel threat to northwestern New Spain in one brief engagement.

Brigadier General Alexo García Conde became field marshal and governor of Nueva Vizcaya, an office he assumed in October of 1813 in Chihuahua. In November of 1817, he was made commandant general of the Western Frontier Provinces. In this position, García Conde occupied a key position in Spanish colonial government in New Spain. While the Frontier Provinces had been split into eastern and western sections and re-subordinated to the overall authority of the viceroy, the commandant general enjoyed considerable latitude of decision, particularly at that period of disorganization in Spain and the top colonial apparatus. Thus, García Conde grew accustomed to making his own decisions.

When the situation crystalized in 1821 on the question of independence or continued royal Spanish rule, Field Marshall Alexo García Conde chose independence. Native of Ceuta, his entire professional career spent in the royal Spanish army in which he had reached maximum rank, decorated with the Order of San Fernando and the Order of San Hermenegildo by his King Fernando VII – this paragon of Spanish virtue defected. He took his command into the rebel camp, ordering residents of all towns in the Western Frontier Provinces to swear fealty to the revolutionary Mexican government.

Field Marshal Alexo García Conde took his decisive step on 24 August 1821, when he adhered to the *Plan de Iguala*, the pronouncement for independence. He guided the Western Frontier Provinces through the transitional period until 1 July 1822. Then he transferred to the capital city as a new lieutenant general decorated with the new Order of Guadalupe and became inspector general of cavalry.[7]

Mariano de Urrea

Another member of the Sonoran provincial elite, Lieutenant Colonel Mariano de Urrea, played a key role in Mexican independence in the Northwest. Mentioned in Chapter 10 as a lieutenant in the Tucson garrison, he commanded the Bacoachi Opata Indian company and the Altar unit[8] after leaving Tucson. When Intendent-General García Conde called for presidial troops to meet the 1810 rebel threat, Urrea led a strong detachment from Altar. After the rout at San Ignacio Piaxtla, Urrea carried on pacification campaigns in Sinaloa and then Nayarit. In 1815 he won promotion to lieutenant colonel and became governor of Colotlán Province. In 1819, he was chief of the Fourth Section of New Galicia, and in June of 1821 he supported the commanding general there in swearing allegiance to the *Plan de Iguala* and independence.[9]

Simón Elías Gonzáles

In the influential Elías Gonzáles lineage, Simón helped take Sonora out of royal control in 1821. Born at Banámichi, he was one of Captain Francisco's grandsons. He served in the Tucson, Buenavista and Bacoachi garrisons and the secretariat of the commandant general of the Frontier Provinces. Promoted to lieutenant in 1805, he took command of the Tubac Pima Company, but remained at Chihuahua until April of 1807. After serving at San Antonio de Bejar in Texas, Simón returned to Chihuahua. He then commanded the Santa Cruz presidio in Sonora in 1814. In 1820, he became adjutant inspector of Sonora. In that office he stepped out of the royal traces and adhered to the *Plan de Iguala* and independence.[10] His lieutenant colonelcy confirmed, he won election as deputy to the first national congress in 1822. He went on to a most distinguished political and military career including terms as governor of the states of Occidente, Chihuahua and Sonora.[11]

Antonio Narbona

A creole born at Mobile in Spanish Louisiana (modern Alabama) joined the Sonoran officers to guarantee independence in 1821. Antonio Narbona first arrived in Sonora as a cadet in the Santa Cruz Company in 1789[12] sponsored by his brother-in-law, Brigadier Enrique Grimarest,[13] who was commandant of arms. Narbona became an ensign at Fronteras on 27 January 1793[14] and captain of Fronteras in 1809. In 1820, he was promoted to lieutenant colonel and made adjutant inspector of the commandancy general with command of the troops in Arizpe. When Lieutenant Colonel Narbona led the garrison in adherence to the *Plan de Iguala*, and independence, his commander, the political and military chief, resigned and left Narbona to take actual command and insure the local success of the revolution. Having secured Arizpe and northeastern Sonora in concert with Simón Elías Gonzáles, Narbona marched on the Gulf of California port of Guaymas where a royalist priest led Tory elements in opposing independence.[15] Narbona later commanded the Sonoran troops and served as governor of New Mexico.

Tucson and the Rebellion

No documentation has come to the author's attention that would indicate that the Tucson garrison resisted independence in 1821, or actively intervened to secure it. Probably post commander José Romero swore fealty to the *Plan de Iguala* at an opportune moment, ordering his subalterns and troops to follow his example, in the same style as García Conde, Urrea, Elías Gonzáles and Narbona.

Little visibly changed with the political transfer of allegiance, but an era had ended. Mexican Tucson would be a rather different place than the Spanish colonial presidio.

Part III
Population Dynamics

13.

Northern Piman Population Trends at Tucson, 1690-1821

THE NATIVE NORTHERN PIMAN INDIANS CONGREGATING at Tucson formed, with their congeners in other native settlements in the lower portion of the Santa Cruz River Valley, the original and one basic ethnic component in urban Tucson's eventual population. It is important, therefore, to understand the numerical trend of that population through historic times. While the author has elsewhere estimated the aboriginal population of the New World just prior to European contact,[1] no trustworthy means of estimating the Tucson Piman population as of A.D. 1500 are at hand. The natives were not literate, and nonwritten evidence of population size is extremely difficult to interpret even if preserved. Once Spaniards reached the Northern Piman homeland and began to produce written documents describing it in various ways, native population trends may be perceived at least dimly through the curtain of time.

A Confluence of Remnants

Paradoxically, while Tucson grew into an important Northern Piman settlement after 1752, Northern Piman population as a whole shrank rapidly during the entire 18th century. Much of the ingathering of Northern Piman Indians at Tucson resulted from the congregation of the remnants of other less fortunate native rancherías weakened by high disease mortality from Spanish-introduced Old World illnesses, which either became endemic or swept through the Northern Piman settlements in life-destroying epidemic episodes.

Infectious epidemics undoubtedly reached the Northern Piman Indian settlements in the Santa Cruz River Valley during the 17th century, and probably during the 16th, but the lack of direct contact between the natives and Spaniards who might have recorded in writing the scale of depopulation during that earlier period makes reconstruction of the process impossible.

Nine Northern Piman settlements can be identified as still existing in the lower Santa Cruz River Valley in 1700 between the *Punta de Agua* where the stream rose to the surface and the *Picacho,* beyond where the water sank under the sand again at *Charco de los Yumas,* at Point of Mountain. Several of those nine aboriginal rancherías possessed very large native populations in 1700. During the 18th century, the Northern Piman Indian inhabitants abandoned all but two of those aboriginal settlements as part of their people died, and the survivors migrated to the two hamlets that endured. Tucson and Bac stood out as the sole surviving Native American settlements long before the end of the 18th century. Both of those settlements persisted, however, only because they were reinforced by extensive accretions of Papago Christian converts from the desert regions to the west of the Santa Cruz River Valley as Jesuit and especially Franciscan missionaries continued energetically to ply the baptismal shell on this frontier of Christendom.

So great was the 18th century diminution of Native American population in the entire Santa Cruz River Valley that it can hardly be imagined by people secure in the modern era of effective public medical prevention of major contagions. Because Spanish frontiersmen in northwestern New Spain often wrote on the basis of short inspection visits, many remained unaware of the dramatic process of Native American depopulation.

When first seen by Father Eusebio F. Kino and his companions, Tucson evidently was so small that no one thought it worthwhile estimating and recording its population. Yet its 18th century history seems unique in the area because it grew in population while the other rancherías declined in numbers. This astonishing reversal of the general population trend in the lower valley seems the more astounding for its having ended in the extinction of all the other settlements save Bac and Tucson in the three-quarters of a century from 1700 to 1775 *before* the Tubac garrison moved to Tucson and provided military protection for the Native American settlement. Tucson simply attracted immigrants from the abandoned settlements and survived at their expense. Clearly its own population did not reproduce itself.

The Statistics of Depopulation

When a Spanish officer enumerated the Indians who had settled peacefully at Tucson in the spring of 1752 following the Pima Revolt, he counted 156 individuals. (See Table 11, Appendix.) Joseph Díaz del Carpio[2] found only 68 unmarried persons compared to 88 married individuals. Native Tucson suffered a serious deficiency in children, which meant that the population was 20 individuals short of reproducing itself, a deficiency of 21.8%. Analysis of family structure shows that the biological situation was very dangerous indeed. A total of 19 of the 44 married women, or 43%, had no reported children. The other 25 married women had 34 children, an average of only 1.36 per family. Even if the unmarried individuals not enumerated with families are allocated to the married women, the average number of hypothetical "children" per family comes to only 1.54. Two children per family would be required to maintain the population.

The prospects for the future of the Tucson population appeared even bleaker than the family analysis indicates. There were 20 unmarried youths 12 years of age and older, but only 14 maidens. That meant that the number of childbearing women would in a few years be less than the number of adult males. Furthermore, Díaz identified only 4 of the younger children as females.

The enumerated 1752 population showed a 152 male per 100 female sex ratio. The mated adults had a 100 sex ratio, of course, but unmated residents of Tucson 12 years of age and older had a 143 ratio, and younger people a 750 ratio. Such sex ratios produce an accelerated rate of depopulation for lack of females to bear children.

The Native Americans of Tucson may well not all have returned by the spring of 1752, yet the enumerated sample was large enough to be representative of family structure unless return movement had been for some unknown reason very selective according to age. In any event, the reliability of the 1752 sampling appears to have been fairly good, because the population dynamics of that year seem consistent with those revealed in later enumerations.

As residents of other lower Santa Cruz River Valley rancherías migrated to Tucson, that settlement's population grew so that by 1765 it contained 200 inhabitants.[3] Yet that "increase" seems to document an appalling interim depopulation, because the 250 Sobaipuris discussed in Chapter 2 had settled at Piman Tucson only three years earlier in 1762. Reflected in these figures was the mortality of the 1764 epidemic in Sonora[4] and possibly emigration of Sobaipuris, if Captain Anza indeed managed to divert some of them to the Buenavista Valley.

By 20 February 1766, Father Neve reported that the population of Tucson had fallen to only 139 individuals, as shown in Table 12 in the Appendix.[5] The total figure was less than the summer seasonal population, almost certainly, but that should not affect the distribution of individuals within families present. The sex ratio for adults was 102 men per 100 women, not far out of balance. The 32 women in existing unions had borne 47 enumerated children, an average of 1.4687 offspring per wife at that time. Ten of these women had no children enumerated, so that 22 women actually had an average of 2.1 offspring each counted.

Because the Jesuit enumerator recorded no ages, nor genetic relationships outside this limited number of marital unions, one cannot discern whether these women had borne additional older children already married or listed with the unmarried population. In any event, the 22 women clearly had borne just enough children to reproduce their own nuclear families. The Tucson Piman population was failing to reproduce itself because about one-third of its females were apparently barren.

All 41 enumerated women, including those listed as widows, had an average of only 1.365 children each. This number fell far short of the total required to replace the adult population. Such a situation was consistent with that reported in 1752.

Depopulation in the Franciscan Period

When Friar Francisco Garcés assumed charge of Tucson Pueblo as a branch of Mission San Xavier del Bac, its population must have been small. He quickly set to work to attract Papago migrants to his mission and its Tucson branch. By 1774, at least, Garcés had begun to resettle Papagos from the desert country at Piman Tucson.[6] The population increased to 239 inhabitants.[7] Anza reported 80 families there in 1774.[8] Families averaged, therefore, three persons each (actually 2.9875). If all of the individuals except the 160 in couples are counted as children (and some surely were widows and widowers), the 80 women were one child shy of reproducing their own number, much less their husbands'. There existed a reproductive deficit of at least 38% below the number required simply to maintain the population.

A few years later, the bishop of Sonora reported that Piman Tucson had 30 married couples in a total population of 82.[9] Not only had total population plummeted, but average family size had also fallen to 2.73 persons. There were then 22 children at most, or at least 38 short of reproducing the married population, a minimum deficiency of 73.3%. The women averaged only 0.7 child each, at most!

Such calculations demonstrate very clearly that the historic continuity of Northern Piman Indian residence at Tucson depended on constant migration to that settlement of Indians from other places. Throughout the 18th century Piman residents of Tucson suffered what is often identified as an urban inability to reproduce their own numbers.

By 1783, the total population of Bac had fallen to 167 persons, and that of Tucson stood at 189,[10] a total of 356 Native Americans in the two settlements.

The family structure of both Bac and Tucson Pueblo in 1783 showed how far the Pima, Sobaipuri and Papago Indians living there were even from reproducing themselves. There were 74 families at Piman Tucson and 77 at Bac. Thus, average family size amounted to only 2.2 persons at Bac, and little better than 2.55 at Tucson. Taken at face value, the Tucson Pueblo figures indicated only 41 children, an average of only 0.554 offspring per family. Apparently the population lacked 107 children of reproducing itself, despite the fact that the populace consisted for the most part of migrants, who should have been relatively young and vigorous.

That may not have been true of the Sobaipuris, reduced by war casualties and epidemic mortality, whom Captain Elías removed from the San Pedro River Valley in 1762, settling 250 at Piman Tucson.[11] It was true, surely, of 99 Nixoras (Native American slaves on this frontier)[12] and Papagos Friars Garcés, Belderrain and Llorens baptized at Bac and Tucson from 26 May 1768 to 1 January 1796. How many were settlers is not clear. Llorens labored mightily to repopulate both places. He baptized one group of 30 Papagos — evidently immigrants to Tucson Pueblo — there in 1795, and then another group of 27 later the same year. Llorens persuaded 134 Aquituni Papagos to come on 19 January 1796, and he christened 51 infants in the group.[13] Some or all of these Desert People fled, forcing Llorens to persuade them all over again. Having already baptized 53 other Papagos in the two places during his first five years in this mission,[14] Llorens clearly accelerated Papago urban relocation 150 years before the U.S. Bureau of Indian Affairs took a hand in this game.

In the fall of 1797, the president of the Franciscan missions in Pimería Alta reported that 211 of the Indians at Tucson were Papago immigrants, while only 78 were "Pimas,"[15] a total of 289 persons. Family structure again told a grim tale of depopulation. The 78 survivors of the valley population and former migrants were 30 offspring short of reproducing themselves. They counted 46 married persons and 8 widows or widowers, a total of 54 adults, but only 24 children and adolescents. This was a deficiency of 55.6% from reproduction.

Even the recent Papago immigrants barely maintained themselves. Their 107 children exceeded their adult population of 104 (88 married, 16 widows and widowers) by a narrow margin. Life at the mission soon sent them into decline.

In the spring of 1798, Llorens baptized more 1795-96 migrants: 25, then 12, then 22, leaving 27 unchristened.[16]

In spite of Llorens' conversion of pagan Papagos, when he enumerated the native population of his mission in 1801, he reported only 119 Native Americans at Bac, and 246 at Tucson Pueblo for a total of 365.[17] (See Table 13, Appendix.) By this time, 213 of the people at Tucson were Papagos, 7 were Gila River Pimas, and only 26 were "Pimas," that is to say, survivors of the native riverine population and all of the pre-1790 immigrants!

The 246 persons living at Piman Tucson in December of 1801 included 130 married persons, 8 widowers and 5 widows, a total of 143 persons of child-producing age or over. Their apparent total living child production had been, however, only 103, or 40 short of reproducing themselves. This was a 28% deficiency, reflecting recent Papago migration. The average number of children per married or widowed female came to only 1.47, counting all children and unmarried adolescents enumerated.

The sex ratio in the Tucson Native American population was 115.8 males per 100 females. Even though more boys probably were born than girls, the sex ratio among children 0-5 years of age was 81.3 males per 100 females. Such a figure suggests high male infant mortality. The sex ratio in the 11-15-year-old group sharply reversed in this population to 220 males per 100 females. Such a ratio suggests selective migration and/or very high mortality of girls at puberty during or just after the smallpox epidemic of 1799.[18]

Ethnic Constitution of the Survivors

At the end of the 18th century, imperial law prohibited settlement of Spaniards, half-castes and even Native Americans from elsewhere in Indian towns.[19] Royal policy was either honored in the breach on the Tucson frontier, or local military officers allowed settlement of non-Native Americans at Bac and Piman Tucson in the interests of defense. As Appendix Table 14 shows, Llorens enumerated 39 Spaniards and half-castes there in 1801.

This citizen population of Bac and Tucson had a sex ratio of 82.4 males per 100 females at this time. Although the citizen population was so small that the ratio could be quite biased, the surplus females index an increasing population while the dearth of females in the Native American population indexed a declining population.

The more dynamic citizen population's ethnic constitution reflects the importance of miscegenation combined with transculturation within mixed-marriage families for eventual dominance of culturally Hispanic populations on this frontier. Only 36.1% of the "citizens" of Bac and Tucson Pueblo in

1801 were identified as Spaniards. The progeny of Native American-European matings formed an equal percentage of the "citizens." Only 28.6% of this group ranked as Mestizos, or half-castes, with 71.4% termed *coyotes* (presumably three-quarters Native American and one-quarter European).

The 1801 enumeration of "citizens" shows, because of its careful ethnic identifications, that several persons of African ancestry had already reached the Tucson area during the 18th century besides Sergeant Francisco Xavier Márquez. Three mulattos, or progeny of European-African matings, comprised 7.7% of the citizenry in 1801.

The process of social transformation appears in Friar J. B. Llorens' ethnic classifications. He labeled three daughters of a Mestizo husband and mulatta wife as Mestizas, apparently following a rule of patrilineal inheritance, and suggesting how the frontier population blended genetic contributions from Europe, Africa and the New World into a socially unified new kind of population.

Third most numerous ethnic group among the "citizens" in 1801 was "Yuma," comprising 20.5% of the total. A glance at the citizen enumeration in Appendix Table 14 reveals, however, that these "Yumas" occupied a very special niche in this population. Each of the three Spanish households included one or two Yuma children between the ages of seven and ten. They worked as servants in these households, much as hacienda Indian children have served in landlord households in provincial areas of the Andes in modern times. These Yuma servants most likely reached Bac and Piman Tucson as war captives of Gila River Pimas or Maricopas who sold them to citizens.[20] The "Yuma" label applied to such juvenile servants doubtless referred more to their general linguistic affiliation than to the Quechan tribe.

Llorens listed four "Yumas" not living in Spanish households with the citizens, suggesting that such captives from tribes beyond the frontier of colonial rule actually contributed progeny to the general Mestizo population with a rapidity that missioned Native Americans did not.

The frontier custom of purchasing Native American captives from friendly Indians was rather explicitly described by a Franciscan official of the College of the Holy Cross at Querétaro a few years earlier:

> The Gila River Pimas, as a result of the frequent campaigns that they carry out against the Apaches, conduct their child and adult women prisoners to the Pueblo of Tucson, where for small interests they leave them among the Indians and citizens. They are catechized and serve to augment the population of the Pueblos. Last October [1795] they conducted some prisoners to the Pueblo of Tucson, where they graciously gave some of them to some Indians whom they recognize as relatives, and sold some. Ten pagan Gila River Pimas being present in said Pueblo (having come to guide us to their country) they saw that one of the Chiefs of the Province seized said prisoners from their masters, and without paying for them the smallest recompense, conducted them to Arizpe. I am a witness of this fact and can prove it whenever ordered to do so.[21]

The Franciscan feared that grave consequences would flow from that official action, from the point of view of both Church dogma and simple humanity. "In the future, the Gila River Pimas will kill the adult women from whose preservation they expect no recompense. Thus will be lost these Souls (which were previously assured for a small payment), offending our Religion, humanity, and against the piety of our Sovereign. . . ." Whatever their Catholic Majesties had decreed from Spain against human slavery, the Spaniards and Mestizos of Tucson practiced it on this remote colonial frontier, augmenting, as the Franciscan observed, the mixed ethnic population.

The Mission: From Bodies to Souls

In 1802, the Bac-Tucson mission population declined by two Native Americans, to 363, and two citizens, to 37. The Indian sex ratio stood at 93.1 males per 100 females.[22] By the end of 1804, the Bac-Tucson Pueblo population had risen to 496 Indians, while citizens fell to 29. The Indian sex ratio had climbed, however, to 112 males per 100 females, heralding future decline.[23]

In 1818, Bac and Tucson had 287 Native Americans and 37 citizens.[24] If there had been no additional immigration to Bac and Tucson Pueblo between 1804 and 1818, the population lost no less than 209 persons during those 14 years. The apparent average loss of 15 persons annually probably was concentrated during 1816 when a smallpox epidemic swept the Pimería Alta mission populations.[25]

During 1819, the population of Tucson Pueblo and Bac increased through additional migration to 318 Indians and 62 Spaniards and mixed-bloods. The crude death rate among the Native Americans, computed from end-of-year population and 35 reported burials, was no less than 110 per 1000 population. In contrast, the birth rate indicated by six baptisms amounted to only 19 per 1000 population. If eight baptisms of heathens denoted immigrant infants, some of the disparity was made up by their fertility, but clearly the Native American population still depended upon immigration to this incipient city at the cost of depopulating other settlements.

The apparent net population loss of 6.1% during the year would eradicate any community not reinforced with migrants in a short time. The birth-death rate difference meant a 9.1% annual population decrease without immigration!

In contrast, the non-Indian population remained, immigration aside, in equilibrium with one birth and one death,[26] indicating the tremendous biological advantage persons of European ancestry enjoyed in the biological and cultural environment of the times in the lower Santa Cruz River Valley.

During 1820, the Native American population dropped to 310 in Bac and Tucson, even though baptisms rose to 21, plus 67 heathens, indicating the two years seem to reflect the variation in birth incidence in a small population. The death rate rose slightly to 119 per 1,000 population, 37 burials being reported. The non-Indian population dropped to 44 through emigration, inasmuch as one birth and only two burials were recorded.[27]

The Native American population of the Tucson area continued to decline until the very end of the period of Spanish colonial rule. This is not a matter of Black Legend hyperbole. The figures presented in this chapter speak for themselves. The Northern Piman Indians still reeled biologically and psychologically from the shock of conquest and foreign domination, plus the deadly impact of Old World diseases. As these Native Americans died, they left lands that they had once inhabited open to Spanish colonization. Spaniards and Mestizos farmed Santa Cruz River Valley fields once tilled by Northern Pimans. They ran their livestock on ranges where Northern Pimans once hunted and collected wild foods. The European population increased, however, much more slowly than the Native Americans died. Consequently, large stretches formerly inhabited remained vacant of habitation although exploited for forage, inviting hostile Apache penetration.

Silent biological conquest of the Northern Pimans brought innumerably more casualties than all the Spanish colonial military actions ever carried out in the aboriginal homeland of these Native Americans. Ultimately, migration of Papagos into the lower Santa Cruz River Valley maintained the Northern Piman ethnic character of Tucson and assured that basic ethnic component would eventually participate in urbanizing Tucson.

The grim reality of Native American depopulation recounted in this chapter identifies one basic factor responsible for the decline of Christian missions in the Southwest.[28] Although this chapter deals with a limited area, the Old World diseases affecting the Native American population of the Santa Cruz River Valley spread widely through the Southwest and beyond. What happened here can be generalized throughout the Southwest, and on a grander scale to the densely populated areas of Latin America. This chapter does not make pleasant reading. Yet it reconstructs accurately a major phenomenon in the pageant of the historic peopling and governing of the Americas by European immigrants. The Christian mission as a frontier institution that emerges in this chapter is not a romantic pastoral scene peopled by happy converts led by congenial pastors. Rather, it is the grim story of rapid population decline.

Contemporary Perceptions and Reactions

This chapter raises some serious questions about the nature of the Christian mission as a frontier institution. One may ask what the missionaries themselves thought about the decimination of Native American populations. Were they concerned only with finding replacements to keep their clientele at a level high enough to continue to merit royal financial support? Were they alarmed and morally disturbed by depopulation?

The author can but say that clerics and civil Crown representatives on the northwestern frontier of New Spain seem to have left very little evidence on paper that they even perceived the scale of Native American depopulation that occurred. One does not encounter in the primary sources on northwestern frontier colonial history the sort of impassioned indictments of colonial policies that abounded in records of the more densely settled areas of high aboriginal civilization in Meso-America and the central Andes.

This is not to say that a few colonial officials did not perceive that Native American depopulation was occurring. Captain Juan Bautista de Anza, the energetic commandant of the Presidio of Tubac, was one of the few Sonoran frontiersmen to perceive the native population decline and comment on it. His remarks appeared in a report he penned for the viceroy on 15 December 1772. Discussing the missions established in Pimería Alta in his father's time, Anza remarked that "although the natives used to number thousands, today they are reduced to a few hundred. . . . " Even worse, Northern Piman depopulation proceeded "at such a rate" based upon Anza's 20 years of observation, that he estimated that "very few Indians of the Pima nation will remain" within 10 to 15 years if the rate continued. Anza presented the Las Casian explanation for native population decline as the one held commonly in his area. He blamed it upon excessive work and domination in the missions, noting that the decline seemed most rapid in the missions, less so in the branches, and the heathens appeared to increase.[29]

A full generation later, a bureaucrat in the Frontier Provinces headquarters staff at Arizpe also sarcastically demonstrated his awareness of what actually went on when he recommended against a requested reimbursement to Mission San Xavier del Bac. Father Diego Bringas had asked that Bac be reimbursed for the cost of settling 134 Papagos from Aquituni at Tucson Pueblo in 1795.

The staff officer dryly pointed out to the commandant general that the royal grant of 1,000 pesos made to each new mission was expressly destined to meet all of its temporal expenses. Furthermore, royal policy stipulated "that for the fastest possible growth of new missions, the old ones are allowed to aid them with seeds and cattle that they may be able to give without running themselves short." The staff officer then delivered his analytical punch line: "The established missions ought to aid and contribute in this way to the foundation and establishment of new ones. With far greater reason, therefore, should Mission San Xavier del Bac collaborate – as it has done – in its own repopulation and increase, and aid insofar as its funds allow the heathen families that have recently joined it."[30]

There was some element of church-state conflict in this exchange. Father Bringas would have liked to see Tucson Pueblo changed from a branch to a full-fledged mission with its own 1,000-peso foundation grant. Civil officials, on the other hand, sought economy. Even within that continual contest for funds and power, however, it seems today a bit odd that Bringas and the other men of God consistently presented resettlement of Papagos as new triumphs of the Faith, new additions of souls to Christendom, without counting the antecedent acceleration of conversion of Native American bodies into souls. It remained for a skeptical civil official at Frontier Provinces headquarters to come right out and state baldly that the frontier missionaries were doing nothing more than repopulate their own missions in an attempt to maintain the numbers of neophytes and by implication, their royal support.

14.

Population Dynamics at the Tucson Military Post, 1776-1797

BEFORE THE ARRIVAL OF THE SPANIARDS, the lower Santa Cruz River Valley had supported a thriving Northern Piman population. Chapter 9 indicated the ethnic diversity contributed to these Pimas by two groups of Western Apaches who settled in peace at Tucson, but the declining statistics discussed in Chapter 13 showed that the addition of Apaches failed to arrest the Native-American depopulation process. In contrast to the debilitated reproductive ability of the shocked and discouraged Pimas, the fecundity of the Spanish soldiers was impressive. This chapter analyzes this rapid growth of the Spanish and Mestizo population at the royal military post in the context of population trends in other Sonoran settlements.

Spanish colonial policy succeeded not merely in military terms in conquering Native Americans – even Apaches – but also in biological terms. Not only did Christian missionaries convert Native Americans, but the original Christians themselves reproduced at a healthy rate. The contemporary Spanish-speaking population of metropolitan Tucson and southern Arizona stems only in part from Christianized Native Americans who learned to speak Spanish. More basically it descends from Spanish or Mestizo forebears who multiplied mightily during the early years of Hispanic settlement.

Population Trends at Piman Tucson

As already pointed out, Native Americans survived in the Tucson area only by migration and ethnic diversification. In 1774, two years before the presidio was established, Piman Tucson held 239 persons. They already included native-born individuals – the Sobaipuris whom Captain Francisco Elías G. had resettled there in 1762, and the Papagos whom Friar Francisco Garcés had persuaded to move in from the desert. By 1797, the Tucson Pueblo population rose to 289 persons, yet only 78 were riverine natives while 211 were migrant Papagos! The age structure of these Northern Pimans militated against their maintaining their own numbers. Despite a 20.9% increase from 1774 to 1797, Piman Tucson required more Native American migrants, as shown by a drop to 246 persons by 1801.

It seems doubtful that the Peaceful Apache population varied significantly between 1793 and 1797. Thus, approximately 100 Western Apaches may be presumed to have lived near the presidio in 1797.

Friar Pedro de Arriquibar enumerated the Spanish-Mestizo population for which he was responsible late in January of 1797.[1] He listed 395 persons.[2]

Thus, the Tucson *area* population grew from 230 Northern Pimans to some 784 persons of diverse origins by 1797. The major portion of that 228% increase resulted from migration to the area of ethnic groups not previously resident there. Spaniards, Mestizos and Mulattos migrated to Tucson in 1776. Western Apaches arrived in 1793. Papagos migrated there with some frequency. Yet the latter failed to maintain a viable local Northern Piman population at Tucson until 1801 or later.

Comparative Population Reports

No data have been found on Apache fecundity. Data are available, on the other hand, concerning Spanish-Mestizo fecundity at Tucson. These data demonstrate that the military post contained a viable biological population increasingly rapidly in size regardless of immigration. Seven reports from other settlements allow comparison of Tucson with some other 1796–1797 Sonoran populations.

One immediately obvious difference between the Arriquibar and other enumerations of the time is the mode of presentation of population information. Some priests whose enumerations have been located followed the natural family model. Derived from Catholic doctrine, this model historically displaced an earlier household model in reporting on New Spain's population.[3] Nearly half of this group of Sonoran priests emphasized ethnic group membership.

At Mission Tumacacori, Reverend Mariano Bordoy classified individuals as married couples, widowers, widows, bachelors, boys, girls, male and female children, making a distinction between Indians and citizens. As a result, reconstructing families from Bordoy's enumeration is difficult,[4] even though he did emphasize matrimony. Noreña[5] followed the same scheme at Yécora, while Legarra[6] reported *only* ethnic group totals from Cucurpe and Tuape. These priests seemed more interested in what Spicer[7] calls "persistent ethnic groups" or peoples, than in doctrinal families.

More than half of this sample of Sonoran priests paid more attention to the "natural family." Francisco Canales, Franciscan chaplain at the Presidio of Altar, reported only an estimated total of 800 persons in 90 military and 60 civilian families. "All its inhabitants are taken for and reputed to be Spaniards."[8] Arriquibar listed the Tucson population in what appear to be household groups. He placed a male at the head of each group listed, several of them alone. Arriquibar gave the military rank of men on his list, but did not record their marital status. One may infer only that men listed with a woman and children were married.[9] Arriquibar did identify sons, daughters and servants within apparent households. Santisteban[10] explicitly reported the Cocospera population by family groups *familias*), which he classified in ethnic groups. Martínez[11] followed the same format at Pitíc, listing *matrimonios* or married couples, with the husband first, followed by wife and offspring.

Only two of these seven priests really employed the doctrinal "natural family" model in enumerating the mission and presidial populations at the end of the 18th century. Two used the old household model, one used a matrimonial model and two used ethnic group models. It would appear that the bishop's instructions left each priest a good deal of leeway in his reporting, and that the men in the missions, presidios and parishes were unfamiliar with a common model for population reporting.

Bordoy systematically indicated the ethnic origin of each individual he listed at ethnically complex Tumacacori Mission, whether Pima, Papago, Apache, Yaqui, Opata, Yuma or Spanish.[12] The Tumacacori Mission population included more ethnic groups than that reported for any of the other missions. Legarra identified only Native Americans at Tuape, but Spaniards, Mestizos and Mulattos at Cucurpe. Both Noreña at Yécora and Martínez at Pitíc listed Spaniards as well as Native Americans – Pimas in the former instance, and Seris in the latter. Although he refused to send the bishop enumerations of residents, Reverend Joseph N. de Messa listed Yaquis at Torim, Vicam, Bacum and Cocorim; Yaquis and seven citizens at Virivis, and Pimas and Guaymas at Belem.[13] Outside the missions, a different motivation led secular clergymen to report differently. At Bacuvirito, Licenciado Sepulveda subordinated population figures to his fee-income totals. He identified Native Americans at the Pueblo of Bacuvirito only. Those living in the placer camps Sepulveda lumped with "Spaniards, Mestizos and Mulattos" as "confessing souls receiving communion" and paying fees. He noted Native Americans separately only because he performed the sacraments for them gratis, "from the bucket" as he put it. Otherwise Sepulveda distinguished only between adults and children.[14] Appendix Table 15 compares the ethnic composition of this small sample of Sonoran settlements in 1796–1797.

Arriquibar furnished no ethnic identification for individuals on his list.[15] The Appendix Table 15 listing of the Tucson population as "Spaniards" is a courtesy decision, therefore, and placing it in the Mestizo-Mulatto column would probably be more accurate. The lack of ethnic identifications on Arriquibar's list of Tucson residents shows that it was not comprehensive. There is rather abundant evidence that Spaniards at the frontier missions and military posts very often utilized captive Indians as domestic servants, as civilian Spaniards at Bac and Tucson Pueblo did in 1801. In fact, so general was this practice in Sonora that the specific term "Nixora" was employed in that province to designate such captives.[16] It appears doubtful, therefore, whether all 19 servants listed by Arriquibar were Spaniards. That they were detribalized Native Americans seems much more likely.

The lack of ethnic identification on Arriquibar's list raises a point of a different order concerning the completeness of his enumeration of the actual population of the Tucson area. Arriquibar listed no Apaches, or none that can be so identified. Thus, his enumeration was in fact not a complete listing of the total population of the area. Arriquibar included only members of the presidial garrison and related persons among those he considered his parishioners. His list excluded both the *Apaches de Paz* living near the fort and missionized Northern Piman-speaking Native Americans across the Santa Cruz River at Tucson Pueblo. While the missionary at San Xavier del Bac

Mission cared for the Northern Pimans at the Pueblo of Tucson and assumed responsibility for the Peaceful Apaches, one might have expected Arriquibar to at least mention the latter. Chaplain Canales was more explicit about the Altar Post, certainly. On the one hand, "Indians have never been established in this Presidio." On the other, Canales described his chaplaincy, which "extends only to the Presidio of Santa Gertrudis del Altar, without other additions of Missions, ranches or haciendas and without embracing any other district or territory."

Undoubtedly this was similar to Arriquibar's perception of his responsibility at the Tucson post. Nonetheless, Arriquibar served in an inter-ethnic area of greater complexity than did Canales. The latter had earlier reported that: "The citizenry cannot be reported precisely because of its proximity to the Mission towns. Sometimes they move from the towns to the Presidio; on other occasions they move from the Presidio to the towns."[17]

Clearly the Arriquibar enumeration of Tucson's population was not a "census" as it has been labeled more than once, for the priest ignored the Native American population of the Tucson area. Colonial census-taking never achieved real success in New Spain. On the other hand, enumerations of parts of the Tucson population similar to that by Arriquibar were made earlier than 1797.

After the reforms Charles III of Spain instituted in his colonial frontier forces, particularly the New Regulations promulgated in 1772,[18] senior army officers periodically visited the Tucson post on inspection tours. An inspection report on a Spanish royal garrison is a lengthy and fairly detailed document. Several of these concerned with the Tucson garrison survive in the national archives of Spain and Mexico. This author[19] has already published one list of officers and men in the Tucson garrison in December of 1778 contained in the 1779 review of Colonel Roque de Medina, also included in this volume. Because the review listed soldiers by name in order to report their economic status – whether they owed the garrison treasury or had money due them – this list can be taken as a reliable record of the military population of the post. A similar report by Colonel Hugh O'Connor listed members of the company at Tubac just before it moved to Tucson. These antedate the Arriquibar listing as post population enumerations.

Even earlier Captain Joseph Díaz del Carpio enumerated the Northern Pimans living at Tucson in 1752 (see Appendix Table 11). That is the earliest known enumeration of Native American population at Tucson. The Arriquibar 1797 enumeration is the first known listing of civilian population related to the post, inasmuch as inspection reports listed only military personnel. It is not, however, a census nor the earliest known enumeration of the Tucson population.

When the bishop of Sonora sent out his circulars asking his priests to report on population, he may well have had in mind receiving something along the lines of a modern census of population. Yet all the priests' reports thus far located leave something to be desired in this respect, especially in their lack of uniform reporting. Still, the reports allow analysis of population trends.

Tucson and Tumacacori

Earlier this author[20] analyzed Native American depopulation in the Santa Cruz River Valley settlements during the 18th century and Spanish fecundity at the Tubac military post that helped to insure permanency to Hispanic settlement in what is now southern Arizona.[21] The differential survival of Native American and European populations in this valley makes comparison of the Tumacacori and Tucson population enumerations of interest, as these formed the northernmost finger of imperial settlement in northwestern Sonoran Indian country along with the Pima Indian Company at Tubac.

Despite differences in reporting between Bordoy at Tumacacori and Arriquibar at Tucson, their enumerations yield information on differential population pyramids in Tumacacori and Tucson. This evidence is of the soundest type, moreover, inasmuch as neither priest was a demographer and we are converting them into what McCall[22] has labeled "witnesses in spite of themselves." It is this category of evidence in which historians have come to repose more confidence than in narratives written to influence readers considering the topic discussed.

It is possible to identify children in both enumerations, as differentiated from married couples, widows and widowers, although with less certainty in the Tucson than the Tumacacori enumeration. The bachelors, spinsters and children in Bordoy's list[23] amounted to 36% of the total reported population of 102. Inasmuch as Bordoy gave the age of each person, it is possible to see that his bachelors ranged up to 24 years of age. At Southern Piman Yécora, bachelors, spinsters and children comprised exactly half of the Native American population Noreña reported, but the sample is very small. Appendix Table 16 compares the youthfulness of people at five Sonoran settlements.

The children Arriquibar listed with couples amounted to 40% of the population he enumerated, 158 of 395 individuals listed.[24] Because Arriquibar did not give the ages of persons on his list, it is impossible to differentiate widowers from bachelors. The Tucson percentage is, therefore, an underestimate compared to the Tumacacori percentage. There are 28 single men on Arriquibar's list. If all are counted as bachelors, this makes the bachelor-spinster-child group in Tucson 47% of its enumerated population.

The true figure for Tucson lies, in other words, between 40 and 47% of the total enumerated population. This is not a great difference from Tumacacori's 36%. Yet it is a sufficient difference to afford one more perspective on the differential dynamics of population trends in the aboriginal population of the Santa Cruz River Valley, even reinforced with Apache, Yuma and Papago replacements, as compared to the Hispanic settlers. The Spanish-Mestizo population was relatively younger, so better able to reproduce itself.

Fecundity at Tucson

Arriquibar listed at Tucson 3 commissioned officers, 9 non-commissioned officers, 6 carbineers, 1 armorer, 2 cadets and 39 enlisted men, for a total of 60 men in the garrison. The families and servants of the 60 members of the unit raised the total population of the post and its direct dependents to 223 persons. Twelve members of the garrison were listed as single. The 48 listed as having families had a total of 163 wives, children and servants reported. This meant that the average military household in Tucson included 4.4 persons at that time. The average military nuclear family size was 4.2 individuals, excluding the servants included in the household figure.

This compares with 4.69 persons per household in the Peruvian Indian agricultural population at Vicos in 1952, and 4.56 persons per household there in 1963, when the total population grew at approximately 1.5% annually.[25] Inferentially, the Tucson growth rate in 1797 was slightly but not greatly lower than the modern Vicos rate, which occurred under health conditions not much different from those in Tucson at the end of the 18th century.

Appendix Table 17 compares household average size in the various ethnic groups in Cocospera, Tumacacori and Pitíc Missions with the Tucson presidial situation at the same time, plus Altar presidio. Only the small colony of Spaniards at the Pitíc Seri Mission and the Altar post families exceeded the Tucson garrison households in average size, indicating the significant differential between Spanish families and native Sonoran Indian families in biological reproductive rates in 1796–1797. The coincidence between the Spanish and Northern Piman household sizes at Cocospera, where Santisteban reported that Native American population had been falling, suggests important differences between mission and presidial environments, the Cocospera and Tucson environments, and/or migration.

Even with the 20% unmarried men in the Tucson garrison, the post population was being more than reproduced by the wives of married soldiers. Tucson's population was growing, in other words, if emigration were balanced by immigration, simply on the basis of the fecundity of garrison spouses, without even taking the civilian population into account. This is clear not only from the average family size, but also from fecundity figures. The 47 women in existing marital unions in the post population in 1797 had produced 105 living children when Arriquibar made his enumeration, an average of 2.2 each. This figure leaves out of account others who had emigrated or established independent households in Tucson, because such cases cannot be identified from the Arriquibar list. In other words, only 21 years after the post was founded, it could maintain and increase its own population. Gross fecundity was undoubtedly considerably higher than the figures given here, inasmuch as Arriquibar enumerated only surviving children still in households at the time, giving no clues as to the prevalence of miscarriages, still-births, and the infant mortality rate.

That miscarriages and other factors depressed fecundity is suggested by the presence of 11 wives, or 23.4% of those enumerated, who had no living children recorded. This number probably included young wives yet to enter their child-bearing years, and older women past child-bearing age, but the proportion does suggest some degree of sterility.

The 36 women, or 76.6% of the garrison mates enumerated, were fecund enough to more than reproduce the adult population. Twelve of these wives had three living children enumerated, and another dozen had two living children. Eight had four children, and two wives had only a single living child still in the household. On the other hand, one wife had five and one had six children at home. This amounted to an average fecundity of 2.9 children per fertile wife in 1797, which must be taken as a rather minimal figure inasmuch as it does not count any older children of these women who might already have left home. This fecundity rate suggests the possibility of a 50% increase in the local population of each child-bearing generation, without immigration from farther south in New Spain.

The apparent sex ratio of children born by women in the Tucson post seems to have been nearly equal. The living children Arriquibar recorded in military garrison families included 52 boys and 53 girls. Appendix Table 18 compares the tertiary sex ratio of the total Tucson population Arriquibar enumerated with 1796 ratios for Spaniards elsewhere in Sonora and three Native American samples. This comparison suggests that the Pima Bajo of Yécora were capable of significant increase by 1796 as were the Spaniards at Cocospera and Tucson, although the nature of the latter settlement as a military post with more single males than a civilian settlement would have masked its biological potential.

Given the small size of the Yécora Mission population reported, the suspicion arises that its sex ratio may well be a product of differential residence at the mission and the scattered Pima Bajo rancherías roundabout, rather than a reflection of the actual total population. Yet the Pima Bajo may have passed their population nadir by 1797 and been recovering numbers.

Successful biological adjustment to life at Tucson and Altar stands in striking contrast to the continued high rate of Native American mortality, low Native American fecundity and Native American population decline reported from Tumacacori and Cocospera and implied in the enumerations elsewhere. This difference between the Spanish or Spanish-Mestizo population, and the Native American populations in their susceptibility to infectious diseases explains in large part why Spain was able to establish and to maintain a permanent outpost of Western Civilization and colonial military power at Tucson at the farther boundary of friendly Native American territory and the hostile edge of inimical Apache country. Biological differences in disease resistance expressed in fecundity rates ultimately determined the cultural characteristics of the population of the Tucson area.

Part IV
Supplementary Data

Contents of Appendix

TABLES, INVENTORIES AND CHARTS

Tables

Inventories of Chapel Furnishings

Charts

Appendix: Tables, Inventories and Charts

TABLE 1

Fifteen U.S. Cities With More Than 5,000 Native American Inhabitants in 1970

Place (SMSA)*	Population	Native Americans	Percent Native American
Los Angeles-Long Beach	7,032,075	24,509	0.3
Tulsa	476,945	15,519	3.3
Oklahoma City	640,889	13,033	2.0
New York	11,571,899	12,160	0.1
San Francisco-Oakland	3,109,519	12,011	0.4
Phoenix	967,522	11,159	1.2
Minneapolis-St. Paul	1,813,647	9,852	0.5
Seattle-Everett	1,421,869	9,496	0.7
Chicago	6,978,947	8,996	0.1
Tucson	**351,667**	**8,837**	**2.5**
San Bernardino-Riverside-Ontario	1,143,146	6,378	0.6
San Diego	1,357,854	5,880	0.4
Albuquerque	315,774	5,839	1.8
Detroit	4,199,931	5,683	0.1
Dallas	1,555,950	5,002	0.3

SOURCE: U.S. Bureau of the Census 1972, 1-324-26.
*SMSA = Standard Metropolitan Statistical Area

TABLE 2

United States Counties With Over 20,000 White Inhabitants With Spanish Surnames in 1950

Rank	County	State	Spanish-Surname Population
1.	Los Angeles	California	287,614
2.	Bexar	Texas	176,877
3.	Hidalgo	Texas	112,422
4.	El Paso	Texas	89,555
5.	Cameron	Texas	81,080
6.	Nueces	Texas	58,939
7.	Webb	Texas	47,525
8.	Bernalillo	New Mexico	43,729
9.	Maricopa	Arizona	42,560
10.	Harris	Texas	39,171
11.	Alameda	California	35,578
12.	San Bernardino	California	35,330
13.	Santa Clara	California	35,306
14.	Fresno	California	32,678
15.	San Francisco	California	31,433
16.	San Diego	California	28,926
17.	**Pima**	**Arizona**	**27,224**
18.	Denver	Colorado	24,950
19.	Orange	California	23,680
20.	Santa Fé	New Mexico	23,034
21.	Ventura	California	21,697
22.	Doña Ana	New Mexico	20,883
23.	San Miguel	New Mexico	20,524
24.	Río Arriba	New Mexico	20,056

SOURCE: Brunsman 1953, p. 3C-59-70.

TABLE 3

Tubac Troopers Who Later Served at Tucson

Name	Age	Birthplace	Social Class	Credits/Debits*	
José Antonio Ureña	29	–	–	49	–
José Marcos Ramírez	40	Fronteras	Spaniard	20	–
Luis Albiso	37	Real de San Juan	Spaniard	19	–
Pasqual Rivera	33	San Luís	Coyote	18	–
José Antonio Palomino	35	San Luís	Morisco	22	–
Juan Miguel Palomino	31	Tubutama	Morisco	22	–
Juan Angel Castillo	46	San Miguel de Guadalupe	Coyote	20	–
Juan Vicente Martínez	26	Buenavista	Spaniard	23	–
Francisco Xavier Espinosa	31	Fronteras	Spaniard	21	–
Francisco Xavier Figueroa	37	Mátape	Coyote	–	5
José Cayetano Mesa	25	Villa de San Miguel	Spaniard	21	–
Modesto Hilario Santa Cruz	23	Real del Mortero	Spaniard	20	–
Ysidro Martinez	27	San Lorenzo	Morisco	–	5
Juan José Villa	32	Pitíc	Spaniard	22	–
Francisco Xavier Márquez	27	Sinaloa	Mulatto	2	–
Francisco Xavier Díaz	26	San Luís	Spaniard	13	–
José María Sosa	28	Tecori	Spaniard	21	–
Ygnacio Arias	27	México	Spaniard	17	–
Juan José Medina	28	Santa Ana	Coyote	18	–
Andrés Salazar	25	Mistepori	Coyote	12	–
José Domingo Granillo	21	Sopori	Coyote	21	–
Miguel Zamora	42	Sinaloa	Coyote	–	8
José Manuel Ayala	42	Villa de Leon	Coyote	22	–
José Ygnacio Martínez	28	San Juan	Coyote	11	–
Juan de Mesa	17	Sinaloa	Spaniard	–	99
Juan Antonio Oliva	19	Tubac	Coyote	–	72
José Ygnacio Zamora	23	Sinaloa	Spaniard	–	63

SOURCES: Social class data from Oliva 13 de Agosto de 1775 No. 3; Financial status data from Oliva 13 de Agosto de 1775 No. 7.
*Credits and debits are rounded to the nearest peso.

TABLE 4

Tucson Garrison Strength in May 1779

Officers	
Captain Don Pedro de Allande	Present
Lieutenant Don Miguel de Urrea	in San Miguel
Ensign Don Diego de Oya	Present
Second Ensign of Light Troops, Don José Francisco de Castro	Present
Chaplain Friar Francisco Perdigon	Present
Armored Troop	
Sergeant José de Tona	1
First Corporals	2
Second Corporals	2
Soldiers	37
Master Armorer	1
Light Troop	
Sergeant Juan Vega	1
Corporals (paid the same as armored troops)	2
Drummer	vacant
Soldiers	17
Indian Scouts	
Corporal	1
Scouts	9
5 officers, 4 present, and	73 troopers

Source: Medina 1779.

TABLE 5

Tucson Company Individual Accounts in 1778

NAMES	Credits† [Pesos]	Debits† [Pesos]
1st Sergeant José de Tona	1	
1st Sgt. Juan de Vegas		3
1st Corporal Joachin Gamunez	1	
1st Corp. Pasqual Ribera*	14	
2d Corp. Francisco Xavier Figueroa*		50
2d Corp. José María Sosa*	50	
3d Corp. José Marcos Ramírez*	1	
3d Corp. Francisco Xavier Espinosa*	1	
Soldiers		
Luis Alviso*	1	
José Antonio Palomino*	107	
Juan Miguel Palomino*	82	
Juan Angel Castillo*	206	
José Caietano Mesa*	54	
Ysidro Martinez*		23
Francisco Xavier Marquez*		34
Francisco Xavier Diaz*		14
Juan José Villa*		
Ygnacio Arias*	17	
Juan Vicente Martinez*	95	
Modesto Hilario Santa Cruz*	46	
Andrés Salazar*	6	
José Domingo Granillo*		2
José Manuel Ayala*	19	
José Ygnacio Martinez*		66
Miguel Zamora*	1	
Fernando Morales	61	
Jose Antonio Treña	165	
Juan de Mesa*	18	
Juan Antonio Oliba*	2	
José Ygnacio Zamora*	76	
Loreto Amezquita	55	
Juan Santos Lopez	30	
Guadalupe Alvarado	1	
Juan Ygnacio Moreno	22	
Juan Simon Vera	78	
Manuel Vicente de Sosa	73	
Pasqual Escalante	3	
Joachin Gallardo	125	
Simon Tapia	149	
Juan Baptista Romero	156	
José Joachin Gongora	7	
Juan José Medina*		36

*Previously served in 1775 Tubac Company.
†Credits and debits are rounded to the nearest peso.

(continued)

TABLE 5 *(continued)*

Tucson Company Individual Accounts in 1778

NAMES	Credits [Pesos]	Debits [Pesos]
Light Troops		
Juan José Tisnado	5	
José Francisco Ribera		32
Blas Antonio Balderrama	13	
José Gerardo Granillo	30	
Juan Miguel Dias	28	
José Procopio Martinez	5	
Sebastian Ygnacio Granillo		19
Francisco Xavier de la Cruz	61	
José Valdés	124	
Gregorio Acuña	62	
Pedro Gamez	59	
Juan José Soto	41	
Antonio Perez	26	
Sebastian Camacho	1	
Ramon Amezquita		9
Antonio Reyes Días		17
Scouts		
Francisco Xavier Miranda*	33	
Ygnacio Soqui*	104	
Salvador Manuel Miranda*		20
Agustín de la Yguera		25
Totals	2,414	445 Pesos
	1	5 reales
	24	04 maravedis

SOURCES: Medina 1779 and Oliva 13 de Agosto de 1775, No. 3 y "Relación."

TABLE 6

Tucson Garrison Strength in November 1782

Captain Don Pedro de Allande	Present
Lieutenant Don Josef María Abate	Present
First Ensign Don Ygnacio Usarraga	Present
Second Ensign Don Juan Antonio Carrillo	Present
Chaplain Don Gabriel Franco	Present
Sergeant Juan Fernandez	1
Another, Josef María Sosa	1
Drummer Juan Gregorio Rios	1
Corporals	4
Carbineers	4
Master Armorer	1
Soldiers	55
5 Officers	67 men

SOURCE: Neve 30 de Noviembre de 1782.

TABLE 7

Tucson Company at 1783 Inspection

Men	Appeared on 1775 Roll	Appeared on 1779 Roll	Commended for May 1782 Act.	Credit† [Pesos]	Debit† [Pesos]
Corporals					
Francisco Usarraga					17
Luis Alvisso	°	°		26	
Francisco Marquez	°	°			25
Ygnacio Arias	°		°	24	
Carbineers					
Mario Santa Cruz				4	
Juan Ramírez					48
Domingo Granillo	°	°	°		55
Juan Oliva	°	°	°		22
Armorer José Ureña	°			41	
Soldiers					
Cadet Don Pedro de Allande					48
Juan Simón Vera		°		16	
Vicente Sosa		°		40	
Bautista Romero		°			9
Joaquín Góngora		°			33
Juan Medina	°	°		8	
Juan Tisnado		°			81
Juan Díaz		°			54
Sevastian Granillo		°			91
Javier Cruz		°			14

†Credits and debits are rounded to the nearest peso.

(continued)

TABLE 7 *(continued)*

Tucson Company at 1783 Inspection

Men	Appeared on 1775 Roll	1779 Roll	Commended for May 1782 Act.	Credit [Pesos]	Debit [Pesos]
Ramón Amesquita		*	*		125
Agustín de la Yguera		*			72
Clemente Mesa					27
Miguel Luque					54
José Chamorro					209
Salvador Miranda		*			54
Francisco Romero					31
Cayetano Canoro					73
Joaquín Berdugo					83
Luis Messa					64
Francisco Castro			*		62
Ygnacio Espinosa					9
Domingo Mesa					150
Juan Ocovoa				15	
Juan Gurrola					18
Javier Castro, first					27
Manuel Ortega					82
Bautista Urquijo					10
Javier Castro, second				10	
Distinguished Don Juan Beldarrain		*	*	17	
Javier Gurrola					67
Procopio Cancio			*		85
Vicente Pacheco			*		44
Martin Mascareno			*		123
Francisco Barreda					24
Francisco Gonzales					63
Joaquin Ortega			*		86
Jose Baldenegro			*		43
Joaquin Acosta					122
Nicolas Anaya					60
Joaquin Lopez					140
Juan de Ortega					18
Simon Soto					104
Manuel Hernandez					108
José Barrera					95
José Ortega					126
Ygnacio Mesa					127
Juan Palomino		*			110
Juan Luque					116
Domingo de la Cruz					53
Juan Castillo		*			62
Juan Bustamante					52
José Tisnado		*			62
Total men reported: 62	7	20	11	205	3,835

SOURCES: Abate 24 de Diciembre de 1783; Medina 1779; Oliva 13 de Agosto de 1775.

TABLE 8

Tucson Garrison Strength in January 1784

Officers	
Captain Don Pedro de Allande	Present
Lieutenant Don José María Abate	Present
First Ensign Don Felix Usarraga	Wounded
Second Ensign Juan Carrillo	Present
Chaplain Don Gabriel Franco	Present
Sergeant Juan Fernandez	1
Sgt. José María Sosa	1
Drummer Juan Gregorio Ríos	1
Corporals	4
Carbineers	4
Armorer Jose Ureña in prison	1
Soldiers	53
5 officers	65 men

SOURCE: Medina 15 de Enero de 1784.

TABLE 9

Tucson Garrison Strength In October 1785

Officers	
Commander, Lt. Col. Don Pedro de Allande y Saabedra	Present
Lieutenant Don Francisco Barrios	Present
First Ensign	Vacant
Second Ensign Don Pedro María de Allande	Present
Chaplain	Vacant
Sergeant Josef María Sosa	1
Sg.t Francisco Márquez	1
Drummer Juan Gregorio Ríos	1
Corporals	4
Carbineers	4
Armorer	1
Soldiers	51
Sick Soldiers	2
3 officers	65 men

SOURCE: Medina 6 de Octubre de 1785.

TABLE 10

Tucson Garrison Strength on 1 January 1817

Company of the Royal Presidio of San Agustín del Tucson, Province of Sonora, First Day of the Month of January of 1817. List and Summary of the Review I, Don Manuel Ygnacio de Arvizu, Lieutenant Colonel (Brevet) and Captain of Said Company Made of the Officers, Troops and Invalids of Which It Is Composed.

	RANKS	NAMES	ASSIGNMENTS
	Captain, Brevet Lt. Col.	D. Manuel Ygnacio Arvizu	Present
	Lieutenant	D. Manuel de León	Present
	1st Ensign	D. José María Elías Gonzáles	In Nueva Vizcaya
	2d Ensign		Vacant
	Chaplain	Friar Pedro Ariquivar	Sick
	Armorer	Ambrosio Araisa	Present
	Drummer	Francisco Usarraga	Present
Bonuses in reales			
135	Sgt. and Bvt. Ensign	D. Manuel Ortega	in Tubac
90	Sgt.	D. José María Gonzáles	sick
6	Sgt.	D. Loreto Ramírez	remount herd
9	Corporal Bvt. Sgt.	D. Salvador Gallegos	on the Coast
90	Corp.	D. Bicente Rodriguez	Present
6	Corp.	D. Ygnacio Marín	Pack-train
	Corp.	D. Antonio Ramírez	On the Coast
	Distinguished	D. Leonardo Leanor	running remount herd
9	Carbineer	D. Pedro Bega	On the Coast
6	Carbineer	D. Francisco Polanco	Present
	Distinguished	D. Francisco Romero	remount herd
9	Carbineer	D. José Martínes	stationed in Arizpe
6	Carbineer	D. Manuel Orosco	on guard duty
	Carbineer	D. Pedro Ramírez	sick
	Cadet	D. Guillermo Narbona	stationed in Arizpe
		Soldiers	
112		Francisco Romero 1st	with King's cattle
6		Juan Morales	Present
6		Miguel Burrola	on the Coast
6		José Grijalva	Present
6		José Telles	on the Coast
6		Bernardino Mesa	on the Coast
6		Antonio Granillo	pack train
6		Juan María Castro	on the Coast
6		Francisco Pacheco	stationed in Arizpe
6		Santos Sierra	on the Coast
6		Juan Diego Lira	in Bacuachi
6		Bautista Romero	remount herd
		Antonio Carrillo	on the Coast
6		Yldefonso Boxorques	on the Coast
		Mariano Rodriguez	remount herd
		Ylario Andrada	on the Coast

RANKS	NAMES	ASSIGNMENTS
	Guillermo Pacheco	sick
	Pedro Granillo	sick
	Juan Martines	in the Hospital
	Francisco Ortega	on the Coast
	Juan Sisneros	remount herd
	Francisco Morales	Present
	Pedro Cuellar	running remount herd
Bvt. Sgt.	Juan Rodriguez	Sick
	Juan Romero	ordinance
	Francisco Gauna	pack train
	Ramón Federico	in the Hospital
	José Soto	on the Coast
	José Ramíres	remount herd
	Manuel Hernandes	Sick
	Cornelio Elías	Sick
	Pedro Siquieros	pack train
	José Romero	with King's cattle
	Ygnacio Urías	remount herd
Distinguished	Gerónimo de Herran	remount herd
	Vicente Sosa	running remount herd
	José Gallegos	Present
	Francisco Amayo	on the Coast
	José León	Sick
	José Carrisosa	Sick
	Ramón Sortillón	with King's cattle
	Juan Tisnado	Present
	Fernando Ruelas	remount herd
	José Solares	ordinance
	José Luque	running remount herd
	Antonio Cuellar	remount herd
	Francisco Romero 2d	Present
	Juan Morillo	running remount herd
	Juan Miranda	pack train
	Juan Salazar	remount herd
	Julian Baldes	Present
	Ygnacio León	Present
Distinguished	D. Francisco Heran	on guard duty
	José Rangel	running remount herd
	Luis Carrillo	Present
	Nepomuceno Duarte	remount herd
	Juan León	remount herd
	José Mendes	on guard duty
	Juan Urtado	pack train
	Francisco Granillo	Present
	José Siqueiros	on guard duty
	Santiago Urtado	pack train
	Juan Ledesma	Present
	Julian Gales	pack train
	Ramón Romero	remount herd
	Pedro Vega	on guard duty
	Roque Balenzuela	on guard duty

(continued)

TABLE 10 *(continued)*

Tucson Garrison Strength on 1 January 1817

	RANKS	NAMES	ASSIGNMENTS
		José Castillo	Present
		Ramón García	pack train
		Balentín Usarraga	Present
		Alvino Ocoboa	Present
		Ygnacio Castelo	remount herd
		Juan Ygnacio Romero	remount herd
		Eulario Luque	on guard duty
		Narciso Ortega	remount herd
		Juan Martínes	on guard duty
		Francisco Días	remount herd
		Mariano Alegría	remount herd
		Invalids	
90	Corp.	José Tisnado	Present
9		Antonio Gonsales	Present
6		Raimundo Ortega	Present
6		Guillermo Saenz	Present
6		Gregorio Ríos	Present
		Nepomuseno Corales	Present
		Juan Martines	Present
		José Bildusea	Present
		Francisco Granillo	Present
		José Palomino	Present
		Salvador Morales	Present
		Marcos Castro	Present
		Total	12
		Summary	
	Capt. Bvt. Lt. Col.	D. Manuel Ygnacio de Arvizu	Present 1
	Lieutenant	D. Manuel de León	Present 1
	1st Ensign	D. José María Elías Gonzáles	Absent 1
	2d Ensign	D.	Vacant
	Chaplain	Friar Pedro Arriquibar	Present 1
	Armorer	Ambrosio Araisa	Present 1
	Drummer	Francisco Usarraga	Present 1
	Sergeant Bvt. Ensign	D. Manuel Ortega	Absent 1
	Sergeant	José María Gonsales	Absent 1
	Sergeant	Loreto Ramíres	Absent 1
	Corporals		Present 1
	Corporals		Absent 4
	Carbineers		Present 1
	Carbineers		Absent 5
	Soldiers		Present 14
	Soldiers		Absent 65
		Total	92

SOURCE: Arvizu 1 de Enero de 1817.

TABLE 11

Native American Population of Tucson, 1752 Enumerated by Captain Joseph Díaz del Carpio

The Chief, married to Ysavel. He has a son.
Sergeant Antonio, married to María Theresa.
Thomas married to María.
Gregorio married to Ysavel.
Juan married to Savina. He has two sons.
Xaver married to Juana. He has two sons.
A pagan named *Miticri*, married to Anna María.
Francisco married to Juana María.
Juan married to María. They have a son.
Xaveer married to Magdalena.
Lorenzo married to Lucía.
Antonio married to Cristina. They have two sons.
Xaver married to Teresa. They have two sons.
Ygnacio married to Theresa. He has a son.
Pedro married to Ysavel. He has a son.
Juan married to María.
Xaveer married to Lucía.
Carlos married to Juana.
Andrés married to Crestina.
Miguel married to Theresa. They have a son.
Ygnacio married to Michaela. He has a son.
Juan married to Ysavel, two daughters, one pagan.
Juan married to María.
Luis married to María Thereza.
Juan Antonio married to Catharina.
Antonio married to María.
Ygnacio married to María. They have a son, Joseph.
Manuel married to Andrea. They have two sons, Miguel & Marcos.
Juan Miguel married to Josepha. They have a son, Pedro.
Juan Pedro married to Marta, and a daughter Martta.
Xavier married to María. He has a son, Lázaro.
Ygnacio married to María. They have two sons, Pedro & Marcos.
Antonio married to María Antonia, with his son Juan Antonio.
Luis married to María. He has a son Juan Ygnacio.
Santiago married to Martha, one son, Pedro.
Ygnacio married to Josepha, with a daughter Ynes.
Juan married to Juana, with two sons Xavier and Francisco.
Lázaro married to Rosa. They have a son.
Lázaro married to Ysavel, and two sons, one pagan.
Ygnacio married to María, and one son Juan.
Xavier married to Ysavel.
Juan Manuel married to Catharina.
Ygnacio married to Catharina.
There are 20 bachelors 12 years and older. There are 14 spinsters.

SOURCE: Díaz del Carpio 1752, fol. 95-95V.

TABLE 12

Native American Population of Tucson in 1766

Enumeration of the Families That Presently Live in Tuxon,
Branch Pueblo of the Mission of San Xavier del Baca,
Made on 20 February 1766

Married [Men]*	Women	Children
Governor Juan	Anna María	–
Mador Salvador	Theresa	1 child
Fiscal Christoval	Anna María	–
Juan Baptista	Juana	3 children
Christoval	Juana Theresa	–
Joseph	Theresa	–
Esteban	Juana	3 children
Thomas	Rosa María	1 child
Salbador	Anna María	3 children
Lorenzo	Luisa	2 children
Juan Domingo	–	–
Xavier	María	3 children
Nicolás	dead	3 children
Juan	María	–
Andrés	Luisa	3 children
Juan Antonio	Christina	1 child
Francisco	Ysabel	–
Xavier	María	1 child
Joseph	Juana	1 child
Thomas	Ynes María	–
Christobal	–	–
Joseph	Juana	3 children
Manuel	dead	3 children
Cipriano	María	2 children
Xavier	Anna María	2 children
Juanico	–	–
Juan Antonio	Josepha	2 children
Juan María	–	–
Miguel	Ysabel	–
Ygnacio	–	–
Xavier	María	2 children
Juanu	–	–
Juan Antonio	Josepha	2 children
Juan María	–	–
Miguel	Ysabel	–
Ygnacio	–	–
Xavier	María	2 children
Juanico	Josepha	3 children
Ygnacio	María	–
Agustín	María	3 children
Carlos	Juana	2 children
Mathias	Magdalena	2 children

Married [Men]*	Women	Children	
	Widows		
	Magdalena	1 child	
	Luisa	–	
	Guadalupe	–	
	Ynes María	1 child	
	Thomasa	–	
	Juana	–	
	María	1 child	
	Juana	–	
	Nicolasa	–	
42	41	56	Total: 139

SOURCE: (Neve) 20 de Febrero de 1766.
*Although the priest headed this column "married," he listed in it men for whom he did not show wives or children. Thus, "Men" is a more accurate heading.

TABLE 13

Native American Population of Tucson, 1801

Enumeration of the Pueblo Ranch of This Mission, San Agustín del Tucson, Which Lies Three Leagues to the North of This Mission Over a Level Road

	[Residents]	[Tribe*]	[Age]	[Estate]
	Families			
1.	Joseph Castro	Pima	41	Married man
	Regina Flores	Pima	19	married woman
2.	Xavier Cardona	Papago	56	married man
	Ysabel Ronda	Papaga	59	married woman
	Francisco Cardona	Papago	12	bachelor
	Getrudes Cardona	Papaga	09	girlchild
3.	Eusebio Villaplana	Gileño	47	married man
	Ana María Reyes	Papaga	65	married woman
4.	Domingo Zuñiga	Papago	38	married man
	Francisca Bueno	Papaga	43	married woman
	Mariano Zuñiga	Papago	03	boychild
5.	Eusebio Jimenez	Papago	59	married man
	Anamaría Mata	Papaga	54	married woman
	Antonio Jimenez	Papago	08	boychild

(continued)

*Llorens distinguished only three "tribes" in the Northern Piman Indian mission population. He lumped all desert-dwellers as "Papago," accurately differentiated Gila River Pimas as "Gileños," and lumped Sobaipuris from both the San Pedro and Santa Cruz River Valleys, and perhaps other riverine natives, as "Pima." His lumping masked actual tribal affiliations.

TABLE 13 *(continued)*

Native American Population of Tucson, 1801

	[Residents]	[Tribe*]	[Age]	[Estate]
6.	Pedro Bustamante	Pima	38	married man
	Guadalupe Anzar	Papaga	33	married woman
	Bautista Anzar	Papago	09	boychild
	Juana Bustamante	Pima	01	girlchild
7.	Ygnacio Trinidad	Pima	19	married man
	Teresa Villaplana	Papaga	17	married woman
	Francisco Villaplana	Papago	11	bachelor
8.	Ygnacio Reyes	Papago	36	married man
	Guadalupe Sortillón	Papaga	31	married woman
9.	Antonio Díaz	Papago	72	married man
	Juana Flores	Papaga	76	married woman
10.	Vicente Lorenza	Pima	47	married man
	María Galbez	Papaga	45	married woman
11.	Miguel Bueno	Pima	43	married man
	Anamaría Delfin	Pima	39	married woman
12.	Pablo Díaz	Gileño	21	married man
	Josepha Buno	Pima	18	married woman
13.	Pedro Solá	Pima	49	married man
	Cristina Galbes	Papaga	43	married woman
	Francisca Solá	Pima	09	girlchild
14.	Felipe Solá	Pima	18	married man
	Felipa Llorena	Papaga	16	married woman
15.	Joseph Romero	Pima	30	married man
	Anamaría Pachecho	Papaga	29	married woman
	Francisco Pacheco	Papago	09	boychild
15.	Miguel Lorena	Pima	55	married man
	Luisa Tapia	Pima	53	married woman
17.	Ygnacio Lorena	Pima	17	married man
	Ygnacia Redondo	Papaga	14	married woman
18.	Antonio Dorado	Pima	60	married man
	Juliana Alba	Pima	58	married woman
	Petra Dorado	Pima	09	girlchild
19.	Eusebio Rubio	Papago	41	married man
	Getrudis Díaz	Pima	37	married woman
	Juaquín Rubio	Pima	09	boychild
	Francisco Rubio	Pima	00	boychild
20.	Agustín Flores	Pima	42	married man
	Juana Reyes	Papaga	51	married woman
	Pedro Reyes	Papago	09	boychild
	Josepha Reyes	Papaga	07	girlchild
21.	Manuel Compañ	Papago	27	married man
	Concepción Díaz	Gileña	23	married woman
	Jacinto Compañ	Papago	02	boychild
22.	Domingo Díaz	Papago	54	married man
	Francisca Varela	Papaga	33	married woman

	[Residents]	[Tribe*]	[Age]	[Estate]
23.	Francisco Díaz	Pima	29	married man
	Christiana Bueno	Papaga	34	married woman
	Francisco Flores	Pima	07	boychild
24.	Miguel Guesca	Papago	31	married man
	Antonia Castro	Papaga	22	married woman
	María Guesca	Papaga	00	girlchild
25.	Francisco Bueno	Papago	62	married man
	Anamaría Redondo	Papaga	49	married woman
	Patricio Redondo	Papago	05	boychild
26.	Miguel Cardona	Papago	35	married man
	Josepha Pacheco	Papaga	31	married woman
	Cristina Cardona	Papaga	09	girlchild
	Susana Cardona	Papaga	05	girlchild
27.	Bautista Urrea	Papago	37	married man
	Rosa Samaniego	Papaga	30	married woman
	Nicolasa Urrea	Papaga	10	spinster
	Encarnación Urrea	Papaga	04	girlchild
28.	Miguel Castro	Papago	29	married man
	Getrudes Reyes	Papaga	26	married woman
	Joseph Castro	Papago	04	boychild
	Rita Castro	Papaga	00	girlchild
29.	Xavier Zuñiga	Papago	36	married man
	Getrudis Cabañas	Papaga	28	married woman
	Eusebio Zuñiga	Papago	11	bachelor
	Getrudes Zuñiga	Papaga	08	girlchild
	María Zuñiga	Papaga	05	girlchild
	Felipe Zuñiga	Papago	00	boychild
30.	Ygnacio Cabañas	Papago	36	married man
	Anastasia Zuñiga	Papaga	33	married woman
	Pedro Cabañas	Papago	14	bachelor
	Xavier Cabañas	Papago	06	boychild
31.	Pablo Orosco	Papago	30	married man
	Catarina Pacheco	Papaga	34	married woman
	Josepha Orosco	Papaga	09	girlchild
	Lorenzo Orosco	Papago	05	boychild
	Ygnacio Orosco	Papago	00	boychild
32.	Xavier Llorenz	Papago	47	married man
	Teresa Perez	Papaga	44	married woman
	María Llorenz	Papaga	11	spinster
	Antonio Llorenz	Papago	09	boychild
	Pomoceno Llorenz	Papago	00	boychild
33.	Francisco Sn Gil	Papago	41	married man
	Teresa Ríos	Papaga	38	married woman
	Dolores Sn Gil	Papaga	00	girlchild
34.	Siprian Compañ	Papago	42	married man
	Rosa Orosco	Papaga	31	married woman
	Dolores Compañ	Papaga	00	girlchild
35.	Antonio Lorena	Papago	50	married man
	Manuela Arriquibar	Papaga	53	married woman
	Ygnacio Lorena	Papago	12	bachelor
	Teresa Lorena	Papaga	09	girlchild

(continued)

TABLE 13 *(continued)*

Native American Population of Tucson, 1801

	[Residents]	[Tribe*]	[Age]	[Estate]
36.	Cristoval Sn Gil	Papago	56	married man
	Josepha Sotillón	Papaga	49	married woman
	Dolores Sn Gil	Papaga	11	spinster
	Joseph Sn Gil	Papago	09	boychild
	Martín Sn Gil	Papago	05	boychild
	Juana San Gil	Papaga	00	girlchild
37.	Xavier Lorena	Papago	58	married man
	Trinidad Castro	Papaga	50	married woman
38.	Joseph Bustamente	Papago	48	married man
	Juana Belarde	Papaga	39	married woman
	Joseph Bustamente	Papago	11	bachelor
	Getrudis Bustamente	Papaga	09	girlchild
39.	Pedro Sánchez	Papago	55	married man
	Ynes Sn Gil	Papaga	56	married woman
	Manuel Sánchez	Papago	13	bachelor
	Josepha Sánchez	Papaga	10	spinster
	Juana Sánchez	Papaga	06	girlchild
40.	Bernardo Crespo	Papago	60	married man
	Catarina Bojorquez	Papaga	47	married woman
	Antonio Crespo	Papago	12	bachelor
	María Crespo	Papaga	09	girlchild
41.	Xavier Villaplana	Papago	15	married man
	Loreta Belarde	Papaga	14	married woman
42.	Francisco Jimenez	Papago	44	married man
	Lucía Villaplana	Papaga	33	married woman
	Lorenza Jimenez	Papaga	07	girlchild
	Francisco Jimenez	Papago	02	boychild
43.	Antonio Crespo	Papago	28	married man
	Christina Almada	Papaga	24	married woman
	María Crespo	Papaga	02	girlchild
44.	Xavier Castro	Papago	55	married man
	Juana Estrella	Papaga	41	married woman
	Cristoval Castro	Papago	13	bachelor
	Ygnacio Castro	Papago	11	bachelor
	Francisco Castro	Papago	08	boychild
	Nicolasa Castro	Papaga	05	girlchild
45.	Ygnacio Ríos	Papago	20	married man
	Josepha Belarde	Papaga	19	married woman
46.	Miguel Robles	Papago	36	married man
	Rosa Montes	Papaga	41	married woman
47.	Miguel Bustamante	Papago	32	married man
	Rosa Castro	Papaga	29	married woman
48.	Xavier Lorena	Papago	23	married man
	Manuela Bueno	Gileña	21	married woman
49.	Xavier Reyes	Papago	16	married man
	Regina Lorena	Papaga	15	married woman

	[Residents]	[Tribe*]	[Age]	[Estate]
50.	Antonio Cabañas	Papago	24	married man
	Juana Jimenes	Papaga	20	married woman
	Manuela Cabañas	Papaga	00	girlchild
51.	Estevan Mesios	Papago	22	married man
	Ysabel Sn Gil	Papaga	19	married woman
52.	Francisco Almada	Papago	29	married man
	Ygnacia Crespo	Papaga	26	married woman
53.	Miguel Medondo	Papago	19	married man
	Guadalupe Cabañas	Papaga	18	married woman
	Pascuala Medondo	Papaga	00	girlchild
54.	Bautista Bustamante	Papago	59	married man
	Rosa Montes	Papaga	55	married woman
	Ygnacio Bustamante	Papago	13	bachelor
	Francisco Bustamante	Papago	11	bachelor
55.	Joseph Orosco	Papago	43	married man
	Anamaría Sánchez	Papaga	41	married woman
	Baustista Orosco	Papago	09	boychild
	Antonio Orosco	Papago	06	boychild
56.	Xavier Compañ	Papago	68	married man
	Josepha Perez	Papaga	63	married woman
57.	Eusebio Belarde	Papago	49	married man
	María Arriquibar	Papaga	44	married woman
	Lázaro Belarde	Papago	12	bachelor
	Catarina Belarde	Papaga	06	girlchild
58.	Marcos Pacheco	Papago	32	married man
	Gracia Belarde	Papaga	29	married woman
	Getrudis Pacheco	Papaga	04	girlchild
59.	Felipe Zuñiga	Papago	53	married man
	Ysabel Llorenz	Papaga	47	married woman
	Mariana Zuñiga	Papaga	11	spinster
	Francisca Llorenz	Papaga	08	girlchild
	Magdalena Zuñiga	Papaga	06	girlchild
60.	Salvador Llorenz	Papago	38	married man
	Josepha Soler	Papaga	52	married woman
	Josepha Llorenz	Papaga	13	spinster
61.	Pedro Ríos	Papago	36	married man
	Carmen Cabañas	Papaga	32	married woman
	Lucía Ríos	Papaga	13	spinster
	Miguel Ríos	Papago	11	bachelor
	Regina Ríos	Papaga	06	girlchild
	Antonio Ríos	Papago	02	boychild
	Ysabel Ríos	Papaga	02	girlchild
62.	Nicolás Guesca	Papago	39	married man
	Josepha Zuñiga	Papaga	36	married woman
	Xavier Guesca	Papago	10	boychild
63.	Manuel Ríos	Papago	68	married man
	Micaela Cardona	Papaga	64	married woman
	Xavier Ríos	Papago	42	bachelor
	Siprian Ríos	Papago	30	bachelor

(continued)

TABLE 13 *(continued)*

Native American Population of Tucson, 1801

	[Residents]	[Tribe*]	[Age]	[Estate]
64.	Miguel Pacheco	Papago	49	married man
	María Escalante	Papaga	59	married woman
	Ygnacio Almada	Papago	16	bachelor
	Francisco Almada	Papago	13	bachelor
65.	Juan Samaniego	Papago	24	married man
	Luisa Cardona	Papaga	26	married woman
	Antonio Cardona	Papago	02	boychild
	Single Individuals			
	Francisco Gutierrez	Papago	56	widower
	Felipe Gutierrez	Papago	14	bachelor
	Xavier Gutierrez	Papago	11	bachelor
	Dolores Gutierrez	Papaga	03	girlchild
	Antonio Castro	Gileño	55	widower
	Luis Rubio	Papago	83	widower
	Ygnacio Urrea	Papago	49	widower
	Teresa Urrea	Papaga	11	spinster
	Miguel Urrea	Papago	06	boychild
	Miguel Castro	Papago	69	widower
	Miguel Velarde	Papago	57	widower
	Ygnacio Belarde	Papago	15	bachelor
	Francisco Belarde	Papago	06	boychild
	Francisco Zuñiga	Papago	78	widower
	Xavier Orosco	Papago	61	widower
	Nicolás Orosco	Papago	17	bachelor
	Bernardino Pacheco	Gileño	23	bachelor
	Salvador Lorena	Papago	32	bachelor
	Juana Urrea	Papaga	71	widow
	Eusebio Urrea	Papago	15	bachelor
	Rosa Lorena	Papaga	57	widow
	Pedro Samaniego	Papago	15	bachelor
	Rosa Villaplana	Papaga	76	widow
	Eusebio Villaplana	Gileño	17	bachelor
	Lucía Montes	Papaga	78	widow
	Cristoval Bueno	Pima	08	boychild
	Ynes Arriquibar	Papaga	41	widow
	Agustín Lorena	Papago	15	bachelor
	Josepha Lorena	Papaga	13	spinster
	Manuel Lorena	Papago	10	boychild
	Getrudes Lorena	Papaga	08	girlchild
	Diego Lorena	Papago	06	boychild
	María Orosco	Papaga	88	heathen
	María Sinarituz	Papaga	90	heathen

SOURCE: Llorens 12 de Diciembre de 1801, ff. 3v-10v.

TABLE 14

Population of Bac and Tucson, 1801

There Follows the Enumeration of the Citizens Who Reside in This Mission [of San Xavier del Bac] and Its Pueblos

	[Residents]	Nationality	Age	Estate
Families				
1.	Ygnacio Gauna	Spaniard	27	married man
	Fermina Burgue.s	Spaniard	41	married woman
	Getrudes Gauna	Spaniard	12	spinster
	Ventura Gauna	Spaniard	12	spinster
	Ramona Gauna	Spaniard	03	girlchild
	Augustín Gauna	Spaniard	01	boychild
	Miguel Gauna	Yuma	10	boychild
2.	Xavier Usarraga	Spaniard	52	married man
	Dolores Azedo	Spaniard	46	married woman
	Marcial Usarraga	Yuma	09	boychild
	Luz Usarraga	Yuma	08	girlchild
	Juan Sisneros	Coyote*	17	bachelor
3.	Patricio de León	Coyote	26	married man
	Guadalupe Martinez	Coyota	29	married woman
	Joseph de León	Coyote	17	bachelor
	Jeronima de León	Coyota	02	girlchild
4.	Gregorio Barrios	Mestizo	31	married man
	Loreta Martinez	Mulatta	35	married woman
	Ysidora Barrios	Mestiza	13	spinster
	María Barrios	Mestiza	06	girlchild
	Francisca Barrios	Mestiza	01	girlchild
5.	Valentín Carrisosa	Coyote	57	married man
	Ylaria Nostroza	Coyota	49	married woman
	Joseph Carrisosa	Coyote	17	bachelor
6.	Pedro Ríos	Spaniard	26	married man
	Josepha Saiz	Spaniard	20	married woman
	Ramona Ríos	Spaniard	04	girlchild
	Joseph Ríos	Spaniard	00	boychild
	Benito Ríos	Yuma	07	boychild
[Single Individuals]				
	Carmen Romero	Coyota	62	widow
	Ygnacio Pacheco	Coyote	27	bachelor
	Manuel Pacheco	Yuma	11	bachelor
	Joseph Pacheco	Yuma	12	bachelor
	Barbara Romero	Yuma	08	girlchild
	Dominga Rodrigues	Mulatta	52	widow
	Ygnacio Ortega	Mulatto	18	bachelor
	Dolores Gastelum	Spaniard	53	spinster
	Antonio Soto Mayor	Spaniard	12	bachelor
	Guadalupe Gastelum	Yuma	08	girlchild

SOURCE: Llorens 12 de Diciembre de 1801. ff. 3v-10v.
*See discussion of term *Coyote,* Chapter 2.

TABLE 15

Ethnic Composition of Eight Sonoran Settlements, 1796–1797

Settlement	Total Reported	Piman	Apache	Yaqui	Opata	Yuma (●) or Seri (■)	Mestizo or Mulatto	Spaniards
		PERCENTAGE OF RESPECTIVE GROUPS						
Tucson	395							100.0
Altar	800							100.0
Tumacacori	102	62.7	1.0	11.8	1.0	1.0●		2.9
Cocospera	138	44.9		12.3				42.8
Cucurpe	521				49.1		43.4	7.5
Tuape	151				100			
Pitíc	234					87.2■		12.8
Yécora	60	86.7						13.3

SOURCES: Tucson, Collins 1970; Altar, Canales 5 de Agosto de 1796; Tumacacori, Whiting 1953; Cocospera, Santiesteban 9 de 7bre de 1796; Cucurpe and Tuape, Legarra 14 de Octubre de 1796; Pitíc, Martínez 11 de Octubre de 1796; Yécora, Noreña 20 de Octubre de 1796.

TABLE 16

Proportion of Unmarried Youths in Sonoran Populations, 1796–1797

(Bachelors, Spinsters & Children)

Settlement	Total	Natives*	Spaniards	Youths	Percent
Tucson	395			158	40.0
Tumacacori	102			37	36.0
		64		30	46.9
		12†		4	33.3
Cocospera	144			62	43.1
		68		30	44.1
		17†		6	35.3
			59	26	44.1
Pitíc Mission	204			112	54.9
			30	21	70.0
Yécora	52			26	50.0

SOURCES: Data in this table are drawn from Collins 1970 for Tucson; Whiting 1953 for Tumacacori; Santiesteban 9 de Setiembre de 1796 for Cocospera; Martínez 11 de Octubre de 1796 for Pitíc, and Noreña 20 de Octubre de 1796 for Yécora.

*"Natives" are Northern Pimans at Tucson, Tumacacori and Cocospera and Southern Pimans at Yécora and Seris at Pitíc.

†Yaquis.

TABLE 17

Average Household Size in Selected Sonoran Settlements, 1796–1797

Settlement	Ethnic Group	House-holds	Number of Persons	Average per Household
Tucson Post	"Spaniards"	48	211*	4.4
	"Spaniards"	48	192†	4.2†
Altar Post	"Spaniards"	150	800	5.3
Cocospera	N. Piman	18	62	3.44
	Spaniards	17	59	3.47
	Yaquis	6	17	2.83
Pitíc Mission	Seris	50	182	3.64
	Spaniards	5	30	6.0
Tumacacori	N. Pimans	22	72	3.27
	Yaquis	4	12	3.0
Totals	"Spaniards"	220	1,100	5.0
	Seris	50	182	3.64
	N. Pimans	40	134	3.35
	Yaquis	10	29	2.9

SOURCES: Data in this table are drawn from Collins 1970 for Tucson; Canales 5 de Agosto de 1796 for Altar; Santiesteban 9 de Setiembre de 1796 for Cocospera; Martínez 11 de Octubre de 1796 for Pitíc; Whiting 1953 for Tumacacori.

*Including servants.

†Family only.

TABLE 18

Tertiary Sex Ratios in Selected Sonoran Settlements, 1796–1797*

Settlement	Males	Females	Ratio Males/Females
Tucson Presidio	221	174	127.0
Tumacacori Mission			
Northern Piman	49	34	144.1
Yaqui	7	5	140.0
Cocospera Mission			
Northern Piman	34	34	100.0
Spaniards	28	31	90.3
Yaqui	11	6	183.3
Pitíc Mission			
Seri	102	101	100.9
Spaniards	15	15	100.0
Yécora Mission			
Southern Piman	23	29	79.3

SOURCES: Collins 1970 for Tucson; Whiting 1953 for Tumacacori; Santiesteban 9 de Setiembre de 1796 for Cocospera; Martínez 11 de Octubre de 1796; Noreña 20 de Octubre de 1796 for Yécora, provided data for this table.

*Figures represent entire enumerated populations.

INVENTORY 1

Itemized List of The Vessels of This Church of the Royal Post of Tucson [1797]

Royal Post of San Agustín del Tucson. January 21, 1797.
Friar Pedro de Arriquibar, Chaplain

Silver

A regular silver chalice with its paten and spoon
A new silver monstrance sent from Mexico by
Captain Don Pedro Allande y Saabedra
A censor with its incense vessel and spoon
Some wine and water cruets with their plate and a handbell

White Cloths

Two well-used albs of fine linen with their amices
Two altar cloths of Brabant linen
Two pairs of double corporals
One short-sleeved sobrepellice with its consecrated stone and four purificators

Chasubles

Two regular chasubles of all colors
One black chasuble with stole, etc.

One white cope with its stole
One black cope with its stole
An antependium of all colors with its pall
Another black antependium with its appropriate pall
One pallium with which to administer the viaticum
One Altar with one small Holy Christ
Two bronze candlesticks
One box where the vestments are kept
One adobe confessional with wooden lattice

SOURCE: Arriquibar 21 de Enero de 1797.

INVENTORY 2

Inventory of the Sacred Vessels, Vestments and Other Valuables Which the Chapel of the Royal Post of Tucson Contains [1820]

Tucson. August 6, 1820. Fr. Pedro de Arriquibar

Wrought Silver

First, one chalice with its paten and spoon*
One monstrance of good workmanship and size*
One gilded cibary and a shell for baptisms
One censor with its incense vessel and spoon*
One plate with its wine and water cruets and handbell*

Main Altar

One Altar lined with coarse linen, of good proportion
One large tabernacle with its key
Five full-round saints of good sculpture
Six small pictures of various saints in their frames
One canvas of the most Holy Virgin of Piety with its gilt frame
Six medium metal candlesticks
Two large, old candlesticks*
Two gilt missal stands with the hymnal and Gospel of St. John
One Holy Christ in half-round and one emplifier
One coarse linen and dressed sheepskin dyed red to cover the altar
One floor carpet of small cords at the foot of the altar
On the Epistle side it has a small, bare altar with an image of the Most Holy Mother of Sorrows and a full-round Holy Christ
On the Gospel side it has another altar without more decoration than an ancient canvas with various painted saints

Sacristy

One table which serves for vesting, with its old covering and a small Holy Christ
One large trunk and a marked box with its keys, and the following:
One pallium in colors, halfway serviceable for the viaticum and processions*
One colored chasuble with its antependium, all already old*
One black chasuble with silver lace and antependium of the same
One colored chasuble with its antependium of the same*
Another purple chasuble with its antependium of the same
Another old red chasuble without antependium
Four altar cloths, white, black, and colored
One well-used colored cope
Three albs, two good and the other old
Another black cope for burials
Five double corporals with their purificators and Ornaments pertaining thereto
Two cloths for the altar, one missal, and one Roman Manual
Two gilt wooden candlesticks on poles with their cross of the same
One napkin which serves for communion and viaticum
One copper holy water pot and its sprinkler of the same
One short-sleeved surplice* and one wooden wafer-box
One iron mold for making wafers, and a chair

Baptistry

One copper baptismal font with its key
One shell of the same
One silver holy oil vial with its little box of the same

Chapel of the Virgin

One large image of Our Lady of Guadalupe with its gilt frame and various personages painted at her feet in devout postures
One medium tabernacle with its key
One small altar and a coarse linen to cover the altar
Four pictures of saints in their gilt frames
One oil-painted antependium and a chandelier
One confessional with two lath lattices*
Another confessional in the body of the church
One wooden pulpit with its stairs of the same
Two holy water fonts

The material structure of this church is of adobes, its roof beamed, and it is small enough inasmuch as it does not hold the people very well, even though in my time there have been added various parts such as the choir loft, baptistry, sacristy, and the Chapel of the Virgin.

SOURCE: Arriquibar 6 de Agosto de 1820.

*Asterisks are Arriquibar's. He probably used them to indicate items which also had appeared on his 1797 inventory.

CHART 1
Diagram of Kinship Relations in the Elías Gonzáles Family

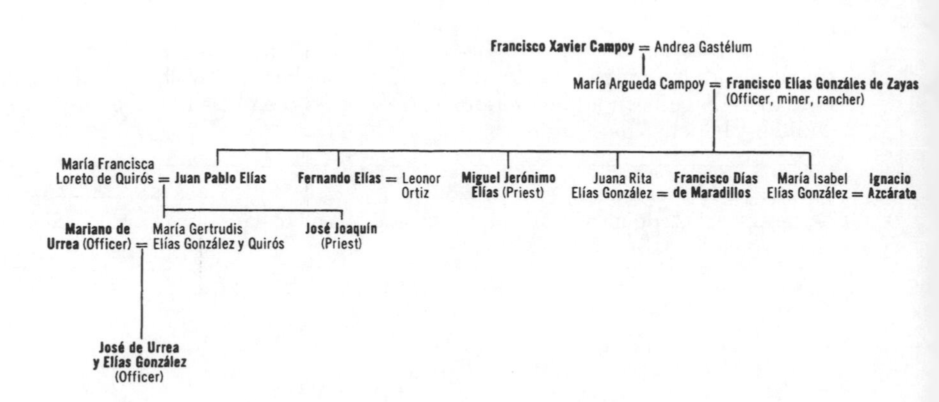

NOTE: Bold Face indicates male.
= indicates marriage
________ indicates siblings
| indicates descent

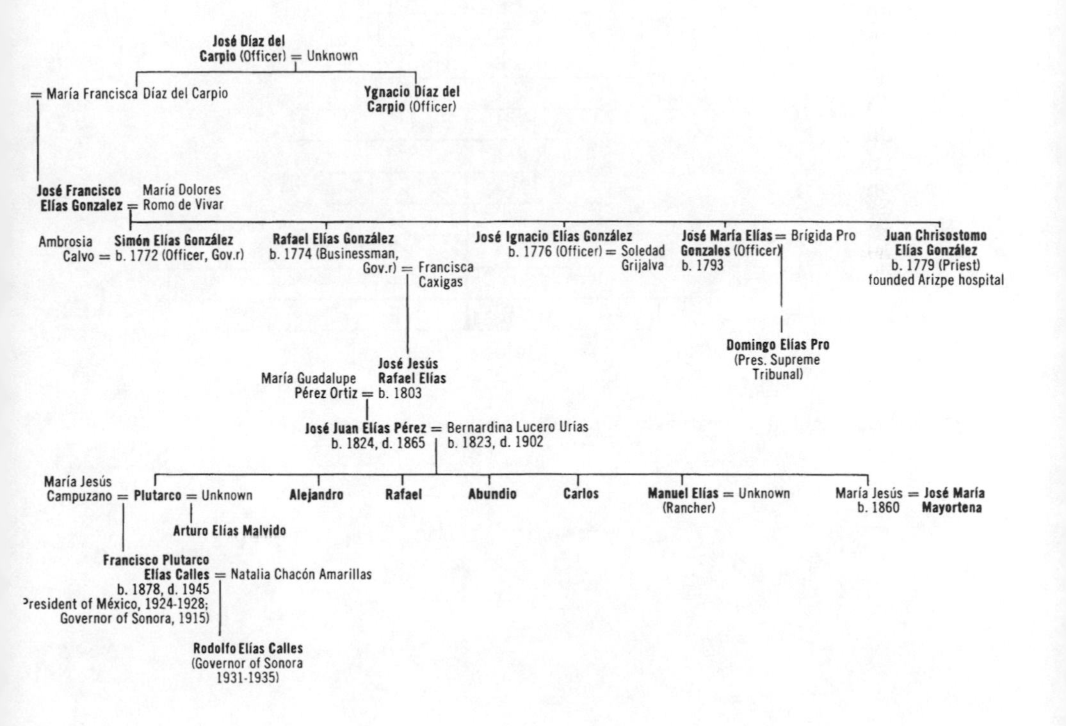

José Díaz del Carpio (Officer) = Unknown
= María Francisca Díaz del Carpio
Ygnacio Díaz del Carpio (Officer)
José Francisco Elías Gonzalez = María Dolores Romo de Vivar
Ambrosia Calvo = Simón Elías González b. 1772 (Officer, Gov.r)
Rafael Elías González b. 1774 (Businessman, Gov.r) = Francisca Caxigas
José Ignacio Elías González b. 1776 (Officer) = Soledad Grijalva
José María Elías Gonzales (Officer) b. 1793 = Brígida Pro
Juan Chrisostomo Elías González b. 1779 (Priest) founded Arizpe hospital
Domingo Elías Pro (Pres. Supreme Tribunal)
María Guadalupe Pérez Ortiz = José Jesús Rafael Elías b. 1803
José Juan Elías Pérez b. 1824, d. 1865 = Bernardina Lucero Urias b. 1823, d. 1902
María Jesús Campuzano = Plutarco = Unknown
Alejandro
Rafael
Abundio
Carlos
Manuel Elías (Rancher) = Unknown
María Jesús b. 1860 = José María Mayortena
Arturo Elías Malvido
Francisco Plutarco Elías Calles b. 1878, d. 1945 (President of México, 1924-1928; Governor of Sonora, 1915) = Natalia Chacón Amarillas
Rodolfo Elías Calles (Governor of Sonora 1931-1935)

CHART 2

Tucson Population Pyramid, 1801*

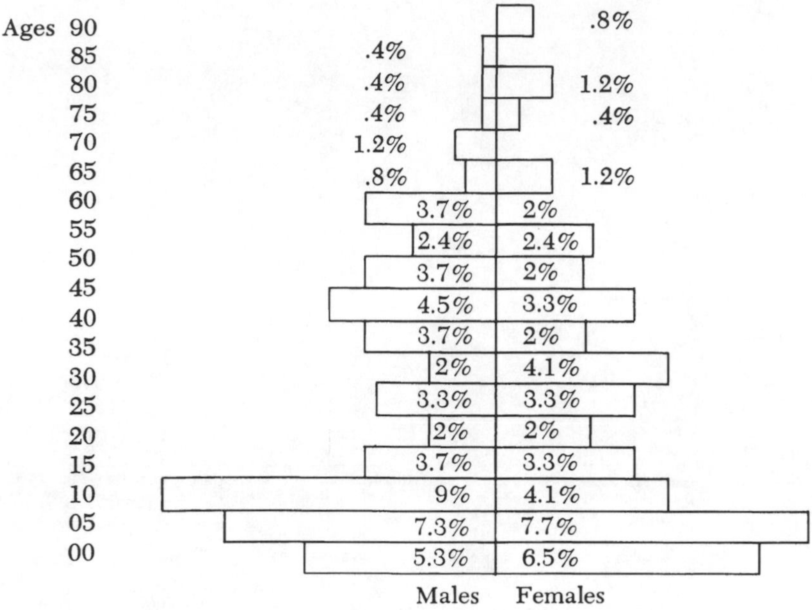

Ages 90
85
80
75
70
65
60
55
50
45
40
35
30
25
20
15
10
05
00

.8%
.4%
.4% 1.2%
.4% .4%
1.2%
.8% 1.2%
3.7% 2%
2.4% 2.4%
3.7% 2%
4.5% 3.3%
3.7% 2%
2% 4.1%
3.3% 3.3%
2% 2%
3.7% 3.3%
9% 4.1%
7.3% 7.7%
5.3% 6.5%

Males Females

*Total enumerated population = 246; figures are percentages of this figure.

Notes to the Chapters

Preface

1. Long 1971, p. 406.
2. U.S. Bureau of the Census 1972, 1-324-26.
3. Brunsman, 1953, p. 3C-59-70.
4. Davis 1869; Defouri 1893; Twitchell 1911-12, 1925; Hackett 1923-37; Meyer 1926; Hammond and Rey 1929, 1953, 1966; Espinosa 1940; Benavides 1945; Dominguez 1956; Thomas 1932, 1935; Schroeder & Matson 1965; others.
5. Burma 1954.
6. Kibbe 1946.
7. Dodson 1951; Madsen 1964; Romano V. 1960, 1965; Rubel 1966.
8. Hawes 1856; Hughes 1875; Powers 1897; Carter 1900; James 1913; Newcomb 1925; Engelhardt 1908-1916; Lummis 1936; Bolton 1926, 1927, 1930.
9. Clark 1959.
10. Few book-length analyses of Arizona's Spanish heritage have previously appeared. John L. Kessell (1970) has published a full-length history of the Jesuit mission at Guebavi. The Native American population of Guebavi died or moved elsewhere (Dobyns 1963), however, so its history forms only a footnote to the process of permanent European settlement within the Gadsden Purchase area and Arizona. Although the Jesuit pioneer Eusebio F. Kino has been the subject of several volumes, his field of action included much of northwestern Sonora as well as southwestern Arizona. Cf. Bolton 1936, 1948; Burrus 1954, 1961.
11. Brunsman 1953 p. 3C-6.
12. As Scholes (1962:22) observed, an earlier emphasis by historians upon "narrative writing, biography or the dramatic event" has contributed to a lack of adequate attention paid to colonial economy and society. Cline (1962:174) at the same time asked for "multi-cultural studies of socio-economic matters...."
13. Heizer and Almquist 1971.
14. Scholes 1962, p. 17.

1. Founding a Jesuit Mission Near Tucson, 1694-1756

1. Chambers 1955, p. 15.
2. Lumholtz 1912, p. 385.
3. *Ibid.*, and author's interviews with many Papagos.
4. Page 1930; p. 13. Warner's Hill took its name from Solomon Warner, who arrived in Tucson on 21 March 1856 with 13 mule-loads of merchandise. When Confederate forces confiscated his goods in 1862, he moved to Santa Cruz, Sonora. After the war, he erected a flourmill on the slope of Sentinel Peak in 1874-75. Bishop Jean B. Salpointe granted him the right of way and water right from the Tucson Pueblo mission property (Lockwood 1943:51, 55). This mill then led some people to refer to Sentinel Peak as "Warner's Hill."
5. Bolton 1948, Vol. I, pp. 127-128. For the convenience of the reader accustomed to the modern form "Tucson," the text will henceforth employ this version of the Northern Piman place name except when quoting a document with an earlier form.
6. *Ibid.*, Vol. I, p. 173; Burrus 1971, p. 348.

7. Smith *et al.* 1966, p. 14; Burrus 1971, p. 562. Carrasco probably copied Kino.
8. Karns 1954, p. 125; Manje 1926, p. 271; Burrus 1971, p. 402. Manje in another manuscript reported "riding through six rancherías each only a harquebus shot distance from one another" (*ibid.*, pp. 245, 430), in the midst of extensive cultivated fields irrigated from many ditches.
9. Bolton, 1948, Vol. I, p. 206, not in 1698 as Page (1930:12) had it; Manje on 1 Nov. 1699, again reported "4 small rancherías" a league apart between Bac and Oiaur (Burrus 1971:452), indicating he settled on the smaller number as more accurate.
10. Page 1930, p. 12, pointed this fact out.
11. Bolton 1948, Vol. I, p. 206.
12. Burrus 1971, p. 430.
13. Castetter and Bell 1942; Maize pp. 30-32, 38, 46, 73, 79; beans pp. 32, 46, 73, 89; cotton pp. 32, 38, 46, 73, 102; squash pp. 38, 73, 100; wheat pp. 114; amaranthus p. 33; chenopodium p. 33; devil's claw p. 113; melons p. 118; tobacco p. 108.
14. Bolton 1948, Vol. I, p. 236.
15. Burrus 1971, p. 452.
16. Bolton 1939, pp. 111, 115, 120, 125, 139.
17. Bannon 1955, p. 1. On 6 July 1591, Fathers Gonzalo de Tapia and Martín Pérez opened the first permanent Jesuit mission in New Spain when they began to convert the Indians of the frontier Province of Sinaloa (Alegre 1956:I:364). Tapia became the protomartyr of his Order in New Spain.
18. Bannon, *op. cit.*, p. 4.
19. *Ibid.*, p. 24; Spicer 1962, pp. 47-49.
20. Bannon 1955, p. 45; Spicer 1962, pp. 49-51, 93.
21. Bolton 1948, Vol. I, p. 110.
22. *Ibid.*, p. 303.
23. Karns 1954, p. 141; Burrus 1971, p. 452.
24. Pinart CPA San Ignacio E 1697. Mission San Ignacio de Cabórica stemmed from Kino's explorations. He first visited it 14 March 1687 and gave it a saint's name. Luis María Pineli began the mission in 1690 (Bolton 1948:I:111, 116, 118). Jorge Hostinski replaced him in 1693 but left that same year (Bolton 1936:270). Then Agustín de Campos took charge and led this mission and its branches until 1736 (Decorme 1941: II:382, n. 11, 386). Thus, Campos began the register cited.
25. Burrus 1961, pp. 30-31.
26. "Sobaipuri" apparently denoted part of the Northern Piman Indian ethnic group residing along both the San Pedro and Santa Cruz Rivers.
27. Pinart CPA San Ignacio B.
28. Bolton 1939, p. 70.
29. Hammond 1929, p. 230.
30. Dunne and Burrus 1955, p. 25, n. 97.
31. Aspurz 1946, Appendix I.
32. Hammond 1929, p. 224.
33. Pinart CPA San Ignacio B 88; E 1697:17-19.
34. Hammond 1929, p. 229.
35. Tarahumara Indians inhabited the upland territory between the eastward-flowing tributaries of the Conchos River and the westward-flowing headwaters of the Fuerte, Mayo and Yaqui Rivers of New Spain (Spicer 1962:3).
36. Bancroft 1889, p. 362 from Pinart CPA San Ignacio E 1697; Dunne and Burrus 1955, p. 38, n. 12.
37. Located on the San Miguel River in Sonora, Mission Santos Reyes de Cucurpe was founded in 1647 (Decorme 1941:II:360, n. 14) by Francisco Guillermo Maluenda, a Belgian Jesuit missionary to the Hymeris tribe, reportedly then occupying Opodepé, Tuape and Cucurpe (Polzer 1972:260, n. 14, 274). By 1662, Maluenda evidently lived at Opodepé as mission headquarters with 200 inhabitants. Cucurpe had only 130 residents, while the other branch at Tuape boasted 260 (Alegre 1959:III:355). As an established mission, Cucurpe served as a staging area for the Jesuit advance into Northern Piman country.
38. Pinart CPA San Ignacio E 1697 fol. 21v. Fabier probably moved to Bac in the spring, departed on 10 August and died on 25 October in San Ignacio.

39. Donohue 1960, pp. 129-130. Kessell (1970:198-99) translates the official inventory of church property at Bac which Ygnacio Xavier Keller conveyed to Rapicani 1 June 1737, with Father Gaspar Stiger as witness. Keller conveyed the Guebavi property on the same date (Kessell 1970:195-97) so the Bac conveyance was a formality for the record, and Rapicani may not yet have seen Bac or Tucson.
40. Mission Santos Angeles de Guebavi was located near the upper Santa Cruz River a short distance north of the present international boundary. It is the only Arizona Spanish mission that has yet received book-length study (Kessell 1970).
41. Kessell 1970, pp. 68-70.
42. Pinart CPA Pueblos de Sta. María 16. Mission Santa María Suamca, located in the headwaters of the Santa Cruz River in modern Mexico, dated from 1732 (Hammond 1929:230-231).
43. Kessell 1970, p. 72.
44. Bancroft 1884, Vol. 1, p. 530, n. 23.
45. The Bancroft Library, University of California at Berkeley, includes this document as number 48 in its Mexican Manuscript collection. It is quoted by permission of the director, the Bancroft Library, University of California, granted 3 January 1972. The translation is mine.
46. Kessell 1970, p. 84.
47. Dunne 1957, pp. 78-79.
48. Donohue 1960, p. 132.
49. Almada 1952, p. 304. Garrucho's original given name was Giuseppe, and he was born at Castel Aragonese (Alegre 1960:IV:404, n. 32).
50. Pradeau 1959, p. 149.
51. *Ibid.*, p. 150.
52. Pinart CPA Magdalena E 1698.
53. Dunne and Burrus 1955, pp. 23-24, n. 88.
54. Aspurz 1946 Appendix I.
55. Bancroft 1889, p. 362.
56. As Kessell (1970:104, n. 37) observed, Bauer's signatures in the San Ignacio registers show that he spent considerable time there. *Cf.* Pinart CPA.
57. Bauer's own writing makes clear that he did not spell his surname Paner or Paver as some have assumed. Pradeau (1959:191) lists Bauer in alphabetical order as Francisco Javier Paver. Pradeau also gives Bauer's birthplace as Bruma, Coruña, Spain, but footnotes Decorme as identifying Bauer as a native of Brunn, Moravia. Decorme was correct.
58. Located in the headwaters of the Altar River, Mission Santa Gertrudis del Saric had Eusebio F. Kino for its first church-builder in 1702-1706 (Bolton 1948:I:373; II:168). Yet no resident missionary seems to have reached Saric until Juan Nentvig went there shortly before the nativistic movement of 1751 (Pradeau 1959:182).
59. Linton 1943.
60. Ewing 1938, pp. 343-344.
61. Mission La Purísima Concepción de Nuestra Señora de Caborca is located near the western end of the Altar River. Father Eusebio F. Kino pioneered contact with its native Northern Pimans. Francisco Xavier Saeta founded the mission on 21 October 1694, then perished in a Northern Piman nativistic movement on 2 April 1695.

    Kino took Gaspar Barrillas there in mid-1698, but he left within a month. Barrillas returned in 1701 but left again in 1702. Domingo Crescoli arrived in 1706 to be followed by Luis Velarde by 1708. Luis Gallardi ministered to the local Native Americans 1720-1722, and Luis Marciano 1722 to perhaps 1727. José Torres Perea came in 1743 but died in 1748. Bartolomé Saenz served in 1748, then Manuel Aguirre, and Tomás Tello. The latter helped set off the 1751 nativistic movement among the Northern Pimans, who killed him (Bolton 1948:I:131-32, 140-41, 145, 164, 175, 303; 1936:538; Alegre 1960:IV:505-507, 501,n25; Bancroft 1884:I:507,n25; 543-544, Burrus 1963:89; Ewing 1945:263). Sonoran military forces defeated California filibusterer Henry Crabb at Caborca in 1857 (Forbes 1952).
62. Ewing 1938, pp. 345-346.
63. Diego Ortiz Parrilla fought Apaches on the northern frontier of New Spain beginning in 1730. Ranking as a captain, he successively commanded the Presidios of San Sabás,

Texas, and Santa Rosa. Promoted to lieutenant colonel, he served with the Veracruz Dragoon Regiment.

Ortiz P. assumed the governorship and captaincy general of the Provinces of Sonora and Sinaloa on 23 June 1749. After supervising the physical construction of the San Miguel de Horcasitas post, he led an expedition against the Seri Indians on Tiburon Island in the Gulf of California. Promoted to colonel, Ortiz Parrilla nonetheless received bitter opposition and criticism from frontier Jesuit missionaries for his policies toward Northern Piman leaders of the anti-mission nativistic movement of 1751. Turning over the governorship at the beginning of 1753, Ortiz Parrilla waited until 1756 for final clearance of his administration. Meanwhile, he commanded the Presidio of Santa Rosa, Coahuila. Promoted to brigadier, Ortiz P. became governor of the Province of Pensacola in 1761, then of Coahuila in 1764. (Almada 1952:542).

64. See Dobyns 1959 for full discussion.
65. Tubutama is located on the east side of the bend in the Altar River where it veers southwest from its southerly course from the U.S.-Mexican border. Mission San Pedro y San Pablo de Tubutama began early in 1691 when Father Eusebio F. Kino installed Antonio Arías as its first priest. He remained until 1693 (Alegre 1960:IV:176; Bolton 1948:I:118). His successor, Daniel Janusque, apparently precipitated the Northern Piman nativistic movement of 1695, although he himself survived it (Bolton 1936:270; Karns 1954:28, 252; Alegre 1960:IV:116, 513, 516; Decorme 1941:II:382, n. 11). Kino sent Ignacio Yturmendi in mid-1701, but he died less than a year later (Bolton 1948: I:303-304). Gerónimo Minutuli came at the end of 1703 (Bolton 1936:525-526) and remained some seven years.

    Tubutama may then have been a branch of San Ignacio Mission for some time. For a decade and a half prior to the Northern Piman nativistic movement of 1751 the German Jacobo Sedelmayr ministered to the Native Americans there (Decorme 1941: II:433). The violent natives burned down the church he had just rebuilt, and beseiged Sedelmayr, Juan Nentvig and their followers in the residence (Ewing 1945:262-263; Decorme 1941:II:440-441). Luis Vivas ministered to the pacified Northern Piman population from 1753 until the expulsion of his Order from New Spain in 1767. Tubutama then became a bulwark of the Franciscan missions in Pimería Alta (Roca 1967: 104-107).
66. Mission San Miguel Arcángel de los Ures lies south of the Sonora River not far west of its big bend from a southerly to southwesterly course toward Hermosillo and the Gulf of California. Baptismal records began in 1636. Ures often served both Jesuits and Franciscans on the northwestern frontier as an administrative headquarters. The mission was secularized with the Pimería Baja missions. The settlement became the Sonoran state capital in 1838-1842, and again in 1847-1879 (Roca 1967:166-171).
67. Sedelmayr 10 Mayo de 1752.
68. Segesser 25 Mayo de 1752.
69. Captain Tomás Belderrain founded the Royal Presidio of San Ygnacio de Tubac in 1752, to pacify the Northern Pimans in the wake of the nativistic movement of 1751. Located on the bank of the Santa Cruz River, the post was established on the site of an earlier Northern Piman settlement. It became the first permanent European settlement within present Arizona. From Tubac, Juan Bautista de Anza would launch his expeditions to Upper California, and Juan Oliva would found the Spanish presidio at Tucson. It has become a state historical park (Dobyns 1959).
70. Guebavi B 95.
71. Salpointe (1880) gave the 49 baptisms at Tubac. Reverend Victor R. Stoner pointed out that they really occurred at Guebavi and Tumacacori (9 March 1954).
72. Pinart CPA Pueblos de Sta. María Soamca fol. 11-11v.
73. Stoner 14 Nov. 1952 personal communication; Guebavi B.
74. Mission Nuestra Señora de la Asunción de Arizpe was located on a plateau west of the Bacanuche River just north of its junction with the Sonora in north-central Sonora. Franciscans from the New Mexico Province began proselytizing in the area about 1642. A Jesuit began visiting the local residents in 1646, and baptismal records began in 1648. Felipe Esgrecho became the first resident Jesuit missionary in 1650. The last Jesuit at Arizpe, Carlos Rojas, served there over 35 years, and greatly improved the still-standing church.

The Spanish king created the Frontier Provinces in 1776, and the first commandant general made Arizpe their capital in 1779. With later administrative changes, Arizpe still remained capital of the Province of Sonora until 1824. It was the capital of the State of Sonora from 1832 to 1838. The first bishop of Sonora, Friar Antonio de los Reyes, made the old mission church the first cathedral in 1783 (Roca 1967:152-158).

75. Roxas Maio 14 de 1755.
76. Kessell 1970, p. 137, inferred this.
77. Roxas Maio 14 de 1755.
78. Pradeau 1959, pp. 138-139. Donohue (1960:133) differs from Almada (1952:253) and Pradeau in saying that Espinosa was ordained in Yucatán in 1741 and entered the Jesuit novitiate on 14 August 1750, after a serious illness, going directly to the missions when his two years as a novice ended.
79. Pradeau (1959:130) thought that Espinosa arrived in Sonora in September of 1756, although Bancroft (1884:I:651) placed him in Pimería Alta in 1751.
80. Kessell 1970, pp. 137-138.
81. Pinart CPA San Ignacio B 186-192; Kessell (1970:138) attributes Espinosa's Bac assignment to Visitor General Utrera, who ordered him to work from Guebavi until the people of Bac built him a house. I infer that Espinosa moved to Bac in mid-April of 1755 on the basis of his signatures in the San Ignacio registers until that time. Kessell (1970:139, 143) conjectures that Espinosa would have joined Governor Juan Antonio de Mendoza's force touring Pimería Alta in January of 1756, but recognizes that it is "not certain" whether Mendoza "personally" saw to Espinosa's installation at Bac. Father Visitor Roxas confirmed Espinosa's residence at Bac in his 30 May 1756 report.
82. Roxas Maio 30 de 1756.
83. Atí comes from *Achi*, a Tautaukwañi dialect Papago settlement in a broad valley west of the Silver Bell Mountains. Father Eusebio F. Kino visited "San Francisco de Adid" on 4 October 1698 (Bolton 1948:I:187-188). He passed by again on 7 November 1699, reporting a population of 800 (Bolton 1948:I:208). His military escort commander, Juan M. Manje, wrote that 100 men and 160 women carrying their children came from "San Francisco de Atí" to visit the travelers at San Serafín de Actún nearby (Karns 1954:142, Burrus 1971:453).

    Anthropologist Ruth M. Underhill (1939:60) recorded the place name as *Archie* or *aatci*, meaning "Narrow Place." Another *achi* on the Altar River south of the present international boundary lay in Kokololoti dialect territory, in all likelihood. It apparently spawned two historic mission branches: Santa Teresa de Adid, which no longer exists, and Las Siete Príncipes de Atil known also in recent times as San Francisco de Atil (Roca 1967:107-110). Inasmuch as Crow's Head's son referred to the people of "Atí" as Papagos, he evidently spoke of the Tautaukwañi Papago settlement.

2. Continued Jesuit Proselytizing 1756-1767

1. The rather consistent generation of nativistic movements by Spanish northward expansion of the frontier of New Spain has yet to be systematically analyzed by either historian or social scientist. Some nativistic movements on this frontier evidently reacted against civil-military imposition of European norms of behavior on Native American populations. Other nativistic movements reacted against clerical imposition of Christian patterns of conduct in the service of Spanish imperialism.

    This constitutes a dimension of the Christian mission as a frontier institution not taken into account by Bolton and other historians of the Spanish borderlands except in a passing reference to "occasional" missionary martydoms (Bolton 1939:132). That the Society of Jesus was not the only Order that generated nativistic movements was proved by the Pueblo Revolt of 1680 against Franciscan missionaries in New Mexico (Hackett and Shelby 1942).
2. Accurate reconstruction of events during the period discussed in this chapter is difficult. The present interpretation differs significantly from my earlier reconstruction (Dobyns 1962). This chapter is therefore provided with ample notes.

3. I draw this inference from the large number of festivals of St. Francis Xavier that came to be celebrated in Sonora during Christian times on 4 October. This is the feast day of St. Francis of Assisi, whereas the feast day of Xavier is 2 December. From this paradox we can infer that the Jesuit missionaries, who expressed fealty to the Jesuit Saint Francis Xavier, saw fit to shift the date of their saint's festival to concur with and incorporate an existing native religious ritual that was immovable, so firmly was it tied to the annual agricultural cycle and the characteristic seasons of the area.
4. Jeffreys 1956.
5. Fathers Kino and Campos most likely first translated the native rite into Catholic forms.
6. Here I depart from my previous reconstruction, which adhered to Pradeau (1959:139), to follow Kessell's (1970:141, n. 46) correct conclusions. Reasons are several. Pradeau erred in placing "paver" at Bac, as evidence above on Espinosa's assignment demonstrates. Pradeau (1959:139) also wrote that Father Bernhard Middendorff had established a "Mission de Santa Catalina" on the Santa Cruz River in September, and claimed that both Middendorff and Bauer strove to change the native celebration. Kessell (1970:141, n. 46) asserts, on the other hand, that Middendorff "did not set foot in the San Xavier-Santa Catalina-Tucson area until after the attack" that came in November.

   Actually, available documents fail to account specifically for Middendorff's whereabouts during October. By his own account, Middendorff "arrived in September 1756 in Mátape, a mission in Sonora among the lower Pimas...." Because of severe diarrhea, his group stayed there three weeks recuperating. Then Middendorff went to Ures (his travel time is not specified, but it must have been short). At Ures he spent an unreported period as a guest of Father Phillip Segesser. Middendorff then continued on to San Ignacio with a large escort – again travel time is not specified (Treutlein 1957:315).

   It does seem unlikely that Middendorff could have founded a mission in September, because he could well have still been in Mátape or on the road from Ures to San Ignacio. Thus, Pradeau's account appears to err with regard to Middendorff; full responsibility for intervention in native ceremonial seems to rest on Espinosa.
7. Pradeau (1959:139) wrote of the "customary celebrations in which they intoxicated themselves celebrating the day of St. Francis the fourth of October," as I translate his text. He is on very firm cultural ground. Underhill (1946:41-67) describes ritual intoxication with fermented giant cactus fruit juice as an aboriginal Northern Piman rain-bringing technique.

   This Native American conventional understanding and actions stemming from it survived at least two centuries of Christian preaching. When I conducted research for the Papago Tribe's suit against the United States before the Indian Claims Commission in the early 1950s, I obtained the cooperation of an elected representative of San Xavier District in lending a pair of fermenting jars to the Arizona State Museum. The hand-made giant cactus juice fermenting vessels constituted part of the ceramic evidence of former Northern Piman land use. When loaned for tribal purposes, these huge *ollas* were stored at a secret (from the priests) *navait* brewing and ritual spot in the desert near Bac. The age-old autumn drinking pattern continues, aided by other factors, in very heavy consumption of alcoholic beverages by Northern Piman pilgrims at the festival of St. Francis held at Magdalena, Sonora, each fall on 4 October (*Cf.* Dobyns 1950; Sheridan 1971).
8. Gardiner 1957, p. 3.
9. *Havañ Mau'au*'s participation in both the 1751 and 1756 uprisings militates against Ezell's (1961:22) conclusion that the Gila River Pimas failed to join the "Papagos" in their various uprisings against Spanish domination. The Gila River Valley and Santa Cruz River Valley natives formed a military unit in the 18th century, when their social structure had yet suffered relatively little from the biological and cultural shocks of the coming of the white man.

   Kessell (1970:141, n. 47) overstates my interpretation of available sources when he asserts that I (1962) credited Oacpicagigua with "an active part" in the 1756 attack on Bac. What I wrote in 1962 was that Spaniards assumed that Luis helped to organize the 1756 revolt. This assumption involves the Spanish concept of "intellectual authorship" of a crime, which does not require active physical participation to establish guilt. Even if Luis had died in jail by the time of the 1756 revolt as Kessell (1970:141, n. 47) suggests, many frontier Spaniards traumatized by the 1751 nativistic movement would still have considered the obviously able and charismatic Luis Oacpicagigua to have been its main "intellectual author."

Moreover, the attitudes of such Spanish frontiersmen would have been reinforced by the guerilla warfare conducted by Oacpicagigua's sons. Not until May of 1760 did Captain Juan Bautista de Anza the younger head a detachment of his Tubac command that surprised a group of guerrillas led by Luis' son Ciprian, killing the latter and eight of his followers (Anónimo 1760).

10. Pradeau (1959:140) clearly utilized the report here translated. He wrote that the Tubac ensign "rescued Father Middendorff and Father Paver, returning both to the Presidio of Tubac. . . ." The anonymous report mentions neither priest in the passage translated here – nor elsewhere.

    Pradeau (1959:140, n. 37) wrote further that the ensign "ought to have been D. Tomás Belderrain, dead in Tubac in 1760 and succeeded in the command by Juan Bautista de Anza," citing the document here translated in part. This seems to be an inexplicable slip. The second paragraph of the anonymous 1760 report clearly gave Tomás Belderrain's correct rank in summarizing attacks on the post by Northern Piman rebels: "Its Captain was Don Thomas de Belderrain, because of whose death Don Juan Bautista de Anza succeeded [him in command] at the beginning of this year" (Anónimo 1760). Belderrain founded the Tubac presidio and commanded it until his death in 1759 (Dobyns 1959, MS p. 240).

    The ensign in 1756 was either Juan C. Ramírez or Juan María Oliva, if Ramírez had already been promoted to lieutenant. Kessell (1970:141) credited Espinosa's rescue to Oliva. To do so, Kessell (1970:141, n. 48) correlated an entry in Oliva's service record with the 1756 engagement with Northern Pimans. Oliva said, "When I was an ensign, about 200 Apache Indians attacked me in the Pueblo of San Xavier del Bac. Having 14 men, I put myself among them and I killed 15" (O'Conor 18 de Agosto de 1775). I think that the available evidence is not conclusive.

11. Anónimo 1760, paragraph 1. Middendorff (Gardiner 1957:3) agreed that "fifteen of the enemy fell" of the force led by "Gabanimo" who fled with 50 survivors to the mountains and canyons.

12. Juan Antonio de Mendoza, a native of Villa de Higuera de Vargas, Castilla, began his military career in 1720 as a cadet of infantry. In 1725, he became captain in the Prince's Regiment. Promoted to lieutenant colonel in 1736, Mendoza became colonel in 1742, fighting in Africa and Italy. He took office as governor and captain general of Sonora and Sinaloa on 30 July 1755.

    After personally leading several expeditions against hostile Native Americans, Mendoza was appointed governor of Puebla. Before leaving Sonora, Mendoza led a relief force to engage Seri Indians attacking miners. One of two Seri leaders killed by Mendoza's expedition dealt the governor a mortal wound before expiring. Mendoza died two days later on 27 November 1760 (Almada 1952:463-464).

13. Och, a member of this group, reported sailing on Christmas and reaching San Juan de Ulloa on 19 March 1756 (Treutlein 1965:20-21, 25), but Pfefferkorn, another companion, years later gave their arrival date as 1755 (Treutlein 1949:260). In yet another account, Treutlein (1957:314) gave 24 December 1755 as the sailing date, but this was quite possibly a typographical error.

14. Treutlein 1949 p. 6, n. 8.

15. Middendorff himself wrote, "We spent four months in going from Mexico to Sonora" (Treutlein 1957:315). The Jesuit Pedro Bueno founded Mission San José de Mátape in 1645 on the banks of the Mátape River, a short stream flowing into the Gulf of California between the Yaqui and Sonora Rivers. In 1867, the Sonoran state government renamed Mátape "Villa de Pesqueira" (Almada 1952:574; Spicer 1962:90).

16. Och also ended up at San Ignacio, where he assisted Father Gaspar Stiger (Treutlein 1965:44) before launching his career as an independent missionary. It is not clear whether Och and Middendorff traveled the final lap together. Och, Pfefferkorn and Gerstner had been delayed in Puebla by orders – later rescinded – to return to Havana.

They did not leave Mexico City until 11 May 1756 (Treutlein 1965:38). Och remembered their receiving orders to go to Upper Pimería after three weeks at Ures Mission in Pimería Baja, whose Swiss missionary Philip Segesser momentarily frightened them with a staged "Indian attack" by his mission Indians just before they reached Ures (Treutlein 1965:43).

17. Decorme (1941:II:443) stated that Mendoza restored Espinosa to Bac after he had been forced to flee. This agrees better with other evidence than Pradeau's (1959:139-40) assertion that Mendoza ordered Bauer to Guebavi and Espinosa to Bac. Donohue (1960:132-133) apparently following Pradeau. Bauer's post-1751 Revolt service at Guebavi as shown in the register for that mission seems to have been uninterrupted, and Middendorff was quite specific that the 1756 rebels sought to slay Espinosa at Bac.
18. Gardiner 1957, p. 3.
19. See Ezell (1963) for ethnic meaning of *Maricopa* and related terms.
20. Gardiner 1957, p. 7.
21. Kessell 1970, p. 142, citing Burrus 1963, p. 70.
22. Treutlein 1957, p. 316. There is some difficulty with Middendorff's account. He wrote that Tucson was named as his future mission "after a campaign of three months." Yet he said he spent only two months with Mendoza, and went among his converts-to-be on the "day before Epiphany in 1757." As his name indicates, Middendorff was yet another German Jesuit, born 14 October 1723, in Vechte, Westphalia. He entered the Society in 1741 (Almada 1952:466; Treutlein 1957:311).
23. Roxas Marzo 15 de 1757.
24. Treutlein 1957, p. 316.
25. Gardiner 1957, p. 8. Och remembered that Middendorff had to "endure" dampness, heat and cold under the sky, but contrary to Middendorff's report of Native American behavior claimed that the "papagos" soon tired of mission life and stole all the food sent to Middendorff because he prohibited their nightly dancing and carousing (Treutlein 1965:44).
26. Treutlein 1957, p. 316. Middendorff reported reaching Bac at daybreak. Retrospectively, Och omitted all mention of hostile Indian attack. He remembered Middendorff as a robust man so weakened by lack of food and shelter that an "inflammatory fever" would have killed him, had he not "been removed" already half dead (Treutlein 1965: 44). Och stated that Middendorff's strength was "somewhat restored" after he ate and slept for "two days and two nights." Pradeau (1959:140) transposed Middendorff's long sleep to Tubac after his supposed rescue by its ensign months earlier.
27. Treutlein 1957; p. 317.
28. Treutlein 1949, p. 8; Aguirre 1856 (Marzo 20 de 1764).
29. Garrucho Junio 21 de 1761.
30. The expansion of Jesuit Indian mission efforts led to creation in 1725 of the post of visitor general. The visitor general of missions became, in effect, a vice-provincial, relieving some of the burdens falling upon the provincial of the Jesuit Mexican Province. Ordinary business arising north of Durango and Guadalajara went to the visitor general after 1725 instead of to the provincial as in the past. Most importantly, the visitor general carried out the arduous duty of personally visiting every Jesuit establishment in the area under his jurisdiction (Donohue 1969: 43).
31. Tomás Ignacio Lizasoaín was born at Pamplona in 1717. He entered the Society of Jesus in 1744-45 after ordination, and reached New Spain in 1750 (Decorme 1941:I: 433). He helped to found a residence and construct a church at San José de Guaymas, where he acted as first superior. The Seris destroyed the place in 1751 (Pradeau 1959: 226; Decorme 1941: II:341, 457).

    Lizasoaín thereafter labored among the Yaquis and acted as visitor. His report on his 1761-1763 inspections provided one of the last general summaries of these frontier institutions before the expulsion of his Order from Spanish dominions (Dunne 1957:25).

    Lizasoaín ordered Mission Yécora transferred from Nueva Vizcaya to Sonora, which was done in 1765 (Pradeau 1959:51). After the Jesuit expulsion in 1767, Lizasoaín became superior of a Jesuit house, and then in 1772 he became the last provincial of the Order for New Spain (in exile) prior to its dissolution. Lizasoaín died on 12 January 1789 (Decorme 1941:I:xvi, 433).

32. A Dutch native in the Spanish royal service, José Tienda de Cuervo became governor and captain general of Sonora and Sinaloa on 16 January 1761. He reached provincial territory on 12 April and arrived at San Miguel de Horcasitas in August. Like his predecessor, Tienda de Cuervo personally led his troops against the Seri Indians, driving them off the mainland onto Tiburón Island. Consequently he won promotion from captain of the Veracruz Dragoon Regiment to lieutenant colonel. War with Great Britain brought Tienda del Cuervo orders to return to his regiment, and he left San Miguel on 9 December 1762. He died two years later in Veracruz (Almada 1952:787).
33. Aguirre Dic. 30 de 1763.
34. Elías Gonzáles 22 de Marzo de 1762. This translation is new. Francisco Elías Gonzáles migrated from his native La Rioja, Spain, to New Spain at an early age. He married in 1729 while farming and ranching at Alamos, Sonora. In 1740, he organized a militia unit to help put down a Yaqui Indian nativistic movement and performed so well that he won a commission as lieutenant of the Janos garrison. Promoted to captain in 1751, he took command of the Terrenate company in 1758 (Almada 1952:239; Philip 17 de Enero de 1758).

    In 1756, Elías commanded the left wing of the Sonoran governor's forces when they attacked the Northern Piman chieftain Crow's Head on the Gila River (Gardiner 1957:5). In spite of his long service on the Native American frontier, Don Francisco presented no documentary record of his services to the royal inspector, the Marqués de Rubí, in 1766. The marqués characterized Elías Gonzáles as applying himself industriously to his mines, "which with notable profit to him he has been benefiting from for some years in this region." On the other hand, the marqués described Elías as totally unfit for the command he held (Rubí 7 de Diz. re de 1766).

    Francisco Elías Gonzáles nevertheless founded a family long prominent in state and national affairs (Almada 1952:239) in Mexico and in southern Arizona. Several of these descendants are mentioned later in this volume. The simplified kinship chart in the Appendix of this book shows major relationships in the Elías Gonzáles lineage (Almada 1952:228-43; Rivera 19 de Sep. de 1801; Salcido 17 de Sep. de 1801; Villa 1948:55-56).
35. Aguirre Dic. 30 de 1763; Treutlein 1965, pp. 49-80.
36. Tienda del Cuerbo 9 de Abril de 1762.
37. Aguirre Dic. 30 de 1763.
38. Ezell 1961, p. 120.
39. Aguirre Dic. 22 de 1763.
40. Aguirre 18 de Febrero de 1764.
41. Aguirre Marzo 23 de 1764.
42. Aguirre 1856, pp. 134-135. (4 de Agosto de 1764).
43. Nentvig 1951, p. 79.
44. Juan Bautista de Anza, born at Fronteras, Sonora, in 1735, was the second frontier officer to bear this name. His grandfather served as lieutenant and captain at Janos Presidio, in Nueva Vizcaya. His father commanded the garrison stationed at Corodeguachi and Fronteras for a score of years.

    Juan Bautista the younger entered the royal military service at Fronteras in 1753. He obtained a lieutenancy 1 July 1755. Five years later, at the age of 25, Anza won promotion to a captaincy and assumed command of the San Ygnacio de Tubac garrison.

    Anza fought Seri, Papago and Apache Indians energetically until late 1773. Then he assembled an exploring expedition and opened a land route from Sonora to Upper California across the Colorado River in the first half of 1774. The viceroy promoted Anza to lieutenant colonel and approved his colonizing California. Anza left Tubac on 23 October 1775, led 240 people to Monterey and returned to Sonora on 1 June 1776.

    This success made Anza a colonel and brought his appointment as commandant of arms of the Province of Sonora in 1777. While attending a council of war at Chihuahua in 1778, he took the oath of office as governor of New Mexico. He began his duties that September.

    Anza achieved a remarkable record in New Mexico. He forced an alliance with the Comanches and other formerly hostile tribes, brought the drought-weakened Hopis into a semi-dependent status for the first time in a century and split the Navajos from the Western Apaches.

In 1786, Anza requested relief and left Santa Fe in November of 1787. Thereupon he returned to the post of commandant of arms of Sonora until his death on 19 December 1788 in Arizpe, where he was buried (Ivancovich 1960:21-24; Dobyns 1959MS: 242-252; Thomas 1932).

45. Aguirre 18 de Febrero de 1764.
46. Juan Claudio de Pineda was born in Sort, Lérida Province, Spain, in 1710. He entered the royal military service on 3 November 1731 as a cadet in the Guadalajara Infantry Regiment. Commissioned ensign on 9 October 1732, Pineda became a lieutenant on 23 December 1740, at which rank he fought in the Italian campaign. Promoted to captain on 17 December 1759, Pineda so improved his unit that the king appointed him lieutenant colonel on 30 December 1760.

    Contrary to his own preferences, Pineda was dispatched to the New World as governor and captain general of Sonora and Sinaloa. En route to his post, he stopped in Mexico City to command the Commercial Regiment, and to accompany the viceroy to Veracruz to deal with the English war threat. Then he reorganized the Puebla provincial militia. Thus, Pineda did not reach Rosario, Sinaloa, until February in 1763, advancing to Culiacán on 2 April and finally relieved Captain Urrea at San Miguel de Horcasitas on 20 May.

    In 1764, Pineda inspected the frontier garrisons and reorganized the militia units. He offered a bounty of three pesos for each Seri Indian captured or killed, and set a price of 300 pesos on the head of the Seri chief. Pineda surveyed Guaymas Bay in 1767 to select sites for the large Sonora Expedition that would shortly endeavor to exterminate the Seris. Then Pineda carried out the secret royal orders expelling members of the Jesuit Order from the area under his jurisdiction. As temporary commander of the Sonora Expedition, Pineda pledged his personal credit to finance it.

    Promoted to colonel in October of 1769, Pineda suffered an attack that left him paralyzed on his left side. The viceroy relieved Pineda on 18 April 1770, and he returned to Mexico City where he died in 1772 (Almada 1952:592-593).
47. Aguirre Marzo 23 de 1764.
48. Aguirre Marzo 26 de 1764.
49. Donohue 1960, p. 135. The total population of 220 was divided into 70 families, plus 58 widows and widowers. This meant only 22 children, far from enough to maintain the population.
50. Aguirre Agosto 11 de 1764; Treutlein 1965.
51. Pradeau 1959, p. 144; Aguirre Hen.o 8 de 1765.
52. Aguirre Abril 26 de 1765. Los Siete Príncipes de Atil Mission, on the north bank of the Altar River between Oquitoa and Tubutama, was a branch of the Tubutama Mission until 1756. Then Father Ignaz Pfefferkorn made it a full-fledged mission, where he remained until poor health forced his transfer in 1762 or 1763 (Treutlein 1949:8-9, 261-263). The Franciscans made Atil a mission beginning in 1768, with Oquitoa as its branch. That relationship was reversed in the 19th century (Roca 1967:109-110).
53. Pradeau 1959, pp. 187-188; Aguirre Mayo 18 de 1765.
54. Aguirre Junio 10 de 1765.
55. Aguirre Junio 30 de 1765.
56. Pinart CPA San Ignacio E 1697 fol. 70; Aguirre Oct.e 5 de 1765.
57. Pinart CPA Bisanig C fol. 105v.
58. Treutlein 1949, p. 263; Pinart CPA Bisanig C fol. 108.
59. Pradeau 1959, p. 188; Treutlein 1949, pp. 9-10. King Charles III of Spain personally decreed the Jesuit expulsion. Charles was born in Madrid on 20 January 1716, the son of King Philip V and Isabel de Farnesio, his second wife. Isabel sought to assure a throne to Charles, Philip's third male offspring. In 1720, the Treaty of the Hague assured his rights to the Dukedoms of Parma, Piacenza and Tuscany. Again in 1731, a treaty between Spain, Austria and England recognized Charles as duke.

    When only 18, he became generalisimo of a Spanish army formed to conquer the Kingdom of Naples. This force defeated the Austrians at Bitonto on 25 May 1734. Naples submitted, and Charles was crowned king at Palermo in July, renouncing his dukedoms to his younger brother. Charles ruled Naples well for 16 years, pacifying the kingdom, building many public buildings, reforming the administration and achieving economic prosperity.

Then Charles' elder half-brother died, and he succeeded Ferdinand VI as king of Spain, returning to Barcelona on 17 October 1759. Charles entered Madrid on 13 July 1760, but his wife died on 27 September. Charles so loved her that he never remarried.

The sunburned, big-nosed king who liked to hunt every day proved to be an able and complex leader for Spain. He beautified Madrid, built bridges and roads, and instituted much social legislation for the benefit of the poor. He introduced German tactics into the Spanish army and founded infantry, artillery and cavalry schools.

Charles III's foreign policy succeeded at times, but failed at others. He warred with England and lost. Later he allied Spain with France and the rebel North American British colonies. He pacified the Mediterranean, concluding treaties with Turkey and Algiers and achieving a truce with Tunisia. He died on 14 December 1788 (Anónimo 1966:11:1031-1038).

60. Anónimo 1966:11:1034 and Kessell 1970a, pp. 181-182.
61. Underhill 1939, p. 57.
62. Aguirre 1856, p. 35 (4 de Agosto de 1764).

3. Garcés' Franciscan Mission Branch 1768-1779

1. Ocaranza 1933, p. 7.
2. Kessell 1970b, pp. 182-183.
3. *Ibid.*, p. 184.
4. *Ibid.*, pp. 186-187.
5. *Ibid.*, pp. 189-190.
6. Garcés 1856, pp. 365-366. Anza was not at home to welcome Garcés because he was campaigning against the Seri Indians on the west coast of Sonora. Garcés' reference to captains and troops at Pitíc meant that Anza and his presidial detachment operated as one unit of the Elizondo expedition mounted to try to terminate the Seri flank threat to the colonial province.
7. Garcés 1856, pp. 367-370 á Gobernador D. Juan de Pineda, extract. I have found that in anthropological field research the new investigator in a specific situation tends to learn fantastically rapidly during the first two or three weeks. Thereafter, the rate of learning may drop greatly, so that months are required to confirm the conclusions reached very quickly at the beginning. For this reason, I consider these two letters from Garcés penned a month after he reached Bac as invaluable descriptions of Bac and Tucson at the beginning of this priest's ministry.
8. Garcés 13 de agosto de 1768, á M. R. P. Guardian.
9. Ocaranza 1933, pp. 11-12. Greenleaf and Wallace (1962:20) exaggerated when they wrote that Garcés "spent most of the next twelve years exploring the Gila and Colorado Rivers." More accurately, Kessell (1970b:182) summarized that Garcés explored "from the Sonoran Desert to the Santa Barbara Channel, from the bottom of Havasupai Canyon to the mesa top at Oraibi."
10. Fontana 1961, p. 8.
11. Arricivita 1792, p. 404.
12. Garcés 1856 (21 de feb.o de 1769).
13. Garcés 1856 (23 de julio de 1769).
14. Rowland 1930, p. 214.
15. Ezell 1955 (translation of archival copy of Anza 1 de mayo de 1770).
16. Coues 1900, Vol. I, pp. 26-30; Garcés Noviembre de 1770.
17. Garcés 20 de Febrero de 1771; Fontana 1961, p. 8.
18. Coues 1900, Vol. I, pp. 30-38; Garcés 8 de Agosto á 26 de Octubre de 1771.
19. Reyes 1856, p. 756.
20. Garcés 1772.
21. Baldonado 1959, p. 23.
22. Garcés 1856 (29 de Julio de 1768 á Juan de Pineda).
23. Galvez, 3 de Junio de 1769.
24. Medina 1779 No. 8.

25. Coues 1900, Vol. I, pp. 39, 46.
26. Baldonado 1959, p. 24. It has been stated (Duell 1919:62) that Friar José del Río accompanied Garcés to Bac. Actually, José del Río took over the mission at Tubutama in 1768 (Pinart CPA Bisanig B fol. 72 and Tubutama B fol. 1-1v). The error arose in translating Arricivita's statement that Father President Mariano Bueno y Alcalde sent his *compañero* – in the sense that del Río was one of the pioneering Franciscans under Bueno's charge, but not meaning that del Río and Garcés occupied the same post – to Querétaro with Garcés' diary of his early explorations (Arricivita 1792:417).
27. Tumacacori B fol. 16v.
28. Garcés 25 de Dic.e de 1776.
29. Arricivita 1792, p. 560.
30. Coues 1900, Vol. I, pp. 9, 63.
31. Garcés 24 de Sep. de 1776.
32. Garcés 25 de Dic.e de 1776.
33. Garcés, 3 de Enero de 1777.
34. Reyes 1784.
35. Garcés 21 de Enero de 1778; Garcés 19 de Feb.o de 1778.
36. Garcés, 11 de Marzo de 1779.
37. Garcés, 23 de Marzo de 1779.

4. Brick-and-Mortar Missionaries, 1779-1790

1. Velderrain and Díaz, Junio 7 de 1775.
2. Tumacacori B, fol. 17v; Entierros fol. 139.
3. Garcés 25 de Dic. de 1776.
4. Tumacacori B fol. 18-20.
5. Hughes 1860, p. 1.
6. *Ibid.*, p. 3.
7. Thomas 1941, p. 151.
8. *Ibid.*, pp. 151, 204; Croix 30 de Nov.e de 1778.
9. Thomas 1941, p. 150.
10. *Ibid.*, p. 204.
11. Arricivita 1792, p. 560.
12. A detachment of the Sonoran Expedition of 1767 and following years found placer gold while pursuing Indians. By 1774, over 500 pounds of nuggets had been recovered, with annual value reaching an estimated 1,000,000 pesos. A gold rush quickly brought Cieneguilla a population over 2,000 (O'Crouley 1972:97-98).
13. The record of Velarde's death and burial is preserved in the fragment of the Cieneguilla burial register housed with other Franciscan mission records in the archive of the Parish of Altar, Sonora. I copied this entry through the courtesy of Reverend Roberto Gonzalez, parish priest in 1952. Paul H. Ezell and Alden W. Jones accompanied me on a document search at that time.
14. Anonymous 1783.
15. Franco 1782.
16. Yturralde 3 de Abril de 1798, fol. 6v.
17. Father Visitor Diego Bringas (15 de Marzo de 1796, fol. 18v) cited Belderrain's death in petitioning for added royal treasury support for posting a second missionary in each of the eight Pimería Alta missions manned by the College of the Holy Cross in Querétaro. He argued that the goal of keeping missionaries from dying unconfessed would by itself justify the doubled expense, although he cited several other reasons for stationing two priests at each mission.
18. Reyes 1784, fol. 223 ff; Habig 1937, p. 156 translation.
19. *Ibid.*, fol. 224.
20. Ezell 1955; Anza 1856.
21. Allande y Saabedra 1785.

5. Franciscans at Work 1790-1821

1. Dobyns and Ezell 1959, p. 154; Llorens Diciembre 12 de 1801.
2. Pinart CPA Oquitoa B 48-50.
3. Yturralde 3 de Abril de 1798, fol. 6v; Moyano 18 de Mayo de 1803.
4. Yturralde 25 de Octubre de 1792.
5. Bringas 15 de Marzo de 1796, fol. 22; Galindo N. 9 de Diciembre de 1796, fol. 27.
6. Hughes 1860, p. 3. In 1814, a Franciscan inspector referred to the Tucson mission branch as "San Agustín del Tucson," as had one in 1774.
7. Habig 1937, p. 166.
8. Salpointe April 21, 1880.
9. Yturralde 3 de Abril de 1798.
10. The festival of Saint Francis Xavier, the church's patron, on December 2.
11. Annotation by Donald Page.
12. Hughes 1860, p. 3.
13. Watson 1931, p. 147. The oral tradition and 1849 statement on relative chronology of the standing Bac church and the Tucson Pueblo structure seem persuading. Some students of Tucson area history have, however, equated the convent that survived into the period of U.S. sovereignty with the house built for Friar Garcés in 1770-1771.

    There are several architectural reasons for rejecting such a correlation. The Garcés house had round defensive towers. It was built so that Tucson's military chaplain was able to climb out on the roof to watch the May Day 1782 battle at the presidio. The structure that survived into U.S. times was, however, rather box-shaped and had no towers. A description written in 1843 reported that this building contained seven ground-floor rooms and a second story with three rooms and an arched, roofed balcony (Quiroga 31 de Mayo de 1843). Moreover, the principal cult celebrated in the structure was that of Our Lord of Esquipulas. This diffused to the Southwest from Guatemala relatively late in colonial times.
14. A Franciscan member of the College of the Holy Cross in Querétaro, Barbastro became *custodio* or chief executive of the *Custodia de San Carlos de Sonora* upon its organization on 23 October 1783. When the king dissolved the *Custodia* a decade later, Barbastro became president of the missionaries at the Pimería Alta missions staffed by his institution (Barbastro 26 de Julio de 1793).
15. Llorens referred to Captain José de Zúñiga's absence leading his 1795 expedition to Zuñi Pueblo in New Mexico.
16. Ensign José María Sosa, mentioned in several chapters of this book.
17. Significant for reconstructing the history of Tucson-area environment is this mid-1795 reference to the island produced by the Tucson irrigation ditches fed by valley-margin springs and the surface-flowing Santa Cruz River. Hydrologic conditions described in the 1 May 1782 battle documents still existed 23 years later.
18. Llorens 2 de Junio de 1795.
19. Arriquibar here employed a term for the first two cards from the bottom of the banker's deck in *monte*. This suggests either that he was not wholly familiar with this card game, or thoroughly so but wished to persuade Barbastro that he was not (or communicate on another level that he and Barbastro were Christian sinners, too).
20. Arriquibar Mayo 20 de 1795, fol. 62v-63.
21. Arriquibar 20 de Mayo de 1795, fol. 63v-64.
22. Moyano 5 de Feb.o de 1805.
23. Geiger 1953, p. 10.
24. Anónimo 1796 Cuadros.
25. Yturralde 4 de Feb.o de 1796.
26. Bringas 15 de Marzo de 1796, fol. 21v.
27. *Ibid.*, fol. 22.
28. Yturralde 4 de Dic.e de 1796.
29. Yturralde 3 de Abril de 1798, fol. 7v.

30. Yturralde 4 de Dic.e de 1796. Early in 1797, college officials had Pimería Alta Mission President Francisco Yturralde sound out Father J. B. Llorens about leading the proposed mission to the Gila River Pimas. The bishop had by that time ordered Llorens to recruit no more neophytes to his mission (Yturralde 1 de Mayo de 1797).
31. Yturralde 3 de Abril de 1798, fol. 7.
32. Yturralde 3 de Abril de 1798, fol. 7v.
33. Oury 1862–1864, p. 63.
34. Brinckerhoff (1967:15) following Greenleaf and Wallace (1962:21) stated that the Franciscans built the two-story convent between 1797 and 1810. He thought that Peaceful Apaches constructed the building, thus providing yet another interpretation of the Tucson oral tradition mentioned in Chapter 4.
35. Because Page's description (1930:21-22) was based on quite detailed interviews with old Mexican-American residents of Tucson who actually worshipped in this church, it is the most accurate which can now be recovered in the absence of contemporary documents. An inventory of equipment made in 1855 substantially confirms Page's description, but is not given here because it properly belongs in the history of Mexican Tucson.
36. Yturralde 3 de Abril de 1798, fol. 6.
37. Pinart CPA Atí 52.
38. Socies Diciembre 14 de 1801, fol. 2.
39. Yturralde 4 de Mayo de 1798.
40. Yturralde 4 de Junio de 1798.
41. Newhall 1954, p. 29; Geiger 1953, pp. 6-10.
42. Cevallos Julio 7 de 1814.
43. This ability of one of a pair of missionaries to proselytize while his companion supervised the mission population had constituted one of Bringas' (Marzo 15 de 1796 fol. 19-19v) arguments for the change.
44. Reverend Victor R. Stoner, 9 March 1954, personal communication from Tumacacori B.
45. Rouset Mayo 12 de 1808.
46. Moyano Diciembre 4 de 1808.
47. Cevallos Julio 7 de 1814.
48. Brinckerhoff 1967, p. 15, n.23.
49. Gonzalez 1820, fol. 143.
50. Perez 1818, fol. 46-47.
51. Gonzalez 1820, fol. 142-143.
52. Gonzalez 4 de Enero de 1821.

6. Founding the Royal Spanish Post of San Agustín del Tucson, 1776-1779

1. Scholes (1962:23) identified this as an area of historical analysis to be cultivated with profit.
2. While I have read many Spanish colonial documents dealing with the Pimería Alta missions, I have encountered no evidence of clerics there raping or living with native women as early Dominicans in Peru were accused of doing (Gutierrez Flores 1970:5-14). Other scandals did occur among the Jesuits in Sonora. Several were criticized for allowing Spanish women in their quarters "on the pretext of making them some remedies, of cooking for them and acting as dispensaresses." (Aguirre Hen.o 7 de 1764). Others caused scandal by keeping loose-living siblings and female "god-children" of marriageable age in their households (Aguirre Marzo 1 de 1764; Aguirre Feb.o 18 de 1764).
3. *Mulatto* is here used to signify the offspring of one European and one African parent.
4. Lafora 1939, p. 155.
5. Garcés 1856 (29 July 1768), p. 366. Translated in Chapter 3.
6. Bolton 1939, pp. 70-71.
7. Ewing 1945, p. 277; Dobyns 1962, pp. 7-10.
8. Bolton 1939, pp. 77-78.

9. Powell 1944, p. 183 etc.
10. The Marqués de Rubí charged with inspecting the frontier defenses of New Spain was Field Marshall Cayetano María Pigatelli Rubí Corbera y San Climent, Baron of Llinás. The Rubí title dated from 30 June 1694 when King Charles II granted it to Joseph Rubí y Bojador for services his father and grandfather had rendered the Crown. Thus New Spain's field marshall belonged to Spain's highest nobility and a family with a long record of royal service in key military commands (Anónimo 1966:52:622-623; 65:1508; Robles 1939:16).
11. Thomas 1941, p. 180; Thomas 1932, p. 315.
12. Thomas 1941, p. 247.
13. Thomas 1932, p. 5.
14. *Ibid.*, p. 6.
15. *Ibid.*, p. 9.
16. Thomas 1941, pp. 172, 207.
17. In the course of establishing the policies recommended by the Marqués de Rubí, O'Connor did not rest for six hectic years, during which he rode over 12,000 miles on horseback inspecting and moving posts and fighting Indians. By the time he reached Sonora in the summer of 1775, O'Connor had ascended to the rank of colonel. Promoted to brigadier, he became governor and captain general of the Province of Yucatán on 24 February 1778. His health undermined by his intensive efforts in northern New Spain, O'Connor died near Mérida on 8 March 1779 (Almada 1952:529-30; O'Conor, Garcés & Fernandez C, 20 de Agosto 1775).
18. O'Conor 1952, pp. 64-65.
19. O'Conor 18 de Agosto de 1775 No. 13.
20. O'Conor, Garcés y Fernández C., 20 de Agosto de 1775.
21. Greenleaf & Wallace 1962, p. 21.
22. O'Conor 1952, p. 75; Moore & Beene 1971.
23. O'Conor y Oliva, 22 de Agosto de 1775. The Presidio of Santa Cruz was located in one of the headwaters valleys of the Santa Cruz River prior to Hugh O'Connor's relocation efforts in 1775. O'Connor, accompanied by Lieutenant Juan M. Oliva, decided to move it north to the west bank of the San Pedro River near a former Sobaipuri village. The post was abandoned by the spring of 1780 after a series of Apache defeats of its garrison. (*Cf.* Croix 30 Nov. 1778.)

    C. C. Di Peso (1953) excavated the ruins of the short-lived military post. Gerald (1968:18) errs in dating occupation of the post to the summer of 1775. O'Connor selected the site on 22 August, two days after he picked the site for the future Presidio of San Agustín del Tucson. Later, O'Connor ordered the Terrenate garrison to move forward as of 10 December 1775, but it seems doubtful whether that garrison carried out O'Connor's orders any more rapidly than did the Tubac garrison. In terms of modern geography, Santa Cruz lies 16 miles south of Benson, Arizona.
24. O'Conor y Oliva, 25 de Agosto de 1775. Don Hugh O'Connor moved the Fronteras garrison forward to a place known as San Bernardino on the basis of his 25 August 1775 inspection with Lieutenant J. M. Oliva. It is 16 miles east of modern Douglas, Arizona, on the west side of the San Bernardino River (Gerald 1968:21).
25. Thomas 1941, pp. 181, 183; (Croix 30 Oct. 1781 paragraphs 414, 420). Moore and Beene 1971, p. 271, n.13. Meanwhile, Juan Bautista de Anza led his second California expedition out of Tubac Presidio on 23 October 1775. He stopped at Tucson the night of 26-27 October, clearly identifying it as a "pueblo" (Bolton 1930:III:6, 9-10). Garcés called Tucson "the last Christian settlement in this direction" (Galvin 1965:5). Thus, the garrison remained at Tubac at the end of October 1775.
26. Moore and Beene 1971, p. 276.
27. Coues 1900, Vol. I, p. 29; Bolton 1931, p. 28. Inasmuch as O'Connor reported that the Altar, Tubac and Tucson garrisons all were to have moved on December 10 (Moore & Beene 1971:276), he clearly had ordered them to do so. I follow Font, however, on the Tubac-Tucson move having actually occurred in 1776. Just when the move was made continues to be a question, but it may have been well into 1776. Father Francisco Garcés mentioned no post at Tucson when he returned from California and the Hopi

Pueblos via the Gila River, reaching his Mission San Xavier del Bac on 17 September 1776 (Galvin 1965:88). Negative evidence cannot be conclusive, yet one would think that Garcés would have mentioned the post had it been moved during his absence. Instead, he continued to recommend that a presidio be established on the Gila and another on the Colorado River (Galvin 1965:93). That the post moved to Tucson in 1776 is indicated also by a list of "Patents and Commissions of Officers of war from 1776 until 1783" for the "Presidio of San Agustín de Tugson" (Archivo General de Indias Audiencia de Guadalajara 505). Had the garrison moved to Tucson in 1775, it seems logical to expect that the scribe would have given 1775 as the initial date for the promotion list.

Friar Pedro Font accompanied Anza's second expedition to Upper California as chaplain, astronomer and diarist (Bolton 1931:IV:ix). Font departed from Mission San José de Pimas, where he was missionary, on 30 June 1775 (*ibid.*, p. 2). After returning to Sonora, Font wrote a short report on the trip at Ures, then repaired to Tubutama Mission to write one five times as long (*ibid.*, p. x). Visiting Santa María Magdalena, the priest was nearly slain by Seris who attacked in 1776. Soon after, Font took up duties as missionary at San Diego de Pitiquito, where he served until his death on 6 September 1781 (Arricivita 1792:561).

28. Medina 1779.
29. Bolton 1930, Vol. III, pp. 6-192.
30. Oliva could sign his name, inasmuch as his signature appears on O'Connor's certifications of inspection of the Santa Cruz and San Bernardino sites. O'Connor (18 de Agosto de 1775) criticized Oliva's illiteracy, however, so signing his name probably constituted the limit of Oliva's ability.
31. Oliva 13 de Agosto de 1775 No. 8.
32. O'Conor 18 de Agosto de 1775.
33. Bucareli 27 de Octubre de 1775.
34. Charles III, 28 de Febrero de 1776.
35. Bucareli 27 de Mayo de 1776.
36. Bolton 1930, Vol. V, p. 392.
37. Bolton 1931, Vol. IV, p. 510. Font referred to Beldarrain on 24 May 1776 as the ensign of Tubac. This could mean that the garrison remained at Tubac. On the other hand, presidial place associations often lingered after a move, so Font could have referred to the unit as the Tubac company even after its advance to Tucson.
38. Thomas 1932, p. 6.
39. Service Record in Medina 1779. Assigned on 11 February he actually assumed command on 12 June.
40. Allande y Saabedra 1785.
41. Gerald 1968, p. 16.
42. Brinckerhoff and Faulk 1965, pp. 26-27.
43. Medina 1779.
44. Croix 23 de Agosto de 1780.
45. Medina 15 de Enero de 1784. Moore & Beene (1971:271, n.13) also give 1783 as the date of wall completion. The source is not apparent, however, inasmuch as the only post-1783 document they cite says nothing about the physical structure. (It is Neve's 26 January 1784 report already published in translation [Dobyns 1964:32] and retranslated below.)
46. Lockwood 1943, p. 3, reported the walls were 18 inches thick. Modern construction allowed Dr. Edward Danson and University of Arizona students to expose the northeast corner of the presidio in 1954 (Chambers 1955:15). They found that the sun-dried bricks employed to make the wall averaged 4 inches thick, 12 inches wide and 18 inches long. Three bricks were laid in adobe mortar to form the base (Greenleaf & Wallace 1962:22). Thus, it slightly exceeded 3 feet in width.
47. Gallego 1935, p. 76.
48. Hughes 1885. Actually, the presidio was between 600 and 700 feet square (Brinckerhoff, personal communication). Greenleaf & Wallace (1962:22) wrote that the walled area was 750 feet square.
49. In Arizona, the Spanish presidio, with its civilian farming-ranching satellite population, and the Mormon irrigated farming village followed similar although independent models of concentrating rural populations in compact settlements within Native Ameri-

can territories. The customary Anglo-American settlement on scattered family farmsteads proved much less adapted to conditions on the Apache frontier.

Both villages followed a pre-existing ideal plan. The Mormon village followed the plan for the "City of Zion" drawn up by Joseph Smith, Sidney Rigdon and Frederick G. Williams in 1833 (Nelson 1930:18). They were probably entirely ignorant of Spanish town and military post planning.

50. Foster 1960, p. 49.
51. Presidial social solidarity resembled that of the Mormon village. Anti-Mormon sentiment and actions by non-Mormons initially fostered in-group solidarity among Mormon villagers, contributing to the success of this form of European land settlement in regions of North America previously occupied only by native inhabitants. While the Paiute Indians posed no great military threat to Mormon villagers, inter-ethnic hostilities did help to reinforce village social solidarity (Nelson 1930:26-27).
52. Mormon leaders had to struggle to achieve identification with an older prestige (Nelson 1930:21).
53. The religious institution formed the backbone of the Mormon village. Nelson (1930: 29) concluded that the geographic and social environment of the Great Basin favored the village settlement plan. Tucson and similar Spanish colonial settlements raise doubts about Nelson's geographic determinism. The Spanish presidio exemplified at Tucson also shared a social environment of European intrusion into Native American territory, thus fostering compact, easily defensible settlements. What the geographic environment may have had to do with favoring village settlement seems much less apparent. Nelson mentions that village settlement fostered common pasturage of harvested fields and common fencing and storage of crops in the village. Yet these are actions governed by the cultural patterns of the people carrying them out independent of environmental imperatives.

    While Spanish documents about Tucson are silent regarding fencing, for example, one can easily doubt after seeing hundreds of unfenced Hispanic American rural villages that fences separated Tucson fields or pastures. Inasmuch as the rich alluvial fields of the Santa Cruz River Valley contained no significant amount of stone to interfere with cultivation, even stone fence rows of the sort common in formerly glaciated mountain areas of Meso-America and South America did not appear at Tucson. Sketches and photographs of this part of the valley in the 19th century make doubtful whether Tucson truck gardeners ever enclosed their rich plots with puddled adobe walls in the fashion of farmers in the rich irrigated valleys of coastal Peru or the Andean highlands.

    The point is that both Spaniards and Mormons settled in villages in environments not very different and affording materials from which fences or walls could be fashioned. Yet Mormons erected fences as did other Northwest Europeans, while the Spaniards apparently did not erect them, like other inheritors of Mediterranean cultural traditions. In other words, cultural antecedents affected village life far more than did environmental factors.
54. Malinowski 1945, pp. 50, 73ff.
55. Spicer 1962, p. 98.
56. Sasaki and Adair (1952:108-109) reported on Navajo settlers on a U.S. Bureau of Indian Affairs irrigation project. They found kinship ties that allowed nuclear families to cooperate in taking turns irrigating were crucial to production success. Beardsley (1964) found that rice-growing led to close parallels in social organization in Japan and Spain. Gallin (1959) reported the same phenomenon on Taiwan.
57. Most Mormon villages shared with Tucson this environmental influence of semi-aridity, so that farming and gardening depended upon irrigation. Nelson (1930) nonetheless did not recognize the need for minimal cooperation in irrigation water management as one influence toward cooperation in Mormon villages as a form of land settlement.
58. Medina 1779.
59. Charles III, 12 de Junio de 1777.
60. Cline (1962:174) suggested that the borderlands bred during that century "a type of frontiersman . . ." who was "insufficiently delineated in the literature. . . ."
61. Medina 1779. Miguel's father, Bernardo de Urrea, was born in Culiacán, Sinaloa, about 1710. Moving to Pitíc (modern Hermosillo), he had become a government official by 1748. In 1751, he organized militia to fight rebel Native Americans, beginning a career

that included participation in over 100 actions against Native Americans. Don Bernardo thrice served as acting governor of the Province of Sonora and Sinaloa and took command of the Sonoran troops on two occasions. Commandant General of the Frontier Provinces Teodoro de Croix granted Don Bernardo's retirement in February of 1777, but the pioneer Urrea did not live to enjoy it (Almada 1952:805-806).

Don Miguel de Urrea's career as an Indian fighter paralleled that of his father in many ways. Despite their success in battle after battle, these frontier officers never won the wars against Native American foes.

62. Charles III, 31 de Agosto de 1776.
63. Bolton 1931, Vol. IV, p. 511; O'Conor 18 de Agosto de 1775.
64. Charles III, 26 de Agosto de 1778 a.
65. Torres Q. 1921, p. 33.
66. *Ibid.*, pp. 12-22.
67. *Ibid.*, p. 12.
68. Spicer 1962, p. 98.
69. *Ibid.*, p. 482.
70. Malinowski 1945, pp. 50, 73-75.
71. Medina 1779.
72. Brinckerhoff and Faulk 1965, pp. 22-23. A soldier's annual pay was 290 pesos (pp. 18-19), or 6.35 *reales* per day.
73. Thomas 1941, p. 152 (Croix 30 de Oct. de 1780 Para. 312).
74. Charles III, 26 de Agosto de 1778 b. Frontier Province Commandant Inspector Hugh O'Connor assigned Márquez to the Tubac unit when he inspected it in 1775, and recommended Oliva for retirement and Beldarrain for dismissal (O'Conor 18 de Agosto de 1775). Tona eventually won a commission as second ensign at Santa Cruz. In 1784, he was promoted to first ensign (Charles III 28 de Marzo de 1784). He rose to the rank of captain and commanded the presidial garrison at San Miguel de Horcasitas at the time of his death late in 1802 or early in 1803 (Charles IV 18 de Marzo de 1803).
75. Parke 1855, p. 30.
76. Oury 1862–1864, pp. 83-84.
77. Bolton 1939, pp. 83-84.
78. Tumacacori B, fol. 137.

7. Fighting Apaches: Offense and Defense 1778-1782

1. Allande y Saabedra 1785 Memorial.
2. Don Pedro de Tueros was captain of the oldest Sonoran presidio when Lieutenant Colonel Juan B. de Anza left the commandancy of arms of Sonora to attend Croix's council of war in Chihuahua. Croix ordered Tueros to assume the military command of the province, which he did in March of 1778 (Thomas 1941:141). After 60 Apaches slew 20 of 34 troopers from Santa Cruz Presidio in open battle, Tueros reinforced that post with a volunteer company (*ibid.*, p. 142). Tueros twice personally led San Miguel de Horcasitas presidials against Seris. Brigadier Jacobo Ugarte y Loyola relieved Tueros on 31 July 1779 (*ibid.*, p. 143).
3. Thomas 1941, p. 143. Thomas sums up Croix's life and Frontier Provinces service.
4. Croix 30 de Nov.e de 1778.
5. Allande y Saabedra 1785 Memorial.
6. *Ibid.*
7. Croix 1780. Croix made Arizpe capital of the Frontier Provinces late in 1779.
8. Spicer 1962, p. 133.
9. Ezell 1961, p. 136.
10. Spicer 1962, p. 427. This process of linguistic unification is one that Spicer did not mention.
11. Croix 7 de Marzo de 1780.

12. Thomas 1941, p. 219 (Croix 30 Oct. 1781, Para. 521).
13. Thomas 1941, p. 220 (Croix 30 Oct. 1781, Para. 528).
14. Thomas 1941, pp. 59-60.
15. Croix 23 de Agosto de 1780. A detachment of the garrison pursued the Apaches when they withdrew, but without result.
16. Croix 23 de Julio de 1780.
17. Croix 23 de Agosto de 1780.
18. Croix 23 de Marzo de 1781.
19. Priestley 1913, pp. 35-39.
20. Abate 2 de Mayo de 1782.
21. Thomas 1932, p. 45.
22. Scholes (1962:23) identified a need for such studies in assessing the historiography of the Southwest.
23. Allande y Saabedra 2 de Mayo de 1782.
24. This tree bears a pod reportedly made into *pinole* in Sonora at one time (Lange, Riley & Lange, eds., 1970:281).
25. Usarraga y Delgado 1782.
26. Velderrain 4 de Mayo de 1782.
27. "Distinguished" was a title of respect for enlisted men of higher social status than common soldiers in the presidial garrisons. "Distinguished" soldiers would normally be commissioned after training.
28. Franco 1782.
29. Charles III, 21 de Febrero de 1783.
30. Usarraga 3 de Mayo de 1782.
31. Allande y Saabedra 1785.
32. Abate, 2 de Mayo de 1782, partial translation.
33. Charles III, 14 de Mayo de 1782.
34. Allande y Saabedra 1785.
35. *Ibid.*
36. Usarraga y Granillo 3 de Mayo de 1782.
37. Usarraga, Fernandez, Cancio y Ortega 1782.
38. Usarraga 3 de Mayo de 1782.
39. Usarraga, Fernandez, Cancio y Ortega 1782.
40. Croix 15 de Mayo de 1782.
41. This was the estimate most generally postulated (Usarraga, Fernandez, Cancio y Ortega 1782).
42. Spicer 1962, p. 547.
43. *Ibid.*
44. Usarraga 3 de Mayo de 1782.
45. Franco 1782.
46. Usarraga y Chacón 1782.
47. Medina 15 de Enero de 1784.

8. Harassing the Western Apaches 1782-1792

1. Brinckerhoff and Faulk 1965, p. 7.
2. Brinckerhoff 1967, p. 8.
3. Sauer 1935, p. 4.
4. Neve 30 de Noviembre de 1782.
5. The king in his 1772 New Regulations specified that ten Indian scouts commanded by a corporal should be attached to each frontier garrison (Brinckerhoff & Faulk 1965:17).
6. Neve 30 de Noviembre de 1782.
7. Neve 26 de Enero de 1784, fol. 2.
8. Croix 27 de Enero de 1783, No. 869.
9. Croix Julio de 1783.

10. Allande 1785. These three campaigns did not go simply "to the Gila River" as stated by Brinckerhoff (1967:8).
11. Medina 15 de Enero de 1784.
12. Medina 1779.
13. Abate 24 de Diciembre de 1783.
14. Brinckerhoff and Faulk 1965, pp. 22-23. Paragraph 5, Title 4, called for each soldier to have one mule, six serviceable horses and one colt.
15. Neve 26 de Enero de 1784, partial translation. Like most superior officers in Spain's colonial service, Phelipe de Neve benefitted from birth on the Peninsula, in the city of Bailén. Governor of the Californias from 1775 to 1782, he moved the capital from Loreto in Lower California to Monterey in Upper California. Neve became adjutant inspector of the Frontier Provinces in the latter year. On 12 August 1783, he succeeded to the command vacated by the Caballero Teodoro de Croix. Again he displayed a penchant for changing capitals. In May of 1784, Neve advised the Chihuahua city government to prepare quarters for him and his staff. He died on the road from Arizpe to Chihuahua City on 21 August 1784 (Almada 1952:505).
16. Neve 5 de Abril de 1784, fol. 1.
17. Tumacacori B., fol. 24.
18. Medina 1779.
19. Neve 5 de Abril de 1784.
20. Treutlein 1949, p. 291.
21. Neve 30 de Noviembre de 1782, emphasis added.
22. Medina 15 de Enero de 1784, emphasis added.
23. O'Conor 1 de Diz.e de 1775, fol. 78v.
24. Neve 8 de Marzo de 1784.
25. Charles III 23 de Agosto de 1784.
26. Thomas 1932, p. 246.
27. *Ibid.*, p. 248. Don Roque de Medina, a captain of cavalry, became adjutant inspector under Frontier Province Commandant General Teodoro de Croix (Thomas 1941:143).
28. Thomas 1932, pp. 248, 254. Don Diego de Borica ranked as a captain commanding San Elezario Presidio when Frontier Province Commandant General Teodoro de Croix assumed command. When the commanding inspector of Nueva Vizcaya died, Croix commissioned Borica to inspect the frontier presidios (Thomas 1941:117).
29. Thomas 1932, pp. 248, 255.
30. Allande 1785.
31. Thomas 1932, p. 255.
32. *Ibid.*, p. 248.
33. *Ibid.*, p. 249.
34. *Ibid.*, p. 256.
35. *Ibid.*, p. 240.
36. Sauer 1935, p. 5.
37. *Ibid.*, pp. 7-8, 12.
38. *Ibid.*, p. 9.
39. *Ibid.*, pp. 10-11.
40. Allande 1785.
41. Sauer 1935, p. 12.
42. Neve 6 de Julio de 1784.
43. Allande 1785.
44. Medina 6 de Octubre de 1785.
45. Charles III 27 de Feb.o de 1784.
46. Viceroy Bernardo de Gálvez gained his initial colonial experience on the frontier of New Spain fighting Apaches, beginning in 1769. He rose rapidly in the royal service with the aid of his uncle, José de Gálvez, one of King Charles III's most powerful ministers. Bernardo returned to Spain after Hugh O'Connor assumed the Frontier Province command. The king sent Bernardo to Louisiana in 1776 with the rank of colonel, and in September of that year a royal order made him acting governor.

    When Spain joined the rebel English North American colonies in 1779, Bernardo de Gálvez conquered the British Gulf posts, including Pensacola and Mobile Bays, as well as taking the Bahamas. In 1783, he participated in councils in Spain, establishing policies for the new Florida and Mississippi frontiers. Toward the end of 1784, he became captain general of Cuba and governor of Louisiana and the Floridas.

When his father died in 1785, Bernardo succeeded him as viceroy of New Spain. He retained jurisdiction over Cuba, Louisiana and the Floridas, and extended his authority over the Frontier Provinces. Not long after promulgating the new Apache policy, however, he died during an epidemic (Worcester 1951:21-22).

47. Bancroft 1889, pp. 378-379. The entire Gálvez Instruction has been translated into English by Donald E. Worcester (1951).
48. Echegaray 12 de Febrero de 1788, fol. 368. The king transferred Echegaray, already a captain of the Third Mobile Company of Nueva Vizcaya to command the Presidio of Santa Cruz in 1785 after the death of Captain Josef Antonio de Vildosola (Charles III 5 de Febrero de 1785).
49. Echegaray 12 de Feb.o de 1788 fol. 370v-371.
50. *Ibid.*, fol. 371v.
51. *Ibid.*, fol. 369.
52. Croix 30 Nov.e de 1778.
53. Croix 23 de Junio de 1780.
54. Medina 27 de Febrero de 1786.
55. Almada 1952:697.
56. Charles III 12 de Octubre de 1788.
57. Arvizu 31 de Diciembre de 1816, fol. 235.
58. Ugarte 10 de Julio de 1788.
59. Romero 24 de Junio de 1788, fol. 425v.
60. Almada 1952:697.
61. Charles III 12 de Octubre de 1788.
62. Arriquibar 6 de Marzo de 1806.
63. Charles III 1 de Octubre de 1788a.
64. Charles III 27 de Feb. de 1784.
65. Hammond 1931, pp. 42, 44.
66. Echegaray 20 de Octubre de 1788, fol. 520-520v.
67. Hammond 1931, p. 46. Captain Echegaray did not survive long in the era of peace. He died in 1796 (Charles IV Sep.re 7 de 1796).
68. Bancroft 1889, p. 379.
69. Brinckerhoff 1967, pp. 19-20. Brinckerhoff (1967:19) concluded that the Spaniards held the Apaches "at bay" for "three decades," one more than Bancroft.
70. Brinckerhoff appears not entirely consistent. In this summary of late colonial times that emphasizes 30 years of peace, Brinckerhoff (1967:19) still writes of "the breakdown of frontier Indian policies." Because Apaches returned to economic raiding after 1830, Brinckerhoff blames the Spaniards – who had not then ruled Mexico for a decade – for not driving enough Apaches to seek peace and for not sufficiently converting to "the Spanish way of life" those who did. Brinckerhoff does mention Mexican independence as one factor making "full execution" of the Gálvez plan impossible. He does not amplify that key Mexican policy-makers abandoned the Gálvez strategy and reverted to inter-ethnic warfare, as well as terminated the subsidy program. In effect, Mexico forced many Peaceful Apaches to return to hunting, gardening and economic raiding.
71. Brinckerhoff and Faulk 1965, p. 7, have not been the only writers who underestimated the effectiveness of Spanish colonial frontier institutions in northern New Spain. Priestly (1917:357) long since set a pattern by considering the Frontier Provinces set up by José de Gálvez as too large, thinly settled and geographically difficult "for successful unification." His conclusion that what he termed a "paucity of Spanish resources" for protecting such a vast territory was felt no more keenly anywhere else may be questioned along with the view of Brinckerhoff and Faulk, in terms of information about military success in the Frontier Provinces presented in this chapter.
72. Almada 1952, p. 67.
73. Charles IV 12 de Agosto de 1789.
74. Charles IV 19 de Mayo de 1792.

75. Charles III 26 de Agosto de 1778c. Born in 1755, José de Zúñiga entered royal service on 18 October 1772 as an officer candidate. He campaigned under O'Connor in 1773–76, and aided in the transfer of the del Norte, Pilares and San Carlos de Cerro Gordo Presidios. After winning his commission dated 26 August 1778, Zúñiga earned promotion to lieutenant on 21 April 1780. He then languished in grade for a dozen years. In 1781, Zúñiga led a group of colonists from Guaymas to Loreto and then Mission San Gabriel. On 8 September 1781, he assumed command at San Diego (Holterman 1956:1).
76. Charles IV 1 de Marzo de 1790.
77. Charles IV 11 de Agosto de 1790.

9. Peace with the Western Apaches 1793-1821

1. Moorhead 1968.
2. Corbalán 1 de Diciembre de 1796 b; Moorehead 1968, pp. 182-183.
3. Moorhead 1968, pp. 183-185.
4. *Ibid.*, pp. 63, 185. Jacobo de Ugarte y Loyola, born in the Peninsular Province of Guipúzcoa in 1728, entered the royal army on 15 April 1742 in the Royal Guards. After fighting in Italy and Portugal as a field grade officer, Ugarte was posted to New Spain. Governor of Coahuila from 5 December 1769, he there received his promotion to brigadier. Thereafter Ugarte served as military governor of Sonora (1779–1782), governor of Puebla (1783–1785) and commandant general of the Frontier Provinces (1786–1787). Those provinces returned to viceregal control on 20 May 1787, and the viceroy made Ugarte directly responsible for Sonora, Sinaloa and the Californias. Although he energetically led the campaign to pacify the Apaches, Ugarte ended Spanish persecution of Tarahumara Indians. Promoted to field marshall, Ugarte left the Frontier Provinces on 14 September 1790 to become intendent governor, captain general and president of the Audiencia of Nueva Galicia in Guadalajara on 14 January 1791.

   The king promoted Ugarte to lieutenant general in 1797, and he died on 20 August 1798, mourned by people of all social classes. One reason was his interest in building institutions behind the frontier. Ugarte initiated the first primary school and the military hospital in Chihuahua City, inaugurated the University of Guadalajara and introduced the first press in the modern State of Jalisco. (Almada 1952:801-802).
5. Moorhead 1968, p. 186. Juan de Ugalde governed Coahuila and Texas once the viceroy regained control of the Frontier Provinces in May of 1787 (Almada 1952:801). El Norte Presidio is modern Ciudad Juárez opposite El Paso, Texas.
6. Moorhead 1968, pp. 188-191.
7. *Ibid.*, p. 191.
8. Escalante 1 de Febrero de 1788; Moorhead 1968, p. 192.
9. Moorhead 1968, p. 193.
10. *Ibid.*, pp. 194-196.
11. *Ibid.*, pp. 198-199.
12. Echegaray 21 de Enero de 1793, fol. 527.
13. *Ibid.*, Nava 29 de Enero de 1793, fol. 529.
14. Nava 14 de Febrero de 1793, fol. 551.
15. Pedro de Nava commanded the Frontier Provinces from 7 March 1791 until 4 November 1802. He finally changed the capital from Arizpe to Chihuahua and again led an administration independent of the viceroy (Almada 1952: 501).
16. Echegaray 21 de Enero de 1793.
17. Corbalán 1 de Diciembre de 1786a. Pedro de Corbalán, born in Barcelona, came to New Spain in 1766 with his relative, the Viceroy Marqués de Croix. Corbalán reached Sonora as subintendent of exchequer with the Sonora Expedition of 1767. Promoted to intendent, Corbalán assumed charge of the royal treasury office at Alamos. Simultaneously, he became governor to replace Juan de Pineda, until the arrival of Sastré in 1772. On 27 July 1776 the king made Corbalán governor of Sonora. After 11 years in that office, he returned to Alamos, where he died in September of 1797 (Almada 1952:184-185).

18. Escalante 26 de Enero de 1787.
19. Garrido 20 de Diciembre de 1787. The Indian agent paid 4 pesos per Spanish bushel of wheat (J. A. de Escalante 31 de Agosto de 1789), 4 pesos 4 reales per bushel of maize (Theran 10 de Febrero de 1789) and purchased cigarettes at 16 packs for a peso (Denofeanto 20 de Marzo de 1789).
20. Escalante Diciembre de 1788.
21. Licendiado Garrido had succeeded Pedro Corbalán as governor of Sonora and Sinaloa in October of 1787 (Almada 1952:185).
22. Escalante Diciembre de 1788.
23. Llorens Junio 2 de 1795, fol. 65.
24. Hernandez 1820, fol. 215.
25. León 29 de Agosto de 1813a.
26. Chapman 1919, pp. 718-719.
27. Carrillo 25 de Febrero de 1819.
28. Narbona 8 de Marzo de 1819.
29. Cordero 1 de Abril de 1819.
30. Venadito 11 de Mayo de 1819.
31. Romero 21 de Mayo de 1819.
32. García Conde 19 de Julio de 1819.
33. Díaz 1873, p. 3.
34. Carroll 1965, p. 10.

10. Peacetime Presidio 1793-1821

1. King Charles IV of Spain, second son of Carlos III and María Amelia, was born 11 November 1748. In 1765, he married María Luisa of Parma, who, with a series of ministers, dominated him when he assumed the throne on his father's death on 14 December 1788. When French revolutionists executed King Louis XVI on 21 January 1793, Charles declared war, and Spanish troops marched into France. Spain spent 680,000,000 reales during the first six months, and in 1794–1795 expenditure was double the government's income. France invaded Spain, occupying Figueras, Fuenterrabía, Pasajes and San Sebastian. Spain ceded part of Santo Domingo in the 22 July 1795 peace treaty.

   Less than two years later, Charles IV allied Spain with the French Directory on 27 June 1797, and declared war on England on 7 October. His foreign policy turned into unmitigated disaster from that time on. Under the 1807 Treaty of Fontainebleau for the partition of Portugal, Napoleon sent troops into Spain. On 19 March 1808, Charles IV abdicated in favor of Crown Prince Ferdinand after trying to flee. Meeting with Napoleon, Charles agreed to cede the Spanish Crown to the emperor in return for a pension. Going to Compiègne, he moved to Rome in 1811, dying there on 20 January 1819 (Anon. 1966:11:1039-1040).
2. Captain George Vancouver met Zúñiga at San Diego on 27 November 1793. The British explorer referred to Zúñiga as former commander of the San Diego post, recently promoted and preparing to leave for his new post (Holterman 1956:2 citing Vancouver 1798:II:470, 473, 482).
3. Moraga 1793.
4. Charles IV 18 de Julio de 1793. A grandson of that Bernardo de Urrea who founded the Presidio of Altar, Mariano was born there in 1765. After serving Altar as a cadet and Horcasitas as an ensign, Mariano was promoted to a lieutenant in the Tucson company on 25 February 1793. He became commanding lieutenant of the Opata Indian Company of Bacoachi on 9 September 1804. On 20 July he ascended to captain in command at Altar.

   The 1810 revolution drastically changed his career. After helping route Gonzalez de Hermosillo at San Ignacio Piaxtla, Urrea assumed command of the Rosario area. In 1812, he went to Tepic. In 1815, he assumed command of the Colotlan Provincial Regiment as lieutenant colonel and acting governor. He went to Apatzingan in 1819 and in 1821 supported General Pedro Celestino Negrete in proclaiming the Plan de

Iguala for independence. Urrea commanded the cavalry during the siege of Durango, taking command of Nueva Vizcaya.

Emperor Iturbide made Urrea a colonel in 1822, and he briefly commanded the Western Frontier Provinces. Removed by Iturbide, Urrea defended himself in Mexico City, then led some of the troops that deposed the emperor.

The next government rewarded Urrea with the title of superior political and military chief of the Provinces of Sonora and Sinaloa, where he took command 31 July 1823. Arrested in 1825 and sent to Mexico City under escort, Urrea joined a Masonic lodge. He tried to raise a rebellion at the end of 1826. Re-arrested, he was exiled. Urrea died in Guayaquil, Ecuador, in 1852 (Almada 1952:810-813; Villa 1948:184).

5. Charles IV 9 de Mayo de 1794. Franco retired with this rank within three years (Charles IV 8 de Junio de 1797).
6. Nava 8 de Agosto de 1794.
7. Hammond 1931, p. 52.
8. *Ibid.*, p. 53.
9. *Ibid.*, pp. 57-58. Antonio Narbona was to become an important post-independence official in Mexico, as outlined in Chapter 10. He was born in 1773 and served in Campeche before coming to Sonora. Narbona's key action for independence came on 6 September 1821. In 1823, as acting head of the Province of Sonora, Narbona suppressed Yaqui and Opata unrest. Promoted to colonel in 1825, he aided in defeating rebel Yaquis. Turning over the Sonoran command to General Figueroa, Narbona became governor of New Mexico in 1826 and 1827. Returning to Sonora, he died in Arizpe in 1830 according to Almada (1952:500). Villa (1948:14) claimed that Narbona was born at Cuaquiárachi, Sonora, and was killed there by Apaches on 23 December 1848, which seems doubtful.
10. Hammond 1931, p. 62.
11. Bringas 15 de Marzo de 1796, fol. 22.
12. Hammond 1931, p. 52.
13. Charles IV, 1 de Julio de 1794.
14. Mata Biñolas 1794.
15. Arvizu 31 de Diciembre de 1816, fol. 233.
16. *Ibid.*, fol. 231.
17. Hammond 1931, pp. 53, 55. Manuel Ignacio de Arvizu was born in Altar in 1760. He we apparently a brother or a son of Manuel Antonio de Arvizu, who became a captain at Altar in 1796 (Charles IV 6 de Diz.re de 1796).

    Manuel Ignacio joined the Altar presidial company in 1779 at 19 years of age. Ten years later he became a cadet and won a commission on 22 January 1794 as second ensign of the Santa Cruz garrison (Charles IV 22 de En.o de 1794). He served almost a decade at that rank, winning promotion in 1803 (Charles IV 11 de Mayo de 1803).

    Arvizu became lieutenant in the Pitíc garrison in 1805, and won a captaincy in 1809 as commander of the Bavispe post. He followed Alejo García Conde south in 1810 to defeat Gonzales Hermosillo at San Ignacio Piaxtla. Arvizu then ascended to lieutenant colonel in 1812 after a dozen engagements against the rebels. In 1814, he commanded a Mobile Company. His later role at Tucson is noted in the text.

    Arvizu adhered to the *Plan de Iguala* on 3 September and won his colonelcy in December. In 1823, Arvizu commanded the State of Chihuahua. Nonetheless, he reportedly returned to the Tucson command in 1825, the same year that he engaged rebel Yaquis. Charged with desertion during the Yaqui campaign, Arvizu was rehabilitated by the federal Congress in 1827, and assumed command of the San Buenaventura garrison. Retired, he died in Arizpe early in 1832 (Almada 1952:84).
18. Almada 1952, p. 806. Villa (1948:177) reported that José was born at Altar on 19 March. José himself considered 19 March his birthday (Castañeda 1928:223) so he may well have been born at Altar and baptized several months later at Tucson.

    Considering the military record achieved by both the Urrea and Elías Gonzales families on the northwestern frontier of New Spain, a brilliant career could have been predicted for their joint offspring. José began his military career on 15 August 1809 as a cadet in the presidial garrison of San Rafael de Buenavista. Over the next 11 years he distinguished himself in various military maneuvers in Mexico, winning regular promotions. He supported the *Plan de Iguala* and received a captaincy on 12 December 1821. Assigned to Huichapan, he supported the *Plan de Casa Mata* that overthrew Iturbide. Then he took part in the siege of San Juan de Uloa, the final Spanish stronghold in Mexico.

Thereafter José initiated a long career as a political-military rebel. Highlights of this unusual lifetime included service as general of brigade of the force moving into Texas to put down the Anglo-American independence movement, two years (6 May 1842–21 May 1844) as governor and military commandant of Sonora, and active service as commandant general of Tamaulipas and Durango during the last years of his life. Low points included periods in prison and exile, and defeats of his several rebellions against the various governments. He died on 1 August 1849 during the cholera epidemic. In sum, Tucson native son José de Urrea y Elías Gonzáles pursued a colorful, active career of political rebellions, defections and disobedience to orders of the central government for 40 years, with occasional flashes of progressive governance, supported always by strong partisans and opposed by bitter enemies (Almada 1952:806-810).

19. Urrea 24 de Agosto de 1798.
20. Ynforme sobre las Misiones del Colegio de Querétaro.
21. Arvizu 31 de Diciembre de 1816, fol. 235. Holterman (1956:3) reports that Zúñiga was captain of Tucson in 1806 when ordered to pay some of Nicolás Soler's debts. Zúñiga served as adjutant inspector of the province at Arizpe at least as early as August 1807 (García H. 7 de Agosto de 1807). The rank of lieutenant colonel that Holterman (1956:3) says Zúñiga held was consistent with the adjutant inspector's post, although a Mexico City 30 May 1810 dispatch placed Zúñiga at Tucson, according to Holterman. Almada (1952:851) wrote that Ignacio Zúñiga received command of Tucson in 1809. Thus, a question of identification arises! Brinckerhoff (1967:11, n. 16) followed Holterman in having José de Zúñiga at Tucson until 1810 and dating his lieutenant colonelcy to that year.
22. Charles IV 11 de Mayo de 1803.
23. Nemesio Salcedo 4 de Septiembre de 1806.
24. Arvizu 31 de Dic.e de 1816, fol. 235. Almada (1952:851) claimed, however, that Ignacio Zúñiga assumed command of Tucson in 1809, and at Pitíc in 1816. I rely on Tucson service records and primary documents for the command record in the text, and conclude that peacetime post command changed very frequently.
25. Manuel de León rose through the ranks like other officers of the colonial period. He served as corporal in the Bacoachi garrison as early as January, 1789. Even as a noncommissioned officer, León enjoyed the advantage of literacy (León 11 de Enero de 1789), bespeaking an early formal education uncommon among presidial soldiers. Service at Bacoachi at that time accustomed León to dealing with Peaceful Apaches from a very early point in his military career. That surely became a major concern of Tucson's officers from 1793 until independence.

    In 1804, León became an ensign and commanded the Pima Indian Company at Tubac (León 1807:3). He continued there at least until 22 December 1808, when he and his wife became godparents to a son born to citizens of Tumacacori (San José de Tumacacori B. f. 45). Some time during the following five years, Manuel de León transferred to Tucson, having been promoted to lieutenant. There he would remain until at least early 1825 (León 16 Febrero de 1825; Urrea 8 de Marzo de 1825).
26. León 29 de Agosto de 1813a, fol. 1-1v.
27. León, 29 de Agosto de 1813b, fol. 2.
28. León 19 de Octubre de 1813, fol. 7.
29. León 29 de Agosto de 1813a, fol. 15v-16.
30. *Ibid.*, fol. 16v-17, 19.
31. León 29 de Enero de 1815, fol. 20v.

32. Arvizu 31 de Diciembre de 1816; Arvizu 1 de Enero de 1817; 1 de Febrero de 1817; 1 de Marzo de 1817. Arvizu was promoted to command Tucson from the captaincy of the Fourth Mobile Company of the Kingdom of Nueva Vizcaya (Bonavía Octubre 5 de 1816). Almada (1952:84) apparently erred in stating that Arvizu assumed command of Tucson in 1818. His text suggests that Arvizu still held the Tucson command when he opted for independence in early September of 1821. Yet he was not in command a year earlier.
33. Arvizu 1 de Marzo de 1817.
34. Stoner and Dobyns 1959, p. 78.
35. Arvizu 1 de Enero de 1817. Baxa. Not translated with the review.
36. Arvizu 1 de Febrero de 1817.
37. Arvizu 1 de Marzo de 1817.
38. Although he is shown on the Tucson company report at the beginning of 1817 (Table 10, Appendix), he may not actually have moved there from El Paso. In any case, at the end of September 1817 he had gone to the San Buenaventura garrison as a lieutenant, so his youthful stay at Tucson was short (Almada 1952:239).
39. Villa 1948, p. 56.
40. Almada 1952, pp. 239-240.
41. Anónimo 1 de Julio de 1817, fol. 419, f. 434.
42. Palerm s.f., p. 73.
43. *Ibid.*, p. 77.
44. *Ibid.*, p. 79.

11. Religion at the Royal Fort of San Agustín de Tucson, 1779-1821

1. Medina 1779, No. 7.
2. Croix 23 de Julio de 1780.
3. Archivo de la Iglesia, Arizpe. Courtesy of Sidney B. Brinckerhoff, Arizona Historical Society.
4. Allande y Saabedra 1785.
5. Haley 1932.
6. Franco 1782.
7. Neve 30 de Noviembre de 1782.
8. Medina 15 de Enero de 1784.
9. Medina 6 de Octubre de 1785.
10. Anónimo Ynforme del Colegio de la Santa Cruz.
11. Moraga 1793.
12. Stoner and Dobyns 1959, p. 75.
13. *Ibid.*, p. 71.
14. *Ibid.*, p. 72.
15. *Ibid.*, p. 73.
16. *Ibid.*, p. 74.
17. Yturralde 24 de Set. de 1795.
18. Friar Lorenzo Simó evidently assumed the chaplaincy of the Bacoachi Opata unit when Arriquibar moved to Tucson. Toward the end of 1796, Simó reported to the bishop of Sonora that he received a 300 peso stipend for ministering to the native Opatas of Bacoachi and baptizing the Peaceful Apaches there "and burying them when they die." Moreover, the Opata company gave him another 100 pesos for ministering to it (Simó 6 de Nov.e de 1796).
19. Bringas 15 de Marzo de 1796, fol. 20.
20. Espiritu Santo 28 de Setiembre de 1820.
21. Stoner and Dobyns 1959, pp. 78-79.
22. Díaz 1873, p. 3.
23. Torres Q., 1921, p. 63.
24. Moreno 2 de Henero á 5 de Febrero de 1797. Manuel María Moreno, a native Sonoran, took the path of formal education in law and religion to high colonial office. His career eventually brought him the titles of provisor and vice-general governor of the Frontier Provinces (1790) and later provisor and vicar-general (1796). (Moreno 20 de Nov.e de 1795; Nava 12 de Agosto de 1796.)

25. Arriquibar 6 de Enero de 1804b.
26. Yturralde 28 de Enero de 1799.
27. Rouset 4 de Agosto de 1803.
28. The decree is discussed at length in Dobyns 1959.
29. From Arriquibar 6 de Enero de 1804a.
30. Arriquibar 6 de Marzo de 1806a.
31. Arriquibar 6 de Marzo 1806b.
32. Haley 1932.
33. Arriquibar 6 de Marzo de 1811a.
34. Arriquibar 6 de Marzo de 1811b.
35. Díaz 1873, p. 3.
36. Tumacacori E f. 13 v.
37. From Rouset 12 de Mayo de 1808, ff. lv-2.
38. Dávalos 18 de Marzo de 1810.
39. McAlister 1957, p. 6.
40. *Ibid.*, p. 93. Appendix One, Table 1.
41. Rouset de Jesús 18 de Diciembre de 1809. The quotations on this topic in the rest of this chapter are my translations of passages in this circular.

12. The End of Spanish Colonial Rule at Tucson, 1821

1. Temple 1830, Vol. I, p. 234.
2. Bancroft 1885, Vol. IV, p. 20.
3. McAlister 1957, p. 5, etc.
4. Bancroft 1885, Vol. IV, p. 714.
5. Almada 1952, p. 294.
6. Bancroft 1885, Vol. IV, p. 238.
7. Almada 1952, p. 295.
8. *Ibid.*, p. 810.
9. *Ibid.*, p. 811.
10. *Ibid.*, p. 242.
11. Elías 18 June 1826.
12. Mata Biñolas 1794.
13. McKenna 28 July 1794.
14. Mata Biñolas 1794.
15. Almada 1952, p. 500.

13. Northern Piman Population Trends at Tucson, 1690-1821

1. Dobyns 1966.
2. Díaz del Carpio 1752 fol. 95-95v.
3. Donohue 1960, p. 135. Aguirre reported 220 persons in 70 families with 58 widowed individuals, leaving only 22 children. This was an age structure of a rapidly declining population.
4. Roxas 15 de Enero de 1765.
5. (Neve) 20 de Febrero de 1766.
6. Tumacacori B, fol. 8.
7. Ezell 1956, p. 153.
8. Bancroft 1889, p. 381; Bolton 1930, Vol. II, p. 241.
9. Reyes 1784, fol. 224v.
10. Anónimo 1783.
11. Elías Gonzáles 22 de Marzo de 1762, translated in Chapter 2.
12. Dobyns, Ezell, Jones and Ezell 1960.
13. Yturralde 4 de Febrero de 1796.
14. Anónimo 1796.
15. Yturralde 3 de Abril de 1798, fol. 7v.
16. Yturralde 4 de Mayo de 1798, 4 de Junio de 1798.
17. Llorens 12 de Diciembre de 1801, ff. 3v-10v.

18. Dobyns 1959, pp. 502, 510-511.
19. Torres Q. 1921, p. 42.
20. Dobyns, Ezell, Jones and Ezell 1957.
21. Bringas 15 de Marzo de 1796, fol. 22-22v.
22. Moyano 18 de Mayo de 1803.
23. Moyano 5 de Febrero de 1805.
24. Perez 31 de Dic. de 1818, fol. 46-47.
25. Dobyns 1959, pp. 511-515.
26. Gonzales 1820, fol. 142-143.
27. Gonzales 4 de Enero de 1821.
28. Scholes (1962:23) complained that historians did "not have adequate reliable information on the basis of which satisfactory judgments" could be made concerning factors in mission "deterioration and decline" over the whole Southwest. Depopulation resulting from introduction of Old World diseases is one general such factor operating throughout the area over a long period of time. Evidence is abundant.
29. Kessell 1972, p. 57.
30. Galindo N., 9 de Diziembre de 1796, f.27v.

14. Population Dynamics at the Tucson Military Post, 1776-1797

1. Dobyns 1972.
2. Collins 1970.
3. Cook and Borah 1971, pp. 136-137.
4. Whiting 1953, pp. 2-3.
5. Noreña 20 de Octubre de 1796.
6. Legarra 14 de Octubre de 1796.
7. Spicer 1971, pp. 795 ff.
8. Canales 5 de Noviembre de 1796.
9. Collins 1970, pp. 16, 18-22.
10. Santisteban 9 de 7bre de 1796.
11. Martinez 11 de Octubre de 1796.
12. Whiting 1953, pp. 7-9.
13. Messa 1 de Nov.e de 1796.
14. Sepulveda 11 de Diciembre de 1796 (Resúmenes).
15. Collins 1970, pp. 18-22.
16. Dobyns, Ezell, Jones and Ezell 1960.
17. Canales 5 de Agosto de 1796.
18. Brinckerhoff and Faulk 1965, pp. 9 ff.
19. Dobyns 1964, pp. 6-11.
20. Dobyns 1962; 1963.
21. Dobyns 1970.
22. McCall 1969, p. 19.
23. Whiting 1953, pp. 8-9.
24. Collins 1970, pp. 18-22.
25. Alers 1975, pp. 425-426.

Bibliography

Printed Works

Aguirre, Manuel de

1856 (20 de Marzo de 1764) "Carta" al Ten.te Cor. Juan de Pineda, *Documentos para la Historia de México.* Serie 4, Tomo I, pp. 124-127. México: Imprenta de Vicente García Torres.

1856 (4 de Agosto de 1764) "Carta del Padre Manuel de Aguirre al Sr. Teniente Coronel, Gobernador y Capitan General, D. Juan de Pineda, en el Año de 764," *Documentos para la Historia de México.* Serie 4, Tomo I, pp. 134-135. México: Imprenta de Vicente García Torres.

Alegre, Francisco Javier (nueva edición por Ernest J. Burrus y Félix Zubillaga)

1956 *Historia de la Provincia de la Compañia de Jesus de Nueva España. Tomo I. Años 1566-1596.* Roma: Institutum Historicum S. J.

1959 *Tomo III. Años 1640-1675.* Roma: Institutum Historicum S. J.

1960 *Tomo IV. Libros 9-10 (Años 1676-1766).* Roma: Institutum Historicum S. J.

Alers, J. Oscar

1965 "Population and Development in a Peruvian Community," *Journal of Inter-American Studies,* 7:4 (Oct.) 422-448.

Almada, Francisco

1952 *Diccionario de Historia, Geografía, y Biografía Sonorense.* Chihuahua: Ruiz Sandoval.

Anónimo

1966 *Enciclopedia Universal Ilustrada.* Madrid: Espasa-Calpe.

Anza, Juan Bautista de

1856 (Mayo 1 de 1770) "Carta al Sr. Coronel D. Juan de Pineda," *Documentos para la Historia de México.* Serie 4, Tomo 2, pp. 118-120. México: Imprenta de Vicente García Torres.

Arricivita, Juan Domingo

1792 *Crónica Seráfica y Apostólica del Colegio de Propaganda Fide de la Santa Cruz de Querétaro en la Nueva España.* México: Felipe de Zúñiga y Ontiveros.

Aspurz, Lázaro de

1946 *La Aportación Extranjera a las Misiones Españolas del Patronato Regio.* Madrid: Publicaciones del Consejo de la Hispanidad.

Baldonado, Luis

1959 "Missions San José de Tumacacori and San Xavier del Bac in 1774," *The Kiva,* 24:4 (April) 21-24.

Bancroft, Hubert Howe, et al.
1884 *History of the North Mexican States and Texas.* Vol. I. San Francisco: A. L. Bancroft Co.
1889 *History of Arizona and New Mexico, 1530-1888.* San Francisco: The History Co. (1962, Albuquerque, New Mexico: Horn & Wallace).
Bannon, John Francis
1955 *The Mission Frontier in Sonora, 1620-1687.* New York: U.S. Catholic Historical Society.
Bean, Lowell John and William Marvin Mason
1962 *The Romero Expeditions 1823-1826.* Palm Springs, California: Palm Desert Museum.
Beardsley, Richard K.
1964 "Ecological and Social Parallels between Rice-Growing Communities of Japan and Spain," *Symposium on Community Studies in Anthropology.* American Ethnological Society, Proceedings of the Annual Spring Meeting.
Beiber, Ralph P. and Averam B. Bender (eds.)
1938 *Exploring Southwestern Trails, 1846-1854.* Glendale, California: Arthur H. Clark Co.
Benavides, Alonso de (ed. by F. W. Hodge, G. P. Hammond and A. Rey)
1945 *Fray Alonso de Benavides Revised Memorial of 1634.* Albuquerque: University of New Mexico Press.
Bolton, Herbert Eugene (ed. and trans.)
1926 *Historical Memoir, or New California by Fray Francisco Palou, O. F. M.* Berkeley: University of California Press.
1927 *Fray Juan Crespi, Missionary Explorer of the Pacific Coast 1769-1774.* Berkeley: University of California Press.
1930 *Anza's California Expeditions.* Berkeley: University of California Press.
1931 *Font's Complete Diary: A Chronicle of the Founding of San Francisco.* Berkeley: University of California Press.
1948 *Kino's Historical Memoir of Pimería Alta.* Berkeley: University of California Press (2d edition).
Bolton, Herbert Eugene
1936 *Rim of Christendom.* New York: Macmillan.
1939 *Wider Horizons of American History.* New York: D. Appleton-Century Co.
Brinckerhoff, Sidney B.
1967 "The Last Years of Spanish Arizona 1786-1821," *Arizona and the West,* 9:1 (Spring) 5-20.
Brinckerhoff, Sidney B. and Odie B. Faulk
1965 *Lancers for the King.* Phoenix: Arizona Historical Foundation.
Brunsman, Howard G.
1953 *Persons of Spanish Surname. United States Census of Population: 1950.* Washington: Government Printing Office, P-E N° 3C.
Burma, John H.
1954 *Spanish-Speaking Groups in the United States.* Durham, North Carolina: Duke University Press.
Burrus, Ernest J.
1954 *Kino Reports to Headquarters: Correspondence of Eusebio F. Kino, S. J., from New Spain with Rome.* Roma: Institutum Historicum Societatis Jesu.

1961 *Kino's Plan for the Development of Pimería Alta, Arizona and Upper California.* Tucson: Arizona Pioneers' Historical Society.
1963 *Misiones Norteñas Mexicanas de la Compañia de Jesus 1751-1757.* México: Antigua Librería Robredo.
1971 *Kino and Manje, Explorers of Sonora and Arizona: Their Vision of the Future: A Study of Their Expeditions and Plans.* Rome: Jesuit Historical Institute.

CARROLL, JOHN ALEXANDER
1965 "The Use and Abuse of Regional History," in C. F. Parker (ed.) *Emergence of a Concept.* Prescott, Arizona: Prescott College.

CARTER, CHARLES F.
1900 *The Missions of Nueva California.* San Francisco: Whitaker and Ray Co.

CASTAÑEDA, CARLOS E. (trans.)
1928 *The Mexican Side of the Texan Revolution (1836) by the Chief Mexican Participants.* Dallas: P. L. Turner Co.

CASTETTER, EDWARD F. and WILLIS H. BELL
1942 *Pima and Papago Indian Agriculture.* Albuquerque: University of New Mexico Press.

CHAMBERS, GEORGE W.
1955 "The Old Presidio of Tucson," *The Kiva,* 20:2-3 (Dec.-Feb) 15-16.

CHAPMAN, CHARLES E.
1919 *Catalogue of Materials in Archivo General de Indias for the History of the Pacific Coast and American Southwest.* Berkeley: University of California Press.

CLARK, MARGARET
1959 *Health in the Mexican-American Culture.* Berkeley: University of California Press.

CLINE, HOWARD F.
1962 "Imperial Perspectives on the Borderlands," in K. R. Toole, J. A. Carroll, A. R. Mortensen & R. M. Utley (eds.) *Probing the American West.* Santa Fé: Museum of New Mexico Press.

COLLINS, KAREN SIKES (ed.)
1970 "Fray Pedro de Arriquibar's Census of Tucson, 1820," *Journal of Arizona History,* 11:1 (Spring) 14-22.

COOK, SHERBURNE F. and WOODROW BORAH
1971 *Essays in Population History: Mexico and the Caribbean Volume One.* Berkeley: University of California Press.

COOKE, PHILIP ST. GEORGE
1878 *The Conquest of New Mexico and California.* New York: G. P. Putnam's Sons (1964, Albuquerque, New Mexico: Horn & Wallace).

CORBALA, MANUEL S.
1970 *Vida y obra de un sonorense: Rodolfo Elías Calles.* Hermosillo (México: Editorial Libros de México).

COUES, ELLIOTT
1900 *On the Trail of a Spanish Pioneer.* New York: Francis P. Harper.

DAVIS, WILLIAM W. H.
1869 *The Spanish Conquest of New Mexico.* Doylestown, Pennsylvania: W. W. H. Davis.

DECORME, GERARD
1941 *La Obra de los Jesuitas Mexicanos durante la epoca colonial, 1572-1767.* México: Antiqua Libreria Robredo de José Porrua e Hijos.

DEFOURI, JAMES H.
1893 *The Martyrs of New Mexico.* Las Vegas, New Mexico: Revisita Católica Printing Office.

DÍAZ, MARIANA
1873 "Tucson A Hundred Years Ago," *Arizona Citizen* (Tucson) June 21, 1873.

DI PESO, CHARLES C. *et al.*
1953 *The Sobaipuri Indians of the Upper San Pedro River Valley, Southeastern Arizona.* Dragoon, Arizona: Amerind Foundation.

DOBYNS, HENRY F.
1950 "Papago Pilgrims on the Town," *The Kiva,* 16:1-2 (Sept.-Oct.) 27-32.
1962 *Pioneering Christians Among the Perishing Indians of Tucson.* Lima: Editorial Estudios Andinos.
1963 "Indian Extinction in the Middle Santa Cruz River Valley, Arizona," *New Mexico Historical Review,* 38:2 (April) 163-181.
1964 *Lance, Ho! Containment of the Western Apaches by the Royal Spanish Garrison at Tucson.* Lima: Editorial Estudios Andinos.
1966 "Estimating Aboriginal American Population: An Appraisal of Techniques with a New Hemispheric Estimate," *Current Anthropology,* 7:4 (October) 395-416.
1972 "The 1797 Population of the Presidio of Tucson: A Reconsideration," *The Journal of Arizona History,* 13:3 (Autumn) 205-209.

DOBYNS, HENRY F. and PAUL H. EZELL
1959 "Sonoran Missionaries in 1790," *New Mexico Historical Review,* 34:1 (Jan.) 152-154.

DOBYNS, HENRY F., PAUL H. EZELL, ALDEN W. JONES and GRETA S. EZELL
1957 "Thematic Changes in Yuman Warfare," *Cultural Stability and Cultural Change,* Proceedings of the Annual Spring Meeting of the American Ethnological Society.
1960 "What Were Nixoras?" *Southwestern Journal of Anthropology,* 16:2 (Summer) 230-258.

DODSON, RUTH
1951 "Don Pedrito Jaramillo: the Curandero of Los Olmos," *Publications of the Texas Folklore Society,* 24.

DOMINGUEZ, FRANCISCO CHÁVEZ ATANASIO, trans. and annot. by ELEANOR B. ADAMS and FRAY ANGELICO CHÁVEZ
1956 *The Missions of New Mexico, 1776.* Albuquerque: University of New Mexico Press.

DONOHUE, J. AUGUSTINE
1960 "The Unlucky Jesuit Mission of Bac," *Arizona and the West,* 2:2 (Summer) 127-139.
1969 *After Kino: Jesuit Missions in Northwestern New Spain 1711-1767.* Rome: Jesuit Historical Institute.

DUELL, PRENTICE
1919 *Mission San Xavier del Bac.* Tucson: Arizona Archaeological and Historical Society.

DUNNE, PETER M.
1957 *Juan Antonio Balthasar, Padre Visitador to the Sonora Frontier 1744-1745.* Tucson: Arizona Pioneers' Historical Society.

DUNNE, PETER M. and ERNEST J. BURRUS

1955 "Four Unpublished Letters of Anton María Benz, Eighteenth Century Missionary to Mexico," *Archivum Historicum Societatis Iseu,* 24.

ENGELHARDT, ZEPHYRIN

1908-16 *The Missions and Missionaries of California.* San Francisco: J. H. Barry Co., 4 vol.

ESPINOSA, J. MANUEL

1940 *First Expedition of Vargas into New Mexico, 1692.* Albuquerque: University of New Mexico Press.

EWING, RUSSELL C.

1938 "The Pima Outbreak in November, 1751," *New Mexico Historical Review,* 13:4 (Oct.) 337-346.

1945 "The Pima Uprising of 1751: A Study of Spanish Indian Relations on the Frontier of New Spain," in *Greater America: Essays in Honor of Herbert Eugene Bolton.* Berkeley: University of California Press, pp. 259-280.

EZELL, PAUL H.

1955 "De Anza Letter Reveals Various Indian Problems," *Arizona Daily Star,* 114:55 (Feb. 24) 2.

1956 "Fray Diego Bringas, a Forgotten Cartographer of Sonora," *Imago Mundi,* 13:151-158.

1961 *The Hispanic Acculturation of the Gila River Pimas.* American Anthropological Association, Memoir 90.

1963 *The Maricopas: An Identification from Documentary Sources.* Tucson: University of Arizona Anthropological Papers No. 6.

FONTANA, BERNARD L.

1961 *Biography of a Desert Church: The Story of Mission San Xavier del Bac.* Tucson, Arizona: Tucson Corral of the Westerners.

FORBES, ROBERT H.

1952 *Crabb's Filibustering Expedition into Sonora, 1857.* Tucson: Arizona Silhouettes.

FOSTER, GEORGE M.

1960 *Culture and Conquest: America's Spanish Heritage.* Chicago: Quadrangle Books.

GALLEGO, HILARIO

1935 "Reminiscences of an Arizona Pioneer," *Arizona Historical Review,* 6:1 (January) 75-81.

GALLIN, BERNARD

1959 "A Case for Intervention in the Field," *Human Organization,* 18:3 (Fall) 140-144.

GALVIN, JOHN (ed.)

1965 *A Record of Travels in Arizona and California 1775-1776.* San Francisco: John Howell – Books.

GARCÉS, FRANCISCO T. H.

1856 (29 de Julio de 1768) "Carta" al Sr. D. Juan Bautista de Anza, *Documentos para la Historia de México,* Serie 4, Tomo 2, pp. 365-366. México: Imprenta de Vicente García Torres.

1856 (29 de Julio de 1768) "Carta al Sr. Gobernador D. Juan de Pineda," *Documentos para la Historia de México,* Serie 4, vol. 2, pp. 367-370. México: Imprenta de Vicente García Torres.

GARCES, FRANCISCO T. H. *(continued)*

1856 "Carta al Sr. gobernador D. Juan de Pineda, Feb.o 21, 1769," *Documentos para la Historia de México,* Serie 4, Tomo 2, pp. 370-372. México: Imprenta de Vicente García Torres.

1856 (Oficio al) "Señor gobernador y capital general" 23 de Julio de 1769, *Documentos para la Historia de México,* Serie 4, Tomo 2, pp. 372-377. México: Imprenta de Vicente García Torres.

GARDINER, ARTHUR D. (trans.)

1957 "Letter of Father Middendorff, S. J. Dated 3 March, 1757," *The Kiva,* 22:4 (June) 1-10.

GEIGER, REV. MAYNARD, O. F. M.

1953 "A Voice from San Xavier del Bac (1802-1805)," Provincial Annals (Province of Santa Barbara) 16:1 (July) 5-11.

GERALD, REX E.

1968 *Spanish Presidios of the Late Eighteenth Century in Northern New Spain.* Santa Fé: Museum of New Mexico Research Records No. 7.

GREENLEAF, CAMERON and ANDREW WALLACE

1962 "Tucson: Pueblo, Presidio, and American City: A Synopsis of Its History," *Arizoniana,* 3:2 (Summer) 18-26.

GUTIERREZ FLORES, PEDRO

1970 "Documentos sobre Chucuito," *Historia y Cultura* (Museo Nacional de Historia, Lima) 4:5-14.

HABIG, MARION A.

1937 "The Builders of San Xavier del Bac," *Southwestern Historical Quarterly,* 41:2 (Oct.) 154-166.

HACKETT, CHARLES W. (ed.)

1923-37 *Historical Documents Relating to New Mexico, Nueva Viscaya and Approaches Thereto, to 1773.* Washington: Carnegie Institution Pub. 330.

HACKETT, CHARLES W. (ed. & annot.) and CHARMION C. SHELBY (trans.)

1942 *Revolt of the Pueblo Indians of New Mexico and Otermin's Attempted Reconquest, 1680-82.* Albuquerque: University of New Mexico Press.

HALEY, J. EVETTS (ed.)

1932 "A Log of the Texas-California Cattle Trail, 1854," by James G. Bell, *Southwestern Historical Quarterly* 35:4 (April) 290-316; 36:1 (July).

HAMMOND, GEORGE P.

1929 "Pimería Alta After Kino's Time," *New Mexico Historical Review,* 4:3 (July) 220-238.

1931 "The Zúñiga Journal, Tucson to Santa Fé, the Opening of a Spanish Trade Route, 1788-1795," *New Mexico Historical Review;* 6:1 (Jan.) 40-65.

HAMMOND, GEORGE P. and AGAPITO REY

1929 *Expedition into New Mexico by Antonio de Espejo, 1582-83.* Los Angeles: Quivira Society No. 1.

1953 *Oñate, Colonizer of New Mexico 1595-1628.* Albuquerque: University of New Mexico Press.

1966 *The Rediscovery of New Mexico 1580-1594.* Albuquerque: University of New Mexico Press.

Hawes, Horace
1856 *The Missions in California, and the Rights of the Catholic Church to the Property Pertaining to Them.* San Francisco: Daily Evening News Office.
Hawley, Florence
1948 *The Indian Problem in New Mexico.* Albuquerque: University of New Mexico, Department of Government, Division of Research.
Heizer, Robert and Alan J. Almquist
1971 *The Other Californians: Prejudice and Discrimination under Spain, Mexico and the United States to 1920.* Berkeley: University of California Press.
Holterman, Jack
1956 "José Zúñiga," *The Kiva,* 22:1 (Nov.) 1-4.
Hughes, Elizabeth
1875 *The California of the Padres, or, Footprints of Ancient Communism.* San Francisco: Choynski.
Ivancovich, Byron
1960 "Juan Bautista de Anza; Pioneer of Arizona," *Arizoniana,* 1:4 (Winter) 21-24.
James, George W.
1913 *The Old Franciscan Missions of California.* Boston: Little, Brown Co.
Jeffreys, M. D. W.
1956 "Some Rules of Directed Cultural Change Under Roman Catholicism," *American Anthropologist,* 58:4 (August) 721-731.
Karns, Harry J. and associates
1954 *Unknown Arizona and Sonora.* Tucson: Arizona Silhouettes.
Kessell, John L.
1970a *Mission of Sorrows: Jesuit Guevavi and The Pimas, 1691-1767.* Tucson: University of Arizona Press.
1970b "The Making of a Martyr: The Young Francisco Garcés," *New Mexico Historical Review,* 45:3 (July) 181-196.
1972 "Anza Damns the Missions: A Spanish Soldier's Criticism of Indian Policy, 1772," *Journal of Arizona History,* 13:1 (Spring) 53-63.
Kibbe, Pauline R.
1946 *Latin Americans in Texas.* Albuquerque: University of New Mexico Press.
Lafora, Nicolás de
1939 *Relación del Viaje que Hizo a los Presidios Internos Situados en la Frontera de la América Septentional Perteneciente al Rey de España.* México: Editorial Pedro Robredo.
Lange, Charles H., Carroll L. Riley and Elizabeth M. Lange (eds.)
1970 *The Southwestern Journals of Adolph F. Bandelier 1883-1884.* Albuquerque: University of New Mexico Press.
Linton, Ralph
1943 "Nativistic Movements," *American Anthropologist,* 45:2 (April) 230-239.
Livermore, Harold
1958 *A History of Spain.* London: George Allen, Unwin.
Lockwood, Frank C.
1943 *Life in Old Tucson, 1854-1864.* Los Angeles: Ward Ritchie Press.

LONG, LUMEN H. (ed.)
1971 *The World Almanac.* New York: Newspaper Enterprise Association, Inc.
LUMHOLTZ, CARL S.
1912 *New Trails in Mexico.* New York: Scribner's. (1971, Glorieta, New Mexico: Río Grande Press.)
LUMMIS, CHARLES F.
1936 *The Spanish Pioneers and the California Missions.* Chicago: McClurg.
MCALISTER, LYLE N.
1957 *The "Fuero Militar" in New Spain.* Gainesville: University of Florida Press.
MCCALL, DANIEL F.
1969 *Africa in Time-Perspective.* New York: Oxford University Press.
MADSEN, WILLIAM
1964 "The Alcoholic Agringado," *American Anthropologist,* 66:2 (April) 355-360.
MALINOWSKI, BRONISLAW
1945 *The Dynamics of Culture Change.* New Haven, Connecticut: Yale University Press.
MANJE, JUAN M.
1926 *Luz de Tierra Incógnita.* México: Talleres Gráficos de la Nación.
MEYER, THEODOSIUS
1926 *St. Francis and the Franciscans in New Mexico.* Santa Fe: Historical Society of New Mexico.
MOORE, MARY LU and DELMAR L. BEENE
1971 "The Interior Provinces of New Spain, The Report of Hugo O'Conor, January 30, 1776," *Arizona and the West,* 13:3 (Autumn) 265-282.
MOORHEAD, MAX L.
1968 *The Apache Frontier: Jacobo Ugarte and Spanish-Indian Relations in Northern New Spain, 1769-1791.* Norman: University of Oklahoma Press.
NELSON, LOWRY
1930 *The Mormon Village: A Study in Social Origins.* Proceedings of the Utah Academy of Sciences, Vol. VII, pp. 11-37.
NENTVIG, JUAN
1951 *Rudo Ensayo.* Tucson: Arizona Silhouettes (reprint from *Records of the American Catholic Historical Society of Philadelphia,* 5:2 (June 1894).
NEWCOMB, REXFORD
1925 *The Old Mission Churches and Historic Houses of California.* Philadelphia: J. B. Lippincott.
NEWHALL, NANCY
1954 "Mission San Xavier del Bac," *Arizona Highways,* 30:4 (April) 12-35.
OCARANZA, FERNANDO
1933 *Los Franciscanos en las Provincias Internas de Sonora y Ostimuri.* México: Autor.
O'CONOR, HUGO DE
1952 *Informe de Hugo O'Conor Sobre el Estado de las Provincias Internas del Norte 1771-76.* México: Editorial Cultura.
O'CROULEY, PEDRO ALONSO (trans. and ed. by SEAN GALVIN)
1972 *A Description of the Kingdom of New Spain 1774.* San Francisco: John Howell – Books.

PAGE, DONALD W.
1930 "Tucson, Pre-Traditional Times to the Founding of the Presidio," in F. C. Lockwood, *Tucson, The Old Pueblo*. Phoenix, Arizona: Manufacturing Stationers.

PALERM VICH, ANGEL
s.f. "Practores Históricos de la Clase Media en México," en *Las Clases Sociales en México*. México: Sociedad Mexicana de Difusión Cultural.

PARKE, JOHN G.
1855 *Report of Lieutenant John G. Parke, Corps of Topographical Engineers, Upon the Portion of the Route Near the Thirty-Second Parallel, Lying Between the Rio Grande and Pimas Villages, on the Gila*. Washington: A. O. P. Nicholson, Printer.

POLZER, CHARLES W. (ed.)
1972 "The Franciscan Entrada into Sonora, 1645-1652: A Jesuit Chronicle," *Arizona and the West*, 14:3 (Autumn) 253-278.

POWELL, PHILIP W.
1944 "Presidios and Towns on the Silver Frontier of New Spain, 1550–1580," *Hispanic American Historical Review*, 24:2 (May) 179-200.

POWERS, LAURA B.
1897 *The Missions of California, Their Establishment, Progress and Decay*. San Francisco: W. Doxey.

PRADEAU, ALBERTO FRANCISCO
1959 *La Expulsión de los Jesuitas de las Provincias de Sonora, Ostimuri y Sinaloa en 1767*.-México: Antigua Librería Robredo de José Porrua e Hijos.

PRIESTLY, HERBERT I.
1913 *The Colorado River Campaign of Pedro Fages, 1781–1782*. Publications of the Academy of Pacific Coast History, 3:3.
1917 "The Reforms of José de Gálvez in New Spain," in H. M. Stephens and H. E. Bolton (eds.) *The Pacific Ocean in History*. New York: Macmillan Co.

REYES, ANTONIO DE LOS
1856 "Memorial y Estado Actual de las Misiones de la Pimería Alta y Baja, Presentado al Excmo. Sr. Virrey D. Fray Antonio María Bucareli y Ursua, en Seis de Julio de 1772 Años," *Documentos para la Historia de México*. Series 3, Tomo 1, pp. 724-765. México: Imprenta de Vicente García T.

ROBLES, VITO ALESSIO
1939 "Liminar Bibliográfico y Acotaciones," *Relación del Viaje que hizo a los presidios internos . . . por Nicolás de Lafora*. México: Editorial Pedro Robredo.

ROCA, PAUL M.
1967 *Paths of the Padres Through Sonora*. Tucson: Arizona Pioneers' Historical Society.

ROMANO V., OCTAVIO IGNACIO
1960 "Donship in a Mexican-American Community in Texas," *American Anthropologist*, 62:6 (Dec.) 966-976.
1965 "Charismatic Medicine, Folk-Healing, and Folk-Sainthood," *American Anthropologist*, 67:5 (Oct.) 1151-1173.

RUBEL, ARTHUR J.
1966 *Across the Tracks: Mexican-Americans in a Texas City*. Austin: University of Texas Press.

SALPOINTE, JEAN B.
1880 "The Church of San Xavier del Bac," *Arizona Star*, April 20, 21, 1880.

SASAKI, TOM and JOHN ADAIR
1952 "New Land to Farm: Agricultural Practices Among the Navaho Indians of New Mexico," in E. H. Spicer (ed.) *Human Problems in Technological Change*. New York: Russell Sage Foundation.

SAUER, CARL
1935 "A Spanish Expedition into the Arizona Apachería," *Arizona Historical Review*, 6:1 (Jan.) 3-13.

SCHOLES, FRANCE V.
1962 "Historiography of the Spanish Southwest: Retrospect and Prospect," in K. R. Toole, J. A. Carroll, A. R. Mortensen and R. M. Utley (eds.) *Probing the American West*. Santa Fe: Museum of New Mexico Press, pp. 17-25.

SCHROEDER, ALBERT H. and DAN S. MATSON
1965 *A Colony on the Move. Gaspar Castaño de Sosa's Journal 1590–1591*. Santa Fe: School of American Research.

SMITH, FAY JACKSON with JOHN KESSELL and FRANCIS FOX
1966 *Father Kino in Arizona*. Phoenix: Arizona Historical Foundation.

SPICER, EDWARD H.
1962 *Cycles of Conquest*. Tucson: University of Arizona Press.
1971 "Persistent Cultural Systems," *Science*, 174:4011 (19 Nov.) 795-800.

STONER, VICTOR R. (edited by HENRY F. DOBYNS)
1959 "Fray Pedro Antonio de Arriquibar, Chaplain of the Royal Fort at Tucson," *Arizona and the West*, 1:1 (Spring) 71-79.

TEMPLE, EDMOND
1830 *Travels in Various Parts of Peru, Including a Year's Residence in Potosí*. London: Henry Colburn & Richard Bentley, 2 vol.

THOMAS, ALFRED B.
1932 *Forgotten Frontiers*. Norman: University of Oklahoma Press.
1935 *After Coronado: Spanish Exploration of New Mexico 1696–1727*. Norman: University of Oklahoma Press.
1941 *Teodoro de Croix and the Northern Frontier of New Spain, 1776–1783*. Norman: University of Oklahoma Press.

TORRES QUINTERO, GREGORIO
1921 *Mexico hacia el fin del Virreinato español: Antecedentes sociológicos del pueblo mexicano*. México: El Pensamiento Vivo de América.

TREUTLEIN, THEODORE E. (ed. & trans.)
1949 *Sonora, A Description of the Province by Ignaz Pfefferkorn*. Albuquerque: University of New Mexico Press.
1957 "Father Gottfried Bernhardt Middendorff, S. J., Pioneer of Tucson," *New Mexico Historical Review*, 32:4 (October) 310-318.
1965 *Missionary in Sonora: The Travel Reports of Joseph Och, S. J., 1755–1767*. San Francisco: California Historical Society.

TWITCHELL, RALPH E.
1911-12 *The Leading Facts of New Mexican History*. Cedar Rapids, Iowa: Torch Press, 2 vol. (1963, Albuquerque, New Mexico: Horn & Wallace.)
1925 *Old Santa Fe: The Story of New Mexico's Ancient Capital*. Santa Fe: Santa Fe New Mexican Publishing Corporation. (1963, Chicago: Río Grande Press.)

UNDERHILL, RUTH M.
1939 *Social Organization of the Papago Indians.* New York: Columbia University Press.
1946 *Papago Indian Religion.* New York: Columbia University Press.
U. S. BUREAU OF THE CENSUS
1972 *1970 Census of Population. General Population Characteristics, United States Summary.* Washington: U. S. Department of Commerce.
VANCOUVER, GEORGE
1798 *A Voyage of Discovery to the North Pacific Ocean, and Round the World . . . Performed in the Years 1790, 1791, 1792, 1793, 1794 and 1795.* London: John Stockdale (1801) 6 vol. 2d ed.
VILLA, EDUARDO W.
1948 *Galeria de Sonorenses Ilustres.* Hermosillo: Impulsora de Artes Gráficos.
WATSON, DOUGLAS S. (ed.)
1931 *The Santa Fe Trail to California, 1849–1852, The Journal and Drawings of H. M. T. Powell.* San Francisco: California Book Club.
WHITING, ALFRED F.
1953 "The Tumacacori Census of 1796," *The Kiva,* 19:1 (Fall) 1-12.
WORCESTER, DONALD E. (trans. & ed.)
1951 *Instructions for Governing the Interior Provinces of New Spain, 1786, by Bernardo de Gálvez.* Berkeley, California: Quivira Society.

Manuscripts

Abbreviations

AGI — Archivo General de Indias, Sevilla, España.
AGN — Archivo General y Público de la Nación, México, D.F.
AGEMS — Archivo del Gobierno Ecclesiástico de la Mitra de Sonora, Catedral de San Agustín, Hermosillo, Sonora.
AHS — Arizona Historical Society, Tucson.
BLUC — The Bancroft Library, University of California, Berkeley.

* * *

ABATE, JOSEF MARÍA
2 de Mayo de 1782. (Report) Tucson. AGI, Guad. 520 (BLUC film).
24 de Diciembre de 1783. Lista de los Créditos y Dévitos que tuvo la citada compañía hasta fin de Dziemb.e de 1783, seqún consta de sus respectivas Cuentas ajustadas hasta dho tiempo. R.l Pres.o de San Agust.n del Tucson. AGI, Guad. 285 (BLUC film).
AGUIRRE, MANUEL
Dic.e 22 de 1763. Carta al P.e Prov.l Fran.co Zevallos. Bacadeguatzi. AGN, Archivo Histórico de Hacienda, Temporalidades, Legajo 17, No. 22 (BLUC film).
Dic.e 30 de 1763. Carta al P.e Prov.l Fran.co Zevallos. Bacadeguatzi. AGN, AHH, Temporalidades, Legajo 17, No. 22.
Hen.o 7 de 1764. Carta al P.e Prov.l Fran.co Zevallos. Bacadeguatzi. AGN, AHH, Temporalidades, Legajo 17 No. 22 (BLUC film).
18 de Febrero de 1764. Carta al Prov.l Fran.co Zevallos. Bacadeguatchi. AGN, AHH, Temporalidades, Legajo 17, No. 22 (BLUC film).
Marzo 1 de 1764. Carta al P.e Prov.l Fran.co Zevallos. Bacadeguatzi. AGN, AHH, Temporalidades, Legajo 17, No. 22 (BLUC film).

Aguirre, Manuel *(continued)*
Marzo 23 de 1764. Carta al P.e Prov.l Fran.co Zevallos. Bacadeguatzi. AGN, AHH, Temporalidades, Legajo 17, No. 22 (BLUC film).
Marzo 26 de 1764. Carta al P.e Prov.l Fran.co Zevallos. Bacadeguatzi. AGN, AHH, Temporalidades, Legajo 17, No. 22 (BLUC film).
Agosto 11 de 1764. Carta al P.e Prov.l Fran.co Zevallos. Bacadeguatzi. AGN, AHH, Temporalidades, Legajo 17, No. 22 (BLUC film).
Hen.o 8 de 1765. Carta al P.e Prov.l Fran.co Zevallos. Bacadeguatzi. AGN, AHH, Temporalidades, Legajo 17, No. 22 (BLUC film).
Abril 26 de 1765. Carta al P.e Prov.l Fran.co Zevallos. Bacadeguatzi. AGN, AHH, Temporalidades, Legajo 17, No. 22 (BLUC film).
Mayo 18 de 1765. Carta al P.e Prov.l Fran.co Zevallos. Bacadeguatzi. AGN, AHH, Temporalidades, Legajo 17, No. 22 (BLUC film).
Junio 10 de 1765. Carta al P.e Prov.l Fran.co Zevallos. Bacadeguatzi. AGN, AHH, Temporalidades, Legajo 17, No. 22 (BLUC film).
Junio 30 de 1765. Carta al P.e Prov.l Fran.co Zevallos. Mochopa. AGN, AHH, Temporalidades, Legajo 17, No. 22 (BLUC film).
Oct.e 5 de 1765. Carta al P.e Prov.l Fran.co Zevallos. Bacadeguatzi. AGN, AHH, Temporalidades, Legajo 17, No. 22 (BLUC film).

Allande y Saabedra, Pedro de
1782 Orden al Alferez Dn Ygnacio Vsarraga. Tucson. AGI, Guad. 520 (BLUC film).
1785 Petición para Promoción y Memorial de Servicios. Tucson. AGI, Guad. 520 (BLUC film).

Anónimo
1760 Breve Resumen de los Desastres, Muertes, Robos y Asolamientos Acaezidos en la Provincia de Sonora Ohstilizada de Apaches, Seris, y Pimas alzados, y en particular desde el año de 1755, hasta el presente de 1760 . . . AGN, AHH, Temporalidades, Legajo 17, No. 69 (BLUC film).
1783 Presidio de San Agustín del Tupson. AGI, Guad. 284 (BLUC film).
1796 Ynforme sobre las Misiones del Colegio Apostólico de Querétaro. AGEMS, Legajo de 1801 y 1802.
1 de Julio de 1817. Veinte y seis cédulas de premios recibidas en la Corte. México. AGN, Provincias Internas, Tomo 207, fol. 419 (BLUC film).

Arriquibar, Pedro de
Mayo 20 de 1795. Oficio al M. R. P. Presidente Fr. Fran.co Antonio Barbastro. Bacoachi. AGEMS, Leg. de 1801–1802.
Henero 21 de 1797. Noticia Yndividual de los Utensilios de Esta Yglesia del R.l Presidio del Tucson. R.l Pres.o de S.n Agustín del Tucson. AGEMS, Año de 1796.
Hen.o 6 de 1804a. Carta al S.or Secretar.o Dn José Dario Rouset. R.l Pres.o del Tucson. AGEMS, Legajo de 1803.
Henero 6 de 1804b. Carta al Obispo. R.l Pres.o de San Agustín del Tucson. AGEMS, Legajo de 1803.
Marzo 6 de 1806a. Carta de Petición al Yllmo Señor el Obispo de Sonora de Dn Juan Romero. R.l Pres.o de San Agustín del Tucson. AGEMS, Legajo 1801–1802B.
Marzo 6 de 1806b. Carta al Obispo. Tucson. AGEMS, Legajo de 1805–1806.
Marzo 6 de 1811a. Carta al Obispo (Petición para José Sosa). R.l Pres.o del Tucson. AGEMS, Legajo del año de 1812.
Marzo 6 de 1811b. Carta al Obispo. Tucson. AGEMS, Legajo de 1812.
Agosto 6 de 1820. Ynventario de los Vasos Sagrados, Ornamentos, y

demas Alajas que contiene la Capilla del R.l Pres.o de Tucson. Tucson. Archive of the Diocese of Tucson (gift from the bishop of Sinaloa).

ARVIZU, MANUEL YGNACIO

31 de Dic.e de 1816. Relación de los Yndividuos de la Compañía del Tucson que tiene cumplidos plasas par los premios señalados en la Real Ordenanza de 4 de Octubre de 1766 . . . AGN, Provincias Internas, Tomo 253, fol. 230-236v.

1 de Enero de 1817. Compañía del Real Presidio de San Agustín del Tucson, Provincia de Sonora. AGN, Provincias Internas, Tomo 206 (AHS film).

1 de Febrero de 1817. Compañía del Real Presidio de San Agustín del Tucson, Provincia de Sonora. AGN, Provincias Internas, Tomo 206 (AHS film).

1 de Marzo de 1817. Compañía del Real Presidio de San Agustín del Tucson, Provincia de Sonora. AGN, Provincias Internas, Tomo 206 (AHS film).

BARBASTRO, FRANCISCO ANTONIO

26 de Julio de 1793. Constancia al P.e Pred.or App.co Fr. Fern.do Madueño...Aconchi. AGEMS, Legajo de 1796.

20 de Junio de 1795. Oficio al Señor Comandante General Dn Pedro de Nava. Aconchi. AGEMS, Legajo de 1801–1802. (in Anónimo 1796).

BONAVIA, BERNARDO

Octubre 5 de 1816. Al Exmo. S.or Virrey de Nueva España. Durango. AGN, Provincias Internas, Tomo 207, fol. 362.

BRINGAS, DIEGO

15 de Marzo de 1796. Súplica al Señor Comandante General. Chihuahua. AGEMS, Legajo de 1801–1802, fol. 17-22v.

BUCARELI Y URSUA, ANTONIO

27 de Octubre de 1775. Oficio al Rey. México. AGI, Guad. 515 (BLUC film).

Mayo 27 de 1776. El Virrey de Nueva España avisa el recibo y dirección dada al R.l Esp.o de Retiro concedido al Teniente de la Comp.a del Presidio de Tubac. No. 2205. México. AGI, Guad. 515 (BLUC film).

CANALES, FRANCISCO

5 de Agosto de 1796. Noticia del Estado en que se halla la Yglesia ó Capilla del Pressid.o de Santa Gertrudis del Altar. Altar. AGEMS, Legajo de 1796.

5 de Noviembre de 1796. Oficio. Real Presidio de Santa Gertrudis del Altar. AGEMS, Legajo de 1796.

CARLOS III, KING OF SPAIN

28 de Febrero de 1776. V. M. Concede retiro de Teniente y Grado de Capitan á Dn Juan María de Oliva. El Pardo. AGI, Guad. 515 (BLUC film).

31 de Agosto de 1776. Presidio de Sn Agustín de Tugson...a Dn Diego de Oya, Nonbram.to de Alferez. AGI, Guad. 506 (BLUC film).

Junio 12 de 1777. Presidio de Tubac, Patentes de Ofiz.s desde 1767. AGI, Guad. 506 (BLUC film).

26 de Agosto de 1778a. Nombramiento de Alferez del Presidio de San Agustín del Tupson – Don Josseph de Castro. San Yldefonso. AGI, Guad. 506 (BLUC film).

26 de Agosto de 1778b. Nombramiento de Alferez del Presidio de Sn

CARLOS III, KING OF SPAIN (continued)
Buenaventura en Nueva España – Dn Pedro Marquez. San Yldefonso. AGI, Guad. 506 (BLUC film).
26 de Agosto de 1778c. Nombramiento de Alferez del Presidio del Norte en N.a España – Dn Josseph de Zuñiga. Sn Yldefonso. AGI, Guad. 506 (BLUC film).
14 de Mayo de 1782. Título de Ten.te del Presidio del Tupson á Dn Josef Abate. Aranjuez. AGI, Guad. 506 (BLUC film).
21 de Febrero de 1783. Nombram.to de Alferez 1° del Presidio de Sn Agustín del Tugson, Dn Félix Usarraga. El Pardo. AGI, Guad. 506 (BLUC film).
27 de Feb.o de 1784. Nombram.to de Alferez de la prim.a comp.a del Presidio de Fronteras, Dn Fran.co Salas Bohorquez. El Pardo. AGI, Guad. 506 (BLUC film).
28 de Marzo de 1784. Nombram.to de Alferez seg.do de la Comp.a del Presidio de S.ta Cruz, p.a Dn Ygn.o Ybarrola, El Pardo. AGI, Guad. 505 (BLUC film).
23 de Agosto de 1784. Nombrm.to de Ten.te de la comp.a volante del Presidio de Sn Agustín del Tucson, Dn Thomás Egurrola. San Yldefonso. AGI, Guad. 506.
5 de febrero de 1785. Patente de Capitan de la Compañía del Presidio de S.ta Cruz. El Pardo. AGI, Guad. 506 (BLUC film).
1 de Octubre de 1788. Nombrm.to de teniente de Presidio de Sn Agustín del Tucson en la Prov.a de Sonora – Dn Franco. Salas Bo.rques. San Yldefonso. AGI, Guad. 506 (BLUC film).
12 de Octubre de 1788. Patente de Capitán del Presidio de San Agustín del Tucson – Dn Pablo Romero. AGI, Guad. 506 (BLUC film).
CARLOS IV, KING OF SPAIN
12 de Agosto de 1789. Patente de Capitán de la Compañía del Presidio de San Agustín del Tupson – Dn Nicolás Soler. Madrid. AGI, Guad. 506 (BLUC film).
1.o de Marzo de 1790. Nombramo.to de Ten.te de la Compañía de Caballería del Presidio de Sn Bernardino de Fronteras – Dn Josef Ign.o Moraga. Madrid. AGI, Guad. 506 (BLUC film).
11 de Agosto de 1790. Nombram.to de Alferez segundo de la Compañía del Presidio de Sn Agustín del Tupson – Dn Juan Felipe Beldarrain. Madrid. AGI, Guad. 506 (BLUC film).
19 de Mayo de 1792. Patente por la q.e se le concede la Compañía del Presidio del Tupcson – Dn Josef de Zuñiga. Aranjuez. AGI, Guad. 506 (BLUC film).
18 de Julio de 1793. Nombram.to de Ten.te de la Compañía de Sn Agustín del Tupcson – Dn Mariano Urrea. AGI, Guad. 506 (BLUC film).
22 de En.o de 1794. Nombram.to de 2° Alferez del Presidio de S.ta Cruz, Dn Man.l Ign.o Arbizu. Aranjuez. AGI, Guad. 505 (BLUC film).
9 de Mayo de 1794. Nombram.to de ten.te de la Comp.a del Presidio de S.ta Cruz, Dn Juan Franco. AGI, Guad. 505 (BLUC film).
1.° de Julio de 1794. Nombramiento de Alferez 2° de la Comp.a del Presidio de Sn Agustín del Tupcson – Dn Antonio Narbona. AGI, Guad. 506 (BLUC film).
Sep.re 7 de 1796. Patente, Capitán de S.ta Cruz, Dn Marcos Reaño. AGI, Guad. 505 (BLUC film).
6 de Diz.re de 1796. Nombram.to de Ten.te de la Compañía Presidial de Orcasitas. AGI, Guad. 505 (BLUC film).
8 de Junio de 1797. Nombram.to de Ten.te dela Comp.a del Presidio

de S.ta Cruz, Dn Josef María del Rivero. AGI, Guad. 505 (BLUC film).

18 de Marzo de 1803. Nombram.to de Capitán de la Compañía Presidial de Sn Mig.l de Orcasitas. AGI, Guad. 505 (BLUC film).

11 de Mayo de 1803. Nombram.to de Alferez de la Compañía Presidial de S.ta Cruz. AGI, Guad. 505 (BLUC film).

CARRILLO, JUAN ALEXO

Febrero 25 de 1819. Al Señor Comandante de Armas Dn Ant.o Narbona. AGI, Papeles de Estado 33, México 14 (BLUC film).

CEVALLOS, JUAN BAPTISTA DE

7 de Julio de 1814. Auto de Visita de 1814. AGN, Misiones, Tomo 11.

CORBALÁN, PEDRO

1 de Diciembre de 1786a. Oficio al S.or Leonardo de Escalante. Arizpe. AGN, Provincias Internas 225 (BLUC film).

1 de Diciembre de 1786b. Padrón del Número de Apaches que se han dado de Paz y se Mantienen en el Pueblo de Bacoachi. Arizpe. AGN, Provincias Internas 215 (BLUC film).

CORDERO, ANTONIO

Abril 19 de 1819. Oficio al Excmo. Señor Virrey Conde del Venadito. Durango, N° 105. AGI, Papeles del Estado 33, México 14 (BLUC film).

CROIX, TEODORO DE

30 de Nov.e de 1778. Extracto de Novedades ocurridas en las Provincias Internas de Nueva España. AGI, Guad. 275 (BLUC film).

1780. Extracto de Novedades ocurridas en las Provincias Internas de Nueva España en los cuatro últimos meses del año de 1779. AGI, Guad. 271 (BLUC film).

7 de Marzo de 1780. Ynstrucción que previene las reglas para el establecimiento de dos Puebos de Españoles é Yndios sobre las Margenes del Río Colorado en territorios de la Nación Yuma. Arizpe. AGEMS, Legajo 1801-1802.

23 de Junio de 1780. Extracto de Novedades Ocurridas en las Provincias Ynternas de N. E. en los tiempos quc cxpresan. AGI, Guad. 271 (BLUC film).

23 de Julio de 1780. Extracto de novedades ocurridas en las Provincias Ynternas de Nueva España en los tiempos que se expresan. AGI, Guad. 271 (BLUC film).

23 de Agosto de 1780. Extracto de Novedades ocurridas en las Provincias Ynternas de Nueva España en los tiempos que se expresan. AGI, Guad. 271 (BLUC film).

23 de Marzo de 1781. Extracto de Novedades ocurridas en las Provincias de Sonora, Nueva Vizcaya, Coahuila, y Texas en los meses de Diciembre, Enero y Febrero últimos . . . AGI, Guad. 271 (BLUC film).

15 de Mayo de 1782. Oficio [commendation of Tucson Garrison]. Arizpe. AGI, Guad. 520 (BLUC film).

27 de Enero de 1783. Extracto de novedades ocurridas en las Provincias Ynternas de Nueva España con los Yndios Enemigos. Arizpe. AGI, Guad. 284 (BLUC film).

Julio de 1783. Extracto de novedades ocurridas con los Yndios Enemigos en las Provincias Ynternas de Nueva España . . . AGI, Guad. 284 (BLUC film).

DÁVALOS, YGNACIO
Marzo 18 de 1810. Circular a RR. PP. Capellanes de los Presidios de la Margen. Arivechi. AGEMS, Legajo de 1810.

DENOFEANTO, ANTONIO
20 de Marzo de 1789. Comprobante para Leonardo Escalante. Bacoachi. AGN, Provincias Internas Tomo 225 (BLUC film).

DÍAZ DEL CARPIO, JOSEPH
Abril 14 de 1752. Padrón General de los Pueblos Situados al Norte de esta Pimería Alta que Yo Don Joseph Díaz del Carpio, Capitán del Real Presidio de San Phelipe Gracia Real alias Terrenate Devo Formar en Virtud de Comisión y Orden del Señor Theniente Coronel Don Diego Hortiz Parrilla, Governador y Capitan General de Estas Provincias . . . AGI, Guad. 419 (BLUC film).

DOBYNS, HENRY F.
1959 Tubac Through Four Centuries. Report to the Arizona State Museum and Arizona State Parks Board.
1970 "Ethnic Differences in the Demography of the Frontier of New Spain," Paper presented at the 39th International Congress of Americanists, Lima.

ECHEGARAY, MANUEL DE
Febrero 12 de 1788. Diario de la Campaña Executada por el Capt.n Don Manuel de Echegaray en el Campo del Enemigo. AGN, Provincias Internas, Tomo 128.
Octubre 20 de 1788. Al S.or Com.te Militar. AGN, Provincias Internas, Tomo 128, fol. 519-520v.
Enero 21 de 1793. Al Comandante General Don Pedro de Nava. AGN, Provincias Internas, Tomo 171, f. 527-528.

ELÍAS GONZÁLES, FRANCISCO
22 de Marzo de 1762. Al S.r Govr. D. Joseph Tienda de Cuerbo. AGI, Guad. 511 (BLUC film).

ELÍAS GONZÁLES, JOSÉ MARÍA
Mayo 20 de 1817. Carta á Juan C. Elías G. Arizpe Parish Archive. University of Arizona Library Sonora-Sinaloa Microfilm Project.

ELÍAS GONZÁLES, SIMÓN
18 de Junio de 1826. Decreto Número 12 del Congreso Constitucional del Estado de Occidente. Fuerte. Bancroft Library, Print 32, Colección de Documentos impresos y manuscritos p.a la Historia de los Estados del Norte de México, Tomo I, regalados por Mons. Alphonse Pinart.

ESCALANTE, JOSÉ ANTONIO DE
Agosto 31 de 1789. Comprobante para Leonardo de Escalante. AGN, Provincias Internas, Tomo 225 (BLUC film).

ESCALANTE, LEONARDO
Enero 26 de 1787. Padrón de Distribución á Apaches de Paz. Bacoachi, countersigned by Corbalán in Arizpe on this date. AGN, Provincias Internas, Tomo 225 (BLUC film).
Febrero 1 de 1788. Nota. En Libro de Caudales: Año 1788. Bacoachi. AGN, Provincias Internas, Tomo 206 (BLUC film).
Diciembre de 1788. Distribución . . . Bacoachi. AGN, Provincias Internas, Tomo 234 (BLUC film).

ESPÍRITU SANTO, FR. BERNARDO DEL
Sept.e 28 de 1820. Carta al M. R. P. Fr. Juan Bañó. Arispe. AGEMS, Letter Book.

Franco, Gabriel
    1782. Declaración de Capellán Gabriel Franco. Tucson. AGI, Guad. 520 (BLUC film).
Galindo Navarro, Pedro
    9 de Diziembre de 1796. Dictamen para le Señor Comandante Gral. Chihuahua. AGEMS, Legajo de 1801–1802.
Gálvez, Josef de
    3 de Junio de 1769. (Order to Commissioners to convey ex-Jesuit Missions to Franciscans) Dado en el Real de los Alamos. AGEMS, Legajo de 1799.
Garcés, Francisco T. H.
    Agosto 13 de 1768. Informe al Muy Reverendo Padre Fray Sebastian Flores, Guardian. San Xavier. Roma, Pontificio Atenio Antoniano Library, Marcellino da Civezza Collection.
    Noviembre de 1770. Diario que se ha formado por el viaje hecho al Río Gila quando los indios Pimas Gileños me llamaron a fin de que Baptisase sus Hijos que estaban enfermos del sarampión. San Xavier, AGN, Historia, Tomo 396.
    Febrero 20 de 1771. Oficio. San Xavier del Bac. Archivo del Colegio de la Santa Cruz de Querétaro Sección H. Guanajuato, Templo Franciscano de Celaya.
    Agosto 8 ál Octubre 26 de 1771. Diario que se ha formado con la ocasión de la entrada que hise á los vesinos gentiles. Caborca. AGN, Historia, Tomo 396.
    1772 Parecer . . . sobre nuevas fundaciones. Archivo del Colegio de la Santa Cruz de Querétaro, Sección H. Guanajuato, Templo Franciscano de Celaya.
    24 de Sep. de 1776. Oficio al M. R. P. Guard.n Diego Ximenez Perez. Tumacacori, Roma, Pontificio Atenio Antoniano Library, Marcellino da Civezza Collection, 201.17.
    25 de Dic.e 1776. Oficio al M. R. P. Guard.n Diego Ximenez Perez. San Ignacio. Roma, Pontificio Ateneo Antoniano Library, Marcellino da Civezza Collection, 201.18.
    3 de Enero de 1777. Oficio al M. R. P. Guard.n Diego Ximenez Perez. Tubutama. Roma, Pontificio Ateneo Antoniano Library, Marcellino da Civezza Collection, 201.19.
    21 de En.o de 1778. Oficio á Don Antonio Bucareli y Ursua. Pueblo de Tucson. AGN, Historia, Tomo 52.
    19 de Feb.o de 1778. Oficio al M. R. P. Guard.n Diego Ximenez Perez. Misión de Tugson. Roma, Pontificio Ateneo Antoniano Library, Marcellino da Civezza Collection, 201.20.
    11 de Marzo de 1779. Carta al Virrey D. Antonio Bucareli. Los Siete Príncipes de Atí.
    23 de Marzo de 1779. Oficio al Gov.r D. Pedro Tueros. Altar. AGI, Guad. 277 (BLUC film).
García Conde, Alexo
    19 de Junio de 1816. Carta á S.or Don Juan Elías Gonzáles. Saltillo. Arizpe Parish Archive. University of Arizona Sonora-Sinaloa Microfilm Project.
    19 de Julio de 1819. Al Exec. Virrey de este Nueva España el Conde de Venadito. AGI, Papeles de Estado 33, México 14 (BLUC film).
García Herreros, José Juaquín
    Agosto 7 de 1807. Oficio al S.or Ayudante Inspector, D. José de Zúñiga. Buenavista. AGEMS, Legajo de 1800 á 1808.

GARRIDO Y DURAN, PEDRO

Diciembre 20 de 1787, Oficio al S.or Dn Leonardo de Escalante. Arispe. No. 1. AGN, Provincias Internas, Tomo 234 (BLUC film).

Febrero 8 de 1788. Oficio al S.or Dn Leonardo Escalante. Arispe. AGN, Provincias Internas, Tomo 234 (BLUC film).

GARRUCHO, JOSEPH

Junio 21 de 1761. Carta al P.e Pro.al Pedro Reales. Oposura. AGN, AHH, Temporalidades, Legajo 17, No. 23 (BLUC film).

GONZÁLES, FAUSTINO

Enero 4 de 1820. Estado de las Misiones de la Alta Pimería en la Provincias de Sonora, Año de 1819. AGN, Misiones, Tomo 3.

Enero 4 de 1821. Estado de las Misiones de la Pimería Alta, Provincia de Sonora, Administradas por el Colegio de la Santa Cruz de Querétaro, Año de 1820. AGEMS, Legajo de 1782.

GUEBAVI

Los Santos Angeles de Guebavi. Libro de Bautismos. Archive of the Diocese of Tucson. Copy in AHS.

HERNANDEZ, MANUEL

1820 (Petición) AGN, Provincias Internas, Tomo 261, ff. 215-221v.

HUGHES, SAMUEL

1860. Statement. AHS. Annotated by Donald W. Page, 16 May 1929.

1885. Dictation. The Bancroft Library, University of California.

LEGARRA, MANUEL DE

Obre 14 de 1796. Padrón de los Vecinos y Ynd.s de esta Misión de los S.tos Reyes de Cucurpe y su visita el Pueblo de Tuape. Tuape. AGEMS, Legajo 1796.

LEÓN, MANUEL DE

Enero 11 de 1789. Comprobante hecho por el Carpintero. Bacoachi No. 2. en Libro de Caudales y Cargo p.a el de Compras, Bacoachi. AGN, Provincias Internas, Tomo 234 (BLUC film).

1807. Oficio al Intendente Alexo García Conde. Tubac. MS in Arizona Historical Society.

Agosto 29 de 1813a. Cabeza del Proceso. Real Presidio de San Agustín del Tucson. AGEMS, Legajo de 1798–1800.

Agosto 29 de 1813b. Extracción de Sagrada. Real Presidio de San Agustín del Tucson. AGEMS, Legajo de 1798–1800.

Octubre 19 de 1813. Auto de Entrega de Autos al Com.te Entrante. Tucson. AGEMS, Legajo de 1798–1800.

Enero 29 de 1815. Atestación de fidelidad de la copia del Proceso. Presidio de Tucson. AGEMS, Legajo de 1798–1800.

Feb.o 16 de 1825. Al S.or Comandante Gral. de Sonora, D. Mariano de Urrea, No. 1. Tucson. Secretaria de Defensa Nacional, Deptamento de Archivo, Correspondencia e Historia, México (courtesy of Dr. Paul H. Ezell).

LLORENS, JUAN BAUTISTA

Junio 2 de 1795. Oficio al M. R. P. Presidente Francisco Antonio Barbastro. Bac. AGEMS, Legajo de 1801–1802.

Diciembre 12 de 1801. Padrón del Pueblo y Misión de San Francisco Xavier del Bac. AGEMS, Legajo de 1801–1802.

MARTINEZ, JUAN FELIPE

Octubre 11 de 1796. Padrón que demuestra el N° de Familias, y Almas que hay en esta Reducción de Yndios Seris en el Pitíc. Año de 1796. Pitíc. AGEMS, Legajo de 1796.

Mata Biñolas, Pedro de
1794 (Service Record of Antonio Narbona). AGI, Guad. 292 (BLUC film).

McKenna, Constantine
28 de Julio de 1794. Partida de Casamiento de Enrique Grimarest y Ana Narbona. Mobile. AGI, Guad. 292 (BLUC film).

Medina, Roque de
Mayo 3 de 1779. Provincia de Sonora, Año de 1779, Real Presidio de San Agustín del Tucson: Revista pasada por el Ayudante Inspector Dn Roque de Medina a la Compañía de cavallería que guarnece el expresado Presidio. AGI, Guad. 271 (BLUC film).
Enero 15 de 1784. Real Presidio de San Agustín del Tucson, Año de 1784, Extracto de la Revista de Ynspección Executada. Real Presidio de San Agustín del Tucson. AGI, Guad. 285 (BLUC film).
Octubre 6 de 1785. Rl. Presidio de Sn Agustín del Tucson. Mes de Octubre de 1785. Extracto de la Revista de inspección executada. AGI, Guad. 521 (BLUC film).
Febrero 27 de 1786. Opatas, Compañía de Bacoachi – Extracto de la Revista de Ynspección. AGI, Guad. 521 (BLUC film).

Messa, Joseph Nicolás de
1 de Nov.e de 1796. Detalle ó relación jurada . . . al Yllmo y Rm.o S.or Ob.po de la administración de su cargo. S.ta Barbara de Virivis. AGEMS, Legajo de 1796.

Moraga, José
1793. Compañía de Cavallería del R.1 Pres.o del Tucson. AGN, Provincias Internas, Tomo 171.

Moreno, Manuel María
20 de Noviembre de 1795. Relación de meritos literarios y servicios personales que hacía el Lic.do dn Manuel María Moreno . . . Hacienda de S. S. Jhp. de Jamaica. AGEMS, Legajo de 1796.
2 de Henero á 5 de febrero de 1797. Sin título (apuntes del viaje de visita episcopal) Fronteras - Santa Cruz - Tumacacori - Tubac - Tucson - S. Xavier - Saric - Tubutama - Oquitoa - Caborca - Cieneguilla. Archivo de la Diocesis de Sinaloa, Catedral de Culiacán. St. Louis University Microfilm, AHS.

Moyano, Francisco
18 de Mayo de 1803. Provincia de Sonora, Misiones de Pimería Alta. Informe de las misiones q.e los Religiosos del Colegio de la Santa Cruz de Querétaro administran en dha provincia . . . hasta el año 1802 . . . Mision de San Antonio de Oquitoa. AGI, Aud. de México, Legajo 2736.
5 de Febrero de 1805. Provincia de Sonora, Misiones de la Pimería Alta: Informe de las misiones q.e los religiosos del Colegio de la Santa Cruz de Querétaro administran en dha. provincia de los años 1803 y 1804. San Antonio de Oquitoa. AGI, Audiencia de México, Legajo 2736.
4 de Diciem.e de 1808. Carta al Yllmo. S.or Dn Fr. Fran.co Rouset dig.no Ob.po de Sonora. Oquitoa. AGEMS, Legajo de 1803.

NARBONA, ANTONIO
8 de Marzo de 1819. Al Brig.r y Comandant General Dn Ant.o Cordero. AGI, Papeles de Estado 33, México 14 (BLUC film).
NAVA, PEDRO DE
Enero 29 de 1793. Oficio al Cap.n Man.l de Echegaray. AGN, Provincias Internas, Tomo 171, fol. 529-530.
Febrero 14 de 1793. Oficio al Exmo. S.or Conde de Revilla Gigedo. Chiguagua. AGN, Provincias Internas, Tomo 171, fol. 551-552.
Agosto 8 de 1794. (Service Records of Sonoran Officers) AGI, Guad. 292 (BLUC film).
Agosto 12 de 1796. Oficio á Dn Fr. Francisco Rouset. Guajoquilla. AGEMS, Legajo de 1796.
(NEVE, JOSÉ)
20 de Henero de 1766. Padrón de las Familias, y Gente q. actualm.te vive en este Pueblo de S.n Xavier. AGN, AHH, Temporalidades, Legajo 17, No. 32 (BLUC film).
20 de febrero de 1766. Padrón de las Familias q. actualm.te viven en el Tuxon Pueblo de Visita de la Miss.n de S.n Xav.r del Baca. AGN, AHH, Temporalidades, Legajo 17, No. 32 (BLUC film).
NEVE, PHELIPE
30 de Nov.e de 1782. Real Presidio de Sn Agustín del Tucson, Año de 1782. Extracto de la Revista de Inspección executada. R.l Presidio de Sn Agustín del Tucson. AGI, Guad. 284 (BLUC film).
Enero 26 de 1784. Al Ex.mo S.or Dn Joseph de Gálvez. No. 76. Arizpe. AGI, Guad. 285 (BLUC film).
Marzo 8 de 1784. Oficio No. 96 al Exmo. Señor Don Joseph de Gálvez. Arizpe. AGI, Guad. 285 (BLUC film).
Abril 5 de 1784. Al Exmo. Señor Dn Joseph de Gálvez. Arizpe. AGI, Guad. 285 (BLUC film).
Julio 6 de 1784. Al Exmo. Señor Dn Josef de Gálvez. Fronteras. AGI, Guad. 520 (BLUC film).
NOREÑA, DOMINGO
Octubre 20 de 1796. Estado en que manifiesta el Número de Almas y clases q. hay en este Pueblo de Yécora. Yécora. AGEMS, Legajo de 1796.
O'CONOR, HUGO
18 de Agosto de 1775. Extracto de Revista de Ynspección Pasada por el Coronel de Ynfantería Dn Hugo Oconor. San Ygnacio de Tubac. AGI, Guad. 515 (BLUC film).
Diziembre 1 de 1775. Diario sequido desde el día siete de Septiembre . . . Real Presidio de Carrizal. AGN, Provincias Internas, Tomo 87 (BLUC film).
O'CONOR, HUGO, FRANCISCO GARCÉS y JUAN FERNÁNDEZ CARMONA
Agosto 20 de 1775. Certificación de Elección del Sitio del Presidio del Tucson. Tucson. AGN, Provincias Internas, Tomo 88, fol. 164 (BLUC film).
O'CONOR, HUGO DE y JUAN MARÍA OLIVA
Agosto 22 de 1775. Certificación de Elección del sitio del Presidio de Santa Cruz. Santa Cruz. AGN, Provincias Internas, Tomo 88, fol. 166 (BLUC film).
Agosto 25 de 1775. Certificación de elección del sitio del Presidio de San Bernardino. Paraje de San Bernardino. AGN, Provincias Internas, Tomo 88, fol. 165 (BLUC film).

Oliva, Juan María de
Agosto 13 de 1775. Pie de Lista de los Soldados de dho Comp.a con distinción de Nombres, edad, Patria, robustez calid.d y zirc.s de cada uno. Real Presidio de Tubac, No. 3. AGI, Guad. 515 (BLUC film).
Agosto 13 de 1775. Relación que Manifiesta el Devito y Crédito que tienen los Soldados que guarnez.n dho Presidio . . . Real Presidio de Tubac, No. 7. AGI, Guad. 515 (BLUC film).
Agosto 13 de 1775. (Service Record Summary) No. 8. Real Presidio de Tubac. AGI, Guad. 515 (BLUC film).

Oury, William S.
1862–1864. Tucson Property Record. Pima County Recorder's Office. Copy in AHS.

Perez, José
1818 Estado Espiritual y Temporal de las Misiones de la Pimería Alta, Provincia de Sonora, Administradas por el Colegio de la Santa Cruz de Querétaro. AGN, Misiones Tomo 13, fol. 46-47.

Pinart, Alphonse Luis (compiler)
Collección de Pimería Alta (Taken from churches) BLUC.
Libro de Bavtismos, Entierros, y Casamientos, del Partido de Atí: 1757.
Libro I de Baptismos para el Pueblo de N. Sra. del Pópulo de Bisanig (1768 ff).
Libro de Casamientos para el Pueblo de N. S.ra del Pópulo del Bisanig.
Libro de Bautismos del Partido de San Ygnacio de Caburica No. 1.
Libro de Entierros deste Pueblo de Sn Yno. Nro. Pe. de la Pimería en que tambien se ponen los del Pueblo de Sn Joseph de Hímuri. 1697–1787.
Bautismos del Partido de Huquitoa de 1757.
Libro de Entierros deste Pueblo de Sn. Yno. Nro. Pe. de la Pimería en que también Visita de Santa Teresa.
Libro de Baptismos de los Pueblos de Sta. María, Sn Pedro, Sta. Cruz, Sn Iago de Optuavo, Sn Andrés de Scug-Bag, Sn Pablo de Baihcat, Sn Tadeo de Baffg-Comarig, S. Juan de Quiburi desde 1732.
Libro de Entierros de Santa María Magdalena desde 1702 (á 1816).
Libro de Baustimos de la Missión de San Pedro y San Pablo de Tubutama y su Visita de Santa Teresa.

Quiroga, Joaquín
31 de Mayo de 1843. Oficio al Secretario del Departamento de Sonora. Cucurpe. Archivo Histórico del Estado, Hermosillo, Carpeton 121.

Reyes, Antonio de los
1784 Informe General que de Orden del Rey con fecha en el Pardo en 31 de Enero de 1784 comunicada por el Excmo. Señor Dn José de Gálvez, he remitido á S. M. por duplicado el Ylo. Señor Obispo de Sonora. AGN, Misiones, Tomo 14, fol. 202-257.

Rivera, Antonio
19 de Septiembre de 1801. Declaración. Arizpe. AGEMS, Legajo de 1801–1802.

Romero, Jose
21 de Mayo de 1819. Oficio al Comandante de Armas Dn Ant.o Narbona. AGI, Papeles de Estado 33, México 14 (BLUC film).

Romero, Pablo
Junio 24 de 1788. Diario de la Operado por el Capn Dn Pablo Romero en

Romero, Pablo (continued)
la Campaña que a Executado de orn del Coronl y Com.te Militar de Armas en Esta Provincia Dn Juan Bap.ta de Anza. AGN, Provincias Internas, Tomo 128, fol. 423-425.

Rouset de Jesus, Francisco
Agosto 4 de 1803. Circular. Culiacán. AGEMS, Legajo de 1803.
Mayo 12 de 1808. Carta al Fr. Francisco Moyano. Culiacán. AGEMS, Legajo de 1803.
Diciembre 18 de 1809. Circular acerca del Ayuno y Comida de Carnes. Culiacán. AGEMS, Legajo del Año 1809.

Roxas, Carlos de
Maio 14 de 1755. Carta al P. Prov.al Ygnacio Calderon. Arispe. AGN, AHH, Temporalidades, Legajo 17, No. 36.
Marzo 30 de 1756. á Mi Am.o P. Prov.al Ygnacio Calderon. Arispe. AGN, AHH, Temporalidades, Legajo 17, No. 36 (BLUC film).
Marzo 15 de 1757. Carta al Prov.al Ygnacio Calderon. Arispe. AGN, AHH, Temporalidades, Legajo 17, No. 8.
Enero 15 de 1765. Carta al Prov.al Fran.co Zevallos. Arispe. AGN, AHH, Temporalidades, Legajo 17, No. 8 (BLUC film).

Rubí, El Marqués de
7 de Diz.re de 1766. Revista. AGI, Guad. 511 (BLUC film).

Salcedo y Salcedo, Nemesio
4 de Set. de 1806. Licencia de Casamiento á Don José Romero. Chihuahua. Arizpe Parish Archive. University of Arizona Sonora-Sinaloa Microfilm Project.

Salcido, José Cayetano
17 de Septiembre de 1801. Certificación. Arizpe. AGEMS, Legajo de 1801–1802.

Santiesteban, Juan de
9 de 7bre de 1796. Padrón de las familias y almas de Yndios ye de Razón que existen en esta Misión de Sn Tiago de Cocospera. Cocospera. AGEMS, Legajo de 1796.

Sedelmayr, Jacobo
10 de Mayo de 1752. Al Sr. Govr. Ures. AGI, Guad. 419 (BLUC film).

Segesser, Phelipe von Brunegg von
25 de Mayo de 1752. Al Señor Governador y Capitán Gral. Ures. AGI, Guad. 419 (BLUC film).

Sepulveda, Juan Manuel
1 de Diciembre de 1796. Informe al Yllmo S.or Obispo de Sonora. . . . Archivo Diocesano de Culiacán. St. Louis University Microfilm, AHS.

Sheridan, Thomas
1971 Female Public Drinking Patterns Among the 1971 Magdalena Pilgrims. Paper in author's files.

Simó, Fr. Lorenzo
Noviembre 6 de 1796. Oficio al M. R. P. Visitador P. P.r Fr. Juan Felipe Martines. Bacoachi. Archivo Diocesano de Culiacán. St. Louis University Microfilm, AHS.

Socies, Bartolomé
Diciembre 14 de 1801. Padrón de los Yndios y Vecinos de la Misión de Nuestra S.ra de los Dolores del Saric. AGEMS, Legajo de 1801–

THERAN, RAFAEL
Febrero 10 de 1789. Comprobante para Leonardo Escalante. Bacoachi. AGN, Provincias Internas, Tomo 225 (BLUC film).

TIENDA DEL CUERBO, JOSEPH
Abril 9 de 1762. Al Marqués de Cruillas. AGI, Guad. 511 (BLUC film).

TUMACACORI
Libro de Bautismos (B), Libro de Casamientos (C), Libro de Entierros (E), de San José de Tumacacori. Archive of the Diocese of Tucson. Copy in AHS.

UGARTE Y LOYOLA, JACOBO
Julio 10 de 1788. Al Exmo. S.or Dn Manuel Antonio Florez. AGN, Provincias Internas, Tomo 128.

URREA, MARIANO DE
Agosto 24 de 1798. Licencia al Soldado Juan Fuentes. Arizpe. Parish Archive. University of Arizona Sonora-Sinaloa Microfilm Project.
Abril 15 de 1807. Al M. R. P. Capellán F. Juan María Torres. Altar. AGEMS, Legajo 1800 á 1808.
Mayo 15 de 1807. Oficio. Altar. AGEMS, Legajo de 1800 á 1808.
Marzo 8 de 1825. Oficio al Exmo. S.or Secretario de Estado y del Despacho de la Grra. y Marina. Arispe. Departamento de Archivo, Correspondencia e Historia, Secretaria de la Defensa Nacional, México (BLUC film).

USARRAGA, YGNACIO FÉLIX
Mayo 3 de 1782. (Report to Captain Allande). Tucson. AGI, Guad. 520 (BLUC film).

USARRAGA, YGNACIO FÉLIX con "El Muchacho Chacón"
1782. Declaración del Muchacho Chacón. Tucson. AGI, Guad. 520 (BLUC film).

USARRAGA, YGNACIO FÉLIX y JOSÉ ANTONIO DELGADO
1782 Interrogatorio: Declaración del Soldado José Antonio Delgado. AGI, Guad. 520 (BLUC film).

USARRAGA, YGNACIO FÉLIX, JUAN FERNÁNDEZ, JOSEPH PROCOPIO CANCIO y JOAQUÍN DE ORTEGA
1782 Declaración de Tropa y Vecinos del Tucson. AGI, Guad. 520 (BLUC film).

USARRAGA, YGNACIO FÉLIX y JOSÉ DOMINGO GRANILLO
1782 Declaración del Soldado José Domingo Granillo. Tucson. 3 de Mayo de 1782. AGI, Guad. 520 (BLUC film).

VELDERRAIN, JUAN BAPT.TA
Mayo 4 de 1782. A S.or Capitán Dn Pedro Allande y Saabedra. San Xavier. AGI, Guad. 520 (BLUC film).

VELDERRAIN (BELDERRAIN), JUAN BAPTISTA y JUAN DÍAZ
Junio 7 de 1775. Partida de Visita. Tecoripa. Roma, Pontificio Ateneo Antoniano Library, Marcellino da Civezza Collection.

VENADITO, CONDE DEL
Mayo 11 de 1819. Oficio al S.or Comand.te Gen.r interino de las Provincias Internas Occidentales. México. AGI, Papeles de Estado 33, México 14 (BLUC film).

YTURRALDE, FRANCISCO
25 de Octubre de 1792. Oficio á los M. R.s PP. Ministros de las Miss.s del Margen. Sta. Theresa. Roma, Pontificio Ateneo Antoniano Library, Marcellino da Civezza Collection 203.22.
7 de Marzo de 1795. Oficio al M. R. P. Guard.n Fr. Juan Ribera. Tubu-

YTURRALDE, FRANCISCO *(continued)*
tama. Roma, Pontificio Ateneo Antoniano Library, Civezza Collection 203.33.
24 de Sep.e de 1795. Oficio al M. R. P. Visitador Fr. Diego Bringas. Roma, Pontificio Ateneo Antoniano Library, Civezza Collection 203.35.
4 de Feb.o de 1796. Oficio al M. R. P. Visitador Fr. Diego Bringas. Roma, Pontificio Ateneo Antoniano Library, Civezza Collection 203.41.
4 de Dic.e de 1796. Oficio al M. R. P. Guard.n Fr. Sebastian Ramis. Tubutama. Roma, Pontificio Ateneo Antoniano Library, Civezza Collection 203.23.
1 de Mayo de 1797. Oficio á M. R. P. Fr. Diego Bringas. Tubutama. Roma, Pontificio Ateneo Antoniano Library, Civezza Collection 203.46.
3 de Abril de 1798. Visita de las Misiones de la Pimería por el P. Yturralde, Presid. Tubutama. Roma, Franciscan Archives. Copy in BLUC.
4 de Mayo de 1798. Oficio al M. R. P. Guard.n Fr. Fran.co Miralles. Tubutama. Roma, Pontificio Ateneo Antoniano Library, Civezza Collection 203.26.
4 de Junio de 1798. Oficio al M. R. P. Guardian Fr. Fran.co Miralles. Roma, Pontificio Ateneo Antoniano Library, Civezza Collection 203.27.
28 de Enero de 1799. Al Yllmo. Señor D. Fr. Fran.co Rouset. Tubutama. AGEMS, Legajo de 1799.

Index

This index is designed to aid those interested in particular individuals who contributed to the development of Spanish colonial Tucson.

C = civilian at Tucson or Bac
G = member of royal garrison
NP = Northern Piman Indian
OFM = member of the Order of Friars Minor (Franciscans)
SJ = member of the Society of Jesus (Jesuits)
W = wife